FEMINIST INTERPRETATIONS OF JEAN-PAUL SARTRE

RE-READING THE CANON

NANCY TUANA, GENERAL EDITOR

This series consists of edited collections of essays, some original and some previously published, offering feminist reinterpretations of the writings of major figures in the Western philosophical tradition. Devoted to the work of a single philosopher, each volume contains essays covering the full range of the philosopher's thought and representing the diversity of approaches now being used by feminist critics.

Already published:

FEMINIST INTERPRETATIONS OF JEAN-PAUL SARTRE

EDITED BY JULIEN S. MURPHY

THE PENNSYLVANIA STATE UNIVERSITY PRESS
UNIVERSITY PARK, PENNSYLVANIA

Library of Congress Cataloging-in-Publication Data

Feminist interpretations of Jean-Paul Sartre / edited by Julien S.
  Murphy.

      p.   cm.—(Re-reading the canon)
    Includes bibliographical references and index.
    ISBN 0-271-01884-4 (cloth : alk. paper)
    ISBN 0-271-01885-2 (pbk. : alk. paper)
    1. Sartre, Jean Paul, 1905– . 2. Feminist theory. I. Murphy,
Julien S., 1956– . II. Series.
B2430.S34F42   1999
194—dc21   98-37145
                                          CIP

It is the policy of The Pennsylvania State University Press to use acid-free paper for the first printing of all clothbound books. Publications on uncoated stock satisfy the minimum requirements of American National Standard for Information Sciences—Permanence of Paper for Printed Library Materials, ANSI Z39.48-1992.

In Memoriam
Phyllis Sutton Morris

Contents

Preface

Nancy Tuana

Take into your hands any history-of-philosophy text. You will find compiled therein the "classics" of modern philosophy. Since these texts are often designed for use in undergraduate classes, the editor is likely to offer an introduction in which the reader is informed that these selections represent the perennial questions of philosophy. The student is to assume that she or he is about to explore the timeless wisdom of the greatest minds of Western philosophy. No one calls attention to the fact that the philosophers are all men.

Though women are omitted from the canons of philosophy, these texts inscribe the nature of woman. Sometimes the philosopher speaks directly about woman, delineating her proper role, her abilities and inabilities, her desires. Other times the message is indirect—a passing remark hinting at women's emotionality, irrationality, unreliability.

This process of definition occurs in far more subtle ways when the central concepts of philosophy—reason and justice, those characteristics that are taken to define us as human—are associated with traits historically identified with masculinity. If the "man" of reason must learn to control or overcome traits identified as feminine—the body, the emotions, the passions—then the realm of rationality will be one reserved primarily for men,[1] with grudging entrance to those few women who are capable of transcending their femininity.

Feminist philosophers have begun to look critically at the canonized texts of philosophy and have concluded that the discourses of philosophy are not gender-neutral. Philosophical narratives do not offer a universal perspective, but rather privilege some experiences and beliefs over others. These experiences and beliefs permeate all philosophical theories whether they be aesthetic or epistemological, moral or metaphysical. Yet this fact has often been neglected by those studying the traditions of philosophy. Given the history of canon formation in Western philosophy, the perspective most likely to be privileged is that of upper-class white males. Thus, to be fully aware of the impact of gender biases, it is imperative that we re-read the canon with attention to the ways in which philosophers' assumptions concerning gender are embedded within their theories.

This new series, Re-Reading the Canon, is designed to foster this process of reevaluation. Each volume will offer feminist analyses of the theories of a selected philosopher. Since feminist philosophy is not monolithic in method or content, the essays are also selected to illustrate the variety of perspectives within feminist criticism and highlight some of the controversies within feminist scholarship.

In this series, feminist lenses will be focused on the canonical texts of Western philosophy, both those authors who have been part of the traditional canon, as well as those philosophers whose writings have more recently gained attention within the philosophical community. A glance at the list of volumes in the series will reveal an immediate gender bias of the canon: Arendt, Aristotle, de Beauvoir, Derrida, Descartes, Foucault, Hegel, Hume, Kant, Locke, Marx, Mill, Nietzsche, Plato, Rousseau, Wittgenstein, Wollstonecraft. There are all too few women included, and those few who do appear have been added only recently. In creating this series, it is not my intention to reify the current canon of philosophical thought. What is and is not included within the canon during a particular historical period is a result of many factors. Although no canonization of texts will include all philosophers, no canonization of texts that excludes all but a few women can offer an accurate representation of the history of the discipline, as women have been philosophers since the ancient period.[2]

I share with many feminist philosophers and other philosophers writing from the margins of philosophy the concern that the current canonization of philosophy be transformed. Although I do not accept the position that the current canon has been formed exclusively by power relations, I do believe that this canon represents only a selective history of the tradition. I share the view of Michael Bérubé that "canons are at once the location, the index, and the record of the struggle for cultural representation; like any other hegemonic formation, they must be continually reproduced anew and are continually contested."[3]

The process of canon transformation will require the recovery of "lost" texts and a careful examination of the reasons such voices have been silenced. Along with the process of uncovering women's philosophical history, we must also begin to analyze the impact of gender ideologies upon the process of canonization. This process of recovery and examination must occur in conjunction with careful attention to the concept of a canon of authorized texts. Are we to dispense with the notion of a tradition of excellence embodied in a canon of authorized texts? Or, rather than abandon the whole idea of a canon, do we instead encourage a reconstruction of a canon of those texts that inform a common culture?

This series is designed to contribute to this process of canon transformation by offering a re-reading of the current philosophical canon. Such a re-reading shifts our attention to the ways in which woman and the role of the feminine is constructed within the texts of philosophy. A question we must keep in front of us during this process of re-reading is whether a philosopher's socially inherited prejudices concerning woman's nature and role are independent of her or his larger philosophical framework. In asking this question attention must be paid to the ways in which the definitions of central philosophical concepts implicitly include or exclude gendered traits.

This type of reading strategy is not limited to the canon, but can be applied to all texts. It is my desire that this series reveal the importance of this type of critical reading. Paying attention to the workings of gender within the texts of philosophy will make visible the complexities of the inscription of gender ideologies.

Notes

1. More properly, it is a realm reserved for a group of privileged males, since the texts also inscribe race and class biases that thereby omit certain males from participation.

2. Mary Ellen Waithe's multivolume series, *A History of Women Philosophers* (Boston: M. Nijhoff, 1987), attests to this presence of women.

3. Michael Bérubé, *Marginal Forces/Cultural Centers: Tolson, Pynchon, and the Politics of the Canon* (Ithaca: Cornell University Press, 1992), 4–5.

Acknowledgments

I would like to express my gratitude to Sandy Thatcher of Penn State Press and series editor Nancy Tuana for being a pleasure to work with on this volume and for their foresight in creating the Re-Reading the Canon series in philosophy. The series presents a much needed forum for feminist work and has already begun to change our understanding of the philosophical canon. The idea for a volume on Sartre originated in San Francisco at a Beauvoir Circle session of the Pacific Division Meetings of the American Philosophical Association. Peg Simons was an early supporter and motivated me to begin. I appreciate her enthusiasm for my work. The authors in this volume have made my task as editor a delightful one. For this book, I was fortunate to receive a sabbatical followed by a leave of absence from the University of Southern Maine that enabled me to be a Visiting Scholar at the University of Washington, Northwest Center for Research on Women from 1994–96. Bill McBride, a long-standing advocate of feminist work on Sartre, has been a generous reader for the book. Amy Geren has been an invaluable research assistant for the Bibliography.

Throughout much of the editing process, I have relied on the good friendships of two Sartreans in particular, Linda Bell and Phyllis Morris. Both Linda and Phyllis have generously given me suggestions on matters great and small for this book and have, on occasion, served as readers. Both women have been pivotal in Sartre studies in America. Linda's books, *Sartre's Ethics of Authenticity* and *Rethinking Ethics in the Midst of Violence: A Feminist Approach to Freedom*, are important contributions to Sartrean feminism. For many years, she has supported my scholarship and nurtured my and others' efforts to use Sartre's philosophy for feminist purposes. Phyllis's book, *Sartre's Concept of a Person: An Analytic Approach*, introduced analytic philosophers to Sartre's work at a time when dialogue between analytic and continental philosophers was difficult. My friendship with Phyllis has been all too brief. I first met her at a Sartre Society sessions at an APA meeting several years ago and admired her relentless interest in Sartre. I have enjoyed her buoyant spirit and her meticulous readings of Sartre. Sadly, Phyllis's battle with cancer ended her life abruptly, a few months after the completion of her chapter included here, her first work on feminism and Sartre. In her last months, she began planning her second book on Sartre and continued to offer suggestions for this volume. She was so full of life and good cheer that I did not fully realize how precious little time remained for her. I am not alone in my appreciation of her efforts over the years to sustain Sartrean scholarship in America. In addition to being an excellent philosopher and devoted teacher at several universities throughout her career, she cofounded the Sartre Society of North America in 1985, served as the North American book review editor for the new journal *Sartre Studies International*, and frequently organized sessions for the Sartre Circle at the American Philosophical Association meetings. This book is dedicated to her memory.

The following works included in the volume are reprinted with permission:

Sonia Kruks, "Identity Politics and Dialectical Reason: Beyond an Epistemology of Provenance," is reprinted by permission of the author from *Hypatia: A Journal of Feminist Philosophy* 10, no. 2 (1995): 1–22. Copyright © 1995 by Sonia Kruks.

Thomas Martin, "Sartre, Sadism and Female Beauty Ideals," is reprinted from *Australian Feminist Studies* 11, no. 24 (1996): 243–52, by permission of the publisher, Carfax Publishing Limited. Copyright © 1996 by Carfax Publishing Limited.

Iris Marion Young, "Gender as Seriality: Thinking About Women as a Social Collective," is reprinted from *Signs: Journal of Women in Culture and Society* 19, no. 3 (1994): 713–38, by permission of the author and the publisher, The University of Chicago Press. Copyright © 1994 by The University of Chicago.

Introduction

This book is the first feminist collection on Jean-Paul Sartre's philosophy. It is of special note that it appears a few years after the Simone de Beauvoir volume in the series. For too long, recognition of Sartre in the philosophical canon was used as a way to dismiss Beauvoir. Sartre was considered the *real* philosopher and Beauvoir's philosophy was allegedly derivative of his. As a corrective measure, feminist philosophers have continually called attention to Sartre's lifelong collaboration with Beauvoir when discussing his work. Her philosophical legitimacy has been such an uphill battle that only after the Beauvoir volume in this series was under way did it occur to me that it was now Sartre who had been (at least temporarily) forgotten. So the tables were turned. In preparation for this book, I found myself asking feminist scholars, What about Sartre?

What is it that Sartre has to say to feminist theory given his lifelong collaboration with Beauvoir? My hunch was that he has deeply influenced feminist scholars, yet little has been written about this by feminists until now.

It is hard to imagine the twentieth century without Sartre. Born in Paris in 1905, he was educated at the École Normale, placed first for his exam for the *agrégation* in philosophy in 1929, and went on to become the most significant French philosopher of the postwar period. He is considered the founder of the popular philosophy existentialism. In his famous philosophical work *Being and Nothingness*, Sartre provided an ontological basis for understanding the human situation, one that assumed us to be radically free. Preceding this were several works taking an existential approach to consciousness (*Transcendence of the Ego*, *The Emotions*, and *The Psychology of Imagination*). Not only a philosopher, he was also a novelist (he wrote *Nausea*; his trilogy, *Roads to Freedom*; and short stories), a playwright (with his most famous play, *No Exit*, and others, including *The Flies*, *The Respectful Prostitute*, *Dirty Hands*, and *The Devil and the Good Lord*), and a winner of but the first to refuse the Nobel Prize in literature. In addition, Sartre brought existentialism to bear on the leading psychological movement, psychoanalysis, and invented a new style of philosophical biography with his studies of the French writers: Baudelaire, Mallarmé, Genet, and Flaubert.

His political works include an analysis of anti-Semitism in France after the war (*Anti-Semite and Jew*), the Soviet invasion of Hungary in 1956 (*The Ghost of Stalin*), and an existential approach to Marxism (*The Critique of Dialectical Reason*), along with countless journal articles, speeches, and interviews. The *Critique* is his most important political work and in it he not only signals the disintegration of Marxism, but offers an early attempt to revive it with an infusion of existentialism. Always on the French Left, Sartre addressed the leading issues of the day, from his participation in the Resistance and his support for decolonization in Indochina and Algeria to the student revolt in May 1968 and beyond. His life, ending in poor health in 1980, was filled with the political struggles of the times. He was the quintessential engaged intellectual, challenging Marx's criticism of philosophy by trying to use philosophy to change the world. That is what impressed me most about him. I remember learning of his death from my professor, Robert Lechner, while waiting for a subway on an elevated platform near DePaul University's Lincoln Park campus. I was a graduate student, soon to write about Sartre for my dissertation, and new to feminism. At the point of one's death, as Sartre himself wrote in *No Exit*, a line is drawn, and thereafter one's life is summed up by others. Little did I foresee that one important piece of that summing up would be this feminist collection.

Why the silence in feminist philosophy around Sartre? Search through the thousands of articles and books on Jean-Paul Sartre and you will find that hardly any take a feminist approach. This is the case with many figures in the philosophical canon, but it is particularly perplexing with Sartre, for he was a contemporary who aligned himself with the oppressed. Even more than that, he was one of the first contemporary philosophers to make gender a philosophical issue. He did this not by writing long chapters in *Being and Nothingness* on the plight of women. In fact, one is hard pressed to find any explicit comments anywhere on women's liberation except for an occasional response to an interviewer's question. Yet, his phenomenological ontology of being-in-situation unmistakably relies on the assumption that situations are gendered in particular ways that disclose some possibilities and not others. Key concepts about sexuality, objectification, and self-deception in *Being and Nothingness* depend upon particular gender assumptions (e.g., the woman on the date, the sexually unresponsive woman, a gay man taunted by the champion of sincerity). Consider how his description of the woman on the date, reluctant to either draw back her hand in a decisive gesture of refusal or openly consent to her suitor's advances, depicts in particular the ambiguity of male-female relationships, not interpersonal relationships in general. As a case of self-deception, it requires assumptions about how the female body is interpreted. Sartre's concepts of "the look" and of bad faith resonate differently for women and men and are understood in part through complex gender relationships. Even before that, Sartre used an example of a woman to illustrate an important philosophical concept. In *Transcendence of the Ego*, to illustrate the spontaneity of consciousness and our radical freedom, he uses Pierre Janet's case of a bride fearful of her own promiscuous desires.

With its rejection of human nature and his emphasis on concrete individuals, his existential philosophy is the first to engage readers of existential phenomenology with the questions of gender, freedom, and the body and, like his later work, has much to offer feminism. This philosopher, who preferred the company of women, did not explicitly link sex with power in his early writings (although that link will be made in his philosophical biography of Jean Genet), and cannot be called a feminist philosopher. Yet, with his attention to women, in his early philosophical and literary works, Sartre was one of the first to make gender a legitimate topic for philosophical analysis (a point still not accepted by conservative philosophers). In doing so, Sartre laid the groundwork for *The Second Sex*, as well as for feminist arguments, appearing much later, that it was indeed philosophy. This does not mean that the ideas in *The Second Sex* were Sartre's, only that it is hard to imagine that the book would be read by philosophers if it had not been preceded by *Being and Nothingness*. Or even that it would have been written at all. As Beauvoir tells it, it was Sartre who suggested that gender was a significant category of analysis, one well worth researching despite her initial impression that she had not suffered from being a woman. Selections from the work were first published in five issues of the journal Sartre founded shortly after the war, *Les Temps Modernes*. *The Second Sex* jump-started the second wave of the women's movement in America and influenced women's liberation struggles around the world.

Feminists challenge a rigid distinction between the personal and the political, and so it is interesting to point out Sartre's personal gender politics, namely, his rather unconventional, egalitarian relationship with Simone de Beauvoir. They were lifelong intellectual allies, reading each other's work before publication, marching together in protests, planning political strategies, traveling to countries in the midst of revolution, such as Cuba, and loving companions from their early days at the École Normale into old age. All the while, they refused the usual institutions of marriage, monogamy, cohabitation, and child rearing. Surprisingly, apart from Beauvoir's extensive autobiographies, only two collaborative publishing projects link their names, Sartre's journal (Beauvoir took a leading role on the board) and her last work, *Adieux: A Farewell to Sartre*, with its chronicle of his last years and her final interviews with him. Given all this, the silence from feminists about Sartre's value is perplexing, having more to do with the historical moment in which Sartre found himself in in his later years than with substantive evaluations of his work.

Though Sartre's influence looms large over the century, he has been temporarily displaced in the past few decades by two trends in particular, poststructuralism and feminism. Only now is he being restored to his rightful position of prominence. Evidence of restoration, in addition to this collection, includes the appearance of his posthumous works: *Notebooks for an Ethics*; *Truth and Existence*; the second volume of *The Critique of Dialectical Reason*; *The Freud Scenario*; the five-volume English translation of *L'Idiot de la famille: Gustave Flaubert de 1821 à 1857; Hope Now: The 1980 Interviews* with Benny Lévy; and his letters to Beauvoir, *The War Diaries, Witness to my Life,* and *Quiet Moments in a War.* Also, there is a new journal devoted to him, *Sartre Studies International,* founded in 1995; several professional groups for Sartre studies such as the Sartre Society of North America, founded in 1985; an eight-volume collection of Sartrean scholarship, *Sartre and Existentialism: Philosophy, Politics, Ethics, the Psyche, Literature, and Aesthetics,* edited by William McBride and published in 1997, and many new books about Sartre. We are in the midst of a Sartre revival. But interest in Sartre's work was not always so great.

The poststructuralists, Foucault the most prominent but also Barthes, Lacan, and Derrida, rejected Sartre's theory of the engaged subject and its modernist implications, choosing instead to emphasize the role of language and institutions in shaping society. Though Sartre's and Foucault's deaths were only four years apart, these men represented two different generations of French philosophy. The popularity of the new French philosophy was widespread but not longstanding. Foucault viewed the modernist emphasis on subjectivity, fundamental to the human sciences, as something that would disappear as quickly as it had appeared at the end of the last century, but that is the likely fate of his (and others') poststructuralist philosophies, defeated by, of all things, the modernist views they opposed.

At the same time as the new French philosophy was on the rise, feminism began to make its mark on university curricula. Women's studies programs were established and feminist courses were created in many academic disciplines, including philosophy. Once again, Sartre received a swift dismissal, though for different reasons. By the time feminist philosophy became a field of inquiry in the late 1970s, Beauvoir's treatise was famous and duly honored by feminist theorists as a significant, if not the key, theoretical text. Beauvoir, not a feminist when she wrote it, had since joined with feminist causes in France. Sartre, on the other hand, blind and in failing health, had finished his all-consuming but little noticed study of the nineteenth-century French novelist Gustave Flaubert. He had not joined any feminist organizations, apparently leaving women's liberation activities to Beauvoir. Even more to the point, the early feminist readings of philosophers were centered on identifying misogynist aspects of their work, and when feminists turned to Sartre's philosophy, he was not spared harsh criticism.

An early task of feminist philosophers was to examine ways in which the established philosophers had dealt with women in their texts. Not surprisingly, gender issues were either ignored or treated uncritically, and often abysmally. Discovering passages of alleged misogyny in famous philosophical texts put feminists in an awkward position. Without fully developed critical tools to analyze claims of misogyny or the effect that such passages had on the understanding of the work as a whole, the compelling choice, in many cases, was to abandon the philosophy altogether. Years later, as is found here in this collection, feminists have developed a more critical use of these tools. But at the time, Sartre was dismissed by many feminists, who turned instead to Beauvoir's writing for an existential analysis of women's oppression.

Accusations of Sartre's misogyny were linked to, among other things, his allegedly gender-based imagery in *Being and Nothingness*. The classic piece attacking Sartre for his sexism was "Holes and Slime: Sexism in Sartre's Psychoanalysis," by Margery L. Collins and Christine Pierce.[1] Writing in 1973, Collins and Pierce extended a much earlier and similar charge of sexism made by William Barrett in his popular book *Irrational Man*, in which Barrett claimed that Sartre's psychology of Being In-itself and Being For-itself were implicitly aligned with traditional gender roles.[2] The In-itself, understood as immanence, could also be read as feminine, whereas the For-itself, meant as volition, was adventurous and masculine. The human project of an individual's choice of self is, in Barrett's view, a masculine project requiring a rupture from nature. Woman, on the other hand, is nature, and as such, is a threat to freedom. To support his case, Barrett pointed to feminine and masculine imagery in Sartre's psychology in *Being and Nothingness* and in his literary works. Barrett also, remarkably, noticed that Sartre's female characters in his novels and plays, and his choice of companion, are anything but "ordinary women." And Barrett himself was not without his own sexist views, which feminists have pointed out, such as when he claims that women's choices of family and children cannot be projects of conscious egos. Still, apart from these inconsistencies, Barrett's initial claim of sexism in Sartre's philosophy began what was to be a heated debate.

Collins and Pierce agreed with Barrett that Sartre's two categories of Being are inherently sexed, even if unintentionally so, and considered Sartre's sexism to be "blatant." Sartre's aim in his psychology was to identify an individual's choice of being through his or her appropriation of the world. One quality of Being he identified as a threat to the For-itself was sliminess, first manifested in slimy things and then extending to psychological and moral attitudes. Although Sartre describes sliminess in many ways, what Collins and Pierce notice is that some of them are feminine, pejoratively so. Sartre's brief discussion of female sexuality in this section centers on the themes of holes, slime, and the obscene, with all three qualities linked to women's bodies (e.g., his statement that "the obscenity of the female sex is everything that gapes open" and his discussion of holes, the desire to fill them, which extends beyond but includes sexual acts and female anatomy). Collins and Pierce read holes-and-slime imagery as representing female behavior and anatomy, respectively; and both threaten (male) freedom. In sum, they claim that in Sartre's philosophy, women personify the unliberated In-itself, whereas men, aligned with Being For-itself, are caught in the throes of conflict and must fend off smothering women to protect their freedom.

The Collins and Pierce essay is the standard piece on sexism in existentialism. It has been widely cited as definitive proof of Sartre's sexism and has been regarded as sufficient grounds for discounting his work. Among those who cite the essay are Dorothy Kaufmann McCall, who considers Sartre ideologically sexist (while also admitting that his philosophy of freedom is compatible with feminism),[3] Naomi Greene, who goes so far as to claim that the sexism of Sartre's philosophy has negatively affected Beauvoir's views of female sexuality in *The Second Sex*,[4] and Jeffner Allen, who calls Sartre's philosophy *patriarchal* existentialism.[5] Citing the holes-and-slime passages, radical feminist Mary Daly calls Sartre "the philosopher of the obscene" and Peggy Holland considers his philosophy "a veto to women."[6] These notorious passages in his psychology aside, I and other feminists, including Allen, Judith Butler, Sonia Kruks, and Michèle Le Doeff, have criticized the patriarchal values implicit in Sartre's early philosophy. Not all feminist philosophers writing on Sartre in past decades were accusatory or dismissive.[7] Sandra Bartky's work on psychological oppression draws heavily on Sartre's analysis of objectification in *Being and Nothingness* and is one important exception.[8] Nonetheless, the holes-and-slime evidence persuaded many of Sartre's sexism and remains a common argument against his work.

Is Sartre guilty as charged? A more extensive understanding of sexism has developed since Collins and Pierce wrote their famous essay. Now, nearly twenty years later, scholars are revisiting the case made against him and largely defend his work. Hazel Barnes, the American translator of *Being and Nothingness*, argues that Sartre's images (for instance, in the holes-and-slime passages), but not his ideas, are sexist.[9] Bonnie Burstow grants that there is some sexism present, namely, that Sartre is guilty of incidental sexism, the sort of oppressive assumptions in his writings commonly found in privileged groups, particularly in men of his time, but she finds charges of his sexism to be overblown and notes that the male anatomy is also aligned with nature, the In-itself.[10] Sartre's point, she reminds us, is that the human body can be obscene. Constance Mui argues that a close analysis of the passages in question does not support the sweeping claims of blatant sexism by Collins and Pierce.[11] All three agree that whatever sexism there is in Sartre's work, it affects neither his ontology nor the feminist work, such as *The Second Sex,* that relies on it.

The debate over how sexist Sartre is might seem quarrelsome to us now, either because it centers on specific interpretations, not the only ones as Burstow shows, of select passages, or is dated, or narrowly focused. Yet, the early charge greatly influenced the reception of Sartre's work among feminists, making our return to the debate necessary. Looking back, perhaps we have been unfair to Sartre. When his work has been more scrutinized for sexism, in some instances, he is held to a higher standard because of his association with Beauvoir. The discussion of holes and slime is an unfortunate part of his early work. But not only should the whole of his life's work not suffer because of it, the criticisms of Collins and Pierce should not be lost either.

Of what use is Sartre's philosophy for feminists? The debate over Sartre's sexism has given way to possible uses of his work for feminist theory. This is no surprise, since some who attacked him also recognized a compatibility between his central ideas and feminist beliefs. In this collection, feminist scholars from a variety of disciplines are taking new approaches to Sartre's work, closing the gap between Sartre and feminism. Essays included here cover Sartre's early and later works, from his first philosophical treatise to his final interviews. In general, feminist philosophers draw heavily upon *Being and Nothingness* and *Anti-Semite and Jew.* These two texts, so centered on freedom and oppression, resonate with feminist theories of liberation. The value of Sartre's early existentialism, the emphasis on experience and embodiment, is not lost on feminists, though some find it more nuanced than it appears, whereas others develop their own more complex accounts. Reflecting a new trend in Sartrean scholarship, some authors put more stress on the lesser known *Critique of Dialectical Reason,* in which Sartre moves well beyond his ideas in the early existential writings. The *Critique,* as feminists show, also has useful political concepts that can be applied to the thorny problems of identity politics as well as feminist praxes. The *Notebooks on Ethics* is also of interest. Recently published, it contains some conventional ideas of Sartre's from the 1940s, particularly on interpersonal relationships, affording new readings for feminists of Sartre's early philosophy. Authors in this volume also address new directions in Sartre's work that are found in his final interviews in *Hope Now*. Not only do the authors provide discussions of Sartre's work in light of contemporary feminism, but they take a variety of different philosophical approaches. Themes covered in this collection include Sartre's sexism, Beauvoir as a collaborator, objectification, embodiment, freedom and oppression, identity and collectivity, friendship, spirituality, and the legitimacy of the final interviews.

The first essay, by Hazel Barnes, extends her earlier defense of Sartre and addresses two major charges from his critics—that his is a wholly male philosophy of no use to women and that his concept of the For-itself offers an unrealistic account of freedom. In response to the first charge, Barnes provides the most comprehensive discussion to date of Sartre's use of women in examples in his philosophical work. She considers how and why Sartre uses a woman in each case, from *Being and Nothingness* to his posthumous works and unpublished lectures. She argues that in only a few cases is Sartre displaying male chauvinism. Most of the time, he is describing common elements of the human situation. In fact, she shows how Sartre occasionally took men to task for making women's lives difficult and condemned the male bad faith that allows for gender oppression. She provides new speculation about why Sartre made little mention of women's liberation.

In the second part of her essay, Barnes argues that not only is Sartre's view of freedom not abstract and unrealistic, as Beauvoir and other critics have maintained, but Sartre's thinking on the interplay of freedom and socialization surpasses that of Beauvoir's in *The Second Sex*, making his work important for feminist theorists. Sartre's three ontological dimensions of the body make it possible for his philosophy to address influences of free choice and socialization. These three dimensions are the body as Being For-itself, the body for others, and my body as I am aware that it is known by others. Each dimension offers possibilities for authentic (erotic and nonerotic) human relationships based on reciprocity. This is a new approach supported, in part, by the *Notebooks*. Sartre is commonly understood to have only a negative view of personal, or at least sexual, relationships because of the emphasis on sadism and masochism in *Being and*

Nothingness and his famous line from *No Exit*, "Hell is other people." Yet in his writings, Sartre clearly understood the importance of social relationships and that cultural expectations and other social forces played a part even in forming authentic relationships. Barnes contends that Sartre has provided a more thorough examination of the ontological complexity of our existence as consciousness in bodies than has any other philosopher, with the possible exception of Merleau-Ponty. This complexity allows him to surpass Beauvoir's work in a second way.

While Beauvoir has declared that one makes oneself a woman, it is Sartre, according to Barnes, who has a theory about how we constitute ourselves as women and men. What is most useful for feminist theorists is Sartre's discussion of the relationship between consciousness and the ego, for this relationship is the site of our freedom. Barnes speculates that the relationship of consciousness to the ego parallels the three dimensions characterizing the relationship of consciousness to the body. She shows how social change is possible within Sartre's later philosophy, and in doing so, she offers us a Sartrean explanation for how consciousness-raising and other feminist forms of radical self-structuring actually work. Not only, then, is Sartre's understanding of freedom not hopelessly abstract, it is of great value to feminist theory.

Barnes has drawn on much of the corpus of Sartre's work to make her case. In doing so, she allows us to see how Sartre's philosophy developed over time. Typically, Sartreans focus on the early writings. These are marked by the beginning of Sartre's relationship with Beauvoir, his military service, and the transformation of his political consciousness by the Occupation. His call to freedom under oppressive circumstances resounds throughout his writings at this time and strikes a chord in feminist readers. In the next seven chapters, the authors take up themes of absence, objectification, embodiment, freedom, and oppression in Sartre's early existential writings.

In Chapter 2, Edward and Kate Fullbrook probe several separations that occur around Sartre's early work, separations that create telling absences. During Sartre's military service, he was separated from Beauvoir, though the two corresponded with each other a good deal about their writings. Sartre was drafting his landmark existentialist text, *Being and Nothingness*, and Beauvoir was writing her novel *She Came to Stay*. First the Fullbrooks note the absence of Sartre from important constructions of the philosophical canon. Next, they show how Beauvoir is an important collaborator for Sartre. They trace the development of Sartre's concept of absence, a central part of his ontology that appears twice in *Being and Nothingness* and also in the *War Diaries,* by comparisons with Beauvoir's phenomenological descriptions of absence in *She Came to Stay.* The Fullbrooks claim that Beauvoir was a major source of Sartre's early philosophical concept of absence, making for an asymmetrical collaboration. Their method of textual comparisons suggests Beauvoir as the origin of at least some of Sartre's existential philosophy. That *Being and Nothingness* is a product of Beauvoir and Sartre's philosophical collaboration and needs to be understood through the cross-textual processes that occurred in its making is a surprising claim, since Sartre gives Beauvoir no credit for the concept of absence in his text. (Did he wish to credit her but she refused to allow it?) The lack of mention of Beauvoir as collaborator in Sartre's text is another telling absence, matched by the same omission in most of Sartrean scholarship. That Sartre's work is commonly understood completely apart from the philosophical work of Beauvoir is the final absence the Fullbrooks address, one not perpetuated in this collection.

A topic of great importance to feminist theory is the objectification of women. Sartre is one of few philosophers who discusses objectification. The phenomenological approach of his early work emphasizes how we experience ourselves, in part, as objects for others and is the topic of the next three chapters. Phyllis Morris (Chapter 3) finds that the concept of objectification has been regarded in a wholly negative light in feminist theory. While there are negative forms of objectification, as Sandra Bartky, Iris Young, and Catharine MacKinnon have pointed out in their discussions of sexual objectification, Morris claims that the concept of objectification is theoretically broader than these discussions suggest. Some forms of sexual objectification are negative precisely because they assume patriarchal strategies of dominance. (And Morris claims that Beauvoir's *The Second Sex,* in its emphasis on patriarchal forms of objectification, influenced later feminists in their negative view of objectification.) Might there be non-dominance-oriented forms of objectification that are necessary for the realization of our full human capacity, Morris asks? If so, such positive accounts of objectification would offer feminist theorists a more thorough account of subject-object relations. In arguing for positive forms of objectification, she boldly advances feminist discussions, especially those of sexual objectification, beyond their current limits. This is no small task. The pornography debates of a decade ago were perhaps the most divisive moment for feminist theorists in recent times. Morris's work, in raising the possibility of positive forms of objectification, debunks the view that assumes objectification per se is morally suspect and points feminists in a new direction.

In order to provide a positive basis for objectification Morris looks not only to the work of the early Sartre, but to its particularly non-Cartesian elements. Presenting a view contrary to some feminist readings, she argues that Sartre's early existential phenomenology works against Cartesianism by refusing an oppositional relationship between the conscious subject and the human body. As she puts it, we are bodily subjects. This means that we are possible objects of perception for others and that we, as subjects, are object related. Objectification then, is a necessary part of being an embodied consciousness. While negative forms of objectification (e.g., the reduction of women to bodily parts) align it with devaluation, it is through objectification that value is brought into the world, and that we are recognized by others as human beings. Further, positive forms of objectification can include (non-dominance-oriented) forms of sexual objectification. While much has been made of Sartre's descriptions of sadism and masochism in *Being and Nothingness*, like Barnes, Morris claims that these do not include all forms of sexual objectification for Sartre. There is the possibility of non–dominance-oriented, reciprocal forms of sexual objectification that move people toward greater recognition of their embodiment without requiring some sort of fragmentation. Sartre's ontological understanding of objectification affords us multiple, complex views of ourselves, but still Morris wonders if the term *objectification* might be too broad to be useful for feminists, especially in critiques of pornography and sexist advertising. She concludes that the term requires more critical articulation if it is to be retained.

Thomas Martin (Chapter 4) takes up the challenge by examining negative forms of sexual objectification, specifically the objectification of women's bodies in the beauty industry. He applies Sartre's account of sadism in *Being and Nothingness* to the issue of female beauty ideals to show their detrimental affects on women. He considers whether women subject to the beauty ideals are in a situation similar to victims of sadism by examining women's phenomenological experience of their bodies as objects for others. Sartre's ontological notions of Being For-itself and Being For-others are central to his account of sadism. Martin differentiates Sartre's descriptions of grace and obscenity in order to show contrasting experiences of the Body For-itself and For-Others. Sartre's account of sadism calls to mind the way in which female beauty ideals affect women, such as the assumption of obscenity, that the body is "constituted of isolated parts." Female beauty ideals not only operate as standards for women's bodies, according to Martin, but can cause women to view their bodies as the central object of their consciousness. Though Martin draws parallels between sadism and the effects of female beauty ideals, he recognizes the two to be quite different. Sartre's analysis of sadism as Martin points out, is part of his theory of intersubjectivity, and hence, cannot be neatly mapped onto an account of a cultural pattern such as beauty ideals. Nonetheless, the striking similarities between the sadist's view of the body, and how it is viewed from the perspective of female beauty ideals offer clues to understanding particular experiences affecting women's consciousness of their bodies.

Some new gynocentric feminist theories of women's embodiment are critical of Sartre's existential theory of embodiment, and of any feminism (such as that of *The Second Sex*) that is seen as based on it. Constance Mui (Chapter 5) assesses the debate in feminist theory between existential and gynocentric views of female embodiment. Existentialists such as Sartre, Beauvoir, and Marcel responded to Cartesian dualism by offering a phenomenology of embodied consciousness, albeit not one that makes much of reproductive differences between women and men. Gynocentric critics charge Sartre with devaluing women's bodily experiences by failing to account for women's uniquely reproductive aspects. They want a feminist theory grounded in an ontology of female embodiment, one that takes seriously the differences in women's and men's reproductive biology. Gynocentric feminists, such as Mary O'Brien, find such differences important for validating women's experiences and claim that existentialists either leave unaddressed issues of female embodiment, or, in the case of Beauvoir, address women's reproductive role negatively. O'Brien validates women's experience by privileging female over male embodiment. She proposes separate ontologies of consciousness corresponding to men and women's reproductive differences that shape different relationships to nature, temporality, and species. Male embodiment, on her view, is marked by discontinuity, separation from nature and species, whereas female embodiment is marked by continuity, a direct connection with nature and the species through reproductive labor.

Mui admits that the existential model for embodiment often assumes a male norm, even for Beauvoir. However, she questions fundamental assumptions of gynocentric feminism by asking if female embodied experience must be incompatible with the existential view of embodiment and if it is inferior to male experience. What she finds particularly troubling in gynocentrism is its monolithic view of women. Must all women and only women share the gender-specific consciousness that O'Brien describes? Mui counters this assumption by pointing out the diversity and complexity of human reproductive experiences not afforded by a gender-specific model of embodiment based on separation or continuity. She questions O'Brien's gynocentrism on many fronts, among them the elevation of women's reproductive consciousness over that of men's, the privileging of continuity, the selection of a model for female reproductive experience, and the familiar reassertion of women's unity with nature as the basis for female authenticity. Like Morris, Mui appreciates the ontological complexity of Sartre's phenomenology. She concludes with a note of skepticism about gender-specific ontologies and considers instead the possibility of broadening traditional existentialism, such as Sartre's, to offer a gender-inclusive account of embodiment.

Sartre's account of freedom and oppression informs the next three chapters. Linda Bell and Sarah Hoagland are interested in feminist ethics. They use clues from the early writings to probe the meanings of authenticity for contemporary forms of oppression. In her essay, Bell (Chapter 6) examines unique features of Sartre's postwar account of anti-Semitism. Two issues in particular are perplexing: Sartre's treatment of Jewish inauthenticity as a unique form of inauthenticity, one without moral blame, and his claim that Jews in anti-Semitic French society cannot afford to be existentialists. Bell wonders whether these features of a uniquely Jewish inauthenticity are applicable to other forms of racism and (hetero)sexism. To what extent are the oppressed to be held morally responsible? In *Anti-Semite and Jew*, Sartre claims that Jews do not have the luxury of circumstance for metaphysical questions about the human condition, leaving Bell to speculate that Jews would not be able to be existentialists. Yet, existentialism is supposedly a philosophy of freedom, one that has embraced a number of liberation movements and one that Bell has found quite useful for addressing her own experiences of sexism in graduate school. To understand Sartre's somewhat baffling view of Jewish inauthenticity, Bell critically analyzes a number of possible explanations for Sartre's unique treatment of anti-Semitism. She argues that the uniqueness of anti-Semitism is in its Manichean aspects. For Sartre, the anti-Semite regards the Jew as the complete embodiment of evil and grants the Jew not a restricted or inferior social place, but no social place at all. The Jew, having available only inauthentic choices, is in an impossible situation. Bell argues for no similar form of inauthenticity for women or other oppressed groups who are relegated to some place, albeit an inferior place, in society, although it bears some resemblance to heterosexism. The similarity that Bell points out lies in the conservative demand for a renouncement of homosexuality, but important differences remain, making Sartre's account of anti-Semitism present an unusual case. For Bell, other oppressed groups are morally responsible for their inauthenticity and may find existentialism helpful for addressing their oppression.

Like Bell, Sarah Hoagland (Chapter 7) finds Sartre's assumption of ontological freedom useful for the oppressed, particularly his notion of authenticity, but she finds limitations in his analysis. Using a philosophical style of storytelling, conversation, and collage, she presents a radical feminist exploration of freedom and resistance. Hoagland asks, "So, how do I move from an ontological understanding of existential freedom to possibilities of political resistance and change under conditions of oppression?" One might find Sartre's early examples of bad faith instructive. Hoagland, however, takes a critical look at the examples from *Being and Nothingness*—the "frigid" woman, the woman on a date, the waiter, and the homosexual—and charges Sartre with arrogance. She claims that he is unable to read the oppressive contexts for choices from anything but the dominant perspective. In each case, Sartre fails to read the context outside of the dominant script. But the dominant script is not the only script possible in oppressive situations. Some allegedly inauthentic choices might be important acts of resistance if viewed from a different perspective. On her view, Sartre fails to provide an adequate account of authentic choices for the oppressed due to his acceptance of certain philosophical assumptions, such as his belief in a unified consciousness and a unitary world of meaning. Hoagland extends existentialism beyond its fundamental assumptions. She shows that authentic choice requires that one know the dominant scripts while using one's agency to generate alternative forms of meaning even within oppressive contexts. This requires multiplicities that allow for alternative readings of choices amid oppression. Further, she asserts that to authentically resist oppression, one must "eradicate the awe one has of an oppressor" and "create new worlds of sense." The idea of playful world travel in the work of María Lugones is a way to create new meanings of otherness, meanings not based on the threat of difference but ones that assume and affirm our intersubjectivity and offer the possibility for political freedom.

Karen Greene's essay (Chapter 8) on freedom and oppression is a transitional piece between the focus on Sartre's early writings and the next five chapters on the later work. Like Bell and Hoagland, Greene is interested in Sartre's early account of oppression, but like the Fullbrooks, she explores Beauvoir's influence on Sartre's account. Greene begins by asking if Beauvoir taught Sartre about freedom, as Sonia Kruks has claimed elsewhere. Kruks goes on to maintain that Beauvoir's analysis of freedom amid oppression surpasses that of Sartre's in the 1940s and foreshadows the development of Sartre's later ideas in the *Critique*. Green takes issue with Kruks's position. For Green, Beauvoir was accurate in acknowledging the Sartrean influences in *The Second Sex*. She shows several close parallels between Sartre and Beauvoir; for instance, their accounts of the origin of oppression in *Anti-Semite and Jew* and *The Second Sex*. Beauvoir differs from Sartre, however, according to Green, in her use of Hegel, Engels, and Lévi-Strauss, rather than primarily in the influence of Merleau-Ponty on Beauvoir, as Kruks suggests. Still, Green contends, these differences do not surpass Sartre's account. Moreover, not only are Sartre's and Beauvoir's approaches to oppression quite similar, they share the same limits. Green concludes that Sartre and Beauvoir place too much emphasis on the attitudes and responsibilities of individuals, neglecting larger social constraints that are imposed on people, make authenticity an impossible option, and fail to emphasize the importance of group solidarity. Not until the *Critique* is there an account of oppression that addresses these points.

The next five chapters are on Sartre's later writings. The authors address new directions in Sartrean scholarship, specifically the usefulness of Sartre's work for countering identity politics, the possibility of friendship as feminist praxis, the discovery of a feminine economy in Sartre's notion of the abandon, and Sartre's influence on feminist spirituality. Two philosophers, Iris Young and Sonia Kruks, appeal to Sartre's *Critique* for insight on one popular form of feminist politics, supported by Sartre's early work, that is problematic for some feminists. In *Being and Nothingness*, writing about class oppression, Sartre claimed that it was important for oppressed people to first identify with the oppression and then to claim it as their own in order to rebel against it (e.g., workers as workers should challenge capitalism). A similar political strategy, now developed in more detail and known as identity politics, has become quite popular among feminists. Identity politics took hold in the feminist movement in counterpoint to monolithic views about women. That all women are not equally situated in the political landscape, a point not recognized by some feminist theorists who possessed a certain measure of race and class privi-lege that was left unexamined in their theorizing, gave rise to identity politics in feminism. Although identity politics has been empowering for many women, critics find several problems with it. Identity politics has been accused of being normalizing, exclusive, and essentialist, among other charges. Most important of all is the challenge posed by it for femi-nist theory: can one legitimately claim anything about women in general? If not, then conceptualizing about women as a single group—indeed the very idea of a women's movement—may be untenable. Because identity politics remains a vital political strategy, this question is an important one that feminists need to address.

Iris Young (Chapter 9) acknowledges the vital role identity politics has played in feminism but is committed to finding some philosophical basis for theorizing about women as a social collective. If we give up understanding women as a social collective, we must identify oppression as an individual problem by either victim blaming or attributing oppres-sion to the attitudes of other individuals. In either case, no attention is paid to the structural and political components of oppression, that Young, like Greene, finds to be important. Young reviews arguments critical of female gender identity by Elizabeth Spelman, Chandra Mohanty, and Judith Butler, but resists concluding that it makes no sense to talk about women as a group. She argues for regarding gender as seriality, in the sense that Sartre gives the term in the *Critique*.

There Sartre identifies levels of internal organization, from relatively unstructured social collectives, which he called a "series" and likened to people waiting for a bus, to elaborate forms of social organization, which he called "groups." Like feminist theorists, Sartre was interested in how individuals come together for political action and, equally important, how political groups, after obtaining a measure of internal organization, fall apart. Sartre realized that if we could not understand why political movements fail, we would not be successful in political transformation. And we cannot understand political movements accurately if we cannot regard oppressed peoples as social collectives. Because women have com-mon constraints yet need not know one another or feel any solidarity with one another, Young proposes that we see them as a series, though a more complex series than Sartre's bus riders. If we understand gender as seriality, Young maintains, we avoid the problems of asserting a common identity. Women can be considered as a social collective without having a common situation or similar attributes. Instead, a social unity is attributed to women based on a set of gender-based structural constraints and relations to the world, such as a sexual division of labor and enforced heterosexuality, that are shaped by history. This perspective avoids false essentialism. Young's innovative application of seriality from Sartre's *Critique* to the complex issues of identity politics affords feminists a feasible solution to many of the problems with identity politics while preserving feminist theory as a legitimate practice.

For Sonia Kruks (Chapter 10), a major problem with identity politics is what she calls its epistemology of provenance. By this she means that identity politics assumes a highly experiential and subjectivist theory of knowledge that is group specific. This again raises a major problem for doing feminist theory. For if we can only speak about that which we directly experience, there can be no common knowledge or solidarity across different identity groups of women. Equally troubling, there can be no collective judgments about sexist practices by those who do not belong to the groups that experience such practices. Like Young, Kruks is committed to finding a way to generalize about women's oppression by concentrating on what women do rather than on female gender identity. She also appeals to Sartre's notion of seriality in the *Critique*. But she differs from Young in her emphasis on the epistemological features of seriality and the dialectical dimensions of human actions.

Kruks finds feminist standpoint theory, as developed by Nancy Hartsock, to be a good but not completely unproblematic alternative to identity politics. A feminist standpoint allows for general claims about women provided they are based not so much on women's subjective experiences as on their specific practices within the social division of labor. Hartsock's standpoint theory, however, has been criticized for obscuring differences between and making false generalizations about women. Kruks is generally in agreement with Donna Haraway's attempts to amend this problem by suggesting that there are multiple feminist standpoints, on the one hand, and some form of common knowledge, on the other, although she is dissatisfied with Haraway's account of how one moves between particular standpoints and common knowledge. This epistemological problem inherent in feminist standpoint theory can be addressed by an appeal to Sartre's Marxist vision of human emancipation and his privileging of differences in the *Critique*. Most important, Sartre has a dialectical concept of reason that Kruks applies to Haraway's account. In Sartre's view of situated knowledges, they arise in a dialectical relationship with other human activities and are communicable because we share common material fields in which we encounter one another's intentional praxes. Through our praxes, then, we are materially and serially connected to each other. Kruks also uses Sartre's concepts of exteriority, interiority, and reciprocity to explain how situated knowledges are translatable for the possibility of common knowledge. Her essay shows one of the ways in which Sartre's later work is vital for solving an epistemological problem in an alternative to identity politics.

Peter Diers (Chapter 11) explores how female friendship might function as an important form of feminist praxis, one with revolutionary potential. Sartre gave little attention to the role of friendship in political transformation. Instead, he outlines processes in the *Critique* by which groups of people united against an oppressive institution can impede political change when the group itself comes to constitute new forms of oppression. Diers asks, If social bonds can have reactionary results, can they also be revolutionary? He finds there to be some hope at the local level if friendships can be a vehicle for personal and social change. He offers an account of how some forms of women's friendships can become feminist praxes by critically discussing the work of two feminist theorists on the topic of friendship; Marilyn Friedman's on the moral dimensions of friendship and Janice Raymond's on the political dimensions of *Gyn/ affection*. With his account of feminist praxis, Diers offers a vital link between Sartre's large historical structures in the *Critique* and the local level of concrete action.

The status of Sartre's final interviews, those with his new young collaborator, Benny Lévy, is one of the most debated aspects of Sartrean scholarship. Readers find Sartre, rather than restating his earlier positions, describing quite different ideas in *Hope Now*. For instance, his comments about authentic humanity and social harmony are not only in sharp contrast with his early existentialism, but close to messianic. His new ideas alarm many of his traditional supporters while bringing new readers to his work. Many scholars and friends of Sartre's, Beauvoir among them, disregard *Hope Now*, holding firm to the idea that Sartre never meant to waver from his core philosophical beliefs. Two scholars who do believe that Sartre continued to develop and change his philosophy even in his final years are Guillermine de Lacoste and Stuart Charmé.

In her essay, Lacoste (Chapter 12) acknowledges a shift in Sartre's thinking reflected in the *Hope Now* interviews with Lévy and his final interviews with Beauvoir in *Adieux*. Lacoste understands this change in

Sartre's thinking as a transition from what Hélène Cixous would call a masculine to a feminine economy. Cixous, a French feminist, contrasts two approaches to pleasure and giving in personal and social relationships: a masculine economy of law and a feminine economy of reciprocal abandon. The feminine economy encourages generosity, openness to others, and positive receptivity. The masculine economy desires to close off openness to others by feelings of obligation and duty. Lacoste traces Sartre's neurotic fear of abandon through his personal life and his philosophy. At the end of his life, Lacoste argues, Sartre finally overcomes his fear of abandonment. As a result, we find new philosophical ideas that reflect a feminine economy of openness and generosity, not possible before in his early work; we even find a celebration of Mother Humanity. By reading Sartre's life and work through Cixous's theoretical categories, Lacoste pieces together not only disparate parts of Sartre's philosophy but also puzzling aspects of his life. In doing so, she offers a reading of Sartre that is not patronizing or dismissive of his new views in old age, and that in seeing these ideas as the culmination of a life's journey from neurosis to health will not quiet the storm of the debate.

In the final essay, Stuart Charmé (Chapter 13) explores common ground between Sartre's work and feminist theology. He contends that the evolution of Sartre's thought, from his early focus on the "desire to be God" to his final search for a model of authentic community in *Hope Now*, has much in common with the development of feminist theology. Despite Sartre's protestations as an avowed atheist, Charmè points out that he never totally rejected the influence of religion on human beings. Beauvoir, on the other hand, has an antireligious feminism. Charmè describes Beauvoir's rejection of religion and shows the ways in which Sartrean philosophy has taken root in the writings of feminists Mary Daly, Carol Christ, Rosemary Ruether, and others. Sartre's essay on the African poets is particularly useful for its account of a non-Western form of spirituality. For Charmè, the final convergence of Sartre's thought with feminist theology can be found in the Lévy interviews. He draws striking parallels between Sartre's notions of authentic community and Mother Humanity and Ruether's emphasis on the God/ess as transformative symbol representing personal, social, and environmental harmony. It is this hint of Sartrean spirituality that most troubles the critics of *Hope Now*. Whether or not Sartre underwent a deathbed conversion in spiritual matters remains controversial, as does the question of how his new ideas coalesce with his previous writings. At the very least, it is uncanny that in his last years, Sartre began speaking a language that feminist theologians find comfortable.

The essays in this collection begin an important and long overdue dialogue between feminist theory and Sartrean philosophy. While the authors differ in their philosophical approaches as well as their feminist politics, each demonstrates the value of the Sartrean project for feminist inquiry. This is the first feminist collection on Sartre, hopefully to be followed by others that may pursue some of the important issues raised here along with other new directions in feminist theory.

Notes

1. Margery L. Collins and Christine Pierce, "Holes and Slime: Sexism in Sartre's Psychoanalysis." *Philosophical Forum* 5 (1973): 112–27. Also in *Women and Philosophy: Toward a Theory of Liberation*, Carol C. Gould and Marx W. Wartofsky (New York: G. P. Putnam's Sons, 1976), 112–27; and in *Women in Western Thought*, ed. Martha Lee Osborne (New York: Random House, 1979), 319–22.

2. William Barrett, *Irrational Man: A Study in Existential Philosophy* (New York: Doubleday, 1962).

3. Dorothy Kaufmann McCall, "Simone de Beauvoir, *The Second Sex*, and Jean-Paul Sartre," *Signs* 5 (1979): 209–23.

4. Naomi Greene, "Sartre, Sexuality, and *The Second Sex*." *Philosophy and Literature* 4 (1980): 199–211.

5. Jeffner Allen, "An Introduction to Patriarchal Existentialism: A Proposal for a Way out of Existential Patriarchy," first published in *Philosophy and Social Criticism* 9 (1982). Also in *The Thinking Muse: Feminism and Modern French Philosophy*, ed. Jeffner Allen and Iris Marion Young (Bloomington: Indiana University Press, 1989); See also Allen, *Sinuosities: Lesbian Poetic Politics* (Bloomington: Indiana University Press, 1996).

6. Peggy Holland, "Jean-Paul Sartre as a NO to Women," *Sinister Wisdom* 6 (1978): 72–79; Mary Daly, *Gyn/Ecology: The Mataethics of Radical Feminism* (Boston: Beacon Press, 1978).

7. See my "The Look in Sartre and Adrienne Rich," *Hypatia* 2, no. 2 (1987): 113–24; reprinted in Allen and Young, *The Thinking Muse: Feminism and Modern French Philosophy*, 101–12; see also Judith Butler, *Gender Trouble: Feminism and the Subversion of Identity* (New York: Routledge, 1990); Sonia Kruks, "Simone de Beauvoir: Teaching Sartre About Freedom," in *Feminist Interpretations of Simone de Beauvoir*, ed. Margaret Simons (University Park: Penn State Press, 1995) 79–96; and Michèle Le Doeuff, *Hipparchia's Choice: An Essay Concerning Women, Philosophy, etc.*, trans. Trista Selous (Oxford: Blackwell, 1991).

8. "On Psychological Oppression" was first published in *Philosophy and Women*, ed. Sharon Bishop and Marjorie Weinzweig (Belmont, Calif.: Wadsworth, 1979), 33–41, and later appeared in Sandra Lee Bartky, *Femininity and Domination: Studies in the Phenomenology of Oppression* (New York: Routledge, 1990).

9. Hazel E. Barnes, "Sartre and Sexism, "*Philosophy and Literature* 14 (1990): 340–47.

10. Bonnie Burstow, "How Sexist Is Sartre?" *Philosophy and Literature* 16, no. 1 (1992): 32–48.

11. Constance Mui, "Sartre's Sexism Reconsidered." *Auslegung* 16, no. 1 (1990): 31–41.

1

Sartre and Feminism

Aside from *The Second Sex* and All That

Hazel E. Barnes

While Sartre's *Critique of Dialectical Reason* could hardly be called a drama, the first volume has a distinct sense of rising and falling action. The dramatic climax comes in the cluster of passages describing the emergence of the group-in-fusion and the formation of the fused group. Rhetorical excitement abounds as Sartre puts us in the midst of the group at white heat, running on "its hundred pairs of legs," shouting with "its hundred mouths," each one of us the same in a body of "myselves" (*des moi-même*). Then, on the bright morning after the battle, when all vote to continue their existence as a pledged group, emotion mounts still higher. This act Sartre declares to be "the origin of humanity." Our committed freedoms unite us. We are brothers, but not like tinned peas in a can. Sartre grandly proclaims, "We are our common creation, we are our own sons."[1] What a thud! Why couldn't Sartre have written, "We are our own children"? The French *enfants* is a nonsexual generic, *fils* is not.

Perhaps one might say that the logic of rhetoric requires the masculine. Sartre's description is loosely based on the taking of the Bastille, the revolutionary group comes into being on the field of battle, and so on. The further we go, the worse it gets. "The origin of humanity" is in a military camp; we pledge ourselves to invoke terror against traitors and defectors. "We?" Sartre may say "we," but I cannot. And where are the women? One may assume that they are cooking a meal for the men busy signing the new constitution. Whatever the women are doing, one can only imagine them. In the text itself there is no room for them. Women are nowhere. To label the formation of this male club the "origin of humanity" is a travesty.

I begin with this dismal illustration because I want to acknowledge at the outset that it is not without reason that some feminists have found Sartre's aggressive masculinity, shown in a passage such as this and in the sexist language of certain rhetorical images in *Being and Nothingness*, sufficient to render suspect, in their opinion, his overt approval of *The Second Sex* and women's liberation. I find this judgment overhasty but understandable. Sartre is not *my* ego ideal either. What I cannot accept is the often heard pronouncement that Sartre's entire philosophy is so irremediably male that it excludes women. Nor the view that it is based on the notion of a purely male consciousness, presented as an all but disembodied, hostile stare. Nor the charge that Sartre's concept of human freedom is so abstract as to be virtually unrelated to the real world. Nor even the conclusion that, while Beauvoir managed to bend Sartre's ontology to suit her own purpose, the only way to find Sartre's philosophy at all useful for feminism today is to concentrate on his later work and regard *Being and Nothingness* as preenlightened Sartre.

In a small, limited response to such attacks on Sartre, I will do two things here: First, I will ask whether Sartre's philosophical writings (I will exclude his literary works) do in fact put us into a wholly male world. He frequently employs examples in which women are present. What do these show us about Sartre's attitude? Second, I want to look once again at Sartre's early description of consciousness in relation to the body and the ego. Is the for-itself in truth a bizarre creation that can exist only on the printed page?

* * *

First then, what are the implications of those examples in which Sartre selects women to clarify or to illustrate points in his philosophy? Without attempting to be exhaustive, I find that a surprisingly large number comes readily to mind. They are of various types:

Among those that refer to women to illustrate negative points, the one most strongly reflecting male bias is, of course, the woman in the café who demonstrates bad faith as she tries to deceive herself with regard to her companion's sexual overtures and her own responses to him.[2] This woman's behavior is by no means unusual. I suspect that Sartre was expressing his frustration in having often encountered it. Yet he could, drawing on even more intimate personal experience, have analyzed the conduct of a self-deceiving male seducer. Perhaps more offensive, because more general, is a remark in *Notebooks for an Ethics*. In the context Sartre is discussing devices in bad faith by which people attempt to protect their unfounded beliefs from rational argument. One of these is the appeal to intuition, which Sartre finds frequent among women, especially "wives or girl friends of professionals (engineers, lawyers, doctors) who regularly beat them in discussion; they can protect their truths only by putting them beyond the control of discussions and discourse, of criticism."[3] Sartre softens his charge by pointing out that resorting to intuition is an inoffensive weapon of the weak. And, of course, he is speaking of the untrained in the presence of experts. Still, the tacit assumption is that only rationality counts; the implication is that women's appeal to other than established forms of reason is a sign of inferiority.

Other examples of women illustrating self-deception are not necessarily reflections of male chauvinism. In *Saint-Genet* Sartre makes an extended comparison of Saint Theresa with two would-be saints, Jouhandeau and Genet. Sartre is unkind to Saint Theresa, labeling her a "fake saint," who in her professed self-abasement risked far less than the other two and was more thoroughly steeped in self-deception.[4] But, if Sartre is unfair to her, surely here the cause is his lack of sympathy for Christianity, not sexual bias. In *Truth and Existence*, Sartre chooses a woman to exemplify a willed ignorance that is almost indistinguishable from bad faith, a woman who will find reasons not to consult a doctor, who refuses even to try to interpret her own symptoms, because she does not want to risk knowing that she has tuberculosis.[5] Sartre could just as easily have imagined a man. But aside from the coincidental fact that he probably had in mind a real woman of his acquaintance, I find it hard to see his choice as expressive of contempt for women. In a couple of examples taken from psychoanalytical studies, Sartre introduces women. From *The Emotions* we recall the woman who fainted at the sight of the bay tree *in order to* (in Sartre's view) repress a painful recollection of an episode that once took place near such a tree.[6] In *The Transcendence of the Ego* Sartre refers to Janet's account of the young bride, who found herself suddenly feeling, in a panic, that she *could,* that she was *free* to call down invitations to men in the street though nothing in her past suggested that she was capable of such behavior.[7] This last example is of special interest. Rather than seeking an explanation of the woman's impulse in a repressed past, Sartre views her as experiencing what he believes is a frightening but potentially liberating revelation of the truth of our condition: no human consciousness is walled in or protected by the ego, it is gloriously and terrifyingly free to restructure its own ego. While hardly an example of authenticity, the young bride is, albeit neurotically, expressing our human reality.

Even with just these examples we would have to acknowledge that Sartre has at least peopled his world with women, introduced them into his discussion; the "men only" setting of the fused group appears to be more the exception than the rule. This impression is strengthened when we examine instances where there is no suggestion of bad faith or of instability, places where Sartre might even more naturally have chosen a man but chose a woman instead. The most familiar is probably not useful to us—from *Psychology of Imagination*, the female entertainer, a real person, Franconay, who impersonated Maurice Chevalier.[8] I think it would be a mistake to argue that here Sartre either elevated women as achievers in invoking the imaginary or downgraded them by implying that imagination is powerful enough even to transform a lowly woman into a man. The significant examples come from *Critique* 1 and from the posthumous works.

In *Critique* 1, Sartre dwells at length on the way that industrial conditions have rendered individuals' ontological freedom meaningless. He refers to a woman factory worker who realizes that she is pregnant. Unable to support a child, she decides to have an abortion. The decision is free in that she *could* have let the child be born even though she knew she would be unable to take care of it. But her circumstances are such that Sartre feels he can say that in having the abortion, the woman "carries out against herself the sentence, which has already been passed on her, which deprives her of free motherhood."[9] Two pages earlier, in another example from a factory, he referred to studies that had been made of the way that the demanding rhythm of the hand-operated machines controlled the mental content of the minds of the women who ran them. Remembering and daydreaming were possible; concerned thought about the women's children or husbands or household problems was not. Sartre mentions that the inner life of men workers was comparably regulated by "the machine in them," but it is women on whom he focuses in showing the extent to which our invented instruments have compelled us to be instrumental to them. Note that in both instances Sartre not only illustrates a general point with a feminine example, but considers how she is affected *as a woman*, not just as a human being. She is not, however, shown to us as a victim of males as such, rather of exploitative capitalism viewed asexually.

In the posthumous writings there are at least three places where women are shown to be deliberately victimized by men. The strangest of these is the relatively long passage in the section on violence in *Notebooks for an Ethics* in which Sartre discusses rape solely in terms of the bad faith and self-destructive behavior of the male perpetrator, without a single reference to the woman's reactions or to the social context of sexual violence.[10] Granted, the man is thoroughly condemned, but one feels that rape here is little more than a mental construct.[11] With little change Sartre could have used his example to illustrate the conduct of a man deciding to take by force a work of art he might have bought legitimately. I give this one to Sartre's negative critics.

On two other occasions, although Sartre's primary intent is to explain the motives of the men in question, he explicitly champions the rights of their women victims. *Truth and Existence* reproaches men with having for centuries tried to protect young girls' innocence (innocence from a male point of view, of course) by keeping them ignorant of their own sexuality.[12] A more fully developed example of keeping a woman ignorant of her own condition occurs in the lectures intended for delivery at Cornell. Sartre imagines a couple whose relationship has been exemplary for the pair's mutual concern, openness and honesty. The husband learns that his wife has cancer and resolves to conceal the truth from her. Sartre condemns him for his "theft of his wife's control over her future" and "his systematic treatment of her as an object." This time we could not say that Sartre could just as well have used a man—a son or a father. For he shows how the husband's motives are not merely a mistaken sympathy. Rather they reflect a desire to keep the couple's life within comfortable social structures. In determining what is best for his wife, the husband reaffirms the pattern of male supremacy; he avoids the need for both of them to confront the truth of a life no longer "free from despair" and the necessity of reinventing themselves and their relationship.[13]

Two other passages, which come from the "Rome Lecture Notes," show Sartre using women to illustrate positive points he wants to make, albeit in negative settings. The first is a curious restatement of Kant's "I ought implies I can." Sartre refers to a study involving high school girls. Questioned about their attitude toward lying, 95 percent of them said they believed it was wrong to lie, and 90 percent admitted that on occasion they did lie. Rather than dismissing this as a banal case of human weakness, Sartre claims that the girls intuitively recognized that truthfulness must be kept as a norm in order to preserve the possibility of not lying. Otherwise there would be only lies. To set up what one believes to be an unconditioned norm, Sartre argues, is to lay claim to one's self-determination.[14] Even a schoolgirl might in some circumstances be willing to die for a norm, and that is the ultimate assertion of freedom. Sartre's second example uses the report of a group of women in Belgium who, in the late 1950s, killed their newborn babies, seriously deformed by the mothers' use of thalidomide during pregnancy. In resolving that it was "better to give death than subhumanity," the women were not merely choosing quality of life as a criterion in preference to the sacredness of life as such. It would be an error, Sartre says, to see here an attempt to establish a categorical imperative. The example is anti-Kantian. One cannot universalize the imperative to reject all newborns with a subhuman future; there are other forms of subhuman existence than physical deformity. The women's hope was that their statement that their children were better off dead than alive would pressure medical and governmental institutions to find such accidents as the thalidomide misadventure unacceptable and to take stronger measures to prevent them. The infanticide was both a response to a specific social crisis and a plan to shape the future. As Sartre puts it, each woman said in effect, "I kill my child today so that tomorrow no mother will be tempted to kill hers." The act was a moral praxis.[15] Despite Sartre's carefully refraining from passing judgment on the rightness or wrongness of the decision, it seems obvious to me that he regarded the Belgian mothers as existentialist heroines of a sort, comparable to his fictional hero-murderer Orestes.

My last of Sartre's examples is the most richly complex, the most difficult to interpret; and, for some reason, I find it the most compelling. For these reasons and because it is less familiar, I will examine it in more detail. In *Critique* 2 Sartre has been carrying further the key notion of *Critique* 1; in other words, the claim that whenever I inscribe an act in worked matter, it develops a potentially alienating aspect, often resulting in so profound a deviation that the world can be said to have stolen my action from me. Now he reminds us about how sometimes our very efforts to express ourselves may betray us—as when by moving overcarefully or trying too hard to put others at their ease, we mar the result we try to attain. This interaction of inward intention and outward manifestation, Sartre says, makes the unity of the person. "It is our very life." Sartre goes on to say that whether or not we, as beholders, have the keys and the wit to discern it, there is manifest in the person before me something that could be called the *meaning* of the person. Now the example:[16]

Sartre invites us to consider the woman now walking by. She "is certainly modest and decent; she works, and her serious face and unobtrusive manner show that she has little taste for scandal. Yet she is dressed in gaudy fabrics and wears a loud, vulgar hat." "The violent clash between the bright red and the apple green" and "the contrast between that 'loud' hat and that casual, unselfconscious head" incarnate the woman's free choice in buying the clothes and deviate it. Treating the woman almost like a literary character, Sartre tells us that it was her indifference, her lack of narcissism and coquetry, that led her to purchase the tawdry articles without ever reflecting on them in relation to herself. "She was thinking of *owning* them—like a bit of that lively joy of which she knows nothing—rather than about *wearing* them." In fact she had bought precisely the sort of clothes that ordinarily street women wear, women who, unlike her, want to attract attention to themselves. A careless passerby may actually accost her as a prostitute. A well-intentioned friend may point out her mistake to her, but the woman, not being rich, will then have to wear "the shirt of Nessus" until the material wears out. The dress and the hat shout "whore" for this woman who has chosen them for what they seemed to be objectively, something to "stand out against the greyness of life." For, Sartre sums up, "that *bad taste*—that '*vulgarity*'—is simply the vague presentiment of beauty."

What are we to make of this passage? I imagine some might find it patronizing, the complacent passing of judgment by a cultured bourgeois man on a woman whose appearance fails to conform to his superior aesthetic standards. One cannot deny the presence of unspoken assumptions concerning sex and class; indeed, the example would lose its point if they were not there. (Personally, I confess to a feeling of relief that the woman's lack of education will protect her from having to play Galatea to Sartre's Pygmalion.) Yet the unexpected, compassionate conclusion starkly suggests the hidden *lacrimae rerum*, the tears of things in our human condition. And what remains with the reader longest? What most strikes us in reading this sketch? Is it the hopeless deviation of a personal choice? Or is it the sudden glimpse of a human impulse, unpredictable at the very heart of the practico-inert, freely reaching out to grasp what if finds valuable? There is that, and there is the revelation to us of Sartre's ability empathically to grasp both the inward reality of an act simultaneously so pathetic and so glorious—and, if you like, so feminine—and the complex deviation of its history.

What conclusions may we draw from this brief consideration of Sartre's use of women in examples? There are a few, remarkably few, traces of what I will call *unintended* male chauvinism. (For anyone but Sartre I would say "unconscious.") One assumption is all pervasive: that the human and the personal have existential priority over sex differentiation. We see this not only in the lack of mention of any determining "femininity" or "masculinity" but positively in the ease with which Sartre chooses, often as if at random, both males and females to illuminate the most basic principles in his phenomenological description of human consciousness in-the-world. There is a recognition of ways in which men have made it difficult for women freely to "make themselves" and a condemnation of the male bad faith that is responsible. We see some evidence that Sartre attempted to grasp the particular quality of the kind of situation that only women confronted. By implication, there seems to be room for women leaders in another sort of fused group. In the case of the Belgian women, there is a suggestion that women's unique experience might lead them to change social practice in a particular instance. There is no more general claim that women, in the name of feminine values, might effectively challenge the prevailing "subhumanity," which Sartre believes to be our present environment. In short, Sartre's *attitudes*, as shown here, are, for the most part, compatible with Beauvoir's in *The Second Sex*. They do not clearly point to a feminism more radical than she proposed there; nor, I add, do they preclude it.

If Beauvoir had not (at Sartre's suggestion, we should not forget) written *The Second Sex*, I doubt that Sartre would have attempted a work of his own on women's condition. (One cannot be sure, of course. This strictly heterosexual intellectual did not hesitate to describe the inner life of the homosexual, convicted felon, Saint Genet.) Sartre allowed his favorite character, Hoederer, to say that he was not interested in the cause of women's liberation. In Sartre's case, I think his making relatively few statements on the subject was not due to lack of interest but to the conviction that this was a specific area for the application of general principles and a sphere for social action rather than for philosophical investigation, just as he firmly believed that the education and the treatment of children within the family called for a revolution in our thinking and practice but never wrote an article devoted to child psychology. In taking over the task herself, Beauvoir built primarily on two major themes in Sartre—the subject-object conflict and his insistence that human beings are not born with a given nature but make themselves. All of this is so fully developed in *The Second Sex* that I will not touch on it here. If there is any point on which all feminists agree, surely it is the view that women historically have been the losers in the conflict and that self-definition must be the first step in any effort by women to develop their potentialities, whether as human beings or as women.

In his later work, Sartre went beyond not only *Being and Nothingness* but also *The Second Sex* in his emphasis on the interplay of freedom and conditioning. A summary statement of his position with regard to the relation between the sexes is found in *Critique 2*. "The sexual relationship . . . is perhaps the deepest incarnation of the relation of reciprocity between human beings, at once as free organisms and as products of the society in which they live." He goes on to say that it is not just the couple but the society that is set up for judgment in this "free incarnation."[17] Embodiment as a free incarnation of organisms, the paradox of men and women declared to be free in a society that has produced them, a society on which a judgment can be brought to bear: this passage could not have come from *Being and Nothingness*. Nevertheless, its roots are there. There has been much misunderstanding of Sartre's view on the relation of a consciousness to its body and its ego. It has been particularly consequential in feminists' judgment of his philosophy. Let us look at his position again, beginning with what he says about the body.

I have noticed that translators (myself included) tend to choose the English work "incarnation" in translating the French cognate, rather than "embodiment," which is the more usual term in philosophical contexts.

Why not use "embodiment"? My guess is that we translators have nonre-flectively responded to our sense that it suggests more of a fixed enrooting than seems right for Sartre. In connotation at least, "incarnation" implies that something is one with its setting and yet more than it. Strictly speak-ing, a consciousness, for Sartre, is nether more nor other than its body. He states firmly, "The body is what this consciousness *is*; it is not even anything except body. The rest is nothingness and silence."[18] The "noth-ingness," we know, makes all the difference. Consciousness both is and is not its body. As intentional activity, consciousness lives its relation with the body in three different ways. Or, as Sartre puts it, the human body has three ontological dimensions: (1) the body as being-for-itself; in nonreflective action my body's instrumentality is so fused with conscious intentions that the two are no more separable than a skier's leg is separa-ble from his skiing; (2) the body-for-others, or my body as others perceive it; and (3) my body as I am aware that it is known by others.

Some critics have argued that the very formulation of the three di-mensions introduces an artificial separation into bodily experience. In particular they find a problem in the fact that I apparently cannot simul-taneously be my body and know it. Now if by this they mean that I cannot at the same instant nonreflectively exist my body (to use Sartre's terminology) and focus on it as an object, this is true; but I do not see it as a problem. Consciousness always fluctuates between the reflective and nonreflective modes, often in lightning flashes within a single minute. Sartre did not say that I cease to have an implicit awareness of my body when I do not focus on it directly. I offer a mundane example of my own:

I am trying to pick apples from a branch just above my head. The apples-to-be-picked, not my body, are the posited object of my conscious-ness. Yet consciousness suffuses the body. My consciousness does not command my arm to stretch out, and so on. Experientially, it is rather that my conscious arm reaches to pull down the branch. Suppose now that a friend, unseen by me, is observing me. The second dimension of my body is actively realized but without the body's ceasing to exist in the first one. It is, of course, the other who realizes the possibilities of my body-for-others. She will not watch my bodily movements as if they were the aimless leapings of a squirrel. She will see me as caught up in the project of picking apples. If suddenly I realize that my body-in-action is known and understood by another, I may say, "You see I'm not quite tall enough. Could you lend me a hand?" I have moved into the third dimen-sion but still exist in the other two; for even as I speak, I am moving my hand toward the apple-to-be-picked as my friend lowers the branch. In fact, no one of the three dimensions is wholly absent at any stage. The body is always present as ground. I am throughout implicitly aware of my body as visible, just as I am aware of the surrounding backdrop of lawn and house even as my consciousness engages itself with the apple tree. Moreover, as I was trying to reach the apples by myself, I assumed the objective point of view of the other in mentally measuring the distance between my fingertips and the apple, the size of stool needed to increase my height, and so on. One aspect may be dominant in the various phases of the experience, but there is no logical nor existential conflict. That consciousness exists its body in three dimensions is self-evident.

Let us look specifically now at the first dimension—the body as being-for-itself. It is here that we can best understand Sartre's statement that consciousness both is and is not its body. Consciousness is not its body in that it nihilates (or transcends) its body as it does everything else, including its own past acts of consciousness. Properly and fully understood, this claim by Sartre has been rightly held to be the cornerstone of at least Beauvoir's feminism; I myself believe it to be essential to any feminism that is not deterministic and regressive. It is also a controversial issue to a few later feminists. If, in some ultimate significant sense, consciousness is not its body, then neither anatomy nor physiology makes us what we are as persons. Judith Butler, in an excellent article, showed how Beauvoir, taking Sartre at his non-Cartesian best (as Butler expresses it), used Sartre's view that consciousness always goes beyond its body as support for the position that—while we are our bodies as we are our situation, our field of possibilities—still, our sex is not the same as our gender.[19] We are born female or male (though some extremists would argue that things are not quite that simple); we become women or men. Gender traits we develop ourselves, partly independently, partly as we yield to social expectations and pressures. So-called feminine qualities are on exactly the same level as cowardliness, generosity, irascibility, and so on, all of which, according to Sartre and Beauvoir, are qualities attributed to behavior but are not fixed structures of a person's being.

I think that no feminist would want to reject the basic distinction between sex and gender. Many, however, have argued that Sartre, in denying the determinism of body over consciousness, has actually postulated a disembodied consciousness, as an ideal if not as an existential reality. That he himself valued the feeling of being in control as opposed to yielding and receiving, I do not deny.[20] This is not the same as believing that a consciousness is, should be, or could be, in any significant sense, disembodied. Quite to the contrary, Sartre argued that consciousness is a revealing presence to the world and that the living body is a consciousness present in the world. Consciousness *is* its body. One's way of being in the world inevitably reflects one's bodily structure and physiological condition—just as one's particular position in space and time delimits the objective possibilities of one's life. Sartre always acknowledged that every freedom is situated. If the body is deformed or diseased, its relation to the world is altered. Beauvoir did not have to bend Sartre's theory to show how woman's usually slighter physique, her menstruation, and her potentiality for voluntary or involuntary pregnancy place her in a situation different from that of a man. The woman with tuberculosis cannot prevent the racking cough and fever from weakening her, but she transcends it in her choice to deny or to acknowledge her condition, to surrender to it, or to fight it; she lives with it or dies with it on her own terms. Sartre said in *Critique* 1 that his philosophy gave full weight to both materiality and consciousness. Even in his late work, and despite his heavy emphasis on the alienating power of the practico-inert, he insisted that some measure of subjectivity always contributes to how we live the situation that has been imposed on us. Similarly, a consciousness, while not being something other than the body, is not its body, is not its body in exactly the same way that in every intentional act, consciousness is aware of not being its object—or, more precisely, aware that the awareness of the object is not the object. We are aware of the many ways by which consciousness at once transcends its body and makes itself one with its body in conduct which, as Sartre sees it, is intentional but not deliberate. Psychosomatic reactions testify to a consciousness's capability of expressing its intentions by means of bodily symptoms. In *The Family Idiot* Sartre examined this mode of passive activity in his study of Flaubert's recourse to hysteria (in the form of a pseudo-epileptic attack) as a way for Flaubert to rebel against his father.

Sartre's description of the second dimension of the body has been largely neglected by commentators although I believe that it is here that he most effectively shows the inextricability of body and consciousness and the possibilities for positive relations between individuals. Obviously, like Sartre, I must speak of the body-for-others in terms of the other's body for me, for this is what I know directly. Sartre begins by establishing that whatever my attitude toward a particular other, the other's body is always meaningful; it is a pathway from or to the other's intentional consciousness. The other's body appears graceful insofar as its movements seem to flow harmoniously from that consciousness, obscene if its flesh seems extraneous to consciousness's intentions. Already in *Being and Nothingness*, Sartre, while denying that one consciousness might ever merge with another, spoke of a "reciprocal incarnation" of consciousnesses in the union of lovers when each one, insofar as possible, sought to reach toward the other's consciousness through the body.[21] Sartre appeared hardly to realize the full implications of what he said here, probably because his controlling purpose at this point was to show that neither love nor sex could satisfy the mistaken passion to be God. In *Notebooks for an Ethics* he explicitly designates the body-for-others as the seat of authentic love (love either erotic or nonerotic as in intimate friendship or emotional devotion to the leader of a cause one believes in).

Three things characterize what Sartre takes to be authentic love. First, I empathically read the other's actions and bodily expressions as manifestations of a free consciousness and grasp them in terms of the other's network of ends and means. I interpret the other's activities within a situation and sometimes more clearly than the other, I grasp the external possibilities and obstacles to the other's projects. I regard with love the very limitations of the other's body—for example, "the gauntness, the nervousness of this politician or that doctor, who properly brushes aside and overcomes the thin, nervous body and *forgets* it."[22] This bodily vulnerability which I sense, Sartre says, *is* the body-for-others. He concludes, "To reveal the other in his being-in-the-midst-of-the-world is to love him in his body."[23] Second, beyond empathic comprehension of the other's attempt to pursue his or her project, I shelter the other's freedom, making the other's goal a part of my own project but in such a way as to offer it support without substituting my own in place of the other's projected goal and chosen means. Finally, in authentic love, we do not have an abstract encounter of two impersonal consciousnesses following through on an existential principle. Sartre writes explicitly, "Freedom as such is not lovable, for it is nothing but negation and productivity. Pure being, in its total exteriority of indifference is not *lovable* either. But the other's body is lovable inasmuch as it is freedom in the dimension of being."[24]

Sartre sums up his expanded view of the body-for-others in words that wholly refute the charge that the negative structures described in *Being and Nothingness* are the sole pattern for human relations. "Here is an original structure of authentic love . . . to reveal the other's being-in-the-midst-of-the-world, to take upon myself this revealing, hence this being—absolutely; to take delight in it without seeking to appropriate it, and to give it shelter in my freedom, and to go beyond it only in the direction of the other's ends."[25]

This discussion of authentic love as a natural (though not necessary) way of living the second dimension, the body-for-others, is utterly radical in its full implications—for feminism as well as generally. To set up the goal of empathically comprehending the other's project and striving to enable its free self-realization is to demand a total transformation of the traditional relationship between a man and a woman and—if extended to the social sphere—the overall pattern of male-female relationships. To comprehend and give shelter to the others' ends and means is to open the door to recognition of what have been called feminine values, whatever their origin.

The third dimension of experience of the body, my body as I am aware that it is known by others, is obviously a necessary mediation between the first two dimensions. My awareness that my body and its acts in the world are perceived and interpreted by others is essential to all communication, and it is my practical defense against solipsism. It is also, when I myself look upon my body as an object (thereby assuming the point of view of the other), the tangible proof of my ongoing existence in space and time. It is as well, of course, the treacherous instrument that shows that the world has stolen my action from me, as we saw in the case of Sartre's ill-dressed woman. The significance of this dimension has already been fruitfully exploited by feminists, with and without specific reference to Sartre.

One important example is an article by Sandra Bartky, "Women, Bodies and Power: A Research Agenda for Philosophy," calling on philosophers, especially phenomenologists, to institute a research program in "how to think the nature of human embodiment." Bartky finds Sartre's words directly relevant. Starting from the premise that "embodied experience is always culturally mediated," Bartky discusses the way that women's relations with their bodies inevitably reflect cultural expectations, resulting all too frequently in an interiorized sense of inferiority. Bartky writes, "How to conceptualize the subjective moment in 'inferiorization'? We learn from Sartre that we exist not only as bodies but as witnesses to our own bodily being, from Beauvoir that this 'doubling' is felt acutely by adolescent girls who learn to appraise themselves as they are shortly to be appraised. Objectification becomes self-objectification." A woman suffering from this sort of self-estrangement, Bartky claims, lives in "a state of inner conflict wherein one is closeted with an enemy who is at the same time oneself. Estrangement from self can be likened to a 'colonization' of consciousness when inner conflict facilitates control from without and where such control is maintained by and in turn maintains a hierarchy of gender."[26]

So, far from postulating a disembodied consciousness, Sartre seems to me to have examined the ontological complexity of our existence as conscious bodies more thoroughly than any other philosopher, with the possible exception of Merleau-Ponty, whose work is hardly thinkable without Sartre as his point of departure.

A human being, a being-for-itself, to use Sartre's term, is more than a consciousness and a body. There is also the ego. Unfortunately, Sartre's discussion of the relation between consciousness and ego has, for the most part, been conducted on so abstract a level that its significance for feminism has been neglected. If for the word "ego" we were to substitute "personality structure" or "self-image," both of which, though not quite synonymous with "ego," are inextricably bound up with it, then it should be evident that to ask how a consciousness stands in relation to its ego is tantamount to asking how one makes oneself a person—or how "one is not born but becomes a woman."

Sartrean consciousness, as pure positional awareness of an object, is, as every reader of Sartre well knows, impersonal, not identical with and not inhabited by an "I" nor a "me." The for-itself is individualized by the body, personalized by the ego. At first thought, the Sartrean ego seems to be strikingly different from the body. It is the product created by consciousness rather than the ground of consciousness; it is psychic, not material; it is passive, incapable of either the mechanical or autonomic action found in the body. Yet the relation of consciousness to ego is surprisingly parallel to that of consciousness to body. Both the ego and the body are "at the horizon of consciousness," both are the "past" and the "surpassed" of a consciousness, both are present as the implicit ground for any future action a consciousness may project for itself. Although we cannot correctly speak of a conscious ego in the way that we can refer to conscious body, still, the ego is a necessary structure for the for-itself to bring into existence. A consciousness could not function sanely without creating an ego. Moreover, although Sartre never made this claim, I will go so far as to say that the relation a consciousness

sustains with its ego is manifest in the three dimensions that Sartre attributed to a consciousness "existing its body."

It should be obvious that in the second and third dimensions, body
and ego are inseparable practically. In Sartre's keyhole example, the
shame that overwhelms the Peeping Tom caught in the act is not due to
the fact that his body has been seen bent over a hole in a door but to his
awareness that he is the agent of an act that the observer (and Tom
himself in other circumstances) deems shameful. In authentic love realized via the body-for-others, I do indeed love a body. But if we are speaking of love and not a purely physical hunger for *any body*, then it is the
body insofar as it is expressive of a personal project, a personality, an ego
which leads me to choose this particular freedom to shelter in mine.[27] In
the first dimension there is a significant difference. Sartre never says that
consciousness *is* the ego, not even in the restricted sense that a consciousness *is* body. But consciousness's mode of not being the ego is closely
similar to its way of not being the body. The ego, I think, can be most
precisely defined as the unification that a consciousness has imposed on
its own experience—feeling, thoughts, actions, and so on. It represents a
point of view—judgments, value colorations—that consciousness has
taken on its own activities. The ego is, as it were, the crystallization of
consciousness's accumulated attitudinal awareness of its history at any
given moment. Thus the ego is the product of a consciousness, not a part
of its structure.

The origin of Sartrean freedom is exactly here—the capacity of consciousness to alter what we call the personality, seen most clearly in radical modification of a "fundamental project," Sartre's term for a person's
basic orientation or choice of a way of being. No act of consciousness
takes place without a psychic structure as ground even though Sartre
insists that the meaning of these structures is continually confirmed, denied, or modified, even in nonreflective acts. In reflection, of course,
psychic data are directly the object—though never the structure—of consciousness. Sartre spoke at times of the ideal of trying to live without an
ego.[28] What he meant by this, as he makes clear in *Notebooks for an
Ethics*, is the resolve never to act in the name of a fixed self-image—as if
I said to myself, "I must not do such and such because I am not the kind
of person who would do it."[29] Criteria for ethical action should be strictly
connected with the act in question and its consequence, not referred
back to an internal "I" or "me" as a substantial subject. But in *The War*

Diaries, Sartre wrote of the necessity of making oneself a person as the only way to avoid the inauthenticity of pretending to be detached from the situation in which one finds oneself in the world.[30] In the *Notebooks for an Ethics* he stated that it is impossible to act without "that always open Me (*Moi*) that is referred to by the enterprise at hand. Always open and always in suspense." The ego exists, he says, in order to be lost.[31] In other words, I cannot live without a sense of my temporal unity as agent, but I must acknowledge, if I am authentic, that the self that is present as explicit or implicit object is always in the making. It is a part of my ongoing project. "Man makes himself" applies in the present tense; the task is complete only at death when it is up to others to judge what self I have made.

The ego is a consciousness's objectification for itself of its relations with the world and with other persons. For the very reason that it is an object, the ego is outside consciousness, outside in the world, as Sartre says, just as the other's ego is.[32] And as an object, it is subjected to others' judgments as well as to my own. Consequently, my ego is affected by the way others view it, just as my body is colored, in my own eyes, by how I know others see it. My ego as I am aware that it is known by the other is melded with all of the psychic data that consciousness continues to unify into a self for itself. But, for Sartre, what comes from others continues to be molded by consciousness. It does not wholly determine consciousness as if it were a foreign body put in control of it. The ego is not simply implanted by the other, nor does it make itself. Nevertheless, quite literally, others can maltreat my ego. In Sartre's later work, he is very much aware that the ingredients out of which a consciousness constitutes an ego are highly contaminated in our subhuman environment. Artists will produce works of art that are uniquely theirs; but if they have only drawing materials at their disposal, their works will not be known for their color.

The Sartrean ego is not a substantial, all but disembodied subject, like the Cartesian ego. It is not, like the Freudian ego, a mere part of a complex psychic structure, only partly aware of what it is doing, governed by instinctual forces filtered through the bewildered conduct of parents. Nor is it, like the alien ego of Lacan, an interiorized residue of otherness at the very heart of the psyche and—in the case of women—half biologically, half psychologically, and wholly mysteriously subject to the phallic word of the father.

Several scholars have recognized that, if examined in the light of Sartre's total work, his view of the personal subject stands midway between the I-substance of Descartes and the dissolution of the subject posited by Deconstructionists. Christina Howells, noting Sartre's statement about consciousness's continual creation of an ego that exists in order to be lost, concludes that for Sartre, "the subject may be deferred, dissolved, and deconstructed, but it is not relinquished."[33] I argue that it remains in the form of an impersonal consciousness that makes us persons. The subject other whom we encounter is a consciousness that differentiates itself in the body and by means of the ego. Betty Cannon has been very effective in demonstrating at length how Sartre's concept of the relation between consciousness and ego both allows for the possibility of profound personality conversions and explains why they are accomplished so seldom and with such difficulty.[34] Sonia Kruks has traced Sartre's development to show how he, influenced by Beauvoir and by Merleau-Ponty as Beauvoir read him, finally succeeded in describing how real men and women are driven by their organic needs to transform "nature into those humanized forms of matter" that both sustain and alienate human praxis. As Kruks puts it, Sartre "finally abandons the notion of the 'absolute subject' (and its absolute freedom) for a notion closer to the embodied and 'impure' subject of Merleau-Ponty and Beauvoir."[35] Still, as Kruks recognizes, the hope of a feminist—or any other—revolution rests on the spark of free subjectivity that remains to challenge social conditioning—as we saw pathetically present in the ill-dressed woman and heroically manifest in the Belgian mothers. I am in agreement with Kruks's analysis except that I would stress that it is not the notion of consciousness per se that has changed for Sartre but his recognition of the necessity to give more weight to external pressures (their coefficient of resistance) on the body and the ego within which and by means of which the for-itself makes itself (in *Being and Nothingness*) or carves out its being in-the-world (in *Critique* 1).

I have kept my discussion gender neutral in examining Sartre's view of the roles of consciousness and ego in the formation of the person. In the most basic sense—ontologically, Sartre might say—all women and men build their personalities in the same fashion, forming a unity out of the flux of experience. But just as we "exist our bodies" in the same three dimensions but individualize ourselves by *how* we exist in our biologically given particular bodies, so every consciousness, out of the varied ingredients each life situation provides, forms and re-forms the person we become. Feminists have written at length about the many ways in which the values of a male-dominated society have been internalized by women, shaping and distorting their view of themselves, stunting their inner growth, victimizing them sometimes to the point of turning them into mystified accomplices. What has been mostly lacking is a psychological or philosophical theory to account for the possibility of resistance and change. In fact, in my opinion, some of the more radical feminists in their emphasis on sexual difference have introduced biological determinants, more flattering but just as preventive of free psychic development as traditional views. If we follow Sartre in holding that the ego (or self) is the product of a basic consciousness and not its originator, then perhaps we can better understand how a woman, out of what the world offers her, makes herself, as woman and as person, and also how she is able to assume a new point of view on the self she has made and to modify it. Just as Freud assumed—without presuming to explain how—that there comes a certain moment during analysis at which patients suddenly find within themselves the power to see their past and present selves in a new light, so, I think, feminists tacitly grant that radical self-restructuring does occur; indeed this is what they aim to accomplish. Sartre offers an ontology to justify that hope.

Conclusion

Sartre apparently regarded women's liberation as a logical consequence of his view that to be human is to be, in some fundamental sense, self-determining. Should we expect that a feminism taking Sartre's philosophy (including, of course, the work written after *Being and Nothingness*) as its starting point would, like Beauvoir's in *The Second Sex*, still be liberal and egalitarian rather than radical and concerned with gender differences? My own view is that if we were to take Sartre's theory of the nature of human reality to its logical conclusions and to ask where such a feminism would be situated in contemporary feminist controversies, we should find ourselves making these judgments:

1. With respect to the social-constructionist versus essentialist debate, a Sartrean-based feminism would hold firmly to the view that forms of sexuality and sexual preferences are socially constructed, not biologically determined. But if we are to be guided here by Sartre, we would not go so far as to see individual choice lost in social conditioning nor wholly

molded by the prevailing discourse. (Sartre recognized that language comes to us already structured by others and that it often deviates or alienates. But he still insisted that it is we who speak language, we are not "spoken by language." Like anything in the practico-inert, language is finally the tool of human praxis.)[36] Those who hold that our preferred form of sexuality is a choice and not a destiny are often told that in this case, opponents of homosexuality, for instance, have the right to declare it culpable and punishable. They do indeed have the freedom to do so, but not with the justification of any natural or divine law that can be objectively declared to support them—not if, as Sartre claims, all values and ethics are human creations.

2. An egalitarian feminism, or one based on sexual differences? Sartre's ontology and psychology do not allow for any kind of sexually determined innate differences in men's and women's mental abilities, ethical values, and so on. This was always Beauvoir's position. Yet both believed that women and minorities, marginal in present society, are in a privileged position to challenge prevailing modes of thought and ought to do so, privileged because as partial outsiders, they are better able to discern what is false or destructive. There is a place for a feminist standpoint in a Sartrean feminism but as the result of what women's experiences have revealed to them, not by virtue of their biology.

It may be interesting, though admittedly not of any practical utility, to wonder what Sartre might think of the growing numbers of transsexuals in the contemporary scene. At first thought, an individual's decision to make himself into a herself, or vice versa, might appear to be the ultimate, crowning manifestation of Sartre's famous dictum that "man makes himself," in other words, that the human being is an ongoing activity of self-creating. On closer examination, however, the reason so often quoted for the transsexual choice, "I was born a male in a female body" (or the opposite), points to an assumed biological and psychological determinism that is quite foreign to existentialism. I suspect that Sartre would argue that there are more imaginative ways than surgery by which to express one's unique sexuality. But I confess that I am in danger here of drifting into fantasy; I will not pursue the matter further.

3. Finally, this feminism would not be liberal but radical, perhaps far more so than many self-styled radical feminists would desire. Among his unpublished papers, Sartre left notes for an ethics that would be consistent with his own existentialism and modified Marxist orientation. Here he introduced as a sort of ideal goal for any authentic ethics, the concept

of "integral humanity." He seems to have had in mind the imperative to create a society that would foster the maximum of human fulfillment and allow the greatest scope for individual freedom, one to replace our existing "subhuman" condition in which the full development of positive human potentialities, he believed, is blighted rather than nurtured.[37] Sartre did not spell out all that he may have intended the concept to convey. His use of the term "integral humanity" is puzzling, since Sartre had formerly been suspicious of attempts to define "the human," viewing them as falsely deterministic when not a disguise for the identification of "human" with the prejudices of a particular group. It seems to me that the later Sartre, while still recognizing the dangers inherent in taking "humanity" as something given for a starting point, sees in it a positive value as an ideal to be realized. This would be consistent with his early assertion that humankind, like every individual, defines and makes itself. At any rate, two things are clear: First, the term entails the possibility of an equality that can sustain and support difference. Second, if we consider it in the light of the millennial musings in which Sartre indulged on various occasions in his life, we realize that for him the establishment of anything resembling a liberated society would demand a total resocialization. None of our present assumptions would escape questioning—not only economic, racial, and ethnic, not only those having to do with sex and gender, but presumptions concerning the single nuclear family, parents' absolute authority over their children, even our definition of what currently passes for "intelligence" and "rationality." This may sound grandiose; it is nothing if not radical. The goal of integral humanity could not be achieved without a profound modification of the feminine condition as it exists now.

If—*par impossible*—Sartre were to find himself living in the kind of society he envisioned, he might well experience considerable discomfort and be forced to work hard at his professed practice of "thinking against himself." It is easy to find traces of his personal limitations in his work. Yet, if we want to make use of Sartre's philosophy—and I think it would be wasteful not to do so—we might remember what he once remarked about writers and their work: "It is the goal which defines the man, not the man who defines the goal."[38] Some feminists have claimed that whereas men's approach to discussion is generally confrontational, women tend to try to understand what the other *wants* to say and to find ways of dealing with it constructively. Whether this conviction is true or not, I should like to see feminists adopt this "women's approach" in a rereading of Sartre.

Notes

1. Jean-Paul Sartre, *Critique de la raison dialectique (précédé de Question de méthode)*, vol. 1, *Théorie des ensembles pratiques* (Paris: Gallimard, 1960), 403, 409, 420, 453; *Critique of Dialectical Reason*, vol. 1, *Theory of Practical Ensembles*, trans. Alan Sheridan-Smith, ed. Jonathan Rée (Atlantic-Highlands, N.J.: Humanities Press, 1976), 372, 381, 395, 436–37. All translations in this essay, unless otherwise indicated, are my own. Where I have translated from the French text, I will, for the reader's convenience, also give references for the equivalent passages in English.

2. Jean-Paul Sartre, *Being and Nothingness: An Essay on Phenomenological Ontology*, trans. Hazel E. Barnes (New York: Washington Square Press, 1972), 96–98.

3. Jean-Paul Sartre, *Cahiers pour une morale* (Paris: Gallimard, 1983), 222; *Notebooks for an Ethics*, trans. David Pellauer (Chicago: University of Chicago Press, 1992), 212.

4. Jean-Paul Sartre, *Saint Genet: Actor and Martyr*, trans. Bernard Frechtman (New York, New American Library, 1971), 206ff.

5. Jean-Paul Sartre, *Truth and Existence*, trans. Adrian van den Hoven, ed. and with an introduction by Ronald Aronson (Chicago: University of Chicago Press, 1992), 33ff.

6. Jean-Paul Sartre, *The Emotions: Outline of a Theory*, trans. Bernard Frechtman (New York: Philosophical Library, 1948), 43.

7. Jean-Paul Sartre, *The Transcendence of the Ego: An Existentialist Theory of Consciousness*, trans. and annotated and with an introduction by Forrest Williams and Robert Kirkpatrick (New York: Farrar, Straus and Giroux, n.d.), 100.

8. Jean-Paul Sartre, *The Psychology of Imagination*, tr. anon. (New York: Philosophical Library, 1948), 34ff.

9. Sartre, *Critique* 1, French text, 291; English, 35.

10. Sartre, *Notebooks*, 179–83.

11. In fairness to Sartre I should point out that he does consider and sarcastically condemn the bad faith of men who pretend to themselves that women secretly want to be taken by force, thus refusing the freedom the men in reality seek to violate.

12. Sartre, *Truth and Existence*, 55.

13. This example I know only through a discussion of it by Robert V. Stone and Elizabeth A. Bowman, who have worked with the manuscript of the lectures Sartre had intended to give but never did deliver at Cornell University in 1965. "Sartre's Morality and History: A First Look at the Notes for the Unpublished 1965 Cornell Lectures," in *Sartre Alive*, ed. Ronald Aronson and Adrian van den Hoven (Detroit: Wayne State University Press, 1991), 53–82. The example discussed is at 65–67. Direct quotations in my text are from the authors' translation or from their paraphrase of Sartre's manuscript.

14. Again I am dependent, in this and in the following example, on the work of Stone and Bowman, who allowed me to read a large section of their translation and summary of Sartre's manuscript intended for a lecture to be given in Rome. Sartre did deliver a lecture on ethics in Rome in 1964; the "Notes" include more material than he actually used. Here I am drawing on Stone's and Bowman's published article "Dialectical Ethics: A First Look at Sartre's Unpublished 1964 Rome Lecture Notes," *Social Text: Theory/Culture/Ideology* 5 (Winter/Spring 1986), 195–215. The example of the high school girls is given at 197.

15. Stone and Bowman, "Dialectical Ethics," 198–202.

16. Jean-Paul Sartre, *Critique of Dialectical Reason*, vol. 2 (Unfinished), ed. Arlette Elkaïm Sartre, trans. Quintin Hoare (New York: Verso, 1991), 290–94.

17. Sartre, *Critique 2*, 262.

18. Sartre, *Being and Nothingness*, 434.

19. Judith Butler, "Sex and Gender in Simone de Beauvoir's *Second Sex, Yale French Studies*, no. 72 (1986), 35–49.

20. This attitude is expressed frequently in various contexts in taped conversations of Sartre and Beauvoir. On one occasion Sartre reproaches himself for overemphasizing his own active role in sexual relations, in which, he theoretically held, both partners ought to be reciprocally active and passive. *Conversations with Jean-Paul Sartre, August–September 1974*. In Simone de Beauvoir's *Adieux: A Farewell to Sartre*, trans. Patrick O'Brian (New York: Penguin Books, 1985), 326.

21. Sartre, *Being and Nothingness*, 508. Monika Langer develops the positive implications of this passage in "Sartre and Merleau-Ponty: A Reappraisal," *The Philosophy of Jean-Paul Sartre* in The Living Philosophers series, ed. Paul Arthur Schilpp (La Salle: Open Court, 1981), 300–25.

22. Sartre, *Cahiers*, 517; *Notebooks*, 501.

23. Ibid.

24. Sartre, *Cahiers*, 523; *Notebooks*, 507. I have discussed the role of the body in authentic love in my "The Role of the Ego in Reciprocity," in Aronson and van den Hoven, *Sartre Alive*, 151–59.

25. Sartre, *Cahiers*, 523–24; *Notebooks*, 508.

26. Sandra Bartky, "Women, Bodies and Power: A Research Agenda for Philosophy," *American Philosophical Association Newsletters on Teaching Philosophy/ Computer Use in Philosophy/ Feminism and Philosophy/ Philosophy and Law/ Philosophy and Medicine*, issue no. 89-1 (Fall 1989), 78–81.

27. I have discussed the close relation between body and ego, in a different context, in "Sartre's Ontology: The Revealing and Making of Being," *The Cambridge Companion to Sartre*, ed. Christina Howells (New York: Cambridge University Press, 1992), 13–38.

28. Sartre, *Cahiers*, 430, 433; *Notebooks*, 414, 417.

29. Sartre, *Cahiers*, 433; *Notebooks*, 417.

30. Jean-Paul Sartre, *The War Diaries of Jean-Paul Sartre, November 1939/March 1940*, trans. Quintin Hoare (New York: Pantheon, 1984), 324–25.

31. Sartre, *Cahiers*, 433; *Notebooks*, 417.

32. Sartre, *The Transcendence of the Ego*, 93–96.

33. Christina Howells, "Conclusion: Sartre and the Deconstruction of the Subject," in her *The Cambridge Companion to Sartre*, 342.

34. Betty Cannon, *Sartre and Psychoanalysis: An Existentialist Challenge to Clinical Metatheory* (Lawrence: University Press of Kansas, 1991).

35. Sonia Kruks, "Simone de Beauvoir: Teaching Sartre About Freedom," in Aronson and van den Hoven, *Sartre Alive*, 285–300. The sentence quoted is at 297.

36. For an instructive discussion of Sartre's and Lacan's views of language, cf. Cannon, *Sartre and Psychoanalysis*, the section titled "Sartre and Lacan on the Nature of Language: Existentialist versus Structuralist Metatheory."

37. See note 14 above. Thomas C. Anderson has offered a helpful commentary on Sartre's intention in these condensed passages and has spelled out more fully the connection between integral humanity, freedom, and personal fulfillment (*Sartre's Two Ethics: From Authenticity to Integral Humanity*. [Chicago and La Salle, Ill.; Open Court, 1993], 156–60). Sartre's reference to the "origin of humanity" in the passage from *Critique 1* from which I quoted at the beginning of the essay is tangentially relevant inasmuch as it underscores the idea of humanity as something achieved rather than given.

38. Sartre, *Cahiers*, 516; *Notebooks*, 501.

2

The *Absence* of Beauvoir

Edward Fullbrook and Kate Fullbrook

The *Absence* of Sartre

Despite the vicissitudes of intellectual fashions, there can be no question
that Jean-Paul Sartre and Simone de Beauvoir were two of the most inter-
nationally significant intellectual figures of the twentieth century. Whatever else might be said about them, their achievements, both jointly and
separately, are of the highest magnitude. In terms of those achievements,
and at the moment we are especially concerned with Sartre's, it is more
than interesting to consider a recent publication. In 1994, Blackwell published a standard reference book with the promising, even enticing title,
A Companion to the Philosophy of Mind.[1] This compendious volume includes fascinating and sophisticated essay-length entries on topics such

as *consciousness, content of consciousness, desire, emotion, imagination, intentionality, perception, perceptual content, psychology and philosophy, the self, self-deception,* and *subjectivity.* The volume's title uses the word *philosophy* without qualification or modification, suggesting, by inference, that it provides a general and thorough overview of the major contributions to the various philosophical fields and topics it discusses. But something rather curious happens when the volume is checked for the range of philosophers and of ideas that it treats. A good illustration of what we have in mind can be seen by noting the philosophers mentioned in essays surveying topics of central interest to Sartre scholars. Under *consciousness,* T. H. Huxley, Daniel Dennett, Thomas Nagel, A. Goldman, John Searle all feature, along with a score of others with whom we confess unfamiliarity. Under *desire,* Socrates, Plato, Spinoza, Hume, and Mill, and Robert C. Stalnaker, P. Geach, Dennis W. Stampe, and Fred Dretske are all cited. Under *emotion,* the philosophers drawn upon include Plato, Aristotle, Spinoza, Descartes, Hobbes, Hume, and William James, and, alongside them, M. Scheler, J. Panksepp, H. Fingarette, P. D. MacLean, and a dozen others. Under *perception,* Aristotle, Descartes, Wittgenstein, and Strawson are all mentioned. *Perceptual content* treats Strawson, Fred Dretske, T. M. Crane, D. M. Armstrong, C. A. B. Peacocke, and others. Under *psychology and philosophy,* Chomsky, Searle, and Dennett are featured along with Goldman, Putnam, T. Burge, and many others. The section titled *the self* draws on Descartes, Locke, Hume, Kant, Wittgenstein, Strawson, as well as Evans, Lewis, McDowell, Parfit, Perry, and so on. Finally, in the entry on *self-deception,* only Pears, Fingarette, and Davidson figure as individually identified referents.

What is more than peculiar when noting the often repeated presence of all these philosophers is the striking *absence* of Sartre, who must be counted in the handful of the most important and influential twentieth-century contributors to the philosophical discussion of all these topics and areas. However, given the range of philosophers who do feature in the Blackwell volume, Sartre's exclusion is not, really, so very surprising. The politics of this situation are well understood. The volume, for all its massive size, its 642 pages and closely printed double-columned format, and its promise of inclusiveness, is a product of seriously partisan and exclusionary intellectual politics. It is a reference work for a particular kind of discourse on intellectual—specifically philosophical—history from which Sartre and numerous other important thinkers are deliberately excluded. As is well known, beginning roughly a century ago, Western philosophers split into two camps: with the continental camp amorphous and quarrelsome, and the Anglo-American camp well organized and rigidly disciplined. Rather than coexisting peacefully, the two sides, especially the Anglo-American, have worked to limit the rival philosophical camp's credibility. It is a sorry state of affairs (although there are now signs of the beginning of a rapprochement), with students of one or the other of the great branches of twentieth-century philosophy often being trained in something approaching ignorance of the alternate tradition. The excision of modern continental philosophers from pertinent entries in Blackwell's otherwise admirable volume represents just one example of the intellectual politics of absence that can so sorrily skew the records of intellectual history. However, the erasure of various philosophers' names, and the failure to register proper credit for their work, is quite a different matter from banning their ideas. One of the noteworthy aspects of Blackwell's *Companion to the Philosophy of Mind* is the presence in it, especially in passages covering recent works, of ideas that most of us would credit to Sartre. The point here is really a very simple one: philosophers, dispossessed of their official identity, are easily dispossessed, as well, of credit for their ideas.

The *Absence* of Beauvoir from Sartrean Studies

One of the admirable qualities of Sartrean scholarship is its tradition of placing Sartre's philosophy in the context of his antecedent and contemporary philosophers. Of course, Sartre himself encouraged this practice through his example in *Being and Nothingness,* with its expositions on the similarities and divergences of his ideas and from those of his philosophical forebears.[2] By doing so, Sartre reminds his readers of how philosophy is intrinsically a collaborative process, even if one's collaborators are long dead, and that new philosophical ideas rarely, if ever, appear without a more or less distinguished genealogy of intellectual precedents behind them. This fine and honest tradition of placing Sartre's ideas and their development within the context of a community of interacting thinkers is especially well served by *The Cambridge Companion to Sartre,* edited by Christina Howells and published in 1992.[3] This work, which runs to four hundred pages, is particularly strong in tracing the interrelationships between Sartre's thought and that of thinkers with whom Sartre's life was roughly contemporary. Writers covered in this way (and in this case it is both welcome and noticeable that the net has been cast so widely as even to encompass a number of analytical philosophers) include the following: Adorno, Althusser, Aron, Barthes, Baudrillard, Carnap, Cassirer, Deleuze, Derrida, Foucault, Freud, Gandillac, Genet, Gide, Stuart Hampshire, R. M. Hare, Heidegger, Husserl, Hyppolite, Jaspers, Kojève, Lacan, Christopher Lash, Lefèbvre, Lévi-Strauss, Lyotard, Mauss, Merleau-Ponty, Popper, Thomas Nagel, Paul Nizan, Ricoeur, Rorty, Ryle, Strawson, and Wittgenstein.

However, for all its wide range and overt generosity, the *Cambridge Companion to Sartre* also displays another vivid case of absence, one that, unfortunately, characterizes Sartre studies generally. In fact, the absent individual does receive one mention in the book in question, but—and again this is characteristic—in the role of the great man's biographer. In terms of historical, factual, and ethical importance, this absence, compared to the presence of the thirty-seven male writers rightly linked with Sartre, far outweighs the previously noted absence of Sartre in the *Companion to the Philosophy of Mind*. In the *Companion to Sartre* only one deeply significant figure is excluded from the reckoning, and that person is both the most important person in the relevant intellectual history and a woman. The excluded one, so eloquent in her absence, is, of course, Simone de Beauvoir.

The tradition in Sartrean scholarship of more or less completely ignoring the presence of Beauvoir in the formation of "Sartrean philosophy" is, again, of course, part of a much larger historical tradition of positioning women at the margins of intellectual history. Here, rather than exploring that tradition and the particular form it takes in the study of Sartre and Beauvoir, we merely note its prevalence. But there is another factor that contributes to the absence of Beauvoir, and, like Sartre's absence from one version of the philosophical canon, it concerns the use of language.

The Third Method

The barrier between continental and analytical philosophy is founded not so much on ideas as it is on attitudes to language in philosophical discourse. What began as a reaction to the self-entangled verbiage of turn-of-the-century neo-Hegelianism—a reaction that few would dismiss as unnecessary, has led to institutionalized extremes of the opposite kind. The standard analytical philosophical essay displays a highly stylized literary form, which takes the mathematician's use of language as its ideal. It is difference of opinion over the worthiness of this ideal that, more than content, often divides the two philosophical traditions.

Within the continental tradition itself, there are also two self-consciously different approaches to the use of language in philosophical investigation. But here the coexistence of these two methodologies is intended to be complementary rather than oppositional. One method takes the familiar form of the essay. The other is one that we will now consider. In his 1945 essay "Metaphysics and the Novel," Merleau-Ponty, writing with special reference to Beauvoir's *She Came to Stay*, commented on the symbiotic relationship between these two philosophical methods.[4] Merleau-Ponty begins his essay by noting that, since the end of the nineteenth century, the boundaries between literature and continental philosophy had dissolved and that "hybrid modes of expression" had developed in response to the opening up of what he calls "a new dimension of investigation."[5]

In his essay, Merleau-Ponty is especially concerned to analyze the impulse behind Beauvoir's success at using fiction as a philosophical medium in *She Came to Stay*. He distinguishes between two kinds of metaphysics. "Classical metaphysics," he writes, "could pass for a speciality with which literature had nothing to do because metaphysics operated on the basis of uncontested rationalism, convinced it could make the world and human life understood by an arrangement of concepts."[6] Even philosophers who begin on the experiential level tend to end by explaining the world on the basis of abstractions. But Merleau-Ponty continues:

> Everything changes when a phenomenological or existential philosophy assigns itself the task, not of explaining the world or of discovering its "conditions of possibility," but rather of formulating an experience of the world, a contact with the world which precedes all thought *about* the world. After this, whatever is metaphysical in man cannot be credited to something outside his empirical being—to God, to Consciousness. Man is metaphysical in his very being, in his loves, in his hates, in his individual and collective history.[7]

"From now on," concludes Merleau-Ponty, "the tasks of literature and philosophy can no longer be separated."

In 1946 Beauvoir published her essay "Literature and Metaphysics," which expands on Merleau-Ponty's thesis. Like Merleau-Ponty, she divides philosophy and philosophers roughly into two camps.[8] One includes Aristotle, Leibniz, Spinoza, and Kant, and holds that philosophical truth exists only in a "timeless and objective" sense. These philosophers, says Beauvoir, regard "as negligible the subjectivity and historicity of experience."[9] They deny the philosophical relevance of the individual and the concrete and, in so doing, implicitly presume that they, as philosophers, are capable of taking a universal rather than merely an individual point of view toward the metaphysical reality they seek to explain. Beauvoir, however, notes Eleanore Holveck, "argues that philosophers pretend to explain all things universally, but in fact these 'universals' are based in the consciousness of some individual thinker who claims knowledge of the universal, a claim that must be justified."[10] For Beauvoir, the universalist presumption is an egomaniacal delusion fostered by masculine privilege.[11] Earlier, in 1944, in *Pyrrhus et Cinéas*, she writes: "Man cannot escape from his own presence nor from the singular world that his presence reveals around him; even his effort to uproot himself from the earth makes him dig a hole for himself. Spinozism defines Spinoza, and Hegelianism Hegel."[12] In the same essay she writes: "The universal mind is without voice, and every man who claims to speak in its name only gives to it his own voice. How can he claim the point of view of the universal, since he *is* not the universal? One can not know a point of view other than one's own."[13] In other words, Beauvoir regarded truth, including metaphysical truth, as always relative to a knowing subject. "Concrete experience," she writes, "envelops at once the subject and object."[14] Beauvoir regards, notes Margaret Simons, any "attempt to describe reality without reference to the experiencing subject . . . as distorting as trying to describe the subject without reference to the context of circumstances."[15] Beauvoir understood, like Merleau-Ponty, like Sartre, although perhaps not always in the same way, that foreswearing the philosopher's traditional universalist pretension carries with it strong methodological implications.

In "Literature and Metaphysics," Beauvoir outlines a philosophical method founded on her antiuniversalism. If it is only possible to see the world from a particular point of view, then philosophical activity must start by looking at particular and concrete descriptions of subjects' relations with the world and with other consciousnesses. Beauvoir called her chosen philosophical territory "the metaphysical dimension" of human reality, that is, "one's presence in the world, for example, one's abandonment in the world, one's freedom, the opacity of things, the resistance of foreign consciousnesses." "To make" philosophy, she argues, is "to be" philosophical in the sense of sensitizing oneself to these individual metaphysical experiences, and then describing them.[16] It is only on the basis of these particular statements that Beauvoir believes that general philosophical statements can legitimately be constructed.[17]

Beauvoir's distinctive philosophical achievement, notes Eleanore Holveck, was "to ground her abstract philosophical positions in the real world of lived experience, a lived experience she created imaginatively in ordinary language that was more concrete, more rich than any abstract philosophical language."[18] Beauvoir's rejection of a priorism and of a universal point of view makes the starting point of a good philosophical argument the description of a particular individual's metaphysical relations with the world, a description that the reader can then compare to her or his own. Beauvoir identifies fiction as the medium most naturally suited to this end. She explains that although the essay can give "to the reader an intellectual reconstruction of their experience, it is this experience itself, such that it presents itself before any elucidation, that the novelist claims to reproduce on an imaginary plane."[19] Beauvoir continues: "In the real world the sense of an object is not a concept knowable by pure understanding: it is the object inasmuch as it unveils itself to us in the global relation that we maintain with it and that is action, emotion, sentiment; one asks of the novelists to evoke this presence of flesh and bone whose complexity, singular and infinite richness, overflows all subjective interpretation."[20]

Beauvoir's essay on method also attacks what she sees as philosophy's traditional authoritarianism and mystification. Against the tradition of the philosophical messiah, whom she calls "the theoretician," she identifies a kind of reader who is willing to accept other people's philosophical propositions only after "a movement of his whole being before forming judgments that he pulls from himself without someone having had the presumption of dictating them to him. It is this that is the value of a good novel. It is capable of inducing imaginary experiences as complete, as disquieting as lived experiences. The reader interrogates, doubts, he takes sides, and this hesitant elaboration of his thought is for him an enrichment that no doctrinal teaching could replace."[21]

Beavoir identifies philosophical fiction that appeals in this way to the reader's liberty as a valuable form of philosophical research. Because of its grounding in the concrete and its implicit appeal to the reader's critical judgement, fiction's approach to the use of language facilitates advancement beyond the traditional dogmatic abstraction of philosophy and philosophers. Speculative philosophical essays are then free to draw upon the results of the concrete inquiries of philosophical fiction in the same way that in science, theoretical papers draw upon the results of empirical research.

This methodology outlined by Beauvoir and Merleau-Ponty in their respective essays has been commented on by, among others, Mary Warnock. She writes: "The methodology of Existentialism . . . consists in a perfectly deliberate and intentional use of the *concrete* as a way of approaching the abstract, the *particular* as a way of approaching the general."[22] Warnock continues: "The existential philosopher, then, must above all *describe* the world in such a way that its meanings emerge. He cannot, obviously, describe the world as a whole. He must take examples in as much detail as he can, and from these examples his intuition of significance will become clear. It is plain how close such a method is to the methods of the novelist, the short-story writer."[23]

For Beauvoir, and in the main for Sartre as well, all real description of the world takes place from the point of view of an individual-in-the-world. In lieu of the abstract and freewheeling impersonality traditional to philosophy, Beauvoir's essay describes a philosophical process whereby the essay draws from and builds on the concrete analysis of fiction, a symbiotic relationship that she sees as similar to that which exists in science between theory and experiment.[24]

This symbiotic relationship is one form that Sartre and Beauvoir's joint philosophical production took. There are dozens of examples of ideas whose development can be traced to this type of interchange between the two philosophers. Because the theme of this paper is absence, we will examine the origins of this concept as a case in point.

The Theory of Absence as a Case History

Explanation of and Comments on the Concept of Absence

Absence is an important subcategory of concrete nothings or, as Sartre calls them, *négatités*. It is important to note the part they play in his philosophical universe. His task in *Being and Nothingness* is to describe phenomenologically how the individual conscious being, or *pour-soi*, engages with nonconscious being, *en-soi*. As Sartre notes, to accomplish this he needs, in the first instance, "to establish a connection between the two regions of being."[25] Given his method of reasoning from the concrete and the particular to the abstract and the general, this means identifying some definite human activity that epitomizes the relation being-in-the-world. For this he identifies the "attitude of interrogation." "In every question," he writes, "we stand before a being which we are questioning. . . . this being which we question, we question *about* something. That *about* which I question the being participates in the transcendence of being."[26] By "the transcendence of being" Sartre means being that is external to consciousness. He goes on: "I question being about its ways of being or about its being. From this point of view the question is a kind of expectation: I expect a reply from the being questioned. That is, on the basis of a pre-interrogative familiarity with being, I expect from this being a revelation of its being or of its way of being. The reply will be a 'yes' or a 'no.' "[27]

But consider a no answer to a questioning of being, such as "Peg is not here." This is a concrete negation, an instance of what Sartre calls nonbeing. His problem—and it must be recalled that the title of Part 1 of *Being and Nothingness* is "The Problem of Nothingness"—is to demonstrate that a nonbeing such as "Peg is not here" is what he calls a "component of the real," that is, something external to consciousness rather than merely a psychological or linguistic construct. His methodology commits him to carry out this demonstration by direct appeal to the concrete and the particular, rather than the traditional a priori. Therefore, Sartre builds the general concept of nothingness on the basis of phenomenological demonstrations that show the real existence of types of concrete nothings, that is, of instances of nonbeing. It is in this strategic context—of demonstrating that human consciousness reveals not only being, but also nonbeing—that the idea of absence first appears in *Being and Nothingness*.

War Diaries

On 1 February 1940, Sartre wrote a few pages in his diary[28] on the concept of absence. The date of this entry is significant, as it indicates that he was considering this topic two days *before* he left for a week-and-a-half leave in Paris. His analysis takes as its concrete basis the consideration of a husband, named Pierre, and his wife. Sartre asserts, a priori, that there is a fundamental or ontological difference between Pierre's absence from his wife and his "simply 'being away from,'" in the sense in which one might say that two towns are 20 kilometers away, or distant, from each other." Sartre says that "being away" and "distance" exist as relations only insofar as they are established by consciousness. He goes on to note in his journal: "But absence belongs to the very heart of things: being absent is a particular quality of an object. In vain will one seek to reduce this quality to a purely mental perspective." His task is to show concretely that absence is not merely a mental attitude or act, but rather "that there exists something like absence." To this end, he declares: "absence is a certain relationship between my being and the Other's being. It is a certain way I have of being given to the Other."[29] His concrete argument for this hypothesis is as follows:

> There can be *absence* of Pierre only in relation to his wife, for example, because here Pierre's existence alters the very being of his wife's for-herself—and in an essential manner. Pierre's presence is constitutive of the *being* of his wife as for-herself, and vice-versa. It is only against the background of this prior unity of being that absence can be given between Pierre and his wife. . . . It's a *new* mode of connection between Pierre and his wife, which appears against the original background of presence. That original background of presence is *lifted* and denied by absence—yet it's what makes the latter possible.[30]

Sartre concludes that lived absence "can be understood *only* as a concrete relation between two existents against a basic background of unity of contact. Pierre's wife is immediately given to Pierre as *not being there*."[31]

Before we consider Beauvoir's roughly contemporaneous writing on absence, two aspects of Sartre's notebook entry on absence should be mentioned. First, he has merely asserted the possibility of the existence of absence between two people: he has not offered any phenomenological description that permits him to argue from the concrete and the particular to the abstract and the general. In fact, at no point does he attempt to describe an absence from the point of view of a person perceiving an absence. In other words, he is still working on the level of the a priori.

Second, at this point, Sartre's abstract concept of absence is surprisingly narrow. It is limited not only to relations between people, but also to between pairs of people for whom the absence of one alters the being of the other "in an essential manner." We want to emphasize that we do not raise these points as criticisms of Sartre. What we are doing here is tracing the development of an idea.

Before examining Sartre's handling of absence in *Being and Nothing-ness*, we want to consider Beauvoir's treatment of the same topic in *She Came to Stay*. By looking at both Beauvoir's letters and her journals, one can clearly establish that she presented a completed and partially revised draft of her novel to Sartre on his arrival in Paris in February 1940 and that, during the next ten days, he spent a considerable amount of time reading it. (Beauvoir's letters also show that Sartre had previously read her unfinished first draft for the novel.) These facts are given further weight by various passages in Sartre's letters. Examples from two of his letters will suffice to support the point. Sartre's letter to Beauvoir of 15 February 1940—his first full letter to her since his return from Paris—ends with the paragraph "You've written a beautiful novel."[32] His letter to Beauvoir on 18 February includes the following reference to a passage that comes near the end of *She Came to Stay*, in chapter 7 of part 2:[33] "I've got plenty to do, which makes me happy: I'm beginning to see glimmers of a theory of time. This evening I began to write it. It's thanks to you, do you realize that? Thanks to Françoise's obsession: that when Pierre is in Xavière's room, there's an object living all by itself without a consciousness to see it. I'm not sure if I'll have the patience to wait for you to see it when someone takes you my notebooks. On that subject, my love, you haven't had the time to tell me what you thought of my theory on *contact* and *absence*. Do tell me."[34]

Beauvoir could not help but be interested in Sartre's comments on absence, because the notion of absence is central to several passages in *She Came to Stay*, including the one to which Sartre's letter refers. But it is a description of absence that comes much earlier in the novel that proved especially significant to Sartre and Beauvoir's joint development of this idea.

She Came to Stay

Before considering this passage, several points must be noted regarding this novel's structure. The character, Françoise, provides the narrative point of view for most of the text. But through the novel's first half, Beauvoir also uses Françoise to personify two philosophical positions: a form of solipsism, and philosophy's traditional and stubborn denial of the body's philosophical relevance. The latter posed an expository dilemma for Beauvoir. She could not offer vivid illustrations of Françoise's embodiment through Françoise's consciousness without that character ceasing to represent the position against which Beauvoir is arguing. Beauvoir finds her way out of this difficulty by using another character, Elisabeth, who has a highly developed awareness of her own and others' bodies, as the narrative focus of a chapter early in the novel.

The brief scene from Beauvoir's novel that we are about to examine shows off the dexterity and suppleness of her philosophical method, and her ability to apply it simultaneously to more than one philosophical idea. Elisabeth, Françoise's friend and rival, enters Françoise's room, knowing that the latter is not there. Chairs are strewn with Françoise's clothes, and her desk piled with books and papers.

> Elisabeth looked at the couch, at the mirror-wardrobe, at the bust of Napoleon on the mantelpiece beside a bottle of eau-de-Cologne, at some brushes and several pairs of stockings. She closed her eyes once more, and then opened them again. It was impossible to make this room her own: it was only too unalterably evident that it remained an alien room.
>
> Elisabeth went over to the looking-glass in which the face of Françoise had so often been reflected and saw her own face.[35]

Then Elisabeth sits down at Françoise's desk.

> A volume of Shakespeare's plays lay open at the page Françoise had been reading when she had suddenly pushed back her chair. She had thrown her dressing-gown on the bed and it still bore, in its disordered folds, the impress of her careless gesture; the sleeves were puffed out as if they still enclosed phantom arms. These discarded objects gave a more unbearable picture of Françoise than would her real presence. . . .
>
> Elisabeth pulled towards her some sheets of paper which were covered with notes, rough drafts, ink-stained sketches. Thus scratched out and badly written, Françoise's thoughts lost their definiteness; but the writing itself and the erasures made by Fran-

çoise's hand still bore witness to Françoise's indestructible existence.[36]

With the very important exception of the bust of Napoleon, all the objects at which Elisabeth looks have an instrumental relation to Françoise's
body—the couch, the chair, the eau-de-cologne, the brushes, the looking
glass, the clothes, the sheets of paper, the books. Similarly, all the observed spatial relations (the chair pushed back, the clothes strewn about,
the folds in the dressing gown, the puffed-out sleeves, the piles of books
and papers, the book left open, the handwriting), have been defined by
Françoise's body. The entire room is haunted by Françoise, who is elsewhere. Its contents, including their spatial arrangements, refer to Françoise's body, which is not there. The reference point of the room's
spatiality, which Elisabeth knows to be Françoise, is missing. Elisabeth
perceives this *absence*, this nonbeing, this concrete nothingness. That
she does so is an objective fact, not an abstract negation, not a negative
judgment, not a mental construct. The bust of Napoleon looks on to
prove the point. Besides Françoise, there is an infinity of people who are
not there in the room. Napoleon and Shakespeare are two of them, but
their not being there is devoid of reference. Only Françoise's body is
missing from the room's spatiality. Only Françoise is perceived as an absence.

This passage from Beauvoir's novel is exactly the sort of required phenomenological account of a perceived absence that is missing from Sartre's entry on absence in his diary. It also—and this is a paradoxical
aspect of the concrete phenomenological approach—describes an absence that implies a category or family of absences much larger than the
one that Sartre defined a priori with his abstractions. The perception of
Françoise's absence is independent of any significant alteration of Elisabeth's being.

Being and Nothingness

The presentation of the phenomenon of absence in *Being and Nothingness*
is one of Sartre's most wonderfully virtuoso and inimitable philosophical
performances. In terms of depth of explanation, it surpasses by a long way
anything Beauvoir wrote on the subject. But Sartre's account also shows
itself as profoundly influenced by and indebted to Beauvoir's exploration

of absence in *She Came to Stay*. First, there is the general point that he no longer holds the view that absence can occur only between two people for whom the absence of the one alters the being of the other "in an essential manner." Second (and more interesting), Sartre has incorporated into his two examples of absence certain key and idiosyncratic elements of the description by Beauvoir that has just been considered.

Sartre's two accounts of absence in *Being and Nothingness* are separated by several hundred pages.[37] The first, the better known of the two, comes in Part 1, chapter 1 where Sartre builds up the general concept of nothingness on the basis of phenomenological demonstrations showing the existence of types of concrete nothings, of instances of nonbeing. These include questioning, fragility, and destruction, but it is Sartre's account of absence that is most frequently cited, and that has most captured the philosophical imagination. Sartre imagines himself entering a café late for an appointment with Pierre. He surveys the room and its occupants and says to himself, "He is not here."[38] Sartre takes as his task the demonstration that this negation arises in some sense from an intuition or perception, and not purely from a judgment or a linguistic construction. His method of achieving this differs considerably from Beauvoir's. Rather than trying to pull his reader directly into the experience of entering a café and finding Pierre not there, he offers a metadescription of the experience. Whereas Beauvoir describes Elisabeth's experience of absence in all its parts *from the point of view of Elisabeth, who is caught up in the experience,* Sartre, for the most part, describes the perceived absence of Pierre from an analytical distance mediated by explications of various concepts. For example, Sartre appeals openly to a nonsensationalist theory of perception, whereas in Beauvoir's description this remains implicit. Sartre writes:

> But we must observe that in perception there is always the construction of a figure on a ground. No one object, no group of objects is especially designed to be organized as specifically either ground or figure; all depends on the direction of my attention. When I enter this café to search for Pierre, there is formed a synthetic organization of all the objects in the café, on the ground of which Pierre is given as about to appear.[39]

This principle of perception is identical to the one that Beauvoir uses to structure her phenomenological description of Elisabeth's experience of

absence; that is, where all the objects in Françoise's room form a synthetic background against which her absence is perceived.

When it comes to demonstrating the cardinal point that the nonbeing, the "flickering of nothingness," that Pierre perceives upon entering the café, is no mere linguistic or mental negation, Sartre draws
directly upon Beauvoir's account. Sartre, only thinly and jokingly disguis-
ing the source of what became one of his most famous examples, turns
Napoleon into Wellington and Shakespeare into Valéry.

> Pierre absent haunts this café and is the condition of its self-
> nihilating organization as ground. By contrast, judgments which
> I can make subsequently to amuse myself, such as, "Wellington
> is not in this café, Paul Valéry is no longer here, etc."—these
> have a purely abstract meaning, they are pure applications of the
> principle of negation without real or efficacious foundation, and
> they never succeed in establishing a real relation between the
> café and Wellington or Valéry. Here the relation "is not" is
> merely thought. This example is sufficient to show that non-
> being does not come to things by a negative judgement; it is the
> negative judgment, on the contrary, which is conditioned and
> supported by non-being.[40]

Sartre's second account of absence, which comes in his chapter on the
body and its section "The Body-for-Others," is more directly based on
Beauvoir's phenomenological description of Elisabeth in Françoise's
room. This time Sartre describes himself waiting for Pierre in Pierre's
room.

> This room in which I wait for the master of the house reveals to
> me in its totality the body of its owner: this easy chair is a chair-
> where-he-sits, this desk is a desk-at-which-he-writes, this window
> is a window though which there enters the light-which-illumi-
> nates-the-objects-which-he-sees. Thus it is an outline complete
> with all its parts, and this outline is an outline with content. But
> still the master of the house "is not there." He is *elsewhere*; he is
> *absent*.
>
> Now we have seen that absence is a structure of *being-there*. To
> be absent is to-be-elsewhere-in-my-world.[41]

Sartre's next paragraph draws on and elucidates another section of *She Came to Stay* that touches on the phenomenon of absence, this time in terms of its relation to presence. In Beauvoir's novel, Françoise, seriously ill and confined to her private room in a nursing home, thinks about her friends, Xavière and Pierre. "Wherever her eyes fell, they caught only absences." A few minutes later she hears them climbing the stairs.

> They were coming from the station, from Paris, from the center of their life; it was a portion of this life that they would spend here. The steps halted outside the door.
> "May we come in?" said Pierre, as he opened the door. There he was, and Xavière was with him. The transition from their absence to their presence had, as always, been imperceptible.[42]

Sartre elaborates on this imperceptibility and then on the difference between a portion of a life spent elsewhere and spent in one's presence.

> . . . the presence or absence of the Other changes nothing.
> But look! Now Pierre appears. He is entering my room. This appearance changes nothing in the fundamental structure of my relation to him; it is contingency but so was his absence contingency. Objects indicate him to me: the door which he pushes indicates a human presence when it opens before him. . . .
> But the objects did not cease to indicate him during his absence. . . . Yet there is something new. This is the fact that he appears at present on the ground of the world as a *this* which I can look at, apprehend, and utilize directly.[43]

Taken together, all these passages on absence illustrate the collaborative and intertextual process that went into the making of *Being and Nothingness*.

Beauvoir Retrieving Beauvoir

In the course of preparing this essay, we located a textual borrowing that undermines—but only partially—the symmetrical reciprocity that we saw as characterizing Sartre's and Beauvoir's philosophical efforts on absence.

It seems that, like Sartre's accounts of absence in *Being and Nothingness*, Beauvoir's description of Elisabeth's perception of absence in *She Came to Stay* draws heavily on a prior piece of writing. The second of the two unpublished chapters of *She Came to Stay*, which Beauvoir wrote between 1937 and mid-1938, and which found their way into print in Claude Francis and Fernande Gontier's *Les Écrits de Simone de Beauvoir* in 1979, contains a scene in which a much younger Françoise is let into Elisabeth's room to wait for her.[44] The descriptions of the two rooms in the two works are essentially the same. In Elisabeth's room a pair of stockings, some brushes, and a bottle of eau-de-cologne are on the mantel piece. A jacket lies across the bed where Elisabeth has thrown it. A book of plays by a famous playwright—this time Sophocles—is open at where Elisabeth had been reading it. Her chair has been left pushed back from her desk. There are various papers covered with her handwriting and embodying her thoughts. But some of the telling touches of the later version are missing or incompletely conceived. For example, Françoise imagines the room's missing inhabitant looking at a Van Gogh print rather than at herself in a mirror. More important, the bust of Napoleon is missing from the mantelpiece. And, perhaps most important of all, the passage lacks the precise philosophical focus of the corresponding one in *She Came to Stay*.

In conclusion, it merits repeating that the concept of absence lies at the heart of Sartre's ontological project. His, like Beauvoir's, conception of human action balances on the interface between being and nonbeing, between what is and what is not but might be. Both philosophers worked to reveal the essential (in the sense of no dependence on personal differences) structure of reality *from the point of view* of the individual human existent. Through phenomenological descriptions of boundary situations between being and nonbeing, and most notably Beauvoir's descriptions of absence, Sartre identifies an objective and fundamental structure of human reality—rather like seventeenth-century epistemologists distinguished between primary and secondary qualities in order to identify objective structures of material reality.

Obviously, all the similarities between Sartre's and Beauvoir's various texts concerned with the topic of absence do not tell the whole story. Like the puffed-out sleeves of Françoise's dressing gown, these textual correspondences themselves point to an absence. For Sartre and Beauvoir, the formative period of their thought on the question of absence lasted at least five years, during which absence must have figured repeatedly as a topic in their conversation. But it also must have been the case that absence was only one of many such topics in their joint and ongoing explorations of philosophical issues. This detailed exploration of this profoundly collaborative and cross-textual process between the two philosophers generally, that half-century of intellectual partnership between equals, is an absence that should be a fundamental presence in the study of both Beauvoir and Sartre.

Notes

1. *A Companion to the Philosophy of Mind,* ed. Samuel Guttenplan (Oxford: Blackwell, 1994).

2. Jean-Paul Sartre, *Being and Nothingness: An Essay on Phenomenological Ontology,* trans. Hazel E. Barnes (New York: Philosophical Library, 1956).

3. *The Cambridge Companion to Sartre,* ed. Christina Howells, Cambridge: Cambridge University Press, 1992).

4. Maurice Merleau-Ponty, "Metaphysics and the Novel," in *Sense and Non-sense,* Hubert L. Dreyfus and Patricia Allen Dreyfus (Evanston: Northwestern University Press, 1964). Simone de Beauvoir, *She Came to Stay,* trans. Yvonne Moyse and Roger Senhouse (London: Flamingo, 1984).

5. Sartre, "Metaphysics and the Novel," 27.

6. Ibid., 27.

7. Ibid., 27–28.

8. Simone de Beauvoir, "Littérature et métaphysique" [1946] in *Existentialisme et la sagesse des nations* (Paris: Nagel, 1948).

9. Ibid., 116. All translations from this text are our own.

10. Eleanore Holveck, "Can a Woman Be a Philosopher? Reflections of a Beauvoirean Housemaid," in *Feminist Interpretations of Simone de Beauvoir,* ed. Margaret A. Simons. (University Park: Penn State Press, 1995), 70.

11. Simone de Beauvoir, *The Prime of Life,* trans. Peter Green (Harmondsworth: Penguin, 1965), 221; "Littérature et métaphysique," 16–17.

12. Simone de Beauvoir, *Pyrrhus et Cinéas* (Paris: Gallimard, 1944), 34–35. All translations from this text are our own.

13. Ibid., 58.

14. Simone de Beauvoir, preface to *America Day by Day,* trans. Patrick Dudley (London: Duckworth, 1952).

15. Margaret A. Simons, "Joining Another's Fight: Beauvoir's Post-Modern Challenge to Racism in *America Day by Day,*" paper delivered to the Midwest Division, Society for Women in Philosophy, October 1994.

16. Beauvoir, "Littérature et métaphysique," 114.

17. Ibid., 119.

18. Holveck, "Can a Woman Be a Philosopher?" 72.

19. Beauvoir, "Littérature et métaphysique," 105.

20. Ibid., 105–6.

21. Ibid., 106–7.

22. Mary Warnock, *Existentialism* (Oxford: Oxford University Press, 1970), 133.

23. Ibid., 136.

24. Beauvoir, "Littérature et métaphysique," 118–20.

25. Sartre, *Being and Nothingness*, 3.

26. Ibid., 4.

27. Ibid., 4–5.

28. Jean-Paul Sartre, *War Diaries: Notebooks from a Phoney War, November 1939–March 1940*, trans. Quintin Hoare (London: Verso, 1984).

29. Ibid., 187.

30. Ibid., 188.

31. Ibid., 188.

32. Ibid., 55.

33. Beauvoir, *She Came to Stay*, 354–55.

34. Jean-Paul Sartre, *Quiet Moments in a War: Letters of Jean-Paul Sartre to Simone de Beauvoir, 1940–1963*, ed. Simone de Beauvoir, trans. Lee Fahnestock and Norman MacAfee (New York: Charles Scribner's Sons, 1993), 61.

35. Beauvoir, *She Came to Stay*, 64–65.

36. Ibid., 65.

37. Sartre, *Being and Nothingness*, 9–11, 341–43.

38. Ibid., 9.

39. Ibid.

40. Ibid., 10–11.

41. Ibid., 341–42.

42. Beauvoir, *She Came to Stay*, 199.

43. Sartre, *Being and Nothingness*, 342.

44. Simone de Beauvoir, "Deux chapitres inédits de 'L'Invitée,'" in *Les Écrits de Simone de Beauvoir*, ed. Claude Francis and Fernande Gontier (Paris: Gallimard, 1979), 306–7.

3

Sartre on Objectification

A Feminist Perspective

Phyllis Sutton Morris

The concept of objectification has acquired a central, and quite negative, role in recent feminist discussions of male dominance. Examples can be

This essay is dedicated to the memory of Eléanor H. Kuykendall. Eléanor read an early version of this essay a few months before her untimely death in 1993. I am grateful to her for the thoughtfulness of her suggestions for revision, and for the generosity of her support over the years.

    I am indebted also to the following for their comments on earlier versions: Hazel E. Barnes, Linda Bell, Constantine Boundas, Norman S. Care, Lorraine Code, Lewis Gordon, Robert Grimm, Richard Gull, Helen Heise, Peter McInerney, Adrian Mirvish, Kenneth Pendleton, Michael Russell, and Susan Vineberg.

    In addition, I was assisted by audience discussion of earlier versions presented to the Sartre Society, meeting with the Pacific Division, American Philosophical Association, March 1992; to the Sartre Society of North America, Peterborough, Ontario, May 1993; to the University of Michigan/Flint faculty colloquium, College of Arts and Sciences, Winter 1994, and to the Detroit Area Feminist Philosophers, February 1997.

found in Sandra Bartky's accounts of sexual and self-objectification,[1] in Iris Young's descriptions of female body experience,[2] and in Catharine MacKinnon's discussions of pornography.[3] I agree with much of what these thinkers say about the unacceptability of certain patriarchal strategies of dominance. These and other feminists have demonstrated convincingly that the concept of objectification can be applied to exploitive strategies. However, the concept of objectification is theoretically broader than those feminist critiques suggest—perhaps to the point of being too diffuse. In this essay, after some brief theoretical background remarks on Sartre, I give a short account of several influential feminist accounts of objectification, and indicate how Sartre's views on objectification, resemble or differ from these, or both. I will offer several considerations to show the theoretical importance to feminists of a more balanced account of subject-object relations. In doing so, I will explore several elements of Sartre's early work on objectification, which he wrote in dialogue with Simone de Beauvoir.[4]

In particular, I want to show that there are positive as well as negative forms of objectification, and that objectification as considered is conceptually linked to a naturalistic (as opposed to a dualistic or supernaturalistic) account of the human person. Most contemporary feminists have rejected Cartesian dualism.[5] Although Sartre is often dismissed as a Cartesian dualist,[6] what is most striking about Sartre's early existential phenomenology is the powerful set of strategies he develops against some fundamental Cartesian claims. Brief discussion of several theoretical considerations will provide background for further discussion of objectification.

A Theoretical Context for Rethinking Objectification

1. According to the standard Cartesian view, the human subject is a nonphysical mental substance separable from, but interacting with, the nonconscious bodily machine.[7] However, for many existential phenomenologists, including Sartre, the continuing subject of conscious experience and action is the human body.[8] A nonphysical, invisible, intangible subject would be hidden from public view. To be a *bodily* subject, however, is *necessarily* to be experientially accessible to others—that is, to be a possible object of others' perception.

2. Furthermore, to be a *conscious* body-subject is necessarily to be object directed. Sartre's existential phenomenology borrowed from Husserl the claim that all consciousness is consciousness of an object. For Sartre, this claim meant a radical rejection of the traditional philosophical account (defended by rationalists and empiricists alike) that construed the mind as a nonphysical substance or private mental theater occupied by mental contents (ideas, images, etc.) that might or might not correspond to physical objects in the external world.[9] Rather, Sartre said that consciousness is a direct *relation* that the bodily subject has to objects.[10]

What counts as an object, for Sartre, can be quite variable. Some of the "objects" included in Sartre's infamous account of "the feminine" are nonstandard; holes have symbolic significance whether understood ontologically or literally. So does slime. A desiring or hoping consciousness can have nonexistent objects, as when we hope for perfect world peace or desire that there be a unicorn in the garden. In these cases, consciousness is a nonstandard type of relation.[11] More obviously, we are conscious of perceptual objects: the fragrant rose, the noisy machine. The object of special attention at some particular time can be a situation, or a specific feature of that perceptual manifold. The key point, however, is that consciousness is not self-contained, as the philosophical tradition (and later Husserl) had assumed. Sartre began his monumental work, *Being and Nothingness*, by announcing that "the first procedure of a philosophy ought to be to expel things from consciousness and to reestablish its true connection with the world".[12] The mind is not a passive, inner receptacle for incoming images, as Hume had believed. Sartre said that bodily subjects are actively aware of value-laden fields of experience through purposive, selective focus on certain aspects of external objects. Clearly, this is not objectivity in the sense of a neutral, aperspectival consciousness. In any case, object-directedness is a fundamental characteristic of all human conscious experience for Sartre.

3. Because the traditional philosophical view—defended, for example, by Cartesians and sometimes by Hume—treated the human mind as a private, self-contained entity with interior mental contents, the very existence of other conscious beings was theoretically problematic. Thus, the alleged problem of other minds emerged.[13] In claiming, however, that the body is the subject of human experience, and that our desires and purposes are played out in a world that includes other people, Sartre emphasizes that our own actions can either support or block the aims of others. *Conflict*, as a continuing possibility of social objectifiability, is

clearly intrinsic to this model, although supportive actions are equally a possibility.[14]

4. A further implication of our embodied subjectivity for Sartre is that because we usually perform actions in public, but only rarely look back to examine these actions, others may know what we do, and what our long-term desires and goals are, better than we do ourselves.[15] We *are* selves not only as bodily subjects, but also as constructed, long-term patterns of purposive actions undertaken in the public realm. Sartre uses the terms *essence, ego,* and *character* to refer to this sense of "self." In this second meaning, the self or ego is not the subject, but is rather an object for others and for ourselves.[16] In both senses, our self-knowledge depends heavily on objectifying responses from other people. Sartre thus rejects the standard Cartesian claim that we can have immediate, indubitable, privileged knowledge of our own mental life. At best, we learn the fundamental human skill of reflection upon what we do through the "mediation"of others who, in making us objects of their judgment, can teach us what we are like.[17]

So far, I have tried to suggest briefly that there are conceptual links between objectification and Sartre's theoretical account of the human person as a bodily subject, conscious of objects in the world, vulnerable to being perceived and impeded in her pursuits by others, and heavily dependent on others' objectifying assessments for her own self-knowledge. Some of these points will be developed more fully in discussing varieties of objectification.

Let us turn now to some forms of objectification that have been important for feminist theory and practice.

Some Dominance-Oriented Forms of Objectification

There are several different approaches to objectification in recent feminist discussion. Simone de Beauvoir's *The Second Sex* emphasized objectification in the historical context of patriarchal power relations;[18] this work seems to have provided the initial impetus for later feminists to think negatively about objectification. Some of the dominance-oriented forms of objectification that have received considerable attention from contemporary feminists are these: women have been objectified (1) as targets of "objective" thinking; (2) as reduced to *parts* of their bodies, which can be used as mere means or instruments; (3) as whole physical objects that lack conscious goals and desires; and (4) as conscious physical beings who have potentially dangerous desires and thoughts. The present section will describe some versions of these, with a view toward locating and clarifying Sartre's position in comparison and contrast with them.

1. One feminist view has linked domineering objectification to the rational ideal of objective thinking.[19] Catharine MacKinnon's criticisms of pornography have been widely discussed by feminists and others in recent years. She claimed that "to look at the world objectively is to objectify it," and that to do so is the epistemological/political stance under conditions of male dominance.[20] She defines objectivity as a "neutral . . . nonsituated, distanced standpoint."[21]

Sally Haslanger has offered a nuanced gloss on, and carefully qualified partial support for, MacKinnon's discussion of the links between objectivity and objectification. Haslanger explores some ways in which the assumption of objectivity may be linked, weakly or strongly, to men's social roles. She notes in particular that within a social hierarchy, dominant males tend to believe in a "Woman's Nature,"[22] and base that belief, furthermore, on what seem to be natural facts rather than recognizing that they are merely observing the results of their social coercion of women.[23]

The link here is compatible with several elements of Sartre's position, although this is not the whole of his account of objectification. Sartre's affinity with the feminist analysis of objective thought as oppressive can be seen in this passage: "Objectivity = the world seen by another who holds the key to it. . . . Nature in me is myself as a transcended objectivity for another. . . . I can never live my nature. Hence the other transforms me into an objectivity by oppressing me and my initial situation is to have a destiny/nature and exist in the face of objectified values."[24] Sartre's critique of objectivity is offered in the context of a discussion of alleged objective, universal ethics, rather than of epistemology, but he cites problems similar to those cited by MacKinnon, Haslanger, and others: a belief in the objectified's destiny or Nature and a misguided claim by the oppressor to have The Truth about values. Sartre's ideas are well known: there is no general human nature, since existence precedes essence; all values and all knowledge are linked to the goals and position (spatial, historical, cultural, etc.) of the individual within his or her world.

Although Sartre's account of links between objectivity claims and oppressive objectification can *in these respects* be seen as compatible with feminist claims, Sartre does not restrict objectification to an oppressive instrument of males who claim to be objective thinkers, as MacKinnon sometimes suggests. For one thing, Sartre's commitment to the Husserlian claim that *all* consciousness is intentional, in the sense that each conscious act is directed toward an object, is the basis for his much broader account of forms of objectification. Other elements of Sartre's position will emerge later.

It might be questioned, however, whether the link between objective thinking and oppressive objectification has as much explanatory breadth as MacKinnon sometimes seems to suggest. Haslanger makes a brief but telling point when she reminds us that empiricism, which relies on observation but does not claim things have permanent "natures," differs from rationalism, which does claim that things have natures but goes beyond observed regularities in so doing.[25] So whereas some philosophers do assume the ideal of objectivity as described by MacKinnon, Haslanger notes that many in the philosophical mainstream do not.

A further doubt about the explanatory power of MacKinnon's approach is mentioned by Haslanger in passing, when she notes that "race, class, and ethnicity" yield gender norms other than that of a capacity for objective thought.[26] While that type of thought is valued among some privileged Western white men, objectification of women—in pornography or otherwise—is practiced far more widely than among members of that group.[27] For that matter, except for some research scientists and judges, it is difficult to think of many professional roles, occupied by privileged, white, Western males, that mandate a neutral stance. Lawyers, for example, are often advocates for consumers, for the environment, or for their clients. CEOs of major profit-making companies exercise forms of rationality clearly connected to their own interests.

Linda Bell discusses another deep problem with MacKinnon's aim of abandoning the value of objectivity: such a rejection would mean that the most careful feminist research and analyses, including MacKinnon's, would be reduced to *mere* perspectives, on a par with the most careless, biased, antifeminist work. Bell's strategy, building on work by many other feminists and by Sartre, is to redefine objectivity: no longer pretending to be "aperspectival" thought, feminist objectivity would identify its crucial perspectival components, and would aim for inclusiveness and openness to criticism and evidence.[28] Bell's approach to this issue is both thoughtful and convincing.

Although Sartre agrees with MacKinnon that assumed objectivity of thought is oppressive in its intent—and could use moralistic attacks on women's reproductive rights as a contemporary example—there seems to be little reason for Sartre or for feminists to place undue emphasis on that particular danger. Other forms of oppressive objectification have been identified by feminists, and to some of these we can now turn.

2. Feminists have remarked on the ways in which women have often been exclusively identified with parts of their bodies. Iris Young's description of breasts as objects includes the following description of what an object is, which is far more restricted than Sartre's account of objects: "The object is determinate and definable . . . passive, inert matter. . . . The object is what can be handled, manipulated. . . . The essential properties of the object are thus all quantities: extension, location, velocity, weight."[29] Feminists have described ways in which women respond to this type of objectification by objectifying themselves through such means as hip reduction, liposuction, breast augmentation, and so on. Thus women collaborate in perpetuating the dominance of males who treat women as bodily parts to be manipulated.[30]

Two of Sartre's most striking examples have been widely discussed by outraged feminists: slime and holes.[31] Strictly speaking, neither of these is an object at all, at least in Young's sense of a thing with definable boundaries. A hole is a receptacle into which an object can be placed to fill the empty space. "The slimy" is not a defined object but instead a quality of some objects or an amorphous mass. That Sartre intends these descriptions to apply at least in part to portions of the female anatomy can be seen from the following: "The slimy . . . is a trap . . . A sickly-sweet feminine revenge."[32] Or again, "The obscenity of the feminine sex is that of everything which 'gapes open.'"[33] These remarks are clearly demeaning to women.

However, whether Sartre's fuller ontological accounts of slime and holes must be considered *hopelessly* sexist is open to question.[34] For instance, Sartre's discussion of the slimy is explicitly intended to symbolize a certain moral quality that he finds disgusting, but he also admits that "the slimy is *myself*."[35] Again, while the hole-that-is-to-be-filled obviously may refer to sexual penetration, it would apply equally well to heterosexual and to male homosexual acts. Sartre also notes that the mouth is a hole.[36] Eating may be an ordinary act of enjoyment or survival, but in the case of eating disorders (to which women seem to be more prone than men), eating may symbolize an attempt to overcome emotional or spiritual emptiness. Sartre speaks of a general human tendency to desire the "spherical plenitude of Parmenidean being."[37] This point is central to Sartre's discussions of the impossible general human project of aiming to be God. Thus, in the case of Sartre's most frequently cited examples of this type of sexism, it can be shown that he had far more general symbols in mind. I make this point in fairness to the complexity of Sartre's theory, not with the idea of establishing Sartre as an *unqualified* feminist.[38]

Nevertheless, body-part forms of dominance-oriented objectification surely do take place, are widespread, and surely need to be examined and challenged. However, we can ask whether this form of objectification takes place only as directed against women. Men also objectify themselves and perceive themselves as objectified by women. In the context of a discussion of seduction, Sartre comments that a woman "turns herself into an object so that the Other transforms himself into an object. Whence the rancor of many people after sex."[39] To take another example, Laurence Thomas has claimed that it is women who are the main source of men's self-objectification—for example, their preoccupation with penis size—and that men could be male in nontraditional, nonpatriarchal ways if they were encouraged to do so by women.[40] Barbara Herman has written about Kant's views of sexuality and marriage; she reminds us that Kant's concerns about sexual relations were based on the moral degradation of persons—both men and women—that occurs when each partner reduces the other to body parts. Such objectification of the other was for Kant "both natural and inevitable in sexual activity," she adds.[41]

Sartre tells a more complicated story. His discussion of sexual desire in *Being and Nothingness* shares a few, but not all, of the characteristics suggested by Kant and Laurence Thomas. Sartre insists that each desires the other as "a human being,"[42] a claim to be developed shortly. He insists that it is only in a *sense* that we desire the body of the other, and furthermore, that what is desired is, to begin with, a conscious "living body as an organic totality" in a situation—not merely "physiological elements" or parts.[43] Whereas our ordinary relations with the world are usually active and instrumental, in the sexual caress the body is cut off from the numerous possibilities of action. Instead, "I make myself flesh in order to impel the Other to realize *for-herself* and *for-me* her own flesh, and my caresses cause my flesh to be born for me in so far as it is for the Other *flesh causing her to be born as flesh*." Sartre describes this as a process of *"double reciprocal incarnation."*[44] He thus believes that sexual relations tend to move people in the direction of being closer to their bodies, rather than directed toward objects and activities in the world outside. So the kind of transformation he finds is away from externality, rather than away from wholeness. He agrees with Kant and Laurence Thomas that what occurs in sexual activity is mutual. Although he acknowledges that there is a desire to use the other, as he describes it the caress is also a self-imposed form of manipulation. Sartre's basic disagreement with Thomas, Kant, and some feminists is with the notion that sexual activity involves merely parts of the body.[45]

3. An additional form of ojectification discussed by some feminists treats women as whole things, inert or nonconscious, rather than as body parts. Various social practices and attitudes have been described that presuppose a lack of conscious mental life among females who are treated as possessed things. For example, Andrea Dworkin discussed examples of men who considered women as stringed instruments whose music is evoked by male lovers or as passive logs in relation to male lovers' performances; "objects do not see or know."[46] Jessica Benjamin—borrowing from Hegel's master/slave parable—says that when the other is seen as an inanimate object, the objectifier, failing to receive the recognition he desires in dominating, is "imprisoned in his mind."[42] Julien Murphy claims that Sartre describes desire for a woman as akin to "desire [for] an inanimate object."[48]

I do not believe, however, that Sartre claims that we see women as inanimate objects, so the response to this version of the objectification thesis can be brief. Sartre says, instead, that we see others immediately as *conscious* bodily objects. This point will be developed more fully in the next section.

4. In addition to the dominance-oriented forms of objectification that are based on treating women or their body parts or both as nonconscious or as merely quantifiable physical things, there is a theoretically more complex type of dominance-oriented objectification. Women can be treated as dangerous "psychic objects," to use Sartre's phrase.[49] In this case, the other is recognized as a *conscious* physical being, with desires and goals that may be dangerous to the perceiver. Sartre's description of "psychic objects" is not always directed toward male-female relationships, and often seems rather to be embedded in the context of a competitive male world in which the appearance of another male is seen as threatening.[50] The male bodily subject has structured his situation with himself as center so as to further his own aims. The other is dangerous in that he

may "decenter" the situation of the first male and block the goals of that subject.[51] Male competition, in its ugliest forms, can be seen as emerging from such perceived threats.

Sartre's analysis can be extended to male relationships with females. To the extent that women have been perceived as having needs and goals that could conflict with the fulfillment of men's goals, subtler methods have been developed. Men do not compete as equals with women. Instead, historically, females have been subjected from infancy to intense pressures—social, philosophical, religious, political, economic—intended in part to shape the desires of women into conformity with the subordinate roles men have demanded of them.[52] "The object is allowed to desire if she desires to be an object: to be formed; especially to be used."[53] Where this has been successful, men's social, economic, political, and educational arrangements have been central and women have remained "willingly" at the periphery in a supporting role.

It is not always the case that men's purposes have prevailed. Sartre's well-known account of sadists and masochists appears to include both men and women as engaged in a rotating struggle for the central position.[54] Consider the fact that there have always been some women who have understood that if they were highly successful in certain roles, they could manipulate men for their own purposes. Sandra Bartky mentions a number of reasons that women might have for transforming themselves into desirable bodies, but seems to omit mention of the hope of real power over men's lives through their sexual response.[55] Bartky does acknowledge the possibility of power in caregiving;[56] as feminists have often recognized, the maternal object may arouse deep fears of dependency in men. Iris Young acknowledges that a woman may enjoy men's staring at her breasts "with a sense of sexual power."[57] However, Young's remark was made in the context of the claim that women become mere objects of the gaze of men, and she does not go on to say that there may be *genuine* power linked to that *feeling* of power.[58] There have been historical examples of women (e.g., Cleopatra, Pamela Harriman) who have possessed real political power through making themselves into highly prized sexual objects. Even in ordinary cases, a woman who deliberatedly objectifies herself may be acting primarily from purposes of her own. As feminists we may believe that this type of power is flawed in that it is embedded within a vast system of exploitation.[59] However, men's terror of women's sexual power over them, as well as their fear of maternal authority, need to be recognized as important motives in patriarchal strategies of objectification.[60] The anger we feel at being made into sex objects is clearly suitable in many situations as directed against many men. However, to the extent that tendencies to objectify women stem from male fear of their purposes and male vulnerability, it might be the case that less-threatening strategies and more reciprocal openness are also needed.[61] (These remarks are *not* intended to imply that men have been damaged as much as women have by historical patterns of objectification, or that openness is always preferable, much less possible.)

So far we have considered the stance of the subject threatened by the appearance of a "psychic object," a man or woman who might disrupt my situation so as to make himself or herself the central subject or agent in relation to that environment: he might cut down my forest or she might get the promotion I earned. Also mentioned was the deeper threat found in the real possibility that the former psychic object will turn his or her gaze from the environing situation toward me, the subject, making me the object of that look, seeing me directly in the light of his or her aims, not of my own. This intensely uncomfortable discovery of myself as having an "outside"—that is, a social self—leads me to struggle to make the other my object instead once more. So conflict often develops.

The Role of Objectification in Reflective Self-Knowledge

Equally important for the purposes of this essay, the discovery of myself as an object for others is a necessary condition, Sartre claims, of developing the distinctively human capacity to reflect on what we are.[62] Our capacity for reflective self-knowledge is developed through the mediation of others who objectify our actions. How does this mediation work: Sartre suggests two ways: through a Look, through verbal judgments, or both. One of Sartre's famous examples is that of looking through a keyhole to see what is going on in the next room, and being discovered in that act by someone whose look reveals me to myself as a Peeping Tom.[63] Before that discovery, I had been attentive only to the situation revealed through the keyhole, and not to my own action. In other works, Sartre gives examples of verbal assessments: young Jean Genet is labeled a thief, and Garcin, in *No Exit*, is called a coward. Sartre's account of how we develop (or self-deceptively try to avoid!) the skill of reflective self-knowledge through the often unwelcome objectifying assistance of others contrasts sharply with the solipsistic Cartesian claim that we have direct, privileged access to our own desires, goals, and motives.

Women have often been distressed to discover that as we challenge traditional feminine roles, we are charged with being unfeminine, uppity, and worse. While that distress is real, I submit that these charges have contributed in an important way to women's self-knowledge concerning what those traditional roles were and who we are—more precisely, who we become as social selves—when we reject or transform those roles. Also, women have sometimes taken great pleasure in deliberately assuming those negative labels: hag, harpy, witch.[64]

There is another value that should not be overlooked. It is not only the case that women are treated as dangerous "psychic objects" by men. This is surely the strategy feminists use when we confront men with their sexist utterances and actions. It is a weapon that has stimulated much anger and resentment, but also—among some men—explicit self-knowledge of what they were doing. Here again, objectification is not a unilateral approach, nor is it wholly without positive value. We can hope to influence the intentions and actions of at least some men through an increase in their self-knowledge of how they have dominated women.

In connection with some dominance-oriented forms of objectification, I have argued that women have objectified men in ways that are analogous to the ways in which men have objectified women. I have also argued for the positive value of objectification, even when it is painful or upsetting, insofar as it contributes to self-knowledge. There are some complications connected to the latter point that need to be mentioned before concluding this discussion.

Sartre's Account of Reflection: Some Objections and Replies

We recall Sartre's claim that other people's assessment of our actions is necessary to the development of the skill of reflecting upon what we are like as social beings. Criticism of that claim has come and might come from several sources.

First, a thinker wedded to the standard Cartesian notion of privileged access is likely to believe that each thinker can know himself or herself directly and indubitably, and that others cannot know the essential, true self. The theoretical considerations cited earlier in this essay need to be recalled: for Sartre, the human person is a bodily subject, vulnerable to being perceived as well as impeded in her activities by others whose projects may conflict with hers. Furthermore, there is a second sense of "self" (namely, ego or character or essence), which Sartre believes is constructed by the bodily subject act by act, usually in the public realm. In neither sense does the person have full indubitable access to what she really is. Recent research on the ways in which people's body images tend to distort their weight or appearance lends some support to Sartre's claim that the bodily subject is "lived" but not directly known by the subject herself.[65] Sartre also cites the common human tendency to produce double evaluations of certain kinds of actions, depending on whether they were performed by oneself or another.[66] Thus, whereas "I am firm of principle, he is a stubborn so-and-so." Without the input of others, our self-evaluations would likely be too favorable, or in some cases, too unfavorable. Sartre's early work gives a fully satisfactory reply to this possible criticism by the defender of Cartesian privileged access, and because feminists have generally rejected Cartesian dualism, and have often embraced the notion that the self is, in some sense, a social construct, Sartre's reply should make sense.

A second, somewhat similar criticism can be given from a Sartrean perspective. Is it not the case that Sartre's traumatic examples of being subjected to the objectifying Look or judgment of another are intended to show that only my own perspective should count, and that the judgments of others on what I do should be rejected or ignored? Will I not be inauthentic if I try to find out from others what I am really like? Is that not the point, really, of Sartre's famous dictum that "hell is other people"?[67] This is a common reading of Sartre, but I believe an inaccurate one. In reply, to begin with, one can take note of Sartre's explicit claim that it is the other who "teaches me who I am."[68] The examples that come to mind, although often involving intense discomfort on the part of the recipient of the Look or judgment, are usually examples of people acting in bad faith. Garcin, in *No Exit*, does not wish to acknowledge that his actions have formed a pattern of cowardice, and yet Sartre is clearly speaking through Inez when she insists that Garcin is defined by what he did, not by what he dreamed of doing.[69] Again, speaking of the bad faith of the violent man, Sartre says that "violence is a refusal of being looked at," in other words, an insistence on being a "pure transcendence" without the facticity of an observable body.[70] The case of young

Jean Genet is more complicated, for he acknowledges the accuracy of the externally applied label "thief," but then *chooses* to form his subjective life goals around that objectifying assessment, and in doing so, might count as a Sartrean example of someone who achieved a degree of authenticity.[71] Much of Sartre's complex account of the self-deceptive form of bad faith, including his account of reflective consciousness, is directed against the view that our own judgments about what we are like is the only relevant one.[72] Sartre's examples need to be understood in that context.

A third objection comes from a feminist perspective. Sartre discusses the Look as if it were gender neutral. However, whereas women are often subjected to unwelcome looks by men whose demeanor defines the woman as a sexual object, a woman who returns that look is not contributing to the man's capacity for reflective self-knowledge, but rather is taken to be wanton.[73] This would certainly be true of certain kinds of looks in certain contexts. Suppose the woman's look were an angry one, rather than one of welcoming pleasure or docility? Even here, a certain kind of man would take that angry look as a challenge to his masculinity from a woman who, he assumed, was inviting a dominating response from him. Excellent feminist work has already been done on Sartre's Look insofar as it is a device for oppression.[74] Some of the ways that looks can contribute to reflective self-knowledge have also been explored.[75]

Another type of response to this objection, however, is to recall that objectification can take the form of verbal judgments, and that this enables feminists to distance themselves from the complexities and uncertainties of specific relationships and to clarify their positions more fully than might be possible during a one-on-one encounter. It would be unusual for reflective self-understanding to occur instantaneously. It is more likely that each of us learns to understand what we are like, not only from important personal encounters, but also from thoughtful reading and conversation about more general social patterns. Thus a woman may learn that her own need to please is a socially instilled feminine trait open to change, as she speaks with other women about their experiences and reads about the ways in which gender patterns are established in children. Again, as women use written language to describe various forms of patriarchal exploitation, they are objectifying men with the hope of producing change in those men who are able to understand how their own actions have contributed to oppressive situations for women. Not all women, and not all men, will see the connection between what they hear or read and what they themselves have done. However, there has been enough evidence of change in recent years to suggest that, given enough time, objectifying assessments may work to deepen reflective understanding and, based on that, to effect changes in attitude and behavior.

Finally, criticism of Sartre's position by feminists could take a quite different turn. One might reject Cartesian dualism, as Sartre does, and one could agree that the self is at least partially a social construct. One might still doubt that others' assessment can aid us in knowing who we truly are, since the actions observed by others take place in a social context already heavily imbued with external values and expectations; assessments of women and other exploited groups are likely to embody exploiters' values, rather than to reveal what members of those groups are really like.[76] Sartre himself has claimed that perception of situations, and of others acting within situations, is shaped by our projects. Haslanger has suggested that "assumed objectivity" is itself a project.[77] How then could I learn to know myself by listening to the voice of another, or worse, to the conflicting voices of many others?

The nest of issues raised here is both too important and too complex to be addressed fully or satisfactorily in this context. A brief reply might take the form of agreeing with the critic that knowledge of ourselves is vastly complicated by the ulterior aims of those who inhabit our social world; Sartre could easily acknowledge this, since he claimed that perception of situations and of others acting within situations is shaped by individuals' own projects. If we lived in a monolithic culture, it might be extremely difficult to develop alternative perspectives, as Beauvoir and others have claimed. In a time, however, such as the present, of heterogeneous cultural values and rapid change, it is likely that each of us occupies various social worlds that elicit not only differing patterns of action but sometimes contrary assessments of single patterns of action. Thus the woman who speaks courageously against sexual harassment by her exploitive male employer (according to one assessment of her speech) is an uppity bitch (according to another evaluation of that same speech). Self-knowledge in such a case must take the form of recognizing that she is constructing herself as a social being within overlapping and often conflicting value frameworks, and that the question of which is the *true* self is no longer central, since she needs to understand what she is doing in relation to many contexts, and to decide which value framework will guide her actions in each. Sartre, speaking against another kind of oppression, notes that anti-Semitism is a phenomenon of "strongly structured" social pluralities.[78] In any case, insofar as feminists seek to occupy a more public role than women have traditionally done, we need to understand that even unwelcome forms of objectifying judgment may contribute to insight about what we are in relation to particular social frameworks.

There are more rewarding forms of objectification, and we turn now to two of these.[79]

Some Fulfilling Forms of Objectification

As already noted, in Being and Nothingness, Sartre does not *seem* to acknowledge even the theoretical possibility of directly experiencing the other as a subject.[80] I experience the other *indirectly* as a subject when he makes an object of me (or sometimes when we both make an object of someone else). Each of us struggles against the uncomfortable recognition of the other's subjectivity by trying to make him the object for our own consciousness. Thus, in this early work, Sartre takes the Hegelian lord/bondsman struggle for dominance as primary in human relations. In The Second Sex, Beauvoir recognized the chance of experiencing the other simultaneously as subject and object, and the rare possibility of a rewarding, reciprocal relationship between a man and a woman or between two women.[81] However, she emphasized the power relations that have developed; men have historically thought of women, and treated them, as alien objects to be dominated, possessed, used, destroyed, or all of these. If Being and Nothingness were the only source of Sartre's early thought on this issue, it might be necessary to argue that he thought intersubjective relations would always be unfulfilling struggles. The French publication (in 1983) of Sartre's ethical notebooks written several years after the publication of his most famous work (in 1947–48), cast new light on the project of Being and Nothingness, as has ongoing research on his unpublished ethical writings. In the 1992 English translation of his Notebooks for an Ethics, Sartre says that that earlier work is "an ontology before conversion,"[82] in other words, descriptive of bad-faith relations. The notebooks often offer a more hopeful account of possible authentic human relations.

In at least two respects, Sartre failed, in Being and Nothingness, to give sufficient theoretical attention to the concept of an object of consciousness. Both have important implications for feminist thought, and both were included in the ethical notebooks written soon after that work.

1. One basic sense in which one might speak of objectifying something or someone is to be *aware of* that thing or person. This might seem at first to be a wholly neutral experience: you see the stop sign, you hear the bird call. Strictly speaking, this type of awareness of something is all that is *immediately* implied in Husserl's formula "all consciousness is consciousness of an object." Is it as neutral as it appears to be? If one recalls the many accounts by and about girls and women who say, for instance, that they are ignored by male teachers in the classroom or by colleagues or supervisors who do not hear what they have to say, then at least part of what feminists might be considered to hope for is *more*, not less, objectification. That is, women want to have the kind of careful and respectful attention given to their ideas that is normally accorded to the utterances of their male counterparts. We surely *want* to be objects of that kind of attention. As we will see, in his early notes on ethics Sartre implicitly suggests the possibility of this form of object-directedness in his more complex account of mutual recognition.

An objection to my point that has been made by Sally Haslanger is that simple awareness of objects is not what feminists *mean* by "objectification." A brief reply is that feminists have generally discussed only negative forms of objectification, and I hope to show that some positive and potentially positive forms also exist. Another reply is that given the hundreds of pages that Sartre wrote in detailing the various structures of ordinary consciousness, it may be misleading to speak of "simple" awareness of anything in Sartre's account. All attentive awareness involves the person's attitudes, values, memories, future goals, and so on. So attention or *lack* of attention to any particular item is itself complex and value laden. Women and girls who object to being ignored by male teachers and colleagues seem to understand that this is the case.

2. An even richer, positive form of objectification is described in a rarely cited section of Hegel's *Phenomenology of Spirit*, a work that Sartre both criticized and borrowed from.[83] Immediately preceding his famous discussion of the life-and-death struggle leading to unequal power relations between lord and bondsman, which inspired many of Sartre's descriptions in *Being and Nothingness*, Hegel tells another, more hopeful story about human relationships.[84] While it is possible for other living beings to be conscious of things, and while this simple awareness of objects is a necessary condition of the distinctively human capacity for *self-consciousness*, the latter type of consciousness emerges, according to Hegel, through social relationships of mutual recognition. There is a fluid dialectical relationship that develops as two people, desiring acknowl-

edgement, discover a "duplication of self-consciousness",[85] that is, some common bond or similarity. Hegel remarks that "a self-consciousness, in being an object, is just as much 'I' as 'object.'" The resulting "'I' that is 'We' and 'We' that is 'I'"[87] is the fundamental ground of social consciousness (or "Spirit") that enters into a genuine community. Hegel insists that the experience of recognition between subjects has to be *mutual* if fully developed self-consciousness is to emerge.[88] Each person discovers that she is both independent and yet mediated in her development to a higher level of self-consciousness by the other for whom she performs the same assistance. It is when mutuality breaks down that inequality develops and the relations of dominance and submission prevail. Sartre's early work borrowed from Hegel the view that self-knowledge develops through social interaction, but his neglect, in *Being and Nothingness*, of the possibility that people could be subject and object simultaneously, appears to have been offset by his later acknowledgement of the theoretical possibility of mutually fulfilling recognition. Sartre writes of a non-alienating form of recognition that does *not* "[constitute] the other as an object."[89] In this context Sartre seems to speak of the other as an object of attention, but not as an object to be controlled. This can occur when I recognize the other's freedom and freely posit his end as worth pursuing because the other's human freedom is valuable and prolongs my own freedom "in the dimension of otherness."[90] Such free mutual recognition is expressed in the generosity of my aid.

In any case, Hegel's marvelous little fable contains multiple resonances, not only for Sartre's early work, but for feminist theory as well. To suggest a few, Hegel provides another alternative to the still-powerful Cartesian model of a self-contained, autonomous consciousness possessed of immediate, privileged knowledge of itself. Hegel's developmental account of self-consciousness shows the centrality of the social context within which we become subjects for ourselves more fully in recognizing others who simultaneously recognize us as subjects and as objects of their own desire for recognition. One might guess that feminist consciousness-raising has embodied such a pattern.

Conclusions

My main purpose in this essay has been to explore the concept of objectification as it was developed by Sartre, with a view toward its theoretical

and practical implications for feminism. I did this by comparing and contrasting several recent feminist versions of the notion of objectification
to Sartre's ideas.

First, I have argued that Sartre's subject-object analysis was developed
in part as an alternative to traditional philosophical theories of the
human person, including Cartesian dualism. Feminists sometimes describe objectification as if it were a terrible practice that should be abandoned. If the present analysis is on target, however, there is a conceptual
link between some forms of objectification and a nondualistic account of
what a person is. For example, the bodily subject is necessarily a possible
object of others' experience. Unless feminists are willing to abandon a
naturalistic account of persons, objectification seems to be here to stay.
Again, feminists have claimed that selves are, at least in part, social constructs. Sartre makes it clear that in defending a version of that view,
human beings are in the midst of sometimes clashing assessments of what
they do, which is a form of objectification.

Second, in discussing some dominance-oriented forms of objectification, I claimed that women have objectified men as well as having been
objectified by them. There is more than a suggestion of passivity in feminist accounts of being objectified. By concentrating on the ways in which
women have been objectified by men, feminists have contributed to a
tendency for women to think of themselves as mere victims of male dominance. We need to see that we have the same objectifying weapons available to us as men do, if battle is our goal. It has been valuable to find
recent feminist work on women's subjectivity and women's agency sharing the spotlight with objectification.[91]

Third, insofar as feminists have agreed that human beings are social
beings, rather than autonomous, self-contained, isolated entities, there
is value in the ways in which objectifying judgments—in other words,
categorizations of our actions—help to increase our self-knowledge even
when that is uncomfortable and even when we discover that we must
then deal with multiple truths about ourselves. There is positive value in
the forms of objectification inherent in attending to what women say and
do. There is value in entering relationships of mutual recognition and
increasing self-awareness through the complex forms of objectification
involved in interpersonal acknowledgement.

Finally, I would like to express some doubts about the wisdom of feminist preoccupation with objectification. I have suggested here that objectification takes positive as well as negative forms, and that there are many

examples of each. Objectification has become such a broad concept that it may have ceased to be useful.[92] In this essay, I have identified several versions of feminist concern for objectification: (1) objectivity of thought; (2) treating women as parts of bodies to be used (3) treating women as mere bodies lacking consciousness; and (4) treating women as dangerous, conscious objects. One might compare the use of the term *objectification* to the following piece of obfuscating military bureaucratese: "Five thousand of the enemy were 'neutralized.' " Here, the term "neutralized" may refer only to the fact that the enemy's weapons have been taken, or something equally innocuous, but it is also a common euphemism for a massacre. Is it not perhaps uninformative or even misleading to place so much weight on this antiseptic-sounding piece of jargon? To return to the main point, is hard-core pornography *really* to be condemned because it "objectifies" women? Is it not rather that that kind of pornography is wrong because it is produced under conditions often violent, painful, coercive, and humiliating, and because it leaves an indelible mark on pervasive social ideas about women's lack of personhood?

The use of the same term, objectification, to refer both to the hardcore pornographer's activities, as MacKinnon and Dworkin have done, and to advertiser's use of deodorant ads,[93] may overinflate the importance of the latter and lull us into believing that the pornography purveyor is socially acceptable. Feminists have presented us with vast amounts of evidence of damage to, and exploitation of, women throughout history—far more than is hinted at by the term objectification. Perhaps that term has become too broad to be useful any longer. *If* the notion of objectification is retained, it needs to be more clearly articulated in all of its complexity and ambiguity. The present essay has made a beginning in that direction.

Notes

1. Sandra Lee Bartky, "Women, Bodies, and Power: A Research agenda for Philosophy," *APA Newsletter on Philosophy and Feminism* 89, no. 1 (1989): 78–81; *Feminity and Domination: Studies in the Phenomenology of Oppression* (New York: Routledge, 1990).

2. Iris Marion Young, *Throwing Like a Girl and Other Essays in Feminist Philosophy and Social Theory* (Bloomington: Indiana University Press, 1990).

3. Catharine K. MacKinnon, *Feminism Unmodified: Discourses on Life and Law* (Cambridge: Harvard University Press, 1987); *Toward a Feminist Theory of the State* (Cambridge: Harvard University Press, 1989).

4. In developing some of the implications of that phenomenological account, I refer primarily to the writings of Jean-Paul Sartre. Although Beauvoir was a constant collaborator with Sartre in the development of existential phenomenology, and was considered by some who knew them both to be the better philosopher, Beauvoir herself usually deferred to Sartre and allowed herself to occupy the public, self-effacing role of "favored critic" of Sartre's ideas. She came to express most of her philosophical ideas in literary form. Deirdre Bair describes in wrenching detail some of Beauvoir's overly modest claims; Beauvoir says of Sartre: "I accepted his formulations as soon as I heard them. . . . It was only natural that I sought to express these ideas within literature. . . . In philosophical terms, he was creative and I am not (Deirdre Bair, *Simone de Beauvoir: A Biography* [New York: Summit Books, 1990], 269; see also 639 n. 26, for a brief description of Sonia Kruks's challenge to the belief that Beauvoir merely parroted Sartre's ideas).

The issue of intellectual influence between Sartre and Beauvoir is a matter of controversy and puzzlement among feminists, Beauvoir scholars, and Sartre scholars. Sartre acknowledges that he found himself, for the first time in his life, "humble and disarmed" by someone and wanted to learn from Beauvoir (*The War Diaries of Jean-Paul Sartre*, trans. Quintin Hoare [New York: Pantheon Books, 1984 (1983)], 78). He credits her with "forcing" him to renounce his early theory that salvation might come through art (Sartre, *War Diaries*, 88). In any case, I do not support those scholars who have unquestioningly assumed that Beauvoir was a mere mouthpiece for Sartre's ideas.

5. See, e.g., Susan R. Bordo, *The Flight to Objectivity: Essays on Cartesianism and Culture* (Albany: State University of New York Press, 1987).

6. E.g., Marjorie Grene, *Sartre* (New York: New Viewpoints, 1973), 104, 161; Judith Butler, *Gender Trouble: Feminism and the Subversion of Identity* (New York: Routledge, 1990), 129; Rosemarie Tong, *Feminist Thought: A Comprehensive Introduction* (Boulder: Westview Press, 1989), 214.

7. The mainstream view of Descartes holds that he claimed that bodies lack sentience. For a recent, careful challenge to this and other key elements of the standard interpretation of Descartes, see Gordon Baker and Katherine J. Morris, *Descartes' Dualism* (New York: Routledge, 1996).

8. Sartre says: it is "not that the psyche is *united* to a body but that . . . the body is its substance and its perpetual condition of possibility" (Jean-Paul Sartre, *Being and Nothingness: An Essay on Phenomenological Ontology*, trans. Hazel E. Barnes (New York: Philosophical Library, 1956 [1943], 338); the body is the "center of action" (320); the body is "that in relation to which the perceived object indicates its distance" (326); the body is the unutilizable instrument referred to by all other instruments (320–25). Sartre says, "We do not use this instrument, for we *are* it" (324). "The body is *lived* and not *known*" (324). I have written elsewhere on Sartre's account of the body (Phyllis Sutton Morris, *Sartre's Concept of a Person: An Analytic Approach* [Amherst: University of Massachusetts Press, 1976], chap. 2; "Sartre on the Transcendence of the Ego," in *Philosophy and Phenomenological Research*, no. 2 [1985]: 179–98," "Sartre on the Self-Deceiver's Translucent Consciousness," *Journal of the British Society for Phenomenology* 23, no. 2 [1992]: 103–19. See also Hazel E. Barnes, "Sartre's Concept of the Self," *Review of Existential Psychology and Psychiatry*, 17, no. 1 (1980–81): 41–65, especially 49–50; Monika Langer, "Sartre and Merleau-Ponty: A Reappraisal," in *The Philosophy of Jean-Paul Sartre*, ed. Paul Arthur Schilpp (La Salle, Ill.: Open Court, 1981). Sartre's account of the body is complex and puzzling; a much fuller account of his views on this is projected.

Iris Young says that Merleau-Ponty attributes to the body the characteristics given by Kant to transcendental subjectivity (*Throwing Like a Girl*, 149). I have argued elsewhere that Sartre does this also ("Sartre on the Transcendence of the Ego").

In spite of their crucial theoretical differences from traditional philosophical dualism, Sartre and Beauvoir often found it difficult to jettison the traditional negative evaluation of, and feeling for, the body. Sartre sometimes described bodily awareness as nausea. Beauvoir's biographer, Deirdre Bair, gives considerable emphasis to Beauvoir's neglect of appearance and of ordinary hygiene (*Simone de Beauvoir*, 43, 181 and passim). Perhaps there is a hint of this negative evaluation in Bartky's reference to "mere bodily beings" (Sandra Lee Bartky, *Femininity and Domination: Studies in the Phenomenology of Oppression* [New York: Routledge, 1990], 42).

9. Jean-Paul Sartre, "Intentionality: A Fundamental Idea of Husserl's Phenomenology," trans. Joseph P. Fell, *Journal of the British Society for Phenomenology* 1, no. 2 (1970 [1947]): 4–5.

10. Sartre, *Being and Nothingness*, 216, 306.

11. See Morris, *Sartre's Concept of a Person*, 18–20 and passim.

12. Sartre, *Being and Nothingness*, li.

13. Michèle Le Doeuff, mistakenly I believe, interprets Sartre as a solipsist (*Hipparchia's choice: An Essay Concerning Women, Philosophy, etc.*, trans. Trista Selous [Oxford: Blackwell, 1991], 62, 100). See Phyllis Sutton Morris, "Sartre on the Existence of Other Minds," *Journal of the British Society for Phenomenology* 1, no. 2 (1970): 17–21.

14. Sartre is best known for the conflictual relations described in *Being and Nothingness*. That work has been described by him as an "ontology before conversion" (*Notebooks for an Ethics*, trans. David Pellauer [Chicago: University of Chicago Press, 1992 (1983)], 6)—that is, conscious relations in bad faith. In this recently translated work, written several years after *Being and Nothingness*, Sartre had a great deal to say about the supportive relations involved in authentic love and in reciprocity (6, 285, 501, 507, 508, 330, and passim).

15. Jean-Paul Sartre, *The Transcendence of the Ego: An Existentialist Theory of Consciousness*, trans. Forrest Williams and Robert Kirkpatrick (New York: Noonday Press, 1957 [1936–37]), 104.

16. Sartre, *Transcendence of the Ego*, 97. For fuller discussion of this and other key senses of "self" for Sartre, see Phyllis Sutton Morris, "Self-Creating Selves: Sartre and Foucault," in the special Sartre issue of the *American Catholic Philosophical Quarterly* 70 (Autumn 1996).

17. Sartre, *Being and Nothingness*, 274.

18. Simone de Beauvoir, *The Second Sex*, ed. and trans. H. M. Parshley (New York: Bantam Books, 1961 [1949]).

19. See Bordo, *The Flight to Objectivity*, for a fine cultural history of the ideal of objectivity, beginning with Descartes.

20. MacKinnon, *Feminism Unmodified*, 50; cf. her *Toward a Feminist Theory of the State*, 124.

21. MacKinnon, *Feminism Unmodified*, 50.

22. Sally Haslanger, "On Being Objective and Being Objectified," in *A Mind of One's Own: Feminist Essays on Reason and Objectivity*, ed. Louise M. Antony and Charlotte Witt (Boulder: Westview Press, 1993), 104.

23. Haslanger, "On Being Objective," 110.

24. Sartre, *Notebooks for an Ethics*, 8–9.

25. Haslanger, "On Being Objective," 114.

26. Haslanger, "On Being Objective," 90.

27. Lewis Gordon has suggested to me some of these complexities in connection with black male–white female relations. Much of the feminist literature on objectification treats objectifiers as those in power within a patriarchal setting—thus, probably, white Protestant males in Western culture. Other males often escape the usual analysis: not only Afro-Americans, but also Hispanics, poor males, and gay males lack power, at least in relation to the reigning patriarchy. Recent analyses, however, of differences between the situations of women of different races, classes, sexual orientation, and cultures show that exploitive objectifiers of women can be other women, nondominant males, or both, as well as powerful males. These important complications lie beyond the scope of the present essay.

28. Linda A. Bell, *Rethinking Ethics in the Midst of Violence: A Feminist Approach to Freedom* (Lanham, Md.: Rowman and Littlefield, 1993), 56–63.

29. Young, *Throwing Like a Girl*, 191.

30. See, e.g., Bartky, *Femininity and Domination*, 28 and passim; however, see Kathy Davis, *Reshaping the Female Body: The Dilemma of Cosmetic Surgery* (New York: Routledge, 1995), chap. 4, for discussion of interviews with women whose decisions to have cosmetic surgery exhibited a strong sense of agency.

31. See, e.g., Margery L. Collins and Christine Pierce, "Holes and Slime: Sexism in Sartre's Psychoanalysis," in *Women and Philosophy: Toward a Theory of Liberation*, ed. Carol C. Gould and Marx W. Wartofsky (New York: G. P. Putnam's Sons, 1976).

32. Sartre, *Being and Nothingness*, 609.

33. Sartre, *Being and Nothingness*, 613.

34. See Hazel E. Barnes, "Sartre and Sexism," *Philosophy and Literature* 14, no. 2 (1990): 340–47; and Bonnie Burstow, "How Sexist is Sartre?" *Philosophy and Literature* 16, no. 1 (1992): 32–48, for thoughtful discussions of Sartre's alleged sexism.

35. Sartre, *Being and Nothingness*, 609.

36. Sartre, *Being and Nothingness*, 613.

37. Sartre, *Being and Nothingness*, 613.

38. It is worth adding that when Sartre spoke directly of his personal convictions, he unreservedly favored equal rights for women, and expressed his warm admiration for their way "of saying or seeing things . . . their way of thinking" (*The War Diaries*, 281).

39. Sartre, *Notebooks for an Ethics*, 181.

40. Informal talk on pornography, Oberlin College, April 1991.

41. Barbara Herman, "Could It Be Worth Thinking About Kant on Sex and Marriage?" in *A Mind of One's Own: Feminist Essays on Reason and Objectivity*, ed. Louise M. Antony and Charlotte Witt (Boulder: Westview Press, 1993), 55.

42. Sartre, *Being and Nothingness*, 384.

43. Sartre, *Being and Nothingness*, 386.

44. Sartre, *Being and Nothingness*, 391.

45. Sartre, *Being and Nothingness*, 390.

46. Andrea Dworkin, *Pornography: Men Possessing Women* (New York: G. P. Putnam's Sons, 1981), 108.

47. Jessica Benjamin, *The Bonds of Love: Psychoanalysis, Feminism, and the Problem of Domination* (New York: Pantheon Books, 1988), 190.

48. Julien S. Murphy, "The Look in Sartre and Rich," in *The Thinking Muse: Feminism and Modern French Philosophy*, ed., Jeffner Allen and Iris Marion Young (Bloomington: Indiana University Press, 1989), 103.

49. Sartre, *Being and Nothingness*, 305, 347.

50. Murphy, "The Look in Sartre and Rich," 103.

51. Sartre, *Being and Nothingness*, 255.

52. See, for instance, Mary Daly, *Gyn/Ecology: The Metaethics of Radical Feminism* (Boston: Beacon Press, 1978), on the Hindu practice of *suttee* and the African practice of clitoridectomy (116, 153–177); Susan R. Bordo, "The Body and the Reproduction of Femininity: A Feminist Appropriation of Foucault," in *Gender/Body/Knowledge: Feminist Reconstructions of Being and Knowing*, ed. Alison M. Jaggar and Susan R. Bordo, New Brunswick: Rugers University Press, 1989), 13–33; Bartky, *Feminity and Domination*, 22 and passim.

53. Dworkin, *Pornography*, 109.

54. Sartre, *Being and Nothingness*, 361–412; cf. Murphy, "The Look in Sartre and Rich," 103.

55. Bartky, *Femininity and Domination*, 75.

56. Bartky, *Femininity and Domination*, 115–16.

57. Young, *Throwing Like a Girl*, 190.

58. Young does comment that the threat of being seen is not merely the threat of objectification for women, but also a lived threat of bodily invasion in the form of rape or unacceptable touching (*Throwing Like a Girl*, 155). This is surely the case in some, if not all, situations for women.

The type of power I have been discussing here is based on what Audre Lorde has called a "male [model] of power" ("Uses of the Erotic: The Erotic as Power," in *Sister Outsider: Essays and Speeches* [Freedom, Calif.: Crossing Press, 1984], 53); that is, power over someone else. Lorde has developed an alternative assessment of women's eroticism as the source of all their creative power—for instance, in work as well as love (55).

59. Martha Nussbaum has pointed out, however, that feminists often think of culture as being much more monolithic than it really is ("Objectification," *Philosophy and Public Affairs* 24, no. 4 [1995]: 249–91 [278]). In a period of rapid change, such as our own, I think we need to recognize more heterogeneity in male-female relationships.

60. Friedrich Nietzsche is sometimes considered to be a quintessential male chauvinist. There is much in his work to support that assessment; however, his position is more complicated. There is not only arrogance, but also fear and resentment against being used as an instrument by women in the following: "Everything about woman is a riddle, and everything about woman has one solution: that is pregnancy. Man is for woman a means: the end is always the child. But what is woman for man? 'A real man wants two things: danger and play. Therefore he wants woman as the most danger-ous plaything' " (Friedrich Nietzsche, *Thus Spoke Zarathustra*, trans. Walter Kaufmann, New York: Viking Press, 1966 [1883], 66). Often overlooked is Nietzsche's description of an ideal marriage based on mutual compassion and inspiration: "Marriage: thus I name the will of two to create the one that is more than those who created it. Reverence for each other . . . is what I name marriage" (70).

61. For an extended treatment of some of these ideas from psychoanalytic and Hegelian perspec-tives, see Jessica Benjamin's *The Bonds of Love*.

62. Sartre, *Being and Nothingness*, 274.

63. Sartre, *Being and Nothingness*, 259–61.

64. See Daly, *Gyn/ecology*, 14.

65. Sartre, *Being and Nothingness*, 324.

66. Sartre, *Being and Nothingness*, 528.

67. This objection was offered by Constantine Boundas.

68. Sartre, *Being and Nothingness*, 274; cf. Jean-Paul Sartre, *The Writings of Jean-Paul Sartre: A Bibliographical Life*, vol. 1, compiled Michel Contat and Michel Rybalka, trans. Richard C. McCleary (Evanston: Northwestern University Press, 1974 [1970]), 99.

69. Jean-Paul Sartre, *No Exit*, in *No Exit and Three Other Plays*, trans. Stuart Gilbert (New York: Vintage, 1948 [1945]), 44. See Linda A. Bell, *Sartre's Ethics of Authenticity* (Tuscaloosa: University of Alabama Press, 1989), 83–84, for further discussion of Sartre's "hell" claim.

70. Sartre, *Notebooks for an Ethics*, 176.

71. Jean-Paul Sartre, *Saint Genet: Actor and Martyr*, trans. Bernard Frechtman (New York: New American Library, 1963 [1952]), 12–13, 641–44.

72. Phyllis Sutton Morris, "Self-deception: Sartre's Resolution of the Paradox," in *Jean-Paul Sartre: Contemporary Approaches to His Philosophy*, ed. H. J. Silverman and F. Elliston (Pittsburgh: Duquesne University Press, 1980); and Morris, "Sartre on the Self-Deceiver's Translucent Con-sciousness."

73. This criticism was offered by Linda Bell.

74. See, e.g., Murphy, "The Look in Sartre and Rich," Bell, *Sartre's Ethics of Authenticity*, 85, 100, 135.

75. E.g., Bell, *Sartre's Ethics of Authenticity*, 41; Murphy, The Look in Sartre and Rich," 111; Morris, "Sartre on the Self-Deceiver's Translucent Consciousness"; Sartre, *The Writings of Jean-Paul Sartre*, 145.

76. I am indebted to Lorraine Code for raising this issue in a private conversation.

77. Haslanger, "On Being Objective," 115.

78. Jean-Paul Sartre, *Anti-Semite and Jew*, trans. George J. Becker (New York: Schocken Books, 1948 [1946]), 149.

79. See Nussbaum, "Objectification," for a different, interesting account of some positive as well as negative forms of objectification. I agree with her remark that "objectification" is a "relatively loose cluster-term" (258).

80. Some Sartre scholars have argued otherwise recently. For instance, Adrian Mirvish has claimed that Sartre's account of the caress in *Being and Nothingness* is based on reciprocal recognition of subjectivity (paper presented to the Sartre Society of North America, Peterborough, Ontario, May 1993). Sartre's talk of reciprocity does not entirely override his other ontological descriptions that show I am either subject in relation to an object, or object for the other's subjective consciousness, at any given time. For instance, in the recently translated *Notebooks for an Ethics*, Sartre speaks at one point of a reciprocity in rights and says, "These moments are distinct. Each one *in turn* [emphasis added] is the subject of rights; that is, there are two distinct movements" (139). What *is* different is that when Sartre occasionally writes about reciprocity in his early works, he emphasizes cooperation rather than the usual conflict. As I will show, at *some* points in his ethical writings, he *also* acknowledges the possibility of direct, as well as indirect, awareness of the other as subject.

81. Beauvoir, *The Second Sex*, xvii, 391.

82. Sartre, *Notebooks for an Ethics*, 6.

83. Georg Wilhelm Friedrich Hegel, *Phenomenology of Spirit*, trans. A. V. Miller (New York: Oxford University Press, 1977 [1807, 1952]). See Robert R. Williams, *Recognition: Fichte and Hegel on the Other* (Albany: State University of New York Press, 1992) for a recent discussion of the section on recognition in Hegel's *Phenomenology*. Jessica Benjamin offers a feminist, psychoanalytic interpretation of Hegel's lord/bondsman (master/slave) fable as a way of accounting for male domination of women. She also explores some interesting possibilities for fulfilling mutual recognition between men and women (*The Bonds of Love*, 219–24) based on Hegel's account. Here, each party is both subject and object, both independent and interdependent in a mutually rewarding relationship.

84. Eléanor Kuykendall called my attention to passages on rape and seduction in Sartre (*Notebooks for an Ethics*, 179–83, 230ff, 427) which have been interpreted by some Sartre scholars as sexist and by other Sartre scholars as nonsexist. My own reading of these passages is that Sartre uses the sections from Hegel on recognition and its failure, leading to a struggle for dominance, as theoretical underpinning for phenomenological descriptions of bad-faith relations, *rather* than as *advocacy* for the rapist's failed desire for recognition or consent, or for the seducer's rotating struggle between slavery and dominance. My reading is based in part on Sartre's claim that *Being and Nothingness* was an "ontology before conversion" to authenticity (*Notebooks for an Ethics*, 6), a point already hinted at in the earlier work at 534 n. 13. More ambiguous are his lengthy discussions of seduction (*The War Diaries*) when he says, for example, "nothing is dearer to me than the freedom of those I love. . . . but the fact is, this freedom is dear to me provided I don't respect it at all. It's a question not of suppressing it, but of actually violating it" (256). A few pages later he adds: "The love that wants freedom in others only so that it can violate it—that form of love is utterly inauthentic. There are other ways of loving" (258).

85. Hegel, *Phenomenology of Spirit*, 110.

86. Hegel, *Phenomenology of Spirit*, 110.

87. Hegel, *Phenomenology of Spirit*, 110. In 1939, in a letter to Simone de Beauvoir describing their personal relationship, Sartre wrote: "You are truly me. My love, we are simply one." (Jean-Paul Sartre, *Witness to My Life: The Letters of Jean-Paul Sartre to Simone de Beauvoir, 1926–1939*, ed. Simone de Beauvoir, trans. Lee Fahnestock and Norman MacAfee [New York: Charles Scribner's Sons, 1992 (1983)], 233).

88. Hegel, *Phenomenology of Spirit*, 112.

89. Sartre, *Notebooks for an Ethics*, 280.

90. Sartre, *Notebooks for an Ethics*, 280.

91. See, e.g., Young, *Throwing Like a Girl*, 165–66, 182–83; Carol Bigwood, "Renaturalizing the Body (with the Help of Merleau-Ponty)," *Hypatia* 6, no. 3 (1991): 54–73; Lois McNay, "The Foucauldian Body and the Exclusion of Experience," *Hypatia* 6, no. 3 (1991): 125–39; Eileen O'Neill, "(Re)presentations of Eros: Exploring Female Sexual Agency," in *Gender/Body/Knowledge: Feminist Reconstructions of Being and Knowing*, ed. Alison M. Jaggar and Susan R. Bordo (New Brunswick:

Rutgers University Press, 1989); Kathy Davis, *Reshaping the Female Body: The Dilemma of Cosmetic Surgery* (New York: Routledge, 1995).

92. Helen Heise has suggested that the notion of objectification may have been important to earlier feminists as intimating a unifying element in women's experiences. This seems right to me. There is a need now, however, to move on to the task of showing how differences in our situations are equally important.

93. Bartky, *Femininity and Domination*, 40.

4

Sartre, Sadism, and Female Beauty Ideals

Thomas Martin

In *Being and Nothingness*,[1] Jean-Paul Sartre gives an analysis of sadism in which he pays particular attention to the relationships between the participants and their bodies. It is my argument in this article that several aspects of this account can be usefully applied to considerations on the effects and functioning of female beauty ideals in Western society. As Sartre's treatment of sadism falls within his wider account of the nature of human existence and intersubjectivity, I shall introduce briefly Sartre's ontology as expounded in *Being and Nothingness* before going on to discuss his treatment of sadism. Following this I shall suggest, firstly, that several parallels can be drawn between aspects of Sartre's account of sadism and the effects and functioning of female beauty ideals and, secondly, that such an exercise is useful because it can reveal at least one of the adverse effects that such ideals can have on women.

Sartre's Ontology

Sartre holds that there are "two radically separated regions of being" (BN xliii); being-in-itself and being-for-itself. Being-in-itself is the mode of being of objects, which are governed by what Sartre calls "the principle of identity" (BN 58). Being-in-itself is self-identical, self-contained, "it does not enter into any connection with what is not itself" (BN xlii). Being-in-itself simply "is what it is" and "is never anything but what it is" (BN xlii). Being-for-itself, on the other hand, is the being of conscious entities, which are, by Sartre's reckoning, humans.[2] Beings-for-themselves have, as the name suggests, being *for* themselves. They are aware of themselves as being, and being is an issue for them.

Beings-for-themselves are not only conscious, but they are also free, and this freedom and consciousness are closely related. Consciousness of an object implies self-consciousness in that one is conscious of oneself as *not* being the object. Therefore consciousness is not based on any positive essence, but on negation, that is, nothing. This zone of nothingness with which consciousness encases its objects, thereby separating being-for-itself from being-in-itself, also acts to separate being-for-itself from the world of cause and effect. Thus being-for-itself is not determined, but free. These three notions, consciousness, nothingness and freedom, are so closely related, and so fundamental, that Sartre can use any of them to define being-for-itself, and in fact he often interchanges them.

Whatever a for-itself is at any particular time is a manifestation of its free spontaneity. A for-itself is continually creating itself, continually moving toward endless possibilities, and being-for-itself is this movement. Although being-for-itself chooses itself, it never actually is what it chooses, but just is the act of choosing. It is with this point in mind that Sartre writes that the for-itself "is a being which is not what it is and which is what it is not" (BN 79). Therefore a for-itself defies the sort of definitions that it is possible to apply to an in-itself. "Anguish" is the result of a for-itself becoming reflectively aware of the fact that it is this constant movement toward the future, that it is responsible for everything that it chooses although it can never be what it chooses, and that it has no choice but to choose. Being-for-itself "is condemned to be free" (BN 439).

Humans have being-for-itself. However, they also partake of an object-like being which can be interpreted as a variety of being-in-itself. Sartre refers to this aspect of human being as being-for-others. Being-for-others is a mode of being in which the self exists outside as an object for others. As such, it cannot be seen as a mode of being in which simple objects such as tables and chairs can partake. Only conscious beings can have being-for-others. However, having said that, being-for-others does share with other examples of being-in-itself the characteristic of being ruled by the principle of identity. Sartre provides the following example to illustrate being-for-others. There is a man who, through jealousy or curiosity, is looking through a keyhole. He is "on a level of non-thetic self-consciousness" (BN 259), which is to say that he does not inhabit his consciousness as a self that is acting in a certain way. He is completely tied up with the panorama that lies on the other side of the door. All that he is aware of is the keyhole and the scene that he sees through it. Suddenly he hears footsteps behind him in the hallway. Immediately he becomes conscious of himself as he may appear to others—a man, on his knees, spying on someone or something through the keyhole of a door; a jealous man or a perhaps a vicious man. He is aware of the presence of a voyeur. He is aware of himself. Just as the people on the other side of the door were objects in his world, he is now an object in the world of an other (BN 259, 260). Sartre writes that "I grasp the Other's look at the very center of my act as the solidification and alienation of my own possibilities" (BN 263).

Although Sartre tends to cast being-for-others in a negative light,[3] it need not always be seen in this way. If the person-object is interpreted positively by the other, the self may experience pride, rather than shame, upon the realisation of its being-for-others.[4] Examples of this might include an actor who receives a standing ovation for her performance, or a man who realises that someone has witnessed him behaving admirably. Apart from this, being-for-others does grant the self some substance. Part of the for-itself's anguish was caused by its unfoundedness, its floating, indeterminate nature. With being-for-others, the self can see itself, through the eyes of others, as really being there and really being something. Being-for-others can have its positive aspects, but it does have negative ones as well. As being-for-others results from the other's free interpretation of the self, the self has little control over this aspect of its being. Certainly, it can attempt to project a certain image in the hope that its being-for-others will turn out the way that it would like, but it can never really be sure of achieving this. The other's status as a freely interpreting being, which is the basis of being-for-others, makes being-for-others a risky and uncertain state.

Whilst a person has both being-for-itself and being-for-others, these two modes of being are not merged into one. As Bell writes, "One simply is the ambiguous being that is being-for-others and being-for-itself."[5] Being-for-others and being-for-itself are two poles of being between which the self oscillates. This ambiguous mode of existence in which one is neither being-for-itself nor being-for-others but both, despite the fact that they are opposed, this tension in being, is what we might term the human condition.

This ambiguity of being is something that the self may try to escape from or resolve. Sartre describes a number of strategies that seek to escape this ambiguity, though I shall consider only one of these here: sadism. The aim of sadism is to secure the freedom of the sadist at the expense of the freedom of the victim. By doing so, the sadist might escape from having a being-for-others which is uncertain and beyond their control. As such, the being of the sadist would not suffer from the ambiguity which characterises the human condition. Thus sadism stands as a strategy aimed at escaping the ambiguity of being.[6]

Sadism, Grace, and Obscenity

Of sadism, Sartre writes that:

> the sadist's effort is to ensnare the Other in his flesh by means of violence and pain, by appropriating the Other's body in such a way that he treats it as flesh so as to cause flesh to be born. But this appropriation surpasses the body which it appropriates, for its purpose is to possess the body only in so far as the Other's freedom has been ensnared within it. (BN 403)

The sadist attempts to appropriate the other's freedom, in order that the sadist may exist as pure freedom, thereby escaping the human condition—"sadism is a refusal to be incarnated and a flight from all facticity" (BN 399). The sadist attempts this by "incarnating" the other's freedom. This entails causing the other's consciousness to become fascinated by their body or, in other words, to have their body act as the pre-eminent object of their consciousness. This is brought about by the infliction of pain upon the body—"In pain facticity invades the consciousness" (BN 399).[7] The sadist inflicts pain through the use of instruments—sadists want to appear as pure freedom, in no way as objects, and use instruments rather than their own bodies toward that end. Sartre writes that:

> the sadist refuses his own flesh at the same time that he uses instruments to reveal by force the Other's flesh to him. . . . [Sadism] enjoys being a free appropriating power confronting a freedom captured by the flesh. (BN 399)

One question that comes to mind at this point is whether or not this scheme flies somewhat in the face of the existentialist concept of embodiment. Sartre certainly holds the view, shared by many, most notably Merleau-Ponty,[8] that the subject is bodily. For example, Sartre writes that "Being-for-itself must be wholly body and it must be wholly consciousness; it cannot be *united* with a body" (BN 305). They cannot be united because unification implies initial separation. Such ideas of embodiment hold that consciousness and body are intimately connected. Now, if this is the case, surely the possession of another's body necessarily entails the possession of their consciousness. So why, then, must the sadist incarnate the victim's consciousness? Surely their consciousness is already incarnate. This is in one sense true, in another false. In order to understand this we must refer to Sartre's concepts of "grace" and "obscenity."

"In grace," Sartre says, "the body appears as a psychic being in situation" (BN 400). In a graceful act the body disappears behind the activity. Sartre gives a prime example of this by describing the grace of a naked dancer. He writes that:

> the supreme coquetry and the supreme challenge of grace is to exhibit the body unveiled with no clothing, with no veil except grace itself. The most graceful body is the naked body whose acts enclose it with an invisible garment while entirely disrobing its flesh, while the flesh is totally present to the eyes of the spectator. (BN 400, 401)

The dancer's body is in our field of vision and her nakedness is there to be seen. But we do not see it because although we are, in a sense, looking at her body, it is her movements that are the object of our gaze. It is the body as action, as story, as emotion that we see, not the body as naked flesh. The graceful body is for-itself; it is flesh as freedom. So, in the case of the graceful body, it could be said that consciousness is incarnate. But this is not the sort of incarnate consciousness that the sadist is after. His interests lie in the obscene body.

Obscenity is the opposite to grace: "The obscene appears when the body adopts postures which entirely strip it of its acts and which reveal the inertia of its flesh" (BN 401). The obscene body is an object in the world, it is in-itself; it is flesh as flesh. The movements of the obscene body are the result of outside forces such as gravity and simple mechanical interactions. Sartre illustrates this point as follows:

> The sight of a naked body from behind is not obscene. But certain involuntary waddlings of the rump are obscene. This is because then it is only the legs which are acting for the walker, and the rump is like an isolated cushion which is carried by the legs and the balancing of which is a pure obedience to the laws of weight . . . it has the passivity of a thing and . . . is made to rest like a thing upon the legs. (BN 401)

Through the use of instruments, particularly the ropes that bind the victim, the sadist forces the victim's body to exist in the obscene mode. It is in this obscene body that the sadist wants the victim's consciousness to be invested. Sadists experience themselves as pure transcendence in opposition to the other who is obscene, inert flesh.

Why is it that it is so crucial to the sadist to force the other to adopt the obscene mode of bodily being? Whilst Sartre does not actually write this, it is possible to construct an answer to this question by reference to the doctrine of the intentionality of consciousness. An important aspect of consciousness is, according to Sartre, that it is intentional. Consciousness itself is inherently empty, existing only as a relation to something else; its object. Consciousness is always consciousness of something. It seems reasonable to assume that this is why the simple capture of a body is not enough to capture a consciousness, even though consciousness may be embodied. To capture a consciousness, one must also have the object of that consciousness. Thus in order to capture a consciousness by way of taking the body, one must ensure that the body is the object of that consciousness.

In the case of the graceful body, the body in the mode of being-for-itself, one certainly finds consciousness and body, but the body is in no way the object for that consciousness. On the contrary, the graceful body is consciousness in the world and is itself intentional, requiring some object in the world in order to exist as such. The obscene body, however, can act as an object of consciousness (both for the sadist and the victim) and this is why it is crucial for the sadist that the victim's body exist in that mode.

Evidence in support of this interpretation comes from Sartre's statement that the sadist makes the other's body "present in pain. In pain facticity invades consciousness, and ultimately the reflective consciousness is fascinated by the facticity of the unreflective consciousness" (BN 399). Earlier in *Being and Nothingness* Sartre had claimed that the body is the facticity of the unreflective consciousness (BN 330), and so it is reasonable to interpret this passage as saying that the sadist causes the other to become reflectively conscious of their body. The other experiences their body as an object that is being acted upon by the sadist.[9]

The passage quoted above is an interesting one because it indicates another element of sadism. Whilst the reflective consciousness is positional and so always posits an object which it itself is not, the object posited is the self in the mode of not being itself. Another way of putting this is to say that the object of reflective consciousness is the self in the mode of being *me* as opposed to being *I*. Sartre writes that the sadist forces the other's "freedom freely to identify itself with the tortured flesh" (BN 403). On this level, the other exists as being-object-for-others. Their presence in the world is as a body-object. In this sense they are their body, but they are so in the mode of not being it. This is just a version of what was earlier referred to as the human condition; that ambiguous relation between being, on the one hand, what one is and, on the other hand, being what one is not. In this case the ambiguity is manifested in the other, on the one hand, being that body upon which the sadist is acting, and on the other hand, not being that body which is an object for their consciousness. The important point here is that sadism presupposes that in neither of these modes of the other's being can the sadist be object for the other. To the extent that the other identifies themselves as being their body as object, they cannot transcend the transcendence of the sadist. To the extent that the other is subject, by virtue of having their body so forcefully present as object to their consciousness they are in no position to objectify the sadist.

The aim of sadism is to gain for the sadist the position of being pure freedom, avoiding any objectification by the other, and thereby escaping the human condition. But sadism is a failure. In so far as the sadist wishes to tie up and appropriate the transcendent freedom of the other, the sadist finds that it is on principle beyond their reach. Where the sadist was seemingly acting upon the other's transcendence, they were in fact dealing with a transcendence transcended. The sadist "can act upon the [Other's] freedom only by making it an objective property of the Other-as-object" (BN 405). As such, the sadist misses the mark, and "discovers his error when his victim *looks* at him; that is when the sadist experiences the absolute alienation of his being in the Other's freedom" (BN 405).

Sadism and the Female Beauty Ideal

So far we have seen what the sadistic strategy entails, the important role that the concepts of grace and obscenity play in that strategy, and that, although it is a failure, the strategy aims at maintaining the freedom of the sadist. What I would now like to do is demonstrate that a number of parallels can be drawn between Sartre's account of sadism and the way in which female beauty ideals operate and affect women in our society.

We are inundated daily by images, visual images in particular, from the mass media. These images carry with them social norms regarding the way in which people are supposed to be, and there is surely no stronger and no more defined a norm than that regarding the way in which women's bodies are supposed to look. The ideal female body is young and slender. Most women that are chosen to appear in the visual media as women that belong there,[10] have bodies that conform to this norm. Women that do not match up to this norm are often portrayed as being sad, farcical, evil, or even just downright offensive. As the media portrays itself as being a mirror to reality, the message to women is loud and clear—conform to these norms or suffer the consequences.[11]

Messages portraying the female body as an object that must be attended to proliferate in the media in advertisements, talk shows, lifestyle programs and even current affairs. There are a vast number of aspects of women's bodies that are indicated as requiring attention. These include lines and wrinkles, bulges and bumps, body hair and rough dry elbows. Messages concerning these aspects of women's bodies are usually in the form of directives; in order to increase one's value as a woman one must ensure that————. By doing so a woman is assured of coming closer to the ideal, of increasing her value.

It is not simply through explicit directives such as these that women are told to experience their bodies as conglomerations of potentially improvable problem areas. The ideal women of the media are seen to have overcome, or simply not have, these problems, and this is another way in which women are shown that they have work to do. Given the backdrop of strongly and widely held values concerning the judging of the worth of women's bodies as objects, we tend to view women's bodies as objects awaiting assessment. Thus, although the "ideal" women in the media may well be doing things, it is not as active bodies that we admire them. It is their bodies as gradable parts that we assess, and these bodies are used as the standards by which other women's bodies are assessed. It is ironic that the ideal body should be judged as an object isolable from action when we consider that the shape and texture of it may be similar to that of an athlete's body. In fact for all intents and purposes, a woman is required to be an athlete in order to achieve the correct body form. But it is not in the midst of such athletic activity that a woman's body is admired. It is after the fact of having achieved that shape that the female body is admired—as flesh.

This ideal form is difficult to achieve, and the requirement upon women to conform to it makes many women invest a great deal of their consciousness upon their bodies. Those that have achieved the required shape and texture have worked and concentrated hard on doing so, and must continue to work and concentrate hard on maintaining it. But it is not only those women with bodies corresponding to the ideal that have their consciousness invested in their bodies. To think so would be to underestimate the pervasiveness of the ideal. Women that are too fat or too thin, too short or too tall, too old or too young, are constantly reminded of their own bodies by their deviation from the ideal that is everywhere flaunted, valued and worshipped. They too have their consciousness invested in their bodies. Their bodies are always present as an object of their consciousness, even for the reason that they realise that their bodies do not conform to the ideal—and with the pervasiveness of the images carrying that message, this realisation is a difficult one to avoid.

A number of parallels can be drawn between Sartre's account of sadism and the operation of female beauty ideals. In sadism, the victim's body is made to exist in the obscene mode through the activities of the sadist which strip it of grace. Gila Hayim describes the obscene body in sadism as being the "body as constituted of isolated parts, and as a thing unrelated to the situation."[12] The female beauty ideal causes women's bodies to adopt the obscene mode of being by way of making their bodies, as objects, as "constituted of isolated parts," a cause for concern. The ideal body as an object for perusal and assessment has certain properties and, as an ideal which carries some weight by virtue of its being generally accepted, stands as a value demanding fulfilment. The message is clear and, due to its continual transmission, it cannot help but be received by the majority of women. Thus, female beauty ideals set women up to view their bodies as being objects for themselves and others. But recall that the sadist did not merely set the other up to experience the other's body as object. The sadist, through the infliction of pain made the other's body demand attention. In the issue of female beauty ideals it is the continual and pervasive nature of the ideal, or messages transmitting it, in conjunction with the persuasive nature of general attitudes toward it, that cause women to experience their bodies as objects, often even as the preeminent object of their consciousness. It is this that parallels the sadist's infliction of pain upon the other's body, as a way to make the body, as flesh, demand the attention of their consciousness. In short, female beauty ideals parallel the procedures of Sartre's sadist in that both result in women, on the one hand, and the sadist's victim, on the other, experiencing their bodies as objects of their consciousness.

Does all of this mean that in witnessing the operation of female beauty ideals we are in fact witnessing Sartrean sadism? The answer to this question is probably "no." Sartre's account of sadism is found in his chapter on concrete relations with others, and is intended as a description of one of the ways in which an individual might deal with the presence of an individual other. It is the description of a face to face encounter, not of a cultural pattern, and I am not sure that we are at liberty simply to transpose the categories and concepts emerging from his account of one-to-one intersubjectivity onto a consideration of a cultural pattern such as the issue of female beauty ideals. However, having said that, if we were to accept Sartre's human ontology, it would not be unreasonable to expect that aspects of that ontology, such as those concerning the crises connected with the human condition and intersubjectivity, will find some sort of expression in the social and cultural realm. As such, the demon-stration that certain parallels can be drawn between Sartre's account of sadism and the issue of female beauty would not allow us to claim that they are identical, but rather that they might serve to illuminate the problem and suggest further directions·of enquiry. One such further di-rection of enquiry that opens up in light of this is the connection be-tween beauty ideals and disability.

Female Beauty Ideals and Female Disability

There exist many examples of procedures, prescribed by female beauty ideals, that have been performed on women, which have resulted in some degree of physical disability. One example of such a procedure is foot-binding, which was practised in China for the thousand years or so prior to the passing of Mandarin society. Foot-binding, which was practised on women, usually when they were about seven years old, was performed as follows. A wide bandage was tightly wound around the foot in such a way that the big toe pointed upwards while the four smaller toes were pressed back, underneath the sole of the foot, while at the same time the heel and the front of the foot were being brought closer together. Apart from the bandages, they also wore tiny shoes which were replaced every few days with an even smaller pair. The young girls were forced to walk and place their weight upon these bound feet, causing the bones to break. Apart from breaking their bones, the foot-binding process led to their toenails falling out, their flesh petrifying, and the bone and muscle struc-tures of their feet becoming completely deformed. The girls were left with painful stumps, which were described somewhat poetically as "lotus hooks" by Chinese scholars. It was extremely difficult and uncomfortable to walk upon these lotus hooks, and running was made virtually impossi-ble. In fact, many women could not even walk at all and either had to crawl or be carried.[13]

Foot-binding was clearly a brutal and crippling practice. Why did women subject themselves and their female offspring to it? The quick answer is that the beauty ideal of the time demanded it. Men found the lotus hook attractive. Women with "goose feet," as the alternative was called, were considered unattractive and unmarriageable. As a Chinese woman's lot was greatly affected by her marital status, and to whom she was married, it was very much in her interests to conform to the ideal.

There are several other examples of beauty ideals that have required women in foreign cultures to subject themselves to, what may seem to us in the West, unusually brutal procedures. These include such things as neck-stretching, body scarification, genital mutilation and skull deformation. However, one need not go so far afield as Africa or the Orient to find examples of beauty ideals with painful or disabling requirements. One excellent example of such an ideal was that which required women to wear corsets in nineteenth-century Europe. The corset was worn for two reasons. Firstly, it exaggerated the "natural" female form, emphasising a narrow waist against wider breast and pelvic areas. Secondly, the wearing of a corset was seen as essential in assisting women to maintain a correct posture, as it was thought that a woman's spine and back muscles were insufficiently strong for her to support her own upper body weight.[14] Ironically, with regard to the latter point, the corset actually tended to cause the problem it had been intended to rectify. As the corsets provided total support for the upper body, women who wore them regularly experienced extensive wasting of the back muscles, such that they in fact could no longer support their own upper body weight without assistance. Apart from causing the wastage of muscles, corsets severely restricted a woman's movement and breathing. Women experienced difficulty in sitting and bending, they suffered fainting fits and were unable to walk unassisted, save for the shortest of distances.

Both foot-binding and corset-wearing caused serious damage to women's bodies and, as such, the beauty ideals that prescribed them can be said to have physically disabled women. But what is the state of play today? A contemporary beauty ideal for women requires that they be slender, muscle-toned and athletic in appearance.[15] Gone are the constrictive garments that forced female body parts to adopt unnatural shapes. It may appear that, far from disabling the body, this current ideal positively enables it. For instance, women conforming to this ideal require no assistance in walking. In fact, it probably makes them physically healthier than most men. In what way, then, could the current ideal be seen as being disabling? The answer to this is connected to the ideal causing women to experience their bodies as objects.

Regarding the motility of the human body, Maurice Merleau-Ponty has written that "In order that we may be able to move our body towards an object, the object must first exist for it, our body must not belong to the realm of the 'in-itself,' "[16] In other words, free activity amongst objects in the world requires that those objects are objects *for* the body—the graceful, intentional body—and that this cannot happen if the body itself is a mere object. This theme has also been taken up by Iris Marion Young, who has used it to explain some features of feminine body comportment. She has claimed that "Feminine bodily existence is an inhibited intentionality"[17] in that it is "frequently not a pure presence in the world because it is referred onto itself as well as onto possibilities in the world."[18] She provides many examples of manifestations of this "inhibited intentionality" in the way that women's bodies interact with the world.[19] One such example is the well known phenomenon of "throwing like a girl." When an athlete throws a ball, it can be observed that they involve their whole body in the process. The feet, legs, pelvis, back, shoulders and arms are all in motion, with the result often being that the throw is fast, far and accurate. In "throwing like a girl," however, one does not involve their whole body in the process. Rather, the feet tend to remain planted on the ground, with the upper body relatively immobile, save for the throwing arm itself. The throw is inevitably short and inaccurate. Young holds that other activities, such as pushing and lifting, are also performed ineffectively and inefficiently when carried out in the "feminine manner." She cites the female experiencing her body as an object as the main reason for this inhibited intentionality. Women experience their bodies as being "looked at" by others as objects. In Sartrean terms, they experience their being-for-others as body-object. As such, it is not only for others that their bodies are objects but, and perhaps more importantly, their bodies are objects for themselves as well. And this is just the sort of situation to which Merleau-Ponty was earlier referring; bodily activity toward objects in the world is inhibited if the body itself is existing as an object.

It almost goes without saying that the body, experienced as an object of the will, rather than the will itself, is the body existing in what Sartre would refer to as its obscene mode. Through the analysis of female beauty ideals undertaken earlier I suggested that female beauty ideals could be seen as acting to make women's bodies exist in this mode. Given the pervasiveness of these ideals, this can then lead us to say that female beauty ideals could be expected to be a contributing factor in what Young terms the "inhibited intentionality" of women's bodily being. Thus, it is in the sense of causing women's bodily existence to have inhibited intentionality that conformity to the contemporary beauty ideal could be

seen as disabling women, despite the fact that it may not be physiologi-
cally or anatomically destructive.[20]

Conclusion

It has been suggested that aspects of Sartre's account of sadism can be
applied to the issue of female beauty ideals. Such an application allows
us to view women subject to beauty ideals as being in a parallel situation
to the victims of sadism. Furthermore, by framing the demands of beauty
ideals in terms of the obscene mode of bodily being, it becomes possible
to see that contemporary beauty ideals, whilst not necessarily specifying
that women should physically damage themselves, can still act to disable
the women subjected to them.[21]

Notes

1. Jean-Paul Sartre, *Being and Nothingness,* trans. Hazel E. Barnes (London: Routledge, 1993).
Further references will appear in the text.

2. Sartre seems to assume that only human beings have being-for-itself, and ignores the possibility that other creatures, such as dolphins and chimpanzees, might have it too. This is a debate
that I don't care to involve myself in at the moment, so I shall follow him in not addressing this
possibility either.

3. For example, he refers to the self's realisation that it has being-for-others as "shame" (BN
260).

4. Arthur C. Danto, *Sartre* (London: Fontana Press, 1985), 102.

5. Linda A. Bell, *Sartre's Ethics of Authenticity* (Tuscaloosa: University of Alabama Press, 1989),
30.

6. Sadism is by no means the only such strategy described by Sartre. For examples of other
strategies see the chapter entitled "Concrete Relations With Others" in *Being and Nothingness*.

7. The term facticity refers to an individual's material and bodily circumstances, including
their past. It is a mode of being-in-itself and is usually spoken of in contrast to transcendence.

8. It should be noted that Merleau-Ponty believed that Sartre's ontology did not adequately
take embodiment into account. For a discussion of Merleau-Ponty's objections to Sartre, see Monika
Langer, *Merleau-Ponty's "Phenomenology of Perception"* (London: Macmillan, 1989), pt. 2, chap. 4.
Although it may be true that Sartre does not develop an account of, or concentrate on, embodiment
to the same degree as Merleau-Ponty, there is ample evidence in *Being and Nothingness* to suggest
that he at least had some notion of embodiment, and that he assumed and used that notion in many
of his discussions.

9. Jacques Salvan seems to be in support of this interpretation when he writes that Sartre's
sadist "wants the other's consciousness to be entirely absorbed and fascinated by body-consciousness

through pain," *To Be and Not To Be: An Analysis of Jean-Paul Sartre's Ontology* (Detroit: Wayne State University Press, 1962), 96.

10. I am referring here to women such as actors, journalists and other "media personalities." One of course does see "non-conforming" female bodies as well, e.g. politicians and other women who somehow make it into the news, but they are subjects of the media, not a part of the media itself.

11. See Susan Bordo, "Reading the Slender Body," in Mary Jacobus, Evelyn Fox Keller and Sally Shuttleworth (eds), *Body/Politics: Women and the Discourses of Science* (New York: Routledge, 1990), 100. Here one finds a graphic description of a television talk show audience's aggressive response to an obese woman who refused to "admit" that the shape of her body made her miserable.

12. Gila J. Hayim, *The Existential Sociology of Jean-Paul Sartre* (Amherst: University of Massachusetts, 1980), 47.

13. For accounts of foot-binding see Jane Ogden, *Fat Chance: The Myth of Dieting Explained* (London: Routledge, 1992), 1–3; April Fallon, "Culture in the Mirror: Sociocultural Determinants of Body Image" in Thomas F. Cash and Thomas Pruzinsky (eds), *Body Images: Development, Deviance and Change* (New York: Guilford Press, 1990), 104–6; and Arline and John Liggett, *The Tyranny of Beauty* (London: Victor Gollancz, 1989), 150–54.

14. Ogden, *Fat Chance*, 3.

15. There also exists alongside this "athletic look" the "super-thin-bordering-on-anorexic-look" (like that of the fashion model, Kate Moss). Fallon has argued that in various periods in history there have existed two beauty ideals simultaneously. One example of this is the period during the 1950s and early 1960s which had both a voluptuous ideal, exemplified by Marilyn Monroe and Jayne Mansfield, and a thin ideal, exemplified by Grace Kelly and Audrey Hepburn, Fallon, "Culture in the Mirror," 84–8. It is my contention that a similar state of affairs exists today, with the "athletic ideal" and the "super-thin ideal" existing side by side. My interest in this paper, however, will be focused on the former.

16. Maurice Merleau-Ponty, *Phenomenology of Perception,* trans. Colin Smith (London: Routledge and Kegan Paul, 1962), 139.

17. Iris Marion Young, *Throwing Like a Girl and Other Essays in Feminist Philosophy and Social Theory* (Bloomington: Indiana University Press, 1990), 148.

18. Young, *Throwing Like a Girl*, p. 150.

19. It should be noted that Young does not claim that all women exist in this way, but rather what she is describing is "the typical situation of being a woman in a particular society, as well as the typical way in which this situation is lived by the women themselves," Young, *Throwing Like a Girl*, p. 144.

20. It has been drawn to my attention by Linda Burns, and I thank her for this point, that Young's article, and mine as well, might be open to the charge of having adopted a masculinist perspective by simply accepting uncritically that the masculine mode of bodily comportment should act as the standard against which all other modes are judged. In claiming that someone with an "inhibited intentionality" can be considered disabled I am claiming that *given* a particular goal (e.g. throwing a ball effectively) which a person could conceivably achieve, the fact that inhibited intentionality frustrates the achievement of that goal allows us to claim that the person concerned is disabled (by virtue of their inhibited intentionality) with regard to that goal. This leaves it an open question as to whether that goal is one that ought to be pursued in the first place.

21. I gratefully acknowledge the comments and suggestions that I received on earlier versions of this paper from Rosalyn Diprose and Genevieve Lloyd of the University of New South Wales, Linda Burns of Flinders University, Birgitta Holm and Zalma Puterman of Uppsala University, and the two anonymous readers from *Australian Feminist Studies*.

5

Sartre and Marcel on Embodiment

Reevaluating Traditional and Gynocentric Feminisms

Constance L. Mui

In recent years, the celebrated works of Simone de Beauvoir and Shula-mith Firestone, once required readings in feminist philosophy courses, have come under rigorous attack by a new generation of feminist philoso-phers who ascribe to the position known as gynocentrism.[1] Gynocentric feminists challenge the basic philosophical assumptions Beauvoir makes in *The Second Sex,* assumptions that Beauvoir openly admits to have taken from Jean-Paul Sartre's early writings. As one critic observes, *The Second Sex* suffers from its author's "rather uncritical . . . embrace (of)

An earlier version of this essay was presented at the annual meeting of the Marcel Society of the American Philosophical Association, Eastern Division, December 1996. I am indebted to Patrick Bourgeois, Julie Connelly Pedersen, and Julien Murphy for their helpful comments.

Sartre's brand of Existentialist philosophy."[2] To be sure, the geocentric feminists' attack on Beauvoir and her followers is ultimately an attack on Sartre's philosophy, particularly on his theory of embodiment that is predicated on his overall ontology of freedom. They fault Sartre for employing a male-centered model that glorifies male consciousness and activity. According to them, it is an inadequate model that not only fails to account for women's unique embodied experience but devalues it. Contending that traditional feminist writings are infected by the same male bias found in the existentialist phenomenology identified with Sartre, gynocentric feminists set out to reclaim women's experience by grounding feminist theory in an ontology of female embodiment, one that exalts the difference in women's reproductive biology. This essay is an attempt to assess the positions that set apart the two generations of feminists, focusing specifically on the different ontologies that underlie them. Just as any serious treatment of Beauvoir's work must address its affinity with Sartrean philosophy, my evaluation of the positions inevitably will consist of an evaluation of Sartre's approach to the problem of embodiment, an approach that is widely shared by twentieth-century phenomenologists, including Gabriel Marcel. Let me begin by tracing the philosophical development of the general view taken by Beauvoir and Firestone, which, in spite of the label "radical feminism," actually represents the more orthodox tradition in feminist scholarship today.

From *The Second Sex* to the more recent interviews before her death, Simone de Beauvoir consistently rejected natural procreation and motherhood.[3] Anyone who has read her work is familiar with her depiction of childbearing as a "painful ordeal" that enslaves woman "in repetition and immanence." Indeed, in *The Second Sex*, she has this to say about woman's reproductive "activity":

> From puberty to menopause woman is the theater of a play that unfolds within her and in which she is not personally concerned. . . . In truth the menstrual cycle is a burden, and a useless one from the point of view of the individual. . . . It is during her periods that [the woman] feels her body most painfully as an obscure, alien thing, . . . the prey of a stubborn and foreign life. Woman experiences a more profound alienation when fertilization has occurred. . . . Gestation is a fatiguing task of no individual benefit to the woman, but on the contrary demanding heavy sacrifices. . . . All that a healthy and well-nourished woman can

hope for is to recoup without too much difficulty after childbirth; but frequently serious accidents or at least dangerous disorders mark the course of pregnancy. . . . Childbirth itself is painful and dangerous.[4]

Clearly, for Beauvoir, procreation is not authentic human activity but a passive "crisis." What is most alarming about Beauvoir's view is her claim that there is, apart from and beyond patriarchal arrangements surrounding woman's fertility, something *inherently* oppressive about woman's reproductive biology. Admittedly, patriarchal control over women's fertility throughout history has placed many undue burdens and hardships on woman's reproductive life. But in Beauvoir's view, the primary agent of enslavement remains woman's own biology, which subjects her to a life of risk and suffering, giving men every opportunity to exert physical force over her.

This position is readily endorsed by Shulamith Firestone. In *The Dialectic of Sex*, a work dedicated to Beauvoir, Firestone considers woman's reproductive role a "natural inequality." "Reproduction of the species," she says, "costs women dearly, not only emotionally, psychologically, culturally but even in strictly . . . physical terms: before recent methods of contraception, continuous childbirth led to constant 'female trouble,' early aging, and death."[5] Thus, following in the tradition established by Beauvoir, Firestone also gives woman's reproductive biology a negative evaluation. It signifies a woman's existence as both repetitive and immanent.

To appreciate the philosophical weight of this position, however, we must keep in mind that, for a theorist such as Beauvoir whose work is so deeply rooted in existential philosophy, woman exists as immanence both ontically *and ontologically*. Admittedly, it could be argued that a woman's prescribed ontic or social existence in patriarchy as the docile housewife renders her immanent because such a role stifles individual creativity. But apart from patriarchy, Beauvoir understands immanence primarily on the ontological level as constituting the very structure of woman's embodied existence from puberty onwards. The concept of immanence is built into Beauvoir's own ontology of female embodiment, which is essentially an extension of the existentialist model of the lived body as a primordial form of transcendence. In order to understand how and why Beauvoir renders woman immanent ontologically, and, more important, why the concept itself is particularly problematic and negative for Beauvoir in the first place, an explication of the existentialists' treatment of human embodiment is necessary. This will enable us to grasp the notions of transcendence and immanence in the proper existential context that Beauvoir intended, so as to dissociate them from their more familiar theological connotations.

On the issue of embodiment, Beauvoir is perhaps as much indebted to Marcel as she is to Sartre, even though *The Second Sex* contains no direct reference to Marcel. One of the most original and poignant accounts of the body as an existential structure is found in the works of Marcel, whose theory, as my essay will suggest, is ultimately given its fullest and most salient expression in Sartrean ontology. The theory of embodiment is not only central to Marcelian thought, but it also marks one of Marcel's more important contributions to the history of philosophy. Philosophers since Descartes have struggled with little success to overcome the problem of mind-body dualism, prompting a disenchanted Sartre to conclude that dualism is something of an "embarrassment" to philosophy. In a decisive attempt to rescue philosophy from Descartes, Marcel developed an original phenomenology of embodiment, one that would later anticipate a similar approach in Sartre and Merleau-Ponty. For Marcel, Cartesian dualism is problematic on two counts—it destroys the unity of self and body, as well as the unity of self and world. Having broken up the self, the body, and the world into three distinct regions, Descartes faces the impossible task of putting Humpty Dumpty back together again. To be sure, Marcel is well aware that Descartes is only a conceptual dualist when it comes to the person, for whom the mind is distinct from the body only in the sense that we could form, in Descartes's own words, "a clear and distinct concept of mind alone as a complete thing."[6] Time and again, Descartes has emphasized that, even though he can conceive of himself as disembodied thought, the mind is nevertheless "substantially united with the body." But what troubles Marcel is precisely this Cartesian notion that the mind or self can be conceived of at all without the body. To him, to conceive of a disembodied self, even if that were possible, is to leave out the very thing that makes the self a self. As far as Marcel is concerned, to say "I think" is to declare myself a bodily being participating in a bodily world. It is this fundamental objection to Descartes that forms the cornerstone of Marcel's theory of embodiment.

Taking a different course, Marcel begins not with doubt but with the indubitable proclamation, "I exist!" It is to proclaim, with exuberance and bewilderment, that "I stand out toward," that I am extended into, the world. In this way, to say that I exist is to refer immediately to a primordial unity of self, body, and world, one that constitutes for Marcel the lived immediacy of participation that cannot be analyzed in terms of the traditional split between I and not-I, within and without. Furthermore, it is a unity that manifests itself as a "mystery," a term Marcel uses to capture the sense of wonder and bewilderment that accompany the proclamation of my existence. Whereas a problem relies on primary reflection to analyze my body as a detached object or instrument, a mystery makes use of secondary or existential reflection to preserve the unity lost in primary reflection, enabling me to take my body as *mine*. Observing the preanalytic status of a mystery, Marcel aptly characterizes any attempt to grasp the unity in question a "metaproblem."

But in what sense is my body to be taken as mine? To be sure, it is mine insofar as I do not reify it into the body-object that it is for others. Not being an object for me, Marcel insists that I do not "have" a body as a possession, but I *am* my body. According to him, "to say that I *am* my body is to negate, to deny, to erase that gap which, on the other hand, I would be postulating as soon as I asserted that my body was merely my instrument."[7] In other words, there is no gap or distance between me and my body-qua-mine, the kind that is established in any subject-to-object relationship. This lack of distance sets the condition of my embodiment: my body, as mine, is never thrown over to the side of objects in the field of my direct consciousness; I am thoroughly and fundamentally connected with my body as subject. Marcel further illustrates this connection by introducing the concept of "sentir." He points out that "my body, in so far as it is properly mine, presents itself to me in the first instance as something *felt*: I am my body only in so far as I am a being that has feelings. From this point of view, . . . my body is endowed with an absolute priority in relation to everything that I can feel that is other than my body itself."[8] As "absolute priority," my body is that by means of which I can feel other objects. It is not itself an instrument or a possession but is what makes possible the instrumentality or possession of anything else whatsoever. The feeling of my body as intimately mine is a primordial feeling, what Marcel calls an "urgefuhl," which is radically distinct from all other feelings and sensations I have with objects. In his *Metaphysical Journal*, Marcel describes this unmediated, original feeling as a kind of "coenesthesia" between me and my body, which means, quite literally, a shared internal perception.

As internal perception, this coenesthetic feeling hovers over any activity I engage in without being the direct focus of my awareness. For example, I feel myself as tired as I move wearily toward the last stretch of a marathon, my attention focused directly on keeping up my pace and finishing the race. Moments later, I feel myself as suddenly energized as soon as I see the finish line that I am about to cross, all the while thinking to myself that the race will finally be over soon. This coenesthetic feeling between me and my body is one in which neither my self nor my body can be objectified or separated from the other. It instantiates my whole being as an embodied subject organizing my bodily activities in the world. Marcel describes this unobjectifiable experience of my embodiment as "submerged" as opposed to "emergent" participation. Submerged participation, he says, is "feeling below the level of thought."[9] That is to say, it is feeling that is not directly reflected upon and has therefore not yet emerged as the object of my consciousness. As Marcel puts it, it is a prereflective feeling "whose very duty is to ignore itself."[10] As the original feeling that lies at the root of all other feelings, it is precisely that which is ignored so that I may engage in a continuous process of (emergent) participation in the world, of opening myself to the world.

Marcel's idea of my body-qua-mine as unobjectifiable mystery, his insistence on the lack of distance or gap between self and body, his depiction of embodied experience as submerged participation, as feeling below the level of thought, and as feeling that is ignored—in short, his entire position on embodiment is, in a sense, brought to its logical conclusion in Sartre's ontology of the body. Indeed, why Sartre should choose to remain silent on his debt to Marcel is a mystery of a different sort. It certainly appears that he has taken Marcel's idea of body-as-subject and made a definitive case for it.

Like everything in *Being and Nothingness*, Sartre's theory of embodiment is an integral part of his elaborate system and cannot be understood apart from it. His main objective is to develop an ontology of human existence *as* freedom, arguing that freedom constitutes the very fundamental structure of human existence. According to this, consciousness *is* freedom in the mode of *being* rather than that of having. A conscious being is said to exist by moving beyond the past toward some future possibility, and through this dynamic activity engages in the ongoing process of self-definition. Unlike the rock that simply is what it is, this fluid existence of moving-beyond-toward (viz. "transcendence") entails that a conscious being can have no fixed identity, since it is always a step ahead of what we could make of it. Conscious being is therefore free in the ontological sense of existing by wrenching away from the principle of identity. All told, to be conscious is to exist as freedom, and to exist as freedom is to be a nonthing—a "nothingness", as it were—since all things have certain congealed identity.

Sartre further strengthens this ontology by demonstrating the complete translucency of consciousness, such that it cannot in any way be contaminated by any opaqueness, any thinglike quality that would compromise its status as nothingness. Thus, Sartre makes an exhaustive case for the traditional theory of intentionality, insisting that consciousness is wholly "of" an object; it is nothing other than the pure intending of its object.[11] He cautions that if anything should inhabit consciousness, it would cloud its lucidity and prevent it from revealing the object precisely as it is. And so, for Sartre, consciousness is empty qua itself, and demands as its support some object that would "fill" it and give it some content. Uninfected by opaqueness of any sort, consciousness as "nothingness" is not unlike a clear bubble that would envelop its object and give it the most honest disclosure. This is the ontological structure behind Sartre's description of consciousness as pure transcendence into the world.

And yet consciousness is always and necessarily *embodied* consciousness insofar as concrete human beings are the only conscious beings that exist in Sartre's godless world. But given that the body, as flesh, is obviously a substantial and opaque thing, how could consciousness be embodied and still remain translucent? Sartre addresses this problem by demonstrating, as Marcel did earlier, that, in its most fundamental dimension, the body is not merely a thing among things; there is not first a disembodied consciousness that would subsequently be conjoined to a corporeal body. Rather, on the most basic level, I do not experience any separation, any psychic distance or gap, between my body and myself: I *am* my body. I do not "have" a body but I "exist" (live) my body as the center of reference through which the world and its things are univocally displayed and revealed to me.[12] Just as I cannot take up a point of view on that which *is* my point of view on the world, I do not apprehend my body in a subject-to-object relation as I do with all things. Paraphrasing the Marcelian description of body-feeling as "submerged" and "ignored" experience, Sartre says that my body-for-me, as the most authentic dimension of my body, is always "the neglected," and "the passed by in silence" while I engage in the pursuit of my projects.[13] In Sartre's words, it is "that which is surpassed by the nihilating For-itself."[14] I touch my hand, for instance, in order to put on a glove to do some gardening; it is to surpass it toward some possibility. And while I am gardening it is only by "forgetting" (surpassing) my hands that I carry out my project to plant the rosebushes. I am not in the same subject-to-object relation with my hands as I am with the gardening tool, for *I am my hands*. Through this account of embodiment, Sartre seeks to preserve the translucency of (embodied) consciousness: I do not apprehend my body as an object but transcend it toward my project at hand.

Here we have Marcel's and Sartre's ontology of embodied consciousness, the indispensable basis of Beauvoir's own ontology of female embodiment, of which Beauvoir herself has reminded us on numerous occasions. For example, she asserts in the introduction to *The Second Sex* that "our perspective is that of existentialist ethics. Every subject plays his part . . . specifically through . . . projects that serve as a mode of transcendence; he achieves liberty only through a continual reaching out toward other liberties. . . . Every individual concerned to justify his existence feels that his existence involves an undefined need to transcend himself, to engage in freely chosen projects."[15] Beauvoir promptly extends this to woman, describing her as "a being whose nature is transcendent action." Likewise, the existentialist position on the body-as-subject is captured in the section on biology, where Beauvoir makes it clear that, from the existentialist perspective, "the body is not a *thing*, it is a situation, . . . the instrument of our grasp upon the world."[16] This commitment to the body-as-subject has some serious consequences for Beauvoir's own ontology of female embodiment, as is evident when she goes on to observe that, for woman, "her grasp on the world is . . . more restricted."[17] Beauvoir then takes pains to describe the course of a woman's complicated reproductive life from puberty to menopause. The female body, with its menstrual cycle and childbearing function, is not something that could be "ignored" or "passed over in silence" so that the conscious female subject could engage single-mindedly in projects of transcendence. Whereas an occasional headache might make it difficult at times for anyone to "surpass" the body,[18] I think it is for Beauvoir the *repetition* of menstrual cycles that drastically alters the primordial relation between a woman and her body. Cycle after cycle, her body makes its presence known by being an object of constant pain and discomfort. Thus Beauvoir observes that woman "feels her body most painfully as an obscure, alien thing."[19] If authentic existence involves the kind of body-to-be-ignored experience that Marcel and Sartre describe, then it is no wonder Beauvoir would conclude that, "woman, like man, *is* her body; but her body is something other than herself."[20] It is this otherness, this alien-ation from her own body, that compromises a woman's project toward a life of "transcendent action" and enslaves her "in repetition and imma-nence." In this way Beauvoir understands immanence as constituting the very ontological structure of female embodiment, something that exists apart from, albeit aggravated by, patriarchal society.

But like a good existentialist, Beauvoir also insists that woman, like man, is not determined by biology. Rejecting Aristotelian essentialism, Beauvoir argues that to be conscious is to be a free being whose identity is never fixed, a being who is always in the process of creating itself. If it is a person's ontological existence as freedom that renders the female body problematical, it is precisely because the person exists as freedom that biology can never define a woman's destiny. After all, Sartre has observed that "what we call freedom is the irreducibility of the cultural order to the natural order."[21] The product of human work, this cultural order has significantly transformed the natural body through technology that aims at alleviating pain and prolonging life. This vote of confidence on human freedom leads Beauvoir to assert that woman is never passive toward her body but has always violently resisted it.[23] This can be seen in the long history of women's struggles for reproductive freedom, a history of which Beauvoir herself was a part.

Beauvoir's feminism has come under attack in recent feminist scholar-ship for its male bias resulting from an uncritical acceptance of Sartrean philosophy. I shall address the specific criticisms later. For the moment I want to point out a major problem associated with the existentialist model so as to clear the way for my own evaluation of Beauvoir's position. It is commonplace for twentieth-century phenomenologists and existen-tialists to hold up a model that is taken from the male experience. Spe-cifically, they describe the experience of an autonomous body, that of a healthy, privileged, conscious adult male unrestricted by the burdens and demands of maternity. Purporting to be gender neutral, they sidestep biological differences between the sexes, and hold up the male experience of transcendence as the norm for authentic human activity. Beauvoir, on the other hand, takes into account the biological differences in question, but uses male embodied experience as the norm against which to identify differences in female embodied experience as immanent and therefore problematic. Indeed, her negative view of the female body might have been tainted by Sartre's description of the body as "an obstacle to be surpassed in order to be in the world," and as the "necessary obstacle of my being."[23] If even the unrestricted male body is portrayed as an obstacle, it is not surprising that Beauvoir would consider the female body a "crisis."

Having noted the inadequacy of the existentialist model, I want to assess Beauvoir's position more closely by turning to two related issues: (1) Is female embodied experience really incompatible with the existentialist view of embodiment? (2) Is it essentially inferior to male experience as Beauvoir suggests? My response to the first question is that *not* all authentic activities require consciousness to transcend the body completely towards its projects. In fact, many of our projects demand precisely that we pay close attention to our body. For example, it has been said that good posture makes a successful golfer. When Nancy Lopez is putting, she is not merely conscious of the ball or the hole, but perhaps more importantly her straight back and elbows. Likewise, the movers who are carrying a piano down a flight of stairs are not simply aware of the piano or the stairs, but the precarious and precise movements of their own bodies lest they should throw their backs out. These examples show that the body need not be ignored or surpassed *completely* in order for me to experience it as uniquely mine. The body as subject requires only that consciousness assumes an intentional structure whereby the body is never taken *wholly* as an object. Admittedly, golfers and movers cannot see the "seeing" of their own bodies; some aspect of their body (e.g., the eyes) is always and necessarily transcended. Even the pregnant woman whose bulging belly has become a constant object might not at the same time be directly aware of her own hand that is caressing it. And so, while our body cannot be taken wholly as an object, it does *not* follow that the body must be wholly transcended in order for consciousness to project single-mindedly toward meaningful and authentic activities. Taking on some aspect of one's own body as the direct object of consciousness does not compromise the lucidity of consciousness, nor does it render its activity less authentic or free. Beauvoir has taken the existentialists' position too narrowly when she assumes that, since woman's body is ontologically speaking more "immanent" in the stimulative sense of being more difficult to surpass completely, female embodied experience therefore leaves something to be desired.

Indeed, the inability to forget or transcend one's own body entirely might not be so negative an experience if we think of Ernest Becker's assessment of midlife crises in *The Denial of Death*.[24] He argues that many people fall into a crisis in midlife because they have led too symbolic an existence and have not managed to fine-tune between the symbolic and the organic aspects of their lives. If a healthy existence requires that we keep a balance between the infinite and the finite, then we must reevaluate the role of transcendence in any ontology of the body. It could be argued that, precisely due to the repetition of menstrual cycles beginning at puberty, a woman is more in touch with her body and is more able to plant her feet more firmly in the often terrifying reality of finitude. All told, it is not clear that the kind of transcendence Beauvoir identifies in the ideal model of male embodiment is ultimately representative of a balanced, resourceful existence. The difference found in female embodiment might not be as negative as Beauvoir would have it.

Recent feminists have sought to reject such negative evaluation of the female body, and to restore value to natural procreation and motherhood as the goal of feminism. This line of thinking, which has flourished in the last decade or so, and is reflected diversely in the writings of Mary O'Brien, Adrienne Rich, Nancy Hartsock, and others, is known as gynocentrism. Gynocentric feminists begin with the premise that women's reproductive biology has a positive value that has been denied and suppressed in patriarchy. They support a feminist philosophy in which woman's body receives not simply a positive but a *higher* evaluation than man's. I have chosen to concentrate on Mary O'Brien's work because it is the most theoretically grounded. Behind her argument lies a provocative ontology concerning the essential nature of woman, embodiment, and consciousness.

In *The Politics of Reproduction*, O'Brien points to the absence of a philosophy of birth as evidence of the dominance of "male-stream thought," and hence the need for "feminist metatheories."[25] She contends that philosophers have not theorized about human reproduction because men are biologically excluded from having any meaningful reproductive consciousness. Insisting that our philosophical tradition is an impoverished tradition based on man's impoverished experience in procreation, O'Brien declares that "feminist theory will be a philosophy of birth and regeneration."[26] Whereas traditional feminists such as Beauvoir have supported a male-centered ontology for all human beings, O'Brien endorses two separate ontologies of consciousness stemming from the fundamental distinction between female and male embodied experience. In her model, it is male consciousness that gets a secondary evaluation.

O'Brien begins with a staunch rejection of Beauvoir's portrayal of pregnancy and childbirth as passive and alienating. She observes that even on

> the biological level, reproductive labour is a synthesizing and mediating act. It confirms women's unity with nature experientially. . . . Labour is inseparable from reproductive process in its biological involuntariness, but it is also integrative. It is a mediation between mother and nature and mother and child; but it is also a *temporal* mediation between the cyclical time of nature and unilinear genetic time. Woman's reproductive consciousness is . . . a consciousness that she herself is born of a woman's labour, that labour confirms . . . species continuity. . . . [It] is continuous and integrative, for it is mediated within reproductive process. The fact that this integration has been labelled as "passivity" by male-stream though is part of the ideology of male supremacy.[27]

With this obvious attack on Beauvoir's depiction of human reproduction, O'Brien is quick to point out that "all women carry the consciousness of this unity" and that it is transmitted through culture.[28] By contrast, male reproductive consciousness is discontinuous because men do not and indeed cannot experience the same mediation of the time gap that women experience in reproductive labor. O'Brien argues that alienation of the male seed at the very start of the reproductive process produces a splintered, alienated male consciousness. And so "man's relationship to history, to continuity over time, is fundamentally problematic. At the primordial level of genetic continuity, . . . men are separated from natural continuity. . . . Men must therefore make, and have made, artificial modes of continuity. . . . [But in essence they] are separated from nature, from the race and from the continuity of the race over time."[29] O'Brien cites paternity, which amounts to the male appropriation of children, as an example of men's artificial mode of continuity. But men can never experience a genuine unity with nature and species because, given O'Brien's argument, the mediation required for such unity is linked directly to the very act of reproductive labor, or the potential of experiencing such labor. Furthermore, men's experience of separation from nature and species is rooted in the very structure of male embodiment, just as the opposite experience of continuity is rooted in female embodiment. The different ways in which they exist in their bodies mean that women and men develop different relationships, and consciousnesses based on those relationships, with the natural world. In this way O'Brien's ontology rejects the traditional model that analyzes consciousness in terms of transcendence and immanence, and employs instead a gynocentric model of continuity and separation. In this ontology, authenticity has less to do with the connection between the intentional structure of consciousness and concrete freedom, but more with the integration of oneself with nature, temporality and species in a harmonious unity.

O'Brien argues that Beauvoir has started off on the wrong foot by failing to question the value arbitrarily placed on male freedom over female reproduction. As a result she equates human reproduction with animal procreation, thus depriving women's reproductive experience of any significance. O'Brien concludes that Beauvoir's uncritical acceptance of Sartre's male-centered ontology is itself a gesture of bad faith. She promptly extends this criticism to Firestone, who argues that women's liberation rests on the ultimate transcendence of female biology. O'Brien points out that this amounts to wanting women to become men. What is most troubling to her is that ectogenesis should be seen as an instrument of women's liberation. In her view, replacing women's reproductive function with technology would destroy the very thing that makes women's experience authentic. What we need is a woman-centered theory of reproductive consciousness that celebrates the difference in female biology, not alters it.

The strength of O'Brien's theory lies in her effort to identify the crucial connection between consciousness and its embodiment. This point is well taken regardless of whether one agrees with the conclusion she draws from it. Such factors as the condition of one's embodiment, the relationship one has to one's own body, and one's sexual orientation could all shape one's consciousness. But O'Brien takes us well beyond this insight when she submits that it is reproductive biology that solely and uniformly determines for each sex the conditions of its embodiment, conditions that in turn give rise to two gender-specific consciousnesses. Although provocative, it is a theory fraught with serious difficulties.

Perhaps the most obvious difficulty in O'Brien's formulation of female reproductive consciousness is its failure to explain why such consciousness should be shared by *all* women as she believes, and why women *exclusively*. In saying that this consciousness is transmitted to all women through culture, O'Brien is allowing that reproductive consciousness is not a strictly biological phenomenon but also a cultural one that would operate on women's collective identity as women. Presumably, women who do not bear children would nevertheless attain it through identification with their own sex. But this is impossible to substantiate, since not all women ascribe to their gender identity. O'Brien's assumption is further challenged by the fact that there are men who identify closely with female experiences, as in documented cases of expecting fathers who are so emotionally connected with the birth process that they actually experience labor pains during the births of their children. It is plainly incongruous that, given the logic of O'Brien's argument, these men should be precluded biologically from attaining the reproductive consciousness of continuity, while such consciousness should be transmitted through culture to all women, including even those who do not identify with their sex and want to have nothing to do with childbearing.

This also calls into question O'Brien's portrayal of male reproductive consciousness as discontinuous and alienated. She bases this on the act of ejaculation—"the physical separation of man from his own seed"—which symbolizes discontinuity and alienation from species as well as nature. Again, this is hardly reliable evidence for such a bold claim. Moreover, if actually or potentially experiencing an act of physical separation is deemed sufficient condition for men's alienated reproductive consciousness, why would women's consciousness not be similarly affected by their own experiences of physical separation during childbirth? More important than rendering O'Brien's position arbitrary, these observations bring out the complexity and diversity in human reproductive experiences, which may consist of moments of continuity and discontinuity for both sexes. I think a more plausible account of reproductive consciousness is to understand it in part as the product of how we have chosen to relate to this diverse range of experiences. And any gender differences found therein would likely be a function of cultural conditioning rather than biology as O'Brien believes.

Equally problematic is O'Brien's assumption that women's reproductive consciousness is not merely different from men's but "better," a value judgment reflected in her assertion that "nature is unjust to men."[30] O'Brien does not explain why the experience of continuity should be assigned more value than discontinuity. To be sure, qualities associated with continuity are not always superior or desirable; sometimes progress is made precisely when women break continuity with the past. Likewise, qualities associated with discontinuity are not necessarily negative either. Quite the contrary, the encounter with discontinuity could itself compel us to find innovative and creative ways to build bridges, to take risks, to reconstruct or synthesize pieces of a disjointed reality. Hence, one could argue that the consciousness of discontinuity, if it existed, could be seen as a positive potential, motivating us to excel in qualities that make us uniquely human.

Finally, whereas O'Brien has criticized Beauvoir for assuming Sartre's ontology of transcendence modeled after the experience of a healthy, privileged male, her own model is no less a biased one representing a healthy, privileged female. Her description of a synthesizing, mediating, and unifying reproductive process is founded on the unmistakably *positive* experience of a woman having a child under the most favorable physical, psychological, and economic circumstances. However, if any connection is to be drawn between consciousness and embodiment, then we must be consistent and allow that issues of how one is embodied, and how one relates to one's own embodiment, would play a significant role in shaping one's consciousness. We must allow that, in some cases, women's reproductive consciousness is a product of their *negative* rather than positive experiences of embodiment. This poses many difficult questions for O'Brien. For example, would a woman whose own mother had died from childbirth and is now threatened by the same fate, have a reproductive consciousness of continuity? Would a diabetic woman who risks losing her eyesight during pregnancy have the same reproductive consciousness of integration? And what about the woman who has an acute fear of pain? Arguably, these women could have a reproductive consciousness of dread rather than synthesis and integration. Likewise, the fear of unwanted pregnancy could bring about a reproductive consciousness of disruption rather than of continuity. By replacing the traditional model of the healthy, privileged male with that of a healthy, privileged female, gynocentric feminists are subject to similar criticisms that they themselves have leveled against the tradition. Still more troubling in O'Brien's gynocentricism is that it has given way to an ethic that purports to make women authentic by reestablishing their essential unity with nature. If we accept O'Brien's definition of women's authenticity in terms of a continuous and integrative consciousness rooted in their reproductive biology, we must also be prepared to accept that women who willfully reject motherhood are denying their own authenticity and are therefore in bad faith. Indeed, this is the danger of locating authenticity in women's wombs.

In this essay I have explicated and critiqued the opposing views that have shaped the debate between traditional and gynocentric feminist philosophers. In closing I wish to address briefly two reasons why I believe gynocentric feminists ought to rethink their strategy to develop a separate ontology for women. First, by accentuating the difference between women and men, their approach takes our focus away from the many qualities that women and men in fact have in common. These qualities, including men's equal ability to nurture others, give women and men the commonality of experience that forms the basis of authentic being-with-others-in-the-world. In the struggle for gender quality, men and women could certainly accomplish a lot more if they did not lose sight of the common threads that bind them together. Rather than constructing a separate ontology based on gender difference, gynocentric feminists should work toward rebuilding the existing ontology in order to encompass a much wider range of shared human experiences.

This brings us to the second point. In evaluating traditional ontology it is important for gynocentric feminists to appreciate it in its proper historical context. As discussed earlier, Marcel and Sartre developed their theory of embodiment as a way to recover the unity of the person that was hopelessly lost in Cartesian dualism. Above all, their concern was to rescue philosophy from Descartes by working out an ontology that would do justice to the intimate relationship of the person as embodied being in a bodily world. It is an ontology that describes the most fundamental structure of consciousness in terms of the prereflective, preanalytic unity of self, body, and world. To be sure, when O'Brien speaks of authentic consciousness as integrative and continuous with nature and species, she owes much to the success of such an ontology in overcoming the notion of a disembodied self that would be detached altogether from other selves and from the world. O'Brien acted prematurely when she issued a blanket dismissal of traditional ontology as male centered and therefore unworthy of feminist considerations. Quite the contrary, it could be argued that, perhaps unmatched by any other philosophical tradition, the works of many existentialists and phenomenologists provide a potentially rich framework and point of reference for feminist discourse. Specifically, I have in mind, for example, Marcel's idea of participation, communion, and presence, Buber's understanding of authenticity in terms of dialogue and the I-Thou relation, Heidegger's portrayal of the "mitsein" as a basic existential, and Sartre's attempt to ground a moral imperative against oppression on ontological freedom, just to name a few. These themes constitute an overall ontology of human existence that in essence could validate women's unique experiences as nurturers, as companions, as relational beings, as resilient fighters for equality and self-determination. These experiences, although largely ignored by the existentialists themselves, could in turn lend support to presuppositions that they have made about the human condition. Observing this affinity between traditional ontology and feminism, it is time for both sides to come together to rebuild a truly gender-inclusive ontology of human existence based not on the male or female model but on a human one.

Notes

1. Iris Marion Young introduced the concept in her essay "Humanism, Gynocentrism, and Feminist Politics" in *Hypatia Reborn: Essays in Feminist Philosophy*, ed. Ezizah Y. al-Hibri and Margaret Simons (Indianapolis: Indiana University Press, 1990), 231–48.

2. Mary O'Brien, *The Politics of Reproduction* (Boston: Routledge and Kegan Paul, 1981), 66–67. This concern is shared by other feminists as well, including Andrea Nye, who devoted an entire chapter in her book to this problem. See *Feminist Theory and the Philosophies of Man* (New York: Croom Helm, 1988), 73–114. See also Michèle Le Doeuff, "Operative Philosophy: Simone de Beauvoir and Existentialism," *Ideology and Consciousness*, no. 6 (1979), 47–58.

3. To get an impression of Beauvoir's later view, see her interview with Alice Schwarzer, in Schwarzer, *After "The Second Sex": Conversations with Simone de Beauvoir* (New York: Pantheon Books, 1982).

4. Simone de Beauvoir, *The Second Sex*, trans. H. M. Parshley (New York: Knopf, 1975), 27–30.

5. Shulamith Firestone, *The Dialectic of Sex: The Case for Feminist Revolution* (New York: Morrow Quill Paperbacks, 1970), 232.

6. *The Philosophical Work of Descartes*, vol. 2 trans. E. S. Haldane and G. R. T. Ross (Cambridge: University Press, 1934), "Reply to Objections 4," 102.

7. Gabriel Marcel, *The Mystery of Being*, vol. 1, trans. G. S. Fraser (London: Harvill Press, 1951), 100.

8. Ibid., 101.

9. Ibid., 140.

10. Gabriel Marcel, *Metaphysical Journal*, trans. Bernard Wall (Chicago: Henry Regnery, 1952), 173.

11. Jean-Paul Sartre, *The Transcendence of the Ego*. Trans. Forrest Williams and Robert Kirkpatrick (New York: Farrar, Straus and Giroux, 1958), 40. Specifically, Sartre states that "All is . . . clear and lucid in consciousness: the object with its characteristic opacity is before consciousness, but consciousness is purely and simply consciousness of being consciousness of that object. This is the law of its existence."

12. Jean-Paul Sartre, *Being and Nothingness*. Trans. Hazel E. Barnes (New York: Philosophical Library, 1956), 323.

13. Ibid., 330.

14. Ibid., 309.

15. *The Second Sex*, xxviii-xxix.

16. Ibid., 34.

17. Ibid.

18. See also Sartre's discussion on pain in his analysis of the body. He argues that, in the first instance, pain is not part of our reflective consciousness. "It is the-eyes-as-pain or vision-as-pain; . . . it is not named in consciousness, for it is not known." Apparently, for Sartre, even in pain, we do not experience our own body as an object. (Ibid., 332–33)

19. Ibid., 29.

20. Ibid.

21. Jean-Paul Sartre, *Search for a Method,* trans. Hazel E. Barnes (New York: Vintage Books, 1963), 152.

22. Beauvoir, *The Second Sex,* 32.

23. Sartre, *Being and Nothingness,* 326, 328.

24. Ernest Becker, *The Denial of Death* (New York: Free Press, 1973).

25. O'Brien, *The Politics of Reproduction,* 20.

26. Ibid., 200.

27. Ibid., 59.

28. Ibid., 50.

29. Ibid., 53.

30. Ibid., 60.

6

Different Oppressions

A Feminist Exploration of Sartre's
Anti-Semite and Jew

Linda A. Bell

Jean-Paul Sartre's *Anti-Semite and Jew* was published shortly after the end of the Nazi occupation of France. Written in France, by a Frenchman, it is about French anti-Semites and French Jews. While this may seem to restrict the application of what Sartre has to say, I felt from my first encounter with the book that his observations and analyses have enor-

An earlier version of this paper was published in *Sartre Studies International* and even earlier ones were read at meetings of The Georgia Continental Circle in Augusta, Georgia, November, 1995, and The North American Sartre Society in Denison, Ohio, May, 1996, and at The Sartre Circle session of the American Philosophical Association in Atlanta, Georgia, December 1996. I have had a great deal of help in writing it, including that of my writers' group, Charlene Ball, Valerie Fennell, Diane Fowlkes, and Elizabeth Knowlton, and am particularly grateful to them for encouraging me to develop the earlier paper by adding an analysis of homophobia to those I had already done of sexism and anti-black racism.

mous potential in helping us to understand sexism and even heterosexism as well as other forms of racism, including possibly different forms of anti-Semitism. Sartre himself even encourages us to draw this conclusion. As long as I consider analyses like that of over-determination, I find no difficulties in doing so; however, two analyses in *Anti-Semite and Jew* challenge this conclusion. The analyses that concern me suggest that uniquely Jewish inauthenticity differs significantly from other forms of inauthenticity and that Jews in anti-Semitic French society cannot afford to be existentialists. Given my reading of other Sartrean analyses of inauthenticity, the first suggestion has long puzzled me; and given my previous fairly uncritical and unexamined assumption that generally what Sartre had to say about anti-Semitism could be said equally well about sexism, the second proposal seems even more baffling and, if applicable to sexism, certainly quite contrary to my own experience.

> In a word, the inauthentic Jews are men whom other men take for Jews and who have decided to run away from this insupportable situation. The result is that they display various types of behavior not all of which are present at that same time in the same person but each of which may be characterized as an *avenue of flight.* . . . It must be understood that the description of these avenues of flight is applied solely to the *inauthentic Jew* (the term "inauthentic" implying no moral blame, of course), and that it should be supplemented by a description of authentic Jewishness.[1]

The second analysis concerns the Jew's relation to what Sartre calls "metaphysical uneasiness" as opposed to "Jewish uneasiness." Sartre distinguishes the two as follows:

> Jews are often uneasy. An Israelite is never sure of his position or of his possessions. He cannot even say that tomorrow he will still be in the country he inhabits today, for his situation, his power, and even his right to live may be placed in jeopardy from one moment to the next. . . . However, it should not be thought that Jewish uneasiness is metaphysical. It would be an error to identify it with the anxiety that moves us to a consideration of the condition of man.

Having distinguished the two, Sartre proposes that Jews—and workers, oppressed minorities, and classes—cannot afford metaphysical uneasiness:

> I should say rather that metaphysical uneasiness is a condition that the Jew—no more than the worker—cannot allow himself today. One must be sure of one's rights and firmly rooted in the world, one must be free of the fears that each day assail oppressed minorities or classes, before one dare raise questions about the place of man in the world and his ultimate destiny. In a word, metaphysics is the special privilege of the Aryan governing classes. Let no one see in this an attempt to discredit metaphysics; when men are liberated, it will become again an essential concern of mankind.[2]

This means that Jews in an anti-Semitic society like France cannot afford to be existentialists since existentialism is precisely a questioning of the condition of human beings and their place in the universe.

The first claim—that specifically Jewish inauthenticity implies no moral blame—is perplexing. Here Sartre seems to refuse to hold Jews responsible for that over which they have control although he expresses no similar hesitation in the cases of the waiter, the woman in the cafe, the homosexual, and even the victim of torture in the various examples of bad faith and responsibility developed in *Being and Nothingness*.

I understood that Sartre sees the Jew as pushed by the democrat to reject and by the anti-Semite to accept an extraordinarily grotesque "nature" of "Jewishness," a "nature" that is constructed by anti-Semitic society, not by the Jew. But just to say that Jews are placed in an untenable situation by others is hardly sufficient to relieve them of responsibility for their responses to the situation. After all, being placed in a difficult or even horrendous situation by others does not, by itself, distinguish the Jew's situation from that of the homosexual or, for that matter, from the victim of torture in Sartre's other discussions. The homosexual and the torture victim are presented in those discussions as responsible, not for what others have done in structuring their extremely problematic positions (as some of Sartre's less generous critics have maintained), but rather for what they themselves do in these untenable situations. They are and are to be held responsible not only for any cooperation, including nonresistance, in creating their positions and allowing them to continue but also for any choices they are able to make within their now limited and circumscribed situations. In other words, Sartre carefully holds these individuals responsible only for what is within their control, not for actions over which they have no control. Yet he seems not to make the same move in the case of the Jew. Why not?

Sartre's discussion of metaphysical uneasiness raises rather difficult issues for me. From my first reading, I was astounded to see him saying, in effect, that the Jew cannot afford to be an existentialist.[3] In fact, I was so astonished that for a long while I was convinced that Sartre could not possibly mean what he says. Yet what he says is perfectly clear and straightforward. Jews cannot afford to question "the place of man in the universe." It follows, then, that they cannot—or, at least, should not—accept the existentialist affirmation that values are not given but created and its consequent denial of any such things as natures preexisting human choice and creation. On the contrary, according to Sartre, only one "sure of one's rights and firmly rooted in the world, . . . free of the fears that each day assail oppressed minorities or classes . . . ," can afford such metaphysical uneasiness.[4]

Since Sartre himself invites me as a reader to apply this analysis to myself should I belong to one of these "oppressed minorities or classes," I could not help but think how liberating the views of existentialism—Sartre's, in particular—were to me when I first encountered them in the midst of a terribly difficult graduate school experience in which both fellow students and faculty were challenging my being there. Their challenges were both to my *right* to be there (in this connection, I was told that I was usurping a male tradition to which women had made no "serious" contributions) and to the *advisability* of my being there (since fellowships like mine, a professor informed me and a number of other graduate students, were "wasted" on women who would only, he said, get married, drop out of school, and have children). My response was totally unlike the Jew's alleged reaction to metaphysical uneasiness. Instead of being worse off because of existentialism, I found therein not only solace but also ammunition for future use against such harassment inasmuch as it was precisely my alleged nature and my socially constructed place in society that I rejected and almost daily had to challenge, particularly faced with the ways these were being used against me by both students and faculty. For my own sanity, I needed to feel metaphysical uneasiness to my very bones; and I thought then that my success in graduate school and perhaps in the field of philosophy required that I somehow mange to make others, particularly my challengers, feel that same uneasiness. Little did I suspect then that someday the government itself might step in on my side by passing a civil rights law that would, at least on the books, outlaw discrimination against women, making a bit less acceptable the sort of harassment to which I was being subjected; but that was, at any rate, totally irrelevant to my relation to metaphysical uneasiness.

Years later and with some important help recently from my students,[5] I have rethought my perplexities concerning these passages from *Anti-Semite and Jew*. I have decided that, from my initial reading until quite recently, I have been making a fundamental mistake, namely, that of assuming that the position Sartre is ascribing to the Jew in France is sufficiently like those of the homosexual in homophobic society, of the black in anti-black racist society, and of the woman in sexist society, that what Sartre says of the Jew in anti-Semitic French society can just as easily be said of each of the others in contemporary U.S. society. In making this assumption, I was uncritically following Sartre's lead. After all, it is Sartre himself who applies his claim about metaphysical uneasiness not just to workers but to oppressed minorities and classes as well. My conclusion now, though, is that Sartre's invitation must be rejected as not consistent with the rest of *Anti-Semite and Jew*.

Rather, Simone de Beauvoir must be recognized as far clearer than Sartre about the distinctness of anti-Semitism when she wrote in *The Second Sex:* "[T]he Jewish problem is on the whole very different from the other two [those of blacks and women]—to the anti-Semite the Jew is not so much an inferior as he is an enemy for whom there is to be granted no place on earth, for whom annihilation is the fate desired."[6] Somehow Beauvoir resisted as Sartre, at least in his references to workers and to "oppressed minorities or classes," did not what Elisabeth Young-Bruehl describes as "the habit, developed during the war [World War II] and immediately afterward, of thinking in terms of prejudice in general and using antisemitism as the basis for generalizing analogies. . . ." This thinking involves, for Young-Bruehl, "[t]he key distortion obscuring the origins and developmental histories of the prejudices themselves": "the idea that prejudice is one," an idea that hides not only the complexity of the prejudices in general but even prevents recognition of the fact that the prejudices directed at each of these groups are themselves complex.[7]

My work in feminist theory has taught me to be wary of generalizations, particularly those about oppressions, the various forms of which are much more complex, both individually and in their interconnections, than I and many others previously took them to be. This complexity makes it extremely problematic to speak of "the black," "the Jew" (even "the French Jew"), "the homosexual," or "the woman." After all, at the very least, blacks and Jews and homosexuals are often women; and when oppressions overlap, the effect is not simply additive. To make this point, Young-Bruehl restricts the word "sexism" to "prejudice directed at women of the same kind, specifically of the mother's kind," calling by other names the prejudices men have toward other women, for example, "sexist-racism" and "sexist-classism."[8]

Even Sartre was aware that the position of the Jew who is female differs from that of a Jew who is male, although he did not examine this difference, spending less that a full page on it and noting only the well-defined role of the Jewess in novels.[9] Unlike Sartre, though, feminists today know how problematic it is even to speak or write of "women," much less of "their" position, since class, race, and sexual orientation frequently have the effect of obliterating some individuals as women, a fact perceptively demonstrated by Elizabeth V. Spelman,[10] and certainly prevent adult female human beings from having much in common.

I shall try to keep all of this complexity in mind as I work with Sartre's texts, using his masculine pronouns when discussing his examples and using female or more gender neutral ones when discussing others in the categories under analysis. This, however, is likely to obscure some issues since it will be necessary to discuss blacks, homosexuals, Jews, and women as though, at least for purposes of discussion, these are separate and separable categories of human beings. Even noting, in the spirit of Sartre, that what I mean is blacks as blacks, homosexuals as homosexuals, Jews as Jews, and women as women is still rather misleading since it continues to affirm a separability of oppressions that simply is not possible.

This is not to say that separability is never possible. Certainly, there is the phenomenon of "passing": at least momentarily, for example, a Jewish woman might be able to "pass" as a non-Jewish white woman, forced to cope only with those obstacles placed in her path, including assumptions about her as a woman, that would normally affect a non-Jewish white woman (of her class or maybe of a higher class if she is "passing" with respect to class as well). Claims that she is now being treated merely "as a woman," however, not only ignore the fact that she is now being treated as a non-Jewish white woman of a certain class but also implicitly treat such women as the norm.

From the perspective of *Anti-Semite and Jew*, the fundamental question to be asked is: Is the Jew's position in society (or in French society in particular) sufficiently like that of homosexuals, blacks, and women (especially in U.S. society) that we can say similar things of all of them? From a more sophisticated stance on the complexity and inseparability of oppressions, a better formulation of the question would be: How do these complex positions differ and do their differences from one another support Sartre's claims about moral blame and metaphysical uneasiness in the case of Jews, or French Jews, but not in some or all of the other cases?[11]

Although the issues raised in the analyses of moral blame and metaphysical uneasiness now seem to me intricately connected, I choose nevertheless to explore possible answers to them separately, at least initially. This reflects my own struggles to understand what Sartre is saying and also enables me to present as clearly as possible what I see to be the critical difficulties.

1. Sartre's Treatment of Jewish Inauthenticity

Why would Sartre not hold Jews morally responsible and therefore subject to moral blame for inauthenticity emerging specifically from their position in anti-Semitic French society? Various possibilities present themselves in the context of *Anti-Semite and Jew*. First, before discussing the Jew, Sartre spends a good portion of the book analyzing the passion of the anti-Semite who, "longing for impenetrability," "attracted by the durability of stone," and "afraid of reasoning," chooses a hate and an anger that call forth the "facts" that supposedly support them and that have the effect of giving the anti-Semite an instant and unearned status. Out of a fear of being free, the anti-Semite makes a choice that at once confirms him, even—or especially—in his mediocrity, as superior, as a "true" Frenchman. Speaking from the perspective of one who makes such a choice, Sartre says:

> By treating the Jew as an inferior and pernicious being, I affirm at the same time that I belong to the elite. This elite, in contrast to those of modern times which are based on merit or labor, closely resembles an aristocracy of birth. There is nothing I have

to do to merit my superiority, and neither can I lose it. It is given once and for all. It is a *thing*.[12]

This analysis of the bad faith of the anti-Semite might tempt us to conclude that Sartre is simply trying to make sure that the creators of the untenable situation of the Jew receive the moral blame rather than those victimized by a situation not of their own making, something like the concern of feminists more recently to shift the blame for rape from the victims, the traditional recipients of blame, to those who actually do the raping. In both cases, the perpetrators' perspective seems to have dominated Western society, with the result that all too many have been ready to believe that it is something about the Jew or the woman that "made" the anti-Semite or the rapist "respond." A later passage from *Anti-Semite and Jew* offers support to the claim that Sartre is simply trying to place the blame properly:

> Whose is the fault? It is our eyes that reflect to him [the Jew] the unacceptable image that he wishes to dissimulate. It is our words and our gestures—*all* our words and *all* our gestures—our anti-Semitism, but equally our condescending liberalism—that have poisoned him. It is we who constrain him to choose to be a Jew whether through flight from himself or through self-assertion; it is we who force him into the dilemma of Jewish authenticity or inauthenticity.[13]

Although care in ascribing proper blame for the situation to which Jews may respond inauthentically is admirable and is most assuredly *part* of what Sartre is doing in his analyses of the anti-Semite and the Jew, it is sufficient only to explain why Sartre discusses the anti-Semite's inauthenticity *before* he examines that of the Jew. Sartre's analyses are themselves sufficient to show that specifically Jewish inauthenticity is derivative, in other words, that it is possible only on the basis of a prior inauthenticity—that of the anti-Semite. As Sartre later says, the Jew is "over-determined": although having "a personality like the rest of us" (and presumably all of the human problems non-Jews have to deal with, including the daily, non-anti-Semitic looks of others), the Jew is confronted with "a phantom personality, at once strange and familiar, that haunts him and which is nothing but himself—himself as others see him [as a Jew]."[14] Surely, Sartre can and should observe that the Jew must deal with this over-determination only because of the prior inauthenticity of the anti-Semite and, moreover, that the Jew should not have to deal with this inasmuch as the anti-Semite's inauthenticity, with its consequent contribution to the creation of the Jews' situation, should not be.

This in itself, though, is not enough to keep the Jew's derivative inauthenticity from being subject to moral blame. After all, we could just as easily free from moral blame others whose bad faith Sartre elsewhere describes and condemns. For example, the inauthenticity of Sartre's woman in the cafe is, like that of the Jew, a response to the inauthenticity of others, in her case, not just her lustful admirer's sexism as he turns her into a body to be used for his own pleasure but also her society's sexism that will condemn her as less than a woman if she does not inspire such desire in men but will denounce her as "loose" if she accepts too readily the advances she inspires. Certainly, we could free from all moral blame the homosexual who denies his homosexuality. After all, it exists only because of the prior inauthenticity of the champion of sincerity and other heterosexists and homophobes who have created a "nature" and destiny for homosexuals, one that over-determines the latter just as much as the "nature" constructed for Jews over-determines them. We could probably do the same for Sartre's waiter by noting that his bad faith is consequent to the social constructions of class and of the position of waiter with which he must cope. Even without granting Sartre's questionable claim that anti-Semitism is "a poor man's snobbery,"[15] we might be able to free many if not all anti-Semites from moral blame for their inauthenticity by pointing not just to the social constructions of class that situate these individuals but also to the prior constructions of anti-Semitism (which would, of course, be enormously tempting to those not particularly gifted or successful as well as to any who confront all of the negatives—the over-determination—of being lower class).

While excusing all of these other individuals from accountability and moral blame for their actions may seem familiar and perhaps even correct to many who have inherited and are still caught up in the worst aspects of the liberal political tradition in the U.S. (for which liberals have quite appropriately been characterized as "bleeding hearts"), all such freeing from moral blame seems quite contrary to the spirit of Sartre's many discussions of bad faith and inauthenticity. Certainly Sartre himself never hints that any of these other individuals is to be recognized as free from moral blame for her or his inauthenticity. Nor should he. Given his concern (and that of feminist theorists and various revolution strategists) for the plight of the oppressed, an emphasis on responsibility for one's own actions focuses much-needed attention on the freedom of the oppressed rather than solely on their victimization and consequent helplessness. This same attention would, of course, require that all of these other individuals be held responsible for those actions over which they have control.

If all we have to go on is the derivative nature of the Jew's inauthenticity, it would be difficult not to conclude that Sartre is simply responding to the situation of the Jew out of something like what is today called "liberal guilt," having recognized that it is the society made up of all Frenchmen (at least, of all Frenchmen as conceived by the anti-Semite) that created and continues to condone the existence of this anti-Semitism. This dismissive reading of Sartre's denial of moral blame is inadequate, though, given that there are, as we shall see, less psychologizing interpretations of his meaning that take into account far more of the text.

A second possibility was suggested by Julien Murphy in an unpublished paper, "Sartre on the Side of Things," on which I commented during a session of the Sartre Circle at the American Philosophical Association meeting in Atlanta, Georgia, in 1989. In this paper, Murphy showed that Sartre's being-for-others is not a simple, unproblematic, unified appearance. One's object-side is visible to a multiplicity of others and consequently subject to a multitude of interpretations, some of which may be diametrically opposed to others. As these various aspects of one's object-side are internalized, they become, according to Murphy, transposed into a cacophony of opposing and unequal "voices." Some of these "voices" have more authority or power because they are supported by others, perhaps by a significant majority. Some "speak" with the authority of institutions.

Following Murphy's suggestion, which seems basically right, we can see that oppression makes it extremely difficult for the oppressed to maintain the ambiguity, the tension of opposites, that, according to Sartre, they are as human beings (in this case, that of being-for-self and being-for-others). Even for the non-oppressed, this ambiguity seems difficult enough to maintain. After all, being-for-others encompasses one's materiality as well as the weight and authority of multiple others and institutions. Being-for-self seems of necessity to be somewhat tentative, subjective, and weak by comparison. In fact, Sartre's own analyses indicate that this is so. His discussion of valuing, for example, evinces his conviction that valuing cannot remain a subjective activity but must embody itself in action. All the weight of objectivity is on the side of being-for-others, and even being-for-self seems to require a continued externalization in the world.

For those who are oppressed, such externalization becomes problematic since with each action embodying the values and choices of the oppressed, institutions and multiple others undermine and deny the action. As Ralph Ellison's novel *Invisible Man* so effectively points out,[16] the oppressed may have difficulty just making themselves visible, much less making themselves visible in any particular way. Whether they attempt to embody the beauty of their non-heterosexual love affairs, the warmth and goodness of their unconventional families, or a valiant resistance to injustice, the loudest "voices" will make it plain that what is observed by the most powerful others is not beauty but vileness and ugliness, not warmth and goodness but base, animalistic, or barbaric behavior, not valiant resistance but primitive, uncultured, or childish behavior. For the oppressed, recognition by others is unlikely to support in any significant way their views of themselves if such views are at odds with the dominant ideology.

This failure to get significant—or perhaps any—recognition of an object-side bearing a resemblance to the way one sees oneself would indeed undermine the latter and make it very difficult to hold on to the ambiguity of being-for-self and being-for-others in an authentic way, recognizing them as possessing an "equal dignity of being," as Sartre says in *Being and Nothingness*, not allowing one to be reduced to the other.[17] Unfortunately, though, this difficulty is not sufficient for explaining his refusal to hold morally responsible the Jew who is engaged in specifically Jewish inauthenticity. After all, the torture victim must likewise find exceedingly difficult holding on to a view of self and a recognition of freedom amid the torturer's denunciations and deliberate use of pain, inflicted with the intention of getting the victim to identify totally with his or her body and way he or she is seen by the torturer. Even so, Sartre is famous for his unrelenting recognition of the torture victim as responsible.

A third and final possibility—and one that for a long time I believed to be the reason for Sartre's denial—involves his denial of race as connected with anything natural or even with the Jew's behavior. This possibility, like Murphy's acknowledgment of the strength of some of the "voices" that constitute one's object-side, emphasizes the way the object-side given to Jews in anti-Semitic society is totally unrelated not only to the way the Jew sees himself or herself but to what the Jew has actually done.

Sartre clearly rejects the existence of race as commonly understood: "that indefinable complex into which are tossed pell-mell both somatic characteristics and intellectual and moral traits, I believe in it no more than I do in ouija boards." Instead, all he can find are "certain inherited physical conformations that one encounters more frequently among Jews than among non-Jews."[18] With this understanding of race, Sartre, too, can turn the tables on the anti-Semite as does Bernard Malamud's "fixer" (a handyman in Tsarist Russia who is accused of a bizarre murder of a Christian child for no better reason than that the handyman is a Jew and in the wrong place at the wrong time) when he easily finds his prosecutor's nose-type in a chart of "Jewish noses."[19] "For lack of a better term," Sartre calls these more frequently encountered conformations "ethnic characteristics" while recognizing that they apply neither exclusively nor universally to Jews. This recognition forces Sartre to conclude that Jews have as a common bond only their *situation* as Jews, "that is, that they live in a community which takes them for Jews."[20] While many have taken umbrage at this, failing as it admittedly does to credit the way Jews have defined themselves, particularly religiously, I see in it rather a carrying out of the anti-Semite's own logic, a logic that recognizes that not all Jews are religious and that nonetheless lumps them all together, *regardless of how they see themselves*.

If this is the case, an individual Jew may—indeed should—react quite differently to the "nature" he or she is given by anti-Semitic society than to other looks. Whereas all of us have "object-sides" revealed to us by the looks of others, the Jew's additional being-for-others-as-a-Jew is something else again. In the case of the sort of object-sides that everyone receives through the ordinary and, as far as possible, non-racialized looks of others, there is generally some connection between the way we are seen and our bodies and actions. The particular other may be a bit myopic or a careless observer; but, still, what is observed usually has at least something to do with the individual observed. In the case of the additional object-side being given to the Jew, there may be absolutely no connection with any aspect of the particular Jew's embodiment or action.

This seems to introduce a radical difference between the socially constructed "nature" that over-determines the Jew and those that over-determine homosexuals and women. It also makes Jewishness differ from class. The radical difference between Jewishness and these other over-determinations, then, is that in the latter there is usually, though certainly not always, something in individuals' situations that connects them with the way they are being seen by others (besides just their having been taken by others to be homosexuals, women, and lower class). In the case of Jewishness, there may be no such connection whatsoever. Such lack of connection would tend to invalidate totally the way the Jew sees herself or himself and, considering the weight and institutional authority observed by Murphy on the side of these "seeings," make it extraordinarily difficult to hold on to this more ephemeral, subjective perspective, much less to acknowledge it as having a "dignity of being" equal to that of one's being-for-others.

If race is not connected with physical features or actions, then a racially oppressive look and the object-side it confers on an individual will be radically different from other looks and the object-sides they reveal. Given this difference, it might make sense to recognize the situations of those who are racially oppressed as quite different from those of others who are over-determined as the result of non-racial oppressions. With this recognition, specifically Jewish inauthenticity could justifiably be treated differently from some other forms of inauthenticity. And this may well be part of what is going on in Sartre's refusal to ascribe moral blame to the former. It would, of course, be necessary to extend this to all who are singled out for similar treatment on the basis of race. After all, what Sartre says about race seems correct and apparently is meant to apply to all allegedly racial distinctions, not just to that of Jewishness.[21]

My hunch, though, is that this is not all that is going on in Sartre's refusal to cast moral blame on specifically Jewish inauthenticity. In order to determine what else might be involved in this refusal, however, I see no other way to proceed than to turn to the second issue raised for me by *Anti-Semite and Jew*, that of metaphysical uneasiness.

2. Jews and Metaphysical Uneasiness/Existentialism

To understand why Jews cannot allow themselves metaphysical uneasiness requires, according to Sartre's analysis, that we understand and take seriously what he calls Jewish uneasiness. The latter uneasiness follows from the Jew's position—or, more accurately, lack of position—in society. The Jew's foothold in any society is precarious: "His history is one of wandering over the course of twenty centuries; at any moment he must be ready to pick up his stick and his bundle." Because of their lack of position, Jews lack a rootedness in the world and have no assuredness of rights. Living in jeopardy, they live in fear, a fear that means that Jews dare not "raise questions about the place of man in the world and his ultimate destiny." Sartre gives this tragic portrait of the inauthentic Jew in anti-Semitic French society:

> Such, then, is this haunted man, condemned to make his choice of himself on the basis of false problems and in a false situation, deprived of the metaphysical sense by the hostility of the society that surrounds him, driven to a rationalism of despair. His life is nothing but a long flight from others and from himself. He has been alienated even from his own body; his emotional life has been cut in two; he has been reduced to pursuing the impossible dream of universal brotherhood in a world that rejects him.[22]

In this portrait of the inauthentic Jew, Sartre may be claiming only that generally those challenging society need some fairly firm ground on which to stand. While this is probably a rather astute psychological observation, it would not be sufficient to undermine existentialism itself as that ground, much as I used it, in graduate school and later, when I launched my attacks against those who tried to push me back into what they perceived as my "place."

Rather, Sartre's point about the Jew's relation to metaphysical uneasiness seems to be more metaphysical than psychological, namely, that there is in the Jew's lack of position something that forbids a grounding in metaphysical uneasiness. The only way to make sense of this more metaphysical claim is to take seriously Sartre's discussion, at the beginning of the book, of the anti-Semite's Manichaean construction of the Jew as radically evil. In this earlier analysis, Sartre suggests that all the inconsistent anti-Semitic charges made against Jews can be understood only against the implicit claim of anti-Semitism: that there is in the Jew "a metaphysical principle that drives him *to do evil* under all circumstances, even though he thereby destroy himself." The Jew is thereby recognized as free in a "carefully limited" way:

> The Jew is free *to do evil*, not good; he has only as much free will as is necessary for him to take full responsibility for the crimes of

which he is the author; he does not have enough to be able to achieve a reformation. Strange liberty, which instead of preceding and constituting the essence, remains subordinate to it, is only an irrational quality of it, and yet remains liberty.[23]

Sartre goes on to observe somewhat sarcastically how convenient it is that all the evil in the universe is located in unarmed and totally defenseless individuals, thus making extraordinarily easy and simple the anti-Semite's doing of "good." In characterizing this anti-Semitism as Manichaean, though, Sartre depicts the uniqueness of this form of racism—and its uniqueness vis-à-vis sexism. He thereby makes obvious, too, why the Jew is uncertain of his position, why the Jew has no position in society. Sartre's recognition of the Manichaeism of anti-Semitism also clarifies why it is that "the situation of the Jew is such that everything he does turns against him."[24]

Whatever the position of women in a sexist society like that of the U.S., it simply is not the case that *everything* they do turns against them and that they have no place. Marilyn Frye is correct when she observes that women are placed in situations where there may be nothing they can do that is unambiguously in their own interest. To cite one of her examples, young women frequently find themselves in a position where they lose whether they are sexually active or inactive: if they are sexually active, they are "whores" or at least "loose" women, hence, supposedly *incapable of being raped*, and if they are sexually inactive, they are uptight, frigid, and thereby *in need of rape*.[25] Even so, there is a place for such women, particularly if they are white, middle-class, and without physical and mental impairments. If these women marry and particularly if they then become pregnant, they are likely to receive affirmation and respect at a level they never previously believed possible.

Most assuredly, this is not to say that such affirmations come at no cost. Clearly, there are various downsides to being a "good woman." As many traditional women discover at the time of divorce, courts frequently ignore women's unpaid labor in their homes and conclude that those with no income of their own from outside jobs have made no financial contribution to any purchases. No matter how complicated the place and ambivalent the approval, though, women—at least non-Jewish white women—have a "place" in sexist U.S. society and receive some approval for staying in this place. Barring overlaps with some other oppressions, it is possible to be a "good woman." Unlike the Jew, such a woman does not have everything she does turn against her just because she is a woman, at least not directly and unambiguously.

Similarly, Laurence Mordekhai Thomas has convincingly demonstrated that during slavery anti-black racism in the U.S. allowed a place for blacks and praised the "good" black who stayed in his or her place.[26] Consequently, albeit in a rather perverse way, slavery valued blacks, at least under certain conditions, and did not involve, as did the Holocaust, a campaign to exterminate. Although many blacks were killed deliberately as well as inadvertently and few if any of their killers suffered any legal or moral recriminations for their actions, extermination was not the goal of slavery.

After slavery, anti-black racism in the U.S. has no doubt become rather more complicated with at least some of its expressions clearly denying blacks any place, certainly any place in the U.S. Still, though, other expressions of such racism have continued to affirm a place, with movies, for example, lovingly portraying the sometimes simpleminded, always loyal black servant to a white family, more devoted to that family than to his or her own, the latter usually being totally invisible both to the white family and to the moviegoer. As Beauvoir observed during her trip to the U.S. in the late 1940s: "Racialists admit for the most part that the negro is not *a priori* evil; it is only when he leaves his natural status that he becomes a danger, if he 'stays put' he can be a 'good nigger' full of estimable qualities." This allegedly natural status is not, however, as she notes, wholly positive in the eyes of those racialists, whence the "vicious circle denounced by Bernard Shaw: 'The proud American nation . . . compels the black man to polish his [its?] shoes, and demonstrate thereby his physical and mental inferiority by the mere fact that he is a shoe polisher.' " Nevertheless, like colonists in all colonial countries, she adds, the white American will tritely maintain: "the proof that the place assigned to him is good for the negro is the fact that he is happy."[27]

The position of homosexuals vis-à-vis place and "goodness" is a bit more difficult to discern. Quite clearly, at least non-Jewish gay males and lesbians generally have a place and a way of being "good"—if they are willing to renounce their homosexuality. Present-day champions of sincerity often approach homosexuals and the "issue" of homosexuality as though all that individuals so designated need to do is acknowledge the error of their ways and live henceforth on the straight and narrow. This, however, is another way of saying, it seems to me, that there may be no such thing as a good homosexual and that homophobia and heterosexism allow them no place.

Perhaps, though, that conclusion is somewhat precipitate. Something, after all, must be said about the fact that so many heterosexuals seem to be attracted to homosexuals, particularly to gay males, and to find them necessary in a variety of ways. The question to be dealt with here is whether this attraction is like that of Sartre's anti-Semite for whom "it is not unusual to see one of these sworn enemies of Israel surround himself with Jewish friends," while insisting that "they are 'exceptional Jews,' . . . that 'these aren't like the rest.' " Sartre analyzes this attraction as follows: "Actually they take pleasure in protecting these few persons through a sort of inversion of their sadism; they take pleasure in keeping under their eyes the living image of this people whom they execrate." Sartre suggests that anti-Semitic women's motivations may be sexual: they "often have a mixture of sexual repulsion and attraction toward Jews." Men, too, though, may find a special sexual signification in the words "a beautiful Jewess," as phrase that Sartre goes on to analyze as "carry[ing] an aura of rape and massacre."[28]

The sexual unavailability of homosexual men to heterosexual women and of lesbian women to heterosexual men suggests that any attraction of the latter to the former in each of these pairs is likely to be somewhat more complicated than that suggested by Sartre in the case of Jews and anti-Semites. And indeed the attractions do seem far more complex. Some heterosexual women may be living vicariously through their attraction or even attachment to a homosexual relationship, identifying with one or alternatively both of the males in it. Some may simply prefer the company of gay males because, as Young-Bruehl observes, "these men are not threatening to them as men and because they make excellent confidants."[29] On the other hand, what many of these heterosexual women find attractive in some homosexual men is no doubt their non-investment in the myths of masculinity endorsed by many heterosexual and even homosexual men. This does not mean that all of these women would want all heterosexual men to be less stereotypically masculine. Though some homophobic women may be attracted to and surround themselves with gay males out of homophobia just as Sartre's anti-Semite surrounds himself with Jews, "exceptions," some homophobia probably enters into the attraction of other heterosexual women to gay males inasmuch as the attraction, based on the gay males' differences from the other men in the women's lives, may exist alongside repulsion against the very thought of gay male sexual attraction and lovemaking. Similarly but often without sexual attraction, a heterosexual woman may find the services of many gay males essential and pretend not to understand what those males may do or might wish to do with other men, an awareness homophobic women probably would find most distressing. In all of these cases, gay males seem to have a place, even a rather positive one; but homophobia allows them a place, it seems, only as long as they keep their gayness a matter of abstract possibility.

Homophobic males' attractions to homosexuals seem even more complicated. These seem to range from the naive to the extraordinarily threatened where lesbians are concerned. The naive reactions fail to take lesbian relationships seriously, assuming that whatever the lesbians may do sexually with each other is simply heterosexual female sexuality of a different form, that is, female sexuality constructed from and inviting the male gaze and even participation. The extremely threatened reactions take lesbian relationships seriously, so seriously in fact that their very existence is seen as endangering all of the homophobe's relationships with women and maybe even his masculinity. It is such individuals who threaten rape, who rape, or who even kill lesbians resisting the male's advances or dressing and acting in ways he recognizes as not intended to invite him sexually. Young-Bruehl notes that "[m]asculine lesbians attract more violence—men war against them as though they were men. . . ."[30]

While I do not pretend to understand all that is going on in such individuals, it seems obvious enough that they are not really attracted to the lesbians or to the women they perceive as lesbians. More likely, the homophobes' sense of power or sense of self is threatened, and they respond accordingly, in a way designed to destroy the threat. Perhaps even those who rape women they take to be lesbians are, as they often profess, attempting to change the women into heterosexuals and thereby to destroy the perceived threat. This suggests something closer to the Manichaeism of the anti-Semitism described by Sartre and helps to make sense of the way, for example, homosexuals were forced to wear pink triangles by the Nazis and were exterminated in death camps along with Jews.

Unlike lesbians, gay males would not be seen as necessarily sexually unavailable by heterosexual men. This would no doubt lead some homophobic, heterosexually-identified men to feel a combination of attraction and repulsion toward gay men. To the extent that many of the most homophobic of these heterosexually-identified men have serious and un-resolved problems about their own masculinity, frequently even about their own heterosexuality, their reaction to gay males is likely to be like that of the anti-Semite to the Jew and would, like the latter, be premised on the destruction of the evil represented by those seen as exerting the attraction, a destruction that may result in killing. On the other hand, the destruction might be achieved by a threat to rape or even an actual rape of a gay male, each designed either to put the gay male in his proper place as not really a man but rather a woman or, like a beating, to make him afraid of ever again revealing or exercising his sexuality. Quite possibly, rather than being an attempt to destroy the gay male or the attraction he is seen as exerting, raping or threatening to rape him may simply evince the strong and unresolved homosexual desire on the part of the homophobe, in which case it would not deny but would rather affirm, however disastrously for the victim, a place for gays.

A different kind of attraction of homophobic males to gay males can be seen in those of the former who attend drag shows. These men make me think of Michel Foucault's description of people in the towns and cities of Europe at one time flocking to see the mad in their cages much as people today go to zoos to see animals in their cages. Foucault sees this treatment of the insane as serving to give the rest of society a sense of what is "normal" and reassurances of their own normality.[31] Perhaps homophobic males who frequent drag shows are using the drag queens in much the same way, namely, as reinforcers of the homophobics' sense of themselves as "normal" males, as masculine, and of society as properly constituted by two clearly distinct genders. To achieve this, the homo-phobes must reconstitute the men performing in the show as women, just as they are presenting themselves for the performance. Such members of the audience can then leave the show comfortably reassured about the way they see themselves and their world. By obliterating the drag queens as men and seeing them rather as the women they appear to be, with their own proper place, the place already assigned to women, this homo-phobic move may destroy what would otherwise by a threat, leaving a thoroughgoing heterosexuality, at least on the surface of things, and a comfortable universe with everything in its place.

The anti-Semite also, as Sartre says, has "a vital need for the very enemy he wishes to destroy" since if there were no Jews, then everyone would be "true Frenchmen"; and this would devalue the distinction, it no longer serving to distinguish the anti-Semite from any others.[32] The anti-Semite, though, unlike the homophobe, cannot obliterate the Jew's threat in any way other than by destroying the person of the Jew. Whether the anti-Semite needs real live Jews to serve his "vital need" is unclear. Perhaps others, such as immigrants, can replace the Jews; or maybe metaphorical "Jews" can be created by the anti-Semite to serve the purpose, for example, by turning "Jewishness" into a mysterious essence penetrating those with "bad" ideas or beliefs or proclivities. In some such way, presumably, homosexuals could, and in Nazi Germany perhaps did, assume this role, thus guaranteeing an ever-fresh supply of "Jews" even for those determined to destroy such individuals.

From this no doubt much too superficial overview of homophobia and the relationships between homophobes and homosexuals, I conclude that homosexuals are more like Jews than are either blacks or women, there being no clear social place for homosexuals and no clear way they can be "good" as homosexuals. Unlike Jews, though, homosexuals seem able to inhabit a number of places, with some ambiguous ways of being "good" as a consequence. Moreover, since the negative treatment of homosexuals is not based on their Manichaean embodiment of evil but rather on their stepping out of their supposedly naturally assigned heterosexual place in the world, homosexuals, like blacks and women but unlike Jews confronting the sort of anti-Semitism examined by Sartre, could profitably use metaphysical uneasiness and existentialism to unsettle these allegedly natural places.

I think this successfully unravels my earlier difficulties with both Sartre's refusal to invoke moral blame on specifically Jewish inauthenticity and his suggestion that Jews cannot afford to be existentialists. After all, unlike my own experience of delight with the metaphysical uneasiness of existentialism, the experience of the Jews Sartre discusses does not include a place assigned to them that is capable of being challenged by being unsettled. Given their "placelessness," Jews would not be advantaged as I was by metaphysical uneasiness since its use against the anti-Semite is probably more likely to support rather than unsettle the anti-Semite's passion. Any appeal to reason and to ambiguity seems likely only to underscore the difference affirmed by the anti-Semite between himself and the Jew. Moreover, given the anti-Semite's choice of passion, confronting challenges and even self-contradiction may serve to confirm rather than destabilize his choice just as, according to Being and Nothingness, one in bad faith may respond to inconsistency and failure by deliberately choosing such inconsistency and failure.[33]

Furthermore and quite apart from the resiliency of the anti-Semite when faced with counterargument, since Jews have no assigned place against which they can levy an existential challenge, all that remains for them is to attempt to undermine the very distinction between good and evil so prominent in the thought of the anti-Semite. But a challenge to this distinction is more likely than not simply to solidify it and to support the invidious way the anti-Semite applies it to the Jew. After all, such a frontal attack on the "good" and consequently on anti-Semitism itself is all too likely to be dismissed as nothing more than the clever dissimulation of "Jewish intelligence," further evidence of the evil of the Jew. This is just one more indication of the way everything in anti-Semitic society turns against the Jew.

Unlike the Jew, a woman who has a place will not experience everything turning against her. Although she may very well experience a great deal turning against her, particularly if she tries to leave her place, even that is likely to happen quite differently from the way things turn against a Jew. For example, a woman may aspire to be a philosopher, may study philosophy, may argue philosophically, and may use, as I did, existentialism in general and metaphysical uneasiness in particular against those why deny not only that she should do such things but even that she *can* do them. Those she challenges are likely to be at least somewhat unsettled even if they, like the anti-Semite, give themselves "the *right* to play," to make frivolous remarks, to offer ridiculous reasons, to be absurd while "they discredit the seriousness of their interlocutors."[34] Their unsettling can occur at least in part because the woman's philosophical life and existential arguments are of a piece. By her very existence as well as by her argument, she is challenging the comfortable categories of those who affirm natures, destinies, and unquestionable male prerogatives; and I suspect that her existence may unsettle and threaten the sexist's choice of passion far more that her arguments have a chance of doing. I think, in fact, that this is just another way of noting the difference between a woman (when race does not enter negatively into the consideration) and a Jew (when gender does not enter negatively into the consideration) and the fact that one has a place—a "natural" one, at that—and the other does not, that one has the possibility of being "good" while the other does not.

The woman's greater chance of unsettling that which she opposes may follow from another aspect of her difference from the Jew. Anti-Semitism of the sort Sartre discusses sets up a universe in which the Jew is the embodiment of all evil, so the person who adopts an anti-Semitic position not only finds it remarkably easy to do "good" but also is less vulnerable to unsettling. While there may seem to be some parallels between the anti-Semite's position and that of the sexist man, similarity quickly gives way to difference. The masculinity of the sexist male is, like the goodness of anti-Semites, established largely by contrast. What "women" are, "men" are not; but women can leave their assigned place, since they have one, whereas Jews, having no "place" to leave, cannot. Whatever a Jew does will be taken by the anti-Semite as evil, but it simply cannot be said that a sexist man will take just anything that a woman does as an exemplification of her nature as a woman. Rather, she may do things that, if recognized, call into question his difference from her and hence his masculinity and ultimately the very "natures" to which he has such a deep and passionate commitment.

Conclusion

Differences between the position of the Jew in French society and that of at least some women in U.S. society may thus support Sartre's claim that Jews cannot afford metaphysical uneasiness and confirm my sense from my own experience not only that many women can afford this uneasiness but that it can be extraordinarily useful to them. These differences, though, challenge Sartre's inclusion in the ranks of those who cannot allow themselves metaphysical uneasiness both the worker and "oppressed minorities or classes."[35] Just as blacks and women are often recognized as each having a "place" and as being "good" so long as they remain there, so, too, I think, are workers, lower classes, and many other oppressed minorities. I can only conclude that Sartre himself at this point in the book errs in seeing too much common ground among Jews, workers, and other oppressed minorities and classes.

Finally, the differences between Jews and some others who are oppressed offer additional insight into Sartre's refusal to ascribe moral blame to Jewish inauthenticity. The Jew's position in anti-Semitic French society is peculiarly impossible. Pressed by the anti-Semite and by the democrat into equally inauthentic alternatives, the Jew's position is further circumscribed by anti-Semitic society so that authenticity itself is tainted and turns against him, even to the extent of supporting the anti-

Semitic society that crushes him psychologically if not physically. Thus, Sartre says:

> [W]hen all is calm, against whom is he to revolt? He accepts the society around him, he joins the game and he conforms to all the ceremonies, dancing with the others the dance of respectability. Besides, he is nobody's slave; he is a free citizen under a regime that allows free competition; he is forbidden no social dignity, no office of the state. He may be decorated with the ribbon of the Legion of Honor, he may become a great lawyer or a cabinet minister. But at the very moment when he reaches the summits of legal society, another society—amorphous, diffused, and omnipresent—appears before him as if in brief flashes of lightning and refuses to take him in. How sharply must he feel the vanity of honors and of fortune, when the greatest success will never gain him entrance into that society which considers itself the "real" one. As a cabinet minister, he will be a Jewish cabinet minister, at once an "Excellency" and an untouchable. And yet he never encounters any particular resistance; people seem, rather, to be in flight before him; an impalpable chasm widens out, and, above all, an invisible chemistry devaluates all that he touches.[36]

This suggests that Sartre is treating the problem of Jewish inauthenticity in much the same way that he elsewhere treats the problem of violence, a problem in which impossible situations also figure strongly.[37] In discussing violence, Sartre condemns the violence of an oppressive status quo. Such violence conflicts with the affirmation of freedom envisioned in his ideal of the city of ends. At the same time, condoning whatever violence is needed to unsettle the status quo is also unacceptable: justifying such violence as a means endorses what he calls "the maxim of violence" (the end justifies the means) which in turn serves as a cornerstone to the status quo. Worse, though, for him, endorsing violence as an acceptable means to an otherwise praiseworthy end compromises and distorts the end to which the violence was to serve as means.

Yet simply to condemn violence in a situation of oppression also supports the status quo and makes the goal of human freedom nothing but an idealistic and ineffectual dream. Those who work to end oppression must therefore adhere to an ethics in which acts of violence are clearly condemned; at the same time, these reformers and revolutionaries must recognize that oppressive societies and the violence of others sometimes place individuals in impossible situations where violence cannot be avoided. Acting against the oppression may of necessity involve violence; but not acting against the oppression affirms, collaborates with, and even reinforces the oppression and its violence.

Perhaps a similar analysis needs to be made of the options available to the Jew in anti-Semitic French society. Because of the prior inauthenticity of others, Jews are in a position where they are pressured to be inauthentic and where even authentic action will turn against them. This is not exactly parallel to the impossible situation in which all of an individual's choices are violent since Sartre quite clearly recognizes that a specifically Jewish authenticity is possible; but the Jew's situation does bear a strong resemblance to impossible situations inasmuch as all options available to the Jew, at least in times of "calm," are problematic in their different ways of deliberately or inadvertently feeding into and affirming the anti-Semitism of the society. Perhaps this recognition, too, ultimately softens Sartre's moral judgment of Jewish inauthenticity.

Even without this promising connection with what Sartre says elsewhere about violence and impossible situations, the recognition that French anti-Semitism denies its victims a place and any sense in which they can be good is an important contribution to our understanding of differences between at least some anti-Semitism and sexism, heterosexism, along with some other forms of racism. With this recognition, we can make sense of puzzling claims in *Anti-Semite and Jew*, particularly that concerning the Jew's relation to metaphysical uneasiness and thus to existentialism itself. We see how acknowledging societal oppression does indeed complicate our relations with one another, even with what we dare ask for and expect from one another in our philosophical pursuits. In this way we come a bit closer as well to understanding the truth of Sartre's claim that "it is quite impossible to treat concrete men as ends in contemporary society."[38]

Notes

1. Jean-Paul Sartre, *Anti-Semite and Jew*, trans. George J. Becker (New York: Schocken Books, 1965), 93.
2. Ibid., 132–33.
3. In commenting on this paper at the inaugural meeting of the Georgia Continental Philoso-

phy Circle on 18 November 1995, Michael B. Smith observed that Judaism itself gave Jews reasons to find existentialism most "remote" and that a sense of metaphysical uneasiness constantly "vexed" them historically. Citing the Book of Job, Smith then says: "Judaism has practically institutionalized metaphysical insecurity, ritualizing the quest and the question into its ceremonies, renewing its scrutiny of the Torah for clues, crying out in the Psalms for reassurance and comfort." These comments raise interesting and important questions: do these aspects of Sartre's account merely reflect the ignorance about Judaism of which he has been frequently accused? is there is a way of being metaphysically insecure that is embedded in Judaism? and, if so, does that religiously embedded metaphysical uneasiness undermine Jews' resistance to anti-Semitism in the way that, according to Sartre, such resistance would be affected by the non-religious sort of metaphysical uneasiness he examines? Important as they are, however, these are questions beyond my competence and beyond the issues I wish to address in this paper.

4. Sartre, *Anti-Semite and Jew*, 133.

5. Particularly Zenia Chavez and others in my spring quarter 1995 Readings in Existentialism, who were willing to keep discussing these issues with me in several consecutive class meetings.

6. Simone de Beauvoir, *The Second Sex*, trans. H. M. Parshley (New York: Vintage Books, 1974), xxvii.

7. Elisabeth Young-Bruehl, *The Anatomy of Prejudice* (Cambridge: Harvard University Press, 1996), 85, 137.

8. Ibid., 414.

9. Sartre, *Anti-Semite and Jew*, 48–49.

10. See Elizabeth V. Spelman, *The Inessential Woman: Problems of Exclusion in Feminist Thought* (Boston: Beacon Press, 1988).

11. Since I am interested in uncovering similarities and differences only to the extent necessary to answer this question, I shall not even try to illuminate all the differences possible—and actual— within each of these oppressions. For an interesting typology of prejudices based on obsessional, hysterical, and narcissistic character types, see Young-Bruehl, *Anatomy*.

12. Sartre, *Anti-Semite and Jew*, 17–19, 22, 27.

13. Ibid., 135.

14. Ibid., 78–79.

15. Ibid., 26.

16. See Ralph Ellison, *Invisible Man* (New York: New American Library, 1953).

17. Jean-Paul Sartre, *Being and Nothingness*, trans. Hazel E. Barnes (New York: Philosophical Library, 1956), 58.

18. Ibid., 61.

19. Bernard Malamud, *The Fixer* (New York: Dell, 1967).

20. Sartre, *Anti-Semite and Jew*, p. 67.

21. For additional analyses of race to support Sartre's analysis, see the work of W. E. B. Du Bois, Lucius Outlaw, and Kwame Anthony Appiah.

22. Sartre, *Anti-Semite and Jew*, 132–33, 135.

23. Ibid., 39.

24. Ibid., 141.

25. Marilyn Frye, *The Politics of Reality* (Trumansburg, Crossing Press, 1983), 3.

26. See Laurence Mordekhai Thomas, *Vessels of Evil: American Slavery and the Holocaust* (Philadelphia: Temple University Press, 1993).

27. Simone de Beauvoir, *America Day by Day*, trans. Patrick Dudley (London: Gerald Duckworth 1952), 186–87.

28. Sartre, *Anti-Semite and Jew*, 47–48.

29. Young-Bruehl, *Anatomy*, 149.

30. Ibid., 150.

31. Michel Foucault, *Madness and Civilization: A History of Insanity in the Age of Reason*, trans. Richard Howard (New York: Vintage Books, 1973), 68–70.

32. Sartre, *Anti-Semite and Jew*, 28.

33. Sartre, *Being and Nothingness*, 69.

34. Sartre, *Anti-Semite and Jew*, 20.

35. Ibid., 133.

36. Ibid., 79–80.

37. For a thorough discussion of Sartre's treatment of violence see Chapter 5—"The Role of Violence in Ethics"—in my *Rethinking Ethics in the Midst of Violence: A Feminist Approach to Freedom* (Lanham, Md.: Rowman and Littlefield, 1993).

38. Sartre, *What Is Literature?* trans. Bernard Frechtman (New York: Harper and Row, 1965), 269.

7

Existential Freedom and Political Change

Sarah Lucia Hoagland

Existential freedom is not political freedom. So how do I move from an ontological understanding of existential freedom to possibilities of political resistance and change under conditions of oppression? This is not a scholastic piece; it is part storytelling, part conversation, and part collage—a playing with ideas from Sartre, Beauvoir, and Fanon that resonate in me. There is much to criticize in Sartre's work, such as his self-absorbed individualism,[1] his notion of transcendence,[2] his reading of female sexuality.[3] So I will make free with ideas I've found, not trying to be faithful to a tradition but faithful instead to my own query.

This work has benefited from the attentive comments of Jackie Anderson, Julien Murphy, and Anne Throop Leighton.

In my experience students are drawn to existentialism. An ethics of freedom seems much more useful to my students, who include former gang-bangers, women in the grips of male violence, and many who survive in the midst of white racism, than an ethics of universal principles and duty or an ethics of the greatest good or an ethics of care. As Linda Bell argues, these theories do little to challenge oppression and violence, particularly when systemic (Bell 1993). But generally it is existentialism that is written off as having no ethics or politics; certainly Beauvoir's *The Ethics of Ambiguity* is not regarded as a central text by many philosophers. That has been the canon's and students' loss. Beauvoirian and Sartrean existentialism was born in war but it is not only wartime. In war, the volatileness of everything becomes so obvious that it is harder to deny, harder to tell oneself another story that lets one look away from existential freedom, uncertainty, and change.

Existential freedom means who we are, our character, is not determined in advance of our birth—existence precedes essence—or by the facticity/material conditions of our existence. There is no immutable human nature, no a priori human essence. Religious theories such as Christianity, as well as biological, Marxist, and psychoanalytic theories, all make claims in various ways about human destiny: spiritual, material, and symbolic claims about who we are and the value and meaning of our lives (note Beauvoir's discussion [1952, bk. 1, pt. 1]. In a sense, Sartrean existentialism in the ideal[4] also makes a claim about our nature—it is our nature to be free/undetermined—but not about our meaning(s) or destiny.

Existential freedom is centrally negative. But it is not the Anglo-European liberal male idea of freedom as absence of restraint or restriction which assumes an already constituted agent, for existential freedom persists in the midst of restraint and oppression. Even the political prisoner being taken to her death is existentially free, though certainly not politically free. Existential freedom is not the idea that if we were just left alone we would be free to make choices, an idea already exposed by Hegel as naive for its failure to consider historical forces affecting our choices.[5] While Sartre gives precious little consideration to such forces, to this aspect of our facticity, his contention is that who we are is not predetermined by those forces. The prisoner, for example, still has the choice to walk proudly to her death, to put up such a resistance that guards are forced to drug her, to go limp and force her jailers to drag her, to curl under in resignation.

I find it interesting that while I did change Sartre's prisoner from male to female, I can't forget that while she is going to her death, she was raped when she was tortured. Jeffner is right, of course, I can't just insert women in existentialism where there were men, at least not without comment (Allen 1989). How does this affect her choices when she walks among men who would annihilate her pride, her resistance, and thereby construct a piece of meat in whom such qualities do not exist? Does she still walk proudly? Yes and no.[6]

Concomitantly, for Sartre, there is no deity, no absolute Value that gives meaning to what we experience, that fixes and determines things, that will right human wrongs, clean up after the human mess we have made. No armageddon, no final day of judgment, no time when evil will be vanquished despite what we do. Whatever exists are values that humans have chosen, have created. And what will exist is a matter of our continued, everyday choices. So long as racism and sexism and anti-Semitism persist, for example, it is because we have chosen them; apparently they are means through which we make our lives meaningful and find a place for ourselves among others. "The process of cultural erasure and domination is a daily affair, carried out by ordinary persons differently located in society in their daily interactions" (Lugones and Price n.d.).

For Sartre, as for Beauvoir, freedom, responsibility, and choice are entwined. As I come to understand the contingent nature of human values, I come to understand that what I choose by virtue of my everyday actions is what I make meaningful. If the woman next door screams and I hear noises from her home and I do nothing about it, I am valuing the ignoring of womanabuse, perhaps because I do not want to incorporate in my life what that acknowledgment would mean. No big daddy is going to come and protect women from womanabuse, in fact big daddy is often a perp. There is only our society, you and me, and so far as a society, we have chosen womanabuse.

> Whether or not [Nicole Simpson's] ex-husband committed the murder, he did continue to assault her, threaten her, stalk her, intimidate her. . . . Nicole Simpson, like every battered woman, knew she would not be believed . . . has to be careful, even with strangers. His friends won't stop him. Neither will yours. . . . Nicole Simpson went to many experts on domestic violence for help but none of them stopped *him*. That's what it takes: the batterer has to be stopped. . . . Wife-beating is not

Amerika's dirty little secret. . . . Wife-beating is commonplace
and ordinary because men believe they have rights over women
that women dispute.

Accounts of wife-beating have typically been met with incre-
dulity and disdain, best expressed by the persistent question,
"Why doesn't she leave?" But after two decades of learning about
battery, we now know that more battered women are killed after
they leave than before. (Dworkin 1997, 44, 42–43)

Those of us who let the screams go unanswered are embracing the
status quo, which is to blame her and ignore him. That is a choice, that
is the value we as individuals in this society create and bring to meaning.
There is nothing, NOTHING, about her nature that determines she be
abused. And there is nothing, NOTHING, about his nature that determines he will abuse.

*Writing this is complex. Women who have been abused will be reading this,
as well as men who abuse. It is easy to focus on women who are abused or
even abusers and let the rest of us approach reports of womanabuse as if we
are at a movie, an audience, inquiring minds. But I want to focus on us, on
the woman's and the man's friends, neighbors, colleagues.* "In order for the
oppressor to get a clear view of an unjustifiable situation, it is not enough
to look at it honestly, he must also change the structure of his eyes"
(Sartre 1974, 229, cited in Murphy 1989). *The possibilities of political
change and resistance involve changing the structure of our eyes.*

Freedom, responsibility, and choice are entwined because existential
freedom, while part of the ontological nature of our existence, is nevertheless something we must choose, embrace, to be authentic; that is central to our moral agency, ability. And there are myriad ways we try to
avoid that, flee choice.

Beauvoir describes a child cast into a universe she did not make; her
choices are to submit or resist. We come to moral possibility when, often
as adolescents, we realize that the world of our parents or those with
authority over us is not ready-made, that there are other values, other
possibilities. From this point on, what we live by is what we choose, from
our everyday actions to momentous decisions. Bad faith, inauthenticity,
is running away from acknowledging our choices, insisting instead, in a
variety of ways, that we had no choice, or that matters calling for choice
have nothing to do with us (Beauvoir 1980, chap. 2).

Beauvoir describes several types who flee choice: the subman who takes refuge in ready-made values and will make himself part of a mob; the serious man who rids himself of freedom by claiming to subordinate himself to unconditional values, putting nothing to question; the nihilist, often a disappointed serious man, who decides, because there is no ultimate justification, to do nothing and mocks those who do; the adventurer who, close to the genuinely free man, nevertheless remains indifferent to the context and becomes a mercenary; the passionate man; the intellectual; the artist; all who set up absolutes. The genuinely free man is one who wills himself free by willing an open future, by willing the freedom of others (Beauvoir 1980, chap. 2).

This time I cannot just insert women, change subman *to* subwoman. *I can't do this not because women don't join mobs (we do). I can't do it because the man considered here is he for whom the world is arranged, for whom it works, or at the very least, to whom it is addressed, and who accepts this without thought. (Many men have been excluded from the world of men in various ways and when trying to engage become Invisible Men, so this man she speaks of is also not everyman.) While many women have claimed significant places in a world of men, nevertheless our worlds are not arranged for us but more properly against us, and so when we flee freedom, it is more complex.*

Sartre gives an example of a woman who goes out with a man for a conversation in the middle of which he grabs her hand and she ignores it (Sartre 1956, 55). Sartre shows here the presumption of a man who believes he has rights over women. For him the situation is nothing but a sexual scene. Apparently a woman would never go out with a man to have an intellectual conversation; *good grief, did he ever understand Beauvoir? (But then I find heterosexuality puzzling in a way Beauvoir did not.)* A woman engages in conversation, a man grabs her hand, she ignores it. Is this bad faith? They agreed to a meal and conversation. He changed the articulated parameters of the encounter in favor of an unspoken game she is to know about and subtly acquiesce to but had no part in agreeing to, and she, parrying his move with a countermove that interrupts (at least momentarily) his agenda, is charged with bad faith.

Beauvoir's subman is not Sartre's woman, though a woman might also be a subman. Still, why she joins the mob will have dimensions that why he joins does not. Andrea Dworkin suggests some right-wing women give meaning to their lives of abuse by joining with their abuser and focusing their rage on a common "enemy," a scapegoat. Their choice is a choice made in the grips of violence. "Using both force and threat, men in all camps demand that women accept abuse in silence and shame, tie themselves to hearth and home with rope made of self-blame, unspoken rage, grief, and resentment" (Dworkin 1983, 95). Certainly under these conditions they can become a mob.

> "You're a Jew," she said, "and probably a homosexual too." I found myself slowly being pushed farther and farther back against the balcony railing. I kept trying to turn myself around as we talked, to pretend that my position in relation to the railing and the fall of several hundred feet was not precarious; I kept talking with them, lowering the threshold of confrontation, searching my mind for pacifist strategies that would enable me to maneuver away from the railing by getting them to turn at least slightly toward it. They kept advancing, pushing me closer and closer to the railing until my back was arched over it. They kept talking about homosexuals and Jews. . . . I knew the hatred was real, but I had not imagined these apparently docile women hating so much that with tiny steps they would become a gang: so full of unexamined hate that they would have pushed me over that railing "accidently" in defense of Christianity, the family, and the happily heterosexual, churchgoing child molester down the block. (Dworkin 1983, 119–20)

Beauvoir's subman is akin to Sartre's anti-Semite. But so is Beauvoir's serious man. He is one who submits himself to a Value, claims it unconditionally, and then feels himself justified coercing others to the Truth and the Way. He becomes a tyrant. He would foreclose the future for others, not just enslaving and exploiting, but enforcing roles and rules for the "betterment" of (his class of) mankind. This is the spirit of seriousness. "He makes himself serious. . . . He is no longer a man, but a father, a boss, a member of the Christian church or the Communist Party. . . . It is natural he makes himself a tyrant. Dishonestly ignoring the subjectivity of his choice, he pretends that the unconditioned value of the object is being asserted through him; and by the same token he also ignores the value of the subjectivity and the freedom of others" (Beauvoir 1980, 48–49).

As a six-year-old, when I became angered by choices I saw adults making—mostly what I saw as hypocrisies, such as adult women acting all cooey in front of adult men and then trying to act authoritatively with me, or older boys just flat out lying about things—I would console myself by saying that some day they would have to face up to what they were doing. It did not occur to me that this might not happen, that they could encounter death and acknowledge nothing. It did not occur to me that people could lie to themselves forever.

In fact, the tyrant is the moral "evil" existentialism recognizes. But if there is no a priori Value, then how is being a tyrant, or an anti-Semite, to be condemned? Doesn't that invoke preexisting Value? Beauvoir makes clear that the difference between the tyrant and the genuinely free person lies not in the particular choices we make, but how we make them: the first "rests in the certainty of his aims," the second constantly questions whether she is really working for freedom (Beauvoir 1980, 133).

As I engage and create feminist meaning and possibilities, I am aware that those who come after choose few things, move in directions I did not imagine, possibly don't particularly care for. Opening possibilities means other women will animate them through their own choices, create their own meaning. Certainly, feminism has changed and gained in complexity in the last twenty-five years. Central to existential freedom is willing an open future for both myself and for others; not trying to determine outcome, not becoming a serious man.

So if there is no predetermined Value, if it is not *what* so much as *how* one chooses, can't one choose to be an anti-Semite? Sartre calls it a choice of self—a choice of self that flees choice. And certainly those who flee choice do create value we live by—racism, for example. But fleeing freedom puts nothing to questions. The anti-Semite chooses a self who avoids engagement, annihilating his subjectivity, his fallibility, avoiding responsibility for change by constructing a scapegoat to explain what goes wrong in his life. Terrorists, illegal aliens, the homeless. Anti-Semitism is not caused by *experience*; one's ideas about the homeless determine how one experiences the woman on the corner with dirty clothes and messy hair leaning on metal crutches holding a sign with her teeth saying "Money for food, please."

I was a child during the McCarthy hearings, and the particulars did not filter through to me until later. But a nation's way of being did. My father explained his world by pointing to communists. I saw the contradiction then: the anti-Semite needs the communist to explain why the world is in disorder. Today it is the illegal alien, the unwed teenage mother, who make sense of his economic situation. As illegal aliens are being shut out and unwed mothers cut off welfare, he is having to invent another scapegoat to avoid addressing the nature of capitalism. "The anti-Semite is in the unhappy position of having a vital need for the enemy he wishes to destroy" (Sartre 1978, 28). "The carrier of the passion needs the victim and so creates the victim; the victim is an occasion for indulging the passion. One passion touches on another, overlays it, burrows into it, enfolds it, is grafted onto it; the configurations of oppression emerge" (Dworkin 1983, 121). Indeed Sartre claims that if the Jew did not exist, the anti-Semite would *invent* him (Sartre 1978, 13).

Walter Kaufman expunges this line from the excerpt of *Anti-Semite and Jew* in his anthology. I imagine why: there is a big difference between saying the anti-Semite invented Jews, and saying the anti-Semite invented a scapegoat. Nevertheless, others pick up on the theme. Franz Fanon: "For it is the settler who has brought the native into existence and who perpetuates his existence" (Fanon 1963, 36). And Beauvoir, with less rage: "One is not born, but rather becomes, a woman" (Beauvoir 1952, 301).

Foucault reminds us we are not simply restricted or repressed by the dominant frame, by the facticity of the world we move in; our freedom to move in the world is also constructed and shaped through disciplinary procedures. Nevertheless, racist construction is not just a product of disciplinary procedures. It is a product of white supremist agendas,[7] most directly, white disciplinary/colonist/imperialist economic agendas. Further, this construction ultimately makes us objects/pawns of dominant agendas. The invention of *woman, native, pervert, black, homeless, hispanic, welfare queen, homosexual, Jew, delinquent, terrorist* goes beyond disciplinary outcome; it also goes beyond scapegoat. These concepts function to preserve the existing structures of human beings and property on the planet, which serves the interests of a particular few. And the anti-Semite manages to further these interests.

"In patriarchal history, one passion is necessarily fundamental and unchanging: the hatred of women." "The United States is built on a hatred of blacks" (Dworkin 1983, 121). No longer having the communists, members of the CIA have invented for us the terrorist, diverting attention from their own terrorist activities—the assassination of Allende, for example, in Chile. Scapegoating is the Amerikan way. It helps folks who seek solace in the dominant story ignore history, that our way of life exists because of slavery and exploitation (Zinn 1990), that we are living on stolen land. (Silko 1977).

So what is invented when the anti-Semite invents an illegal alien? (After all, what European gentile U.S. citizens are descended from legal aliens?) When he invents the homeless person? The homosexual? When he invents the gang member? A woman? When he invents the unmarried woman on welfare?

And what does one so invented do? Sartre faults the woman for playing the heterosexual femme in a game of masculine aggression—the woman who ignores the man who grabs her hand. Or is it for *not* playing the heterosexual femme? Sartre faults the Jew for trying to run in the midst of a holocaust: "We have shown that the Jews have neither community of interests nor community of beliefs. They do not have the same father-land; they have no history. The sole tie that binds them is the hostility and disdain of the societies which surround them. Thus the authentic Jew is the one who asserts his claim in the face of the disdain shown toward him" (Sartre 1978, 91, also 67).

Oh really? So when one is oppressed is the only way to be authentic to accept one's victim status and the part therein assigned? Sartre here *does* seem to be saying that the anti-Semite invented not a scapegoat, but Jews themselves. While I find Sartre's analysis of the anti-Semite compelling, his portrayal of the authenticity of the oppressed, on the other hand, is arrogant.[8]

Sartre develops the idea of inauthenticity or bad faith as part of his analysis of consciousness. If there is no essence that precedes our existence, then we are nothing and become something only through our choices. That becoming, however, must always be transcended. If I rest in something I've done, for example, as author of *Lesbian Ethics*, I make myself into an object and thereby resist change/transcendence. In a very significant way, I am not now the author of *Lesbian Ethics*.[9] Similarly, I am always aware that I am a teacher, but I am also not a teacher—to the extent that I am aware of myself as a teacher, I am not a teacher, I am a creature aware of myself being a teacher. And that is the only way I can be a teacher, continually looking at myself as a teacher and questioning not only what I think I'm doing and how successful I am at that, but also what others see me as doing.

My mother watched me, from a distance. And I became aware of being watched, of Big Brother watching, of teachers watching, being used, once, by a teacher as a model for appropriate behavior when a little boy acted out—I did not put up a fuss when punished but went back to what I had been doing before my infraction, but he put up a fuss and started crying when he was punished and the teacher pointed to me as an example of what he should have done. Never again could I come under the teacher's criticism without having to decide

*whether to claim solidarity with the boy and fuss, or validate the teacher by
returning to my business. As a child I was always not quite the something I
was seen as being. I liked that, I liked standing outside just a bit. But I also
grossly resented the loss of spontaneity, of total absorption in my task, by
having to take into account the agenda of others.*

Sartre posits *mauvaise foi* against Freud's unconscious, arguing that to
explain self-deception one has two problems: (1) one must know the
truth in order to conceal it, but this duality must be suppressed; and (2)
that which does the self-deception must be conscious of its self-
deception. To avoid the paradox, Freudian psychoanalysis posits the idea
of an unconscious. Consciousness can be deceived by the unconscious,
and that explains how someone both does and does not want something
or does and does not know something. However, Sartre argues, Freud only
postpones the paradox, he doesn't solve it: Freud posits an unconscious in
order to explain the duality of the deceiver and the deceived being in
one person, but he still needs a censor to determine what gets through
from the unconscious to the conscious. So psychoanalysis has gained
nothing:

> The very essence of the reflexive idea of hiding something from
> oneself implies the unity of one and the same psychic mechanism
> and consequently a double activity at the heart of that unity,
> tending on the one hand to maintain and locate the thing to be
> concealed and on the other hand to repress and disguise it. Each
> of the two aspects of this activity is complementary to the other;
> that is, it implies the other in its being. By separating conscious-
> ness from the unconscious by means of the censor, psychoanalysis
> has not succeeded in dissociating the two phases of the act . . .
> [but] has merely localized this double activity of repulsion and
> attraction on the level of the censor. (Sartre 1956, 53)

Moreover, "how can the repressed drive 'disguise itself' if it does not
include (1) the consciousness of being repressed, (2) the consciousness
of having been pushed back because it is what it is, (3) a project of
disguise?" (53; for an excellent comparison of Freudian, Lacanian, and
existential psychoanalysis, note B. Cannon 1991). *Bad faith*, Sartre argues, is more useful for explaining the phenomenon many call "self-deception" than is positing an unconscious.

But then Sartre provides his examples of bad faith and my irritation begins; first a "frigid" woman guilty of detachment. This is a woman in a heteropatriarchy that defines women as whores or virgins and at a time when there was no safe birth control. *Gee, I wonder why she acts as she does. Let me see if I can figure this out.* "In the face of the woman denying forthrightly that she experiences pleasure in coitus with her husband, thepsychiatrist's observation that she *dreads* the experience, and the woman's report that she deliberately averts her attention from the act and the sensations, Sartre insists that what she dreads and tries to distract herself from is 'pleasure' and that the woman is self-deceived" (Frye 1983, 55).

Next we have the woman trying to have a conversation with a man (the game of sex), a waiter adapting to his job (the game of class), and a homosexual consumed with guilt (the game of heterosex). The waiter tries to bury himself in facticity, the woman and the homosexual try to transcend it. Sartre is here treating the dominant script as if it were reality. It is a script, it is part of our facticity, but it is not the only realm of sense, of meaning, the only logic by which people act. Freudian psychoanalysis, or Jungian, becomes counterrevolutionary as well; psychoanalysis grounds its interpretations in dominant scripts.

My rage at being read, walking down the street through heterosex. If I smiled at the whiteman, it was a comeon. If I turned my head in anger, it was a comeon. If I ignored him, it was a comeon. And if I were deeply oblivious, lost in my own thought, I would be rudely interrupted in order that the games could proceed. When it is a blackman I pass, he is also entrapped by dominant scripts, and the situation becomes noisy with readings. Let's start with the city, is it Chicago? What part of Chicago? . . . I find myself on a roller coaster of scripts.

In resisting the dominant construction of us, we run "a perilous course between falling back into and thereby perpetuating the constructs created by the [oppressor] and transcending those constructs altogether" (Murphy 1989, 105). Betty Cannon articulates these aspects of human reality and two ways of animating bad faith:

> On the one hand, there is facticity—the contingent world which I did not create but which I must choose to live in some fashion or other. Facticity includes my own past as well as external circumstances. On the other hand, there is freedom—my choice of objects in the world as a way of realizing my own fundamental project of being. A full recognition of my freedom includes the recognition that nothing—neither myself nor traditional values

nor god—has a priori status as value. Instead I create value through valuing. I fall into bad faith if I take one or both of two dishonest positions about reality: If I pretend to be free in a world without facts or to be a fact in a world without freedom. (B. Cannon 1991, 46)

For those under oppression it is bad faith, counterrevolutionary, either to pretend that one is nothing but dominant scripts, or to pretend one can simply transcend dominant scripts. For example, in my reading of male-to-female transsexuals I don't see a significant difference from whites who imagine themselves black. And I don't see a significant difference between men who do drag shows and whites putting on blackface. I know white women who hate that they are white, search continuously to find a hidden black relative in their past, who regard white women with contempt, who have "felt black" since who knows when, who would turn their skin black in a second if they dared. I applaud the desire to transform racial and sexual meanings. I just don't think crossing over does it. I want to see men who have "felt they were 'women' " challenging the boundaries of what it means to be a man. Not to cross over and claim that they must be women, I want them to inhabit new ways of being a man. Wearing a dress as a man, not as a transvestite. Not female impersonation but being a man in a new mode. Commenting on avant-garde performance that draws on indigenous cultures, Coco Fusco writes: "What may be 'liberating' and 'transgressive' identification for Europeans and Euro-Americans is already a symbol of entrapment within an imposed stereotype for Others" (1995, 46).

I want transsexual men to work to change the meaning of *man* as I try to change the meaning of *woman* and of *white*. No, this is not simply a matter of individual actions any more than it is a matter of individual liberation. But our everyday actions matter. Our everyday actions add up to the values we choose. And to those born and raised male in the United States, I say putting on women's clothes and claiming to be women invokes too much of the history, the facticity, of male privilege—men determining what is proper to being a woman. I need to see a rejection of the dominant definition of what it means to be a man before I can see the play as liberatory, as a committed political choice rather than simply an effort to transcend women's history. *In choosing to be woman, are you choosing to embrace a history of rape, a history in which you are deeply implicated? Do you volunteer at battered women's shelters? What are you doing about the Promise Keepers?* So far what I see is someone oppressed differently from me pretending to be free in a world without facts.

But perhaps I am wrong.

From the other direction, there are those who pretend the oppressed are facts in a world without freedom. For example, Richard Wright and LeRoi Jones see the black man as castrated under slavery. Ralph Ellison challenges Jones: "A slave, writes LeRoi Jones, cannot be a man [*sic*]. But what might one ask of those moments when he feels his metabolism aroused by the rising sap in the spring. What of his identity among other slaves? With his wife? And isn't it closer to the truth that far from considering themselves only in terms of that abstraction, a slave, the enslaved really thought of themselves as men who had been unjustly enslaved?" (Warren 1974, 331). For Ellison, even under the most extreme conditions of oppression, one is more than what the oppressors invented. He challenges the stereotype that U.S. blacks have been deprived of a sense of identity and are self-haters, insisting instead on their will, even under slavery, to develop discipline and achieve individuality (Warren 1974, 330). Although seen as a 60s sellout because he focused on universal man (McPherson 1974, 55), Ellison affirmed: "I don't recognize any white culture, I recognize no American culture which is not the partial creation of black people. I recognize no American style in literature, in dance, in music, even in assembly-line processes, which does not bear the mark of the American Negro" (McPherson 1974, 44). In approaching oppression, Ellison does not see passive victims.

The problem with Richard Wright's portrait in *Native Son* is that Bigger Thomas is a passive pawn of sexist racism (Conversation, Jackie Anderson). The portrait leaves no conceptual room for resistance. Radical analyses such as those offered by Marxism and radical feminism border this danger. To avoid the dominant game of blaming the victim, radical theorists can fall into victimism. "Victimism . . . creates a framework for others to know her not as a person but as a victim, someone to whom violence was done" (Barry 1979, 45).

María Lugones argues that "it is a desideratum of oppression theory that it portray oppression in its full force, as inescapable, if that is its full force." She argues that given the logic of capitalism, she does not see how the subjectivity of class consciousness and class struggle is possible.

Similarly Marilyn Frye's account of arrogant perception whose end is the service of others. "As depicted, the arrogantly perceived woman cannot be an agent of her own liberation" (Lugones 1990, 501).

Yes, but when I initially engaged radical feminist analysis I was elated. Something was articulated not articulated before, giving shape to what had lived in my peripheral consciousness. With radical feminist analysis I could bring these things into direct consciousness and detect patterns, discuss this with others, collectively, and reassess my choices. Young women in my classes today seem to hear only victimism. What I heard let me know myself to be someone who persisted in these conditions, even resisted, let me know myself to be an amazon warrior.

María Lugones does not challenge the depictions of oppression as inescapable because she thinks that much of their explanatory power resides in this inescapability. But she also considers it desirable that oppression theory be liberatory: "The ontological or metaphysical possibility of liberation remains to be argued, explained, uncovered" (Lugones 1990, 501–2). The negotiation between characterizing oppression and articulating the subjectivity of those living under such conditions is complex and ambiguous.

So I ask again, what does one invented do?

For one thing, begin to see the logics of resistance that occur everywhere the dominant agenda is glitched. Lesbian mosquitoes, women marbles. I don't have a program here, I especially do not have a set of rules. We are existentially but not politically free; women still exist, in the dominant script for men, and people of color still exist, in the dominant script, for whites. What does it mean to authentically claim this facticity and also authentically transcend it? My dispute with Sartre has to do with his apparent assumption when assessing inauthenticity that the behavior of we who are caught in dominant invention makes sense only within the confines of the script that invented us; that there is only one world of sense. The woman in the café refusing to acknowledge the man's hand can be read as inauthentic only within the dominant discourse of masculine meaning.

A popular slogan of the early 1970s: If you're not part of the solution, you're part of the problem. And during the movement phase of a political culture[10] the existential idea that not choosing is still choosing is crucial to making it clear that everyone is implicated in the dominant script, whether we asked for it or not. But this idea is double edged; it can also hold us within the parameters of the dominant discourse, keep our imagination limited to dominant boundaries of sense and logic. What counts as what one chooses? How does the woman prisoner walk proudly among her rapists? What does the Invisible Man do?

Resistance mostly doesn't materialize in the dominant frame, it is mystified. Women's resistance, sabotage, is most often portrayed as insanity. So was slave sabotage and resistance. (Note Osofsky 1969 for example) *Femininity* normalizes male domination and paints a portrait of women as subordinate and naively content with being controlled, *femininity* functions to obscure female resistance. A feminine being is by nature passive and dependent. It follows that those to whom the label is applied must by their very nature seek protection (domination) and should be subjected to authority "for their own good." It is a matter of logic, then, that those who refuse to be controlled are abnormal (Hoagland 1988, 39–46). The existential possibilities for those under oppression don't emerge within the dominant frame of meaning. Yes, I am a radical feminist, and the conceptual coercion/appropriation/assimilation by the dominant frame at times overwhelms me. What is one invented to do?

In addressing oppression, Beauvoir tells us that freedom "realizes itself only by engaging in the world" (Beauvoir 1980, 78). When that is interrupted by oppression, condemning some to "mark time hopelessly in order merely to support the collectivity," the oppressed have "only one solution: to deny the harmony of that mankind from which an attempt is made to exclude him" (83).

Frantz Fanon addresses colonial violence and oppression: the use of weapons in the initial invasion; the destruction of the *aboriginal* and creation of the *native* who serves the *settler*—the settler who can only exist through *oppression*; missionary education where children are forced to learn through colonial categories and produce for the sake of those categories; the theft of resources; and the construction of "white man's burden" whereby *natives* are "protected" from themselves. "The aesthetic expressions of respect for the established order create around the exploited person an atmosphere of submission and inhibition which lightens the task of policing considerably" (Fanon 1963, 38). For Fanon, the colonized can be free only through an equal and opposite act of violence. "From birth it is clear that this world can only be called into question by absolute violence" (37). He argues that the "native's challenge is not a rational confrontation of points of view" (41). For the native, objectivity is always directed against him" (77). In other words, resistance is mystified, and in the dominant discourse he is either insane or a terrorist.

"At the level of individuals, violence is a cleansing force, it frees the native from his inferiority complex" (Fanon 1963, 94). Oppression penetrates and festers. I must act to throw off internalized racism/sexism/anti-Semitism/heterosexism/self-hatred. For Fanon, I will not be able to erase the idea that the colonist is better than me and that I must be cared for, until he comes down in my estimation enough that I can do him violence . . . until I change the structure of my eyes.

This is not about the capacity to do violence, for we are adept at horizontal violence. It is about the ability to eradicate the awe one has of an oppressor, to reject his script of himself and of oneself. In eradicating the native, in emerging from the construction of the native, Fanon argues that one must also destroy the settler. The process of decolonization involves the creation of new men [sic], but this creation is not supernatural, rather the "thing" which has been colonized becomes a "man" during the same process by which it frees itself. (Fanon 1963, 36–37)

This last sentence suggests that Fanon, like Wright and Jones, sees only passive victims under colonialism, and the only possibility of resistance to be the overthrow of colonizers. I find the argument for violence compelling, particularly when I think of women living in the grips of male violence. "Men don't take us seriously because they are not physically afraid of us" (Ellen Willis, cited in Kaye 1981). As Jeffner says, constrained to "nonviolence," women are precluded from claiming and creating a self in the world (Allen 1986). And certainly there needs to be the eradication of the native and the settler.[11] Still, I question that one oppressed becomes a man only through the process of violent overthrow. And I disagree that this is the only possibility of resistance. When we recognize as resistance only those acts that overthrow dominators, we miss a great deal.

For some who are scapegoated, another response to foreclosure under oppression lies in choosing to live, particularly when the agenda of the oppressor is plain genocide, not slavery and genocide. What does it means to choose life in a world of oppression, particularly when one is not in the movement stage of a political culture? What is this existential choice? Why would anyone consider, much less acknowledge, life a choice? Talking of his days as a gang-banger, Luis Rodriguez writes, "Death seemed the only door worth opening, the only road toward a future. We tried to enter death and emerge from it" (1993, 125).

There were several cans of clear plastic—what we called *la ce pe*—around us. We each had paper bags and sprayed into them—and I had already dropped some pills and downed a fifth of Wild Turkey. I then placed the bag over my mouth and nose, sealed it tightly with both hands, and breathed deeply.

Dew fell off low branches as if it were breast milk. Birds shot out of the tropical trees which appeared across from us. . . . I was transported away from what was really there—yet it felt soothing. Not like the oil stains we sat in. Not like the factory air that surrounded us. Not this plastic death in a can. . . .

Then everything faded away—the dew, the water, the birds. I became a cartoon, twirling through a tunnel, womb-like and satiated with sounds and lines and darkness. I found myself drifting toward a glare of lights. My family called me over: Seni, Mama, Papa, Tía Cucha, Tío Kiko, Pancho—everybody. I wanted to be there, to know this perpetual dreaming, this din of exquisite screams—to have this mother comfort surging through me. . . .

Everything crashed. Everything throbbed. I only knew: I had to get to the light, that wondrous beacon stuffed with sweet promise: Of peace. untroubled. The end of fear. *Don't close the door, Mama. I scared. It's ok, m'ijo. There's no monsters. We'll be here. Don't be scared.* . . .

I tried to get up but fell back to the ground. A kind of grief overwhelmed me. I was no longer this dream. I was me again. I wished I did die. . . .

I crept toward a paper bag but Baba kicked it out of my reach. Later I found myself stepping down a street. Baba and Wilo had pointed me in the direction of home and I kept going. I hated being there. I didn't know what to do. God I wanted that light, this whore of a sun to blind me, to entire me to burn—to be sculptured marble in craftier hands. (103–5)

Escaping from the dominant frame is escaping from a self-hating construction of one's subjectivity, finding a place where one can't be touched anymore.

The choice to live is a choice to feel, to emerge from numbness, to know one will know hurt, again, to care, and care about others. With the death trip one feels nothing, doesn't care—that's a survival tactic, to decide you don't care; it don't matter whether you live or die. Choosing to care about whether you live or die is choosing to remain connected to the consequences. In situations where you're out of control, that's a terrifying commitment, because you are choosing to stay connected to something you do not control (Conversation, Anne T. Leighton). Luis Rodriguez's choice to live is not that of the anti-Semite.

When one is invented, the possibility of resistance depends on the creation of new worlds of sense (even when one is engaged in violent revolution). But that activity is fraught with danger. "If you step outside of the narrow borders of what they call reality, you step into chaos" (Ellison 1980, 576). One faces "intimate terrorism": it is possible one will be unable to make new sense:

> She has this fear   that she has no names   that she has many names   that she doesn't know her names   She has this fear that she's an image   that comes and goes clearing and darkening   the fear that she's the dreamwork in side someone else's skull . . . She has this fear that if she digs into herself   she won't find anyone. . . . (Anzaldúa 1987, 43)

Drawing on Gloria Anzaldúa's work, María Lugones argues that as la mestiza goes between structures, where agency is not key, and comes to the Coatlicué state, she can develop resistant thinking, the possibility of liberatory imagination, between structures and boundaries where habitual thinking fails. Only in the borderlands, the place between structures, can one begin to enact liberatory imagination (Lugones 1994). Only here, when not hooked on the structures of rationality of the dominant culture, can one conceive new worlds of sense. *Resisting oppression involves changing the structure of our eyes, our understanding.*

In discussing Black womanist ethics, Katie Cannon argues: "The cherished assumptions of dominant ethical systems predicated upon both the existence of freedom and a wide range of choices have proven to be false in the real-lived texture of Black life. Thus Black women have created and cultivated a set of ethical values that allow them to prevail against the odds, with moral integrity, in their ongoing participation in the white-male-capitalist value system" (K. Cannon 1988, 75). "They resented the white man's message of docility which acted to render them defenseless in the face of white violence. Living under a system of cheating, lying and stealing, enslaved Blacks learned to consider these vices as virtues in their dealings with whites" (K. Cannon 1988, 76).

And so resisting also involves messing with dominant sense. Playing the trickster is one way of exercising existential freedom. One can play the fool, playing on others' ignorances/privileges, by playing with structures. "One can be at the same time in a 'world' that constructs one as stereotypically latin, for example, and in a 'world' that constructs one as latin. Being stereotypically latin and being simply latin are different simultaneous constructions of persons that are part of different 'worlds.' One animates one or the other or both at the same time without necessarily confusing them, though simultaneous enactment can be confusing if one is not on one's guard" (Lugones 1987, 11). That is, a latina can play the Latin-American as gringos construct her—stereotypically intense—or she can play the "real" thing. An angla who knows nothing of her world will not be able to tell the difference.

An angla who knows nothing of her world becomes a fool. She must become a self-conscious critical practitioner in dominant culture to know, to understand, the trick. And that means reading oneself and others not through the dominant script, finding the dominant script lacking. María Lugones articulates a means of interacting that undermines standard ethical notions of responsibility (from deontological, utilitarian, and care ethics) in which we act to stay in charge, in control, and for which a lack of reciprocity is central:[12] the ethics of seriousness. Through playful world travel, we go into another's world without trying to destroy it and encounter a gaze that introduces ambiguity, brings new knowledge, and thereby makes change possible (Lugones 1987).

María Lugones argues for plural selves in multiple structures of oppression. This notion of multiplicity is distinct from postmodern fragmentation, which results from dominant scripts constructed out of dominant agendas such that when one responds, one becomes fragmented—as a woman, as a latina, as a worker, when one is all three. "Racist/colonialist perception is narcissistic, it denies independence to the seen, it constructs its object imaginatively as a reflection of the seer. It robs the seen of a separate identity (Lugones n.d.a., 9). Consequently, when one inhabits more than one identity, one becomes fragmented. The notion of multiplicity or plurality, on the other hand, concerns the subjectivity of she who enacts selves in different situations—the maid of the job, the woman who comes home to tell her family about the absurdities she saw in rich people's houses and dispel the awe.

This notion of multiplicity also challenges Sartre's assumption of unified consciousness. Exploring failures of intentionality as well as possibilities of ambiguity and resistance, however, María Lugones's work does not take the route Sartre objects to in Freud of appealing to an unconscious. Instead she allows for memory to operate across selves and the concept of mistake is applicable in her work (Lugones 1990). One can meaningfully say of a self within a particular situation: "I made a mistake."

The woman prisoner, going to her death, may be grafted onto the agendas of her rapists, but she has the possibility of memory of her resistant self, a self that keeps her from descending into the facticity of the present moment; she is not simply the self inscribed in the agendas of her torturers. A right-wing woman has such a possibility as well, the possibility of changing the structure of her eyes and the nature of her choices of loyalty. And the one caught in two or more worlds, finding herself victim and resister and also oppressor and resister can learn to change the structure of her reasoning, learn to recognize other logics, learn how her reasoning is implicated in the oppression of others, where she has been complicit, mistaken, and also how her reasoning is resistant to oppressive agendas.

But none of this is isolated activity. "The look of the oppressor is broken when the oppressed connect with each other for understanding and transforming our lives" (Murphy 1989, 107). The possibility of resistance involves shifting constructed loyalties, from the abuser to the woman abused, from the colonialist to the indigenous person, from master to slave. This is how we stop choosing womanabuse or racism. And that involves, as Sartre and Beauvoir argue, resisting the dominant demand that one be either serious or sincere. Making meaning, sense, is crucial for survival, and occurs when, sometimes spontaneously, many turn away from the meaning of the oppressor and enact new meaning. This is an aspect of existential freedom. When Martin Luther King, Jr., was murdered, black students shifted from white concepts of "Negro" and made new meaning: "Black is beautiful."[13]

In my life, I choose women and lesbians. But if there is no fixed nature, *black*, or *woman*, or *lesbian*, or *straight*, what does it mean to choose women or to choose lesbians or to choose Latinos?

In choosing to be a feminist and a lesbian, I make meaning. In fact, by looking to lesbian lives, we find values of female agency and community distinct from those promoted under heterosexualism where female agency is constructed in terms of self-sacrifice, and where community is understood as hegemonic and difference a threat. For example in heteropatriarchy, self-sacrifice is contrasted with selfishness, a good woman being self-sacrificial, caring; she who chooses herself is selfish. Implicit in this dichotomy is the idea that choice involves loss—she must choose between two things (herself or her husband/children) and sacrifice one (herself). Behind this is an imperialist idea—that everything that exists is ours or ought to be—so when we choose between two things, we lose something that is ours. Among lesbians, however, nothing was ours; everything lesbian that exists has been created out of nothing by lesbians—publishing houses, journals, bookstores, coffeehouses, festivals where new values are explored, lesbian motherhood, and so on. So from lesbian lives we can understand that agency is creative, not sacrificial. Choice is a source of enabling power: where I focus my attention and put my energy, there I create meaning (Hoagland 1988, 1992, 1998).

Still, this activity is ambiguous and fraught with danger. It can unwittingly bring with it dominant values.

> As a lesbian of African descent . . . I am angry with a kind of existential rage at this culture that refuses to acknowledge anything about me or my culture that is not negative. I am angry at the refusal of this culture to recognize anything about me other than the fact that I am "black." I am angry that my folks have never been acknowledged for all that we have given to this country in free labor, cultural contributions and the unspeakably significant role that we have had in the "making of America." I am angry that I am still and will for many generations be a "nigger." I am angry that I must live this in lesbian community as I live it elsewhere. I am also clear that my friends who are not women of color are not my enemies. (Jackie Anderson, Institute of Lesbian Studies Retreat, 1997)

This activity of meaning creation can also turn into its own orthodoxy, seriousness, with demand for cultural and racial authenticity (which is the inauthenticity, the bad faith, of trying to be a fact without freedom). "There is an understanding of only two logics that are markedly distinct, in fierce opposition: racist logic and resistant logic, both active in the home-grown seer as realistic resistance requires. There is no inside understanding of the variety of resistant logics. This lack of fluency in resistant logics accounts in part for the drawing of very tight, inflexible, boundaries around one's circle" (Lugones n.d.a., 13). This means that "those who are not insiders to homeplaces are seen by those within, with the eyes of the oppressor. The choice between only two exclusive logics dictates this adoption. But it is paradoxical that those who cultivate resistant perception with respect to each other would thoroughgoingly internalize oppressive perception of those outside their circle" (Lugones, n.d.a., 15).

In other words, while we animate our own resistant logic, we fail to see others with resistant eyes. Instead we judge them through dominant values, the Norm. For example, how can a critical academic perceive the peripheral economy of gangs as resistance to cultural extermination? How does an aging hippie perceive the resistance in hip hop culture? How does a homeboy understand a lesbian feminist? How does a bulldagger understand a tortillera? How does Sartre understand a woman trying to have a conversation with a man?

And so María Lugones argues for playful world travel. Coming to know others not of one's chosen grouping outside the construction of the dominant agendas means understanding what it is to be the other, and what it is to be ourselves *in their eyes*. Through the attending of playful world travel we become subjects to each other (Lugones 1987). Notoriously, Sartrean and Hegelian attending makes us objects of each other, for the other is approached as if only one value can be enacted, so difference becomes a threat (Hoagland 1988, 235–36). Perhaps for this reason Sartre is limited to gauging authenticity through dominant logic.

María Lugones argues that interdependency (not a Hegelian objectifying/agonistic dependency, but an interdependency of subjects), being with others (and not through the logic of the dominant discourse), is necessary if we are to remake ourselves into active, creative selves, if we are to (re)construct our agency. And this interdependency is part of what I think of when I think about the Sartrean idea of willing an open future, willing the freedom of others. Willing the freedom of others necessarily involves working to end the institutions of oppression, of course. And it involves working for others' possibilities. But there is something more significant, much deeper.

María Lugones notes that "la torillera exists en la comunidad only as a pervert. Perversion constitutes her and marks her as outside of countenanced relationality." Moving into the Lesbian Movement, she becomes a Latina/Lesbian. This movement is a "fantastic flight" because "the eyes that see her coming out, remake her in their own imagination." As such she is fragmented, not yet a tortillera. As a result, she acts out in lesbian community (Lugones, n.d.b., 8, 10). What is the necessity of willing the freedom of others, the existential *and* the political freedom? If many lesbians, lesbians of color, tortilleras, bulldaggers, marimachas, swing girls, can only act out in lesbian community and are forced into the closet in their own, then they are caricatures and I am no(t yet) lesbian. My capacity to be lesbian requires a relationality proscribed by dominant agendas.

I no longer look at oppression as something that can be thrown over, I look at it as something persistent, a way of life. Something I choose to resist without promise of final success. But within that awareness lies existential freedom holding the possibility of change, of resistant engagement with others, of exploring resistant logics to see what parts are liberatory. There is always resistance. Failure to see that is to collaborate with the dominant agenda, to accept dominant logic and meaning as all there is. Sartrean and Beauvoirian existential freedom focuses us on our choices, and grounds the possibility of changing the structure of our eyes through engagement, the possibility of relationality, and hence the ever present possibility of political change.

Notes

1. Even though for Sartre our self is relational in a way Descartes's cogito is not—for Descartes, one does not even need an other to come to self-consciousness—Sartre's primary project is self-absorbed. *Nausea* is a perfect example, as is Camus's stranger, as is Sartre's claim, "This war is my war" (Sartre 1975, 52ff). Beauvoir and Fanon explore relatedness (Beauvoir 1980; Allen 1989, Murphy 1995; Fanon 1963).

2. As Jeffner Allen writes: "The Christian saint leaves earthly life by a death in which he becomes God-like. The existential antihero, condemned to carry the weight of the world on his shoulders evades the complexities of that world by immersion in melancholy, despair, and dread" (Allen 1989, 77).

3. In particular, his conception of "holes and slime [as] obscene qualities of the In-itself which are identified, in anatomy and behavior, with the female" (Collins and Pierce 1976, 119).

4. That is, if one simply ignores his treatment of women and other oppressed peoples.

5. Indeed, Carole Pateman argues that the liberal ideal of freedom as expressed through contract is actually a matter of securing subordination (Pateman 1988).

6. The movie *Death and the Maiden* is a good example of how men would annihilate her subjectivity, even those who love her and are beholden to her, in this case dismissing her as insane (Dorfman 1992).

7. Note Roediger's history of U.S. white laborers, who in the process of being subordinated by management under industrialized capitalism in a way they had never been as farmers, made choices that valued/constructed whiteness to symbolize the hard worker, whereas blackness and Mexicanness came to symbolize laziness in U.S. consciousness (despite the intense labor of chain-gang or migrant work).

8. I mean to invoke Marilyn Frye's notion of the arrogant eye who sees everything as either "for me" or "against me." The arrogant perceiver does not countenance the possibility that the

Other is independent, indifferent (Frye 1983, 67). Note, also, Michael Walzer's (1995) new preface to *Anti-Semite and Jew*.

9. Mary Daly talks complexly about the authors of the various books whose authors are Mary Daly (1992).

10. Thanks to Geoff Bryce and María Lugones for this understanding, Escuela Popular Norteña, July 1995. Political movement is only one stage in a political culture. There are other stages. And in those other stages, one of which we are currently in, different strategies are called for, and different indices of success pertain.

11. Monique Wittig argues a similar point with regard to *men* and *women*. "For what makes a woman is a specific social relation to a man, a relation that we have previously called servitude" (Wittig 1992, 20). Following Beauvoir's argument that one is not born, but rather becomes, a woman, Monique Wittig argues that lesbians are not women (32, note Hoagland 1988).

12. The mother model of the ethics of care, for example, even as it attempts to encourage empathy and make place for reciprocity, still does not develop a reciprocity capable of challenging managers, caretakers, dogooders who find their identity through assuming the authority to control others. And so it gives rise to the managerial type of thinking of utilitarianism without even lip service to the rights of those others to check the arrogating perception of the caregiver. (Hoagland, n.d.)

13. This was particularly significant in its rejection of white Amerika's mode of self-appraisal, which is always comparative: the United States is good because we have something better than someone else.

References

Allen, Jeffner. 1989. "An Introduction to Patriarchal Existentialism: A Proposal for a Way out of Existential Patriarchy." In Allen and Young 1989.

———. 1986. "Looking At Our Blood: A Lesbian Response to Men's Terrorization of Women. In her *Lesbian Philosophy: Explorations*. Institute of Lesbian Studies, P.O. Box 25568. Chicago, IL 60625.

Allen, Jeffner, and Iris Marion Young. 1989. *The Thinking Muse: Feminism and Modern French Philosophy*. Bloomington: Indiana University Press.

Anzaldúa, Gloria. 1987. *Borderlands/La Frontera: The New Mestiza*. San Francisco: Spinster/aunt lute.

Barnes, Hazel E. 1968. *An Existentialist Ethics*. New York: Knopf.

Barry, Kathleen. 1979. *Female Sexual Slavery*. Englewood Cliffs, N.J.: Prentice-Hall.

Beauvoir, Simone de. 1989. *The Ethics of Ambiguity*. Trans. Bernard Frechtman. Secaucus, N.J.: Citadel Press.

———. 1952. *The Second Sex*. New York: Vintage.

Bell, Linda. 1993. *Rethinking Ethics in the Midst of Violence: A Feminist Approach to Freedom*. Lanham, Md: Rowman and Littlefield.

Cannon, Betty. 1991. *Sartre and Psychoanalysis: An Existential Challenge to Clinical Metatheory*. Lawrence: University Press of Kansas.

Cannon, Katie. 1988. *Black Womanist Ethics*. Atlanta, Ga: Scholars Press.

Collins, Margery L., and Christine Pierce. 1976. "Holes and Slime: Sexism in Sartre's Psychoanalysis." In *Philosophy and Women: Toward a Theory of Liberation*, ed. Carol C. Gould and Marx W. Wartofsky. New York: G. P. Putnam's Sons.

Daly, Mary. 1992. *Outercourse*. San Francisco: HarperCollins.

Dorfman, Ariel. 1992. *Death and the Maiden*. New York: Penguin.

Dworkin, Andrea. 1997. "In Memory of Nicole Brown Simpson." In her *Life and Death: Unapologetic Writings on the Continuing War Against Women*. New York: Free Press.

———. 1983. *Right Wing Women*. New York: G. P. Putnam's Sons.

Ellison, Ralph. 1980. *Invisible Man*. New York: Vintage.

Fanon, Frantz. 1963. *Wretched of the Earth*. New York: Grove Press.

Foucault, Michel. 1979. *Discipline and Punish*. New York: Vintage.

Frye. Marilyn. 1983. "In and Out of Harm's Way: Arrogance and Love." In her *The Politics of Reality: Essays in Feminist Theory*. Trumansburg, N.Y.: The Crossing Press.

Fusco, Coco. 1995. "The Other History of Intercultural Performance." In *English is Broken Here: Notes on the Cultural Fusion in the Americas*. New York: New Press.

Hersey, John, ed. 1974. *Ralph Ellison: A Collection of Critical Essays*. Englewood Cliffs, N.J.: Prentice-Hall, Inc.

Hoagland, Sarah L. 1998. "Lesbian Ethics." In *The Blackwell Companion to Feminist Philosophy*, ed. Alison Jaggar and Iris Young, 402–10. Oxford: Blackwell.

———. 1988. *Lesbian Ethics: Toward New Value*. Institute of Lesbian Studies, P.O. Box 25568. Chicago, IL 60625.

———. N.d. "Heterosexualism, Power, and the Academic Mother Model of Care Ethic. Unpublished ms.

———. 1992. "Why Lesbian Ethics?" *Hypatia* 7, no. 4: 195–206.

Kaufman, Walter. 1956, 1975. *Existentialism From Dostoyevsky to Sartre*. New York: New American Library.

Kaye. 1981. "Women and Violence." In *Fight Back! Feminist Resistance to Male Violence*, ed. Frédérique Delacoste and Felice Newmann. San Francisco: Cleis Press.

Kruks, Sonia. 1995. "Simone de Beauvoir: Teaching Sartre About Freedom." In Simons 1995.

Lugones, María. N.d.a. "Boomerang Perception and the Colonizing Gaze: ginger reflections on horizontal hostility." Unpublished ms.

———. 1994. "On Borderlands/La Frontera: An Interpretive Essay." In *Adventures in Lesbian Philosophy*, ed. Claudia Card. Bloomington: Indiana University Press.

———. N.d.b. "El Pasar Discontinuo de la Cachapera/Tortillera del Barrio a la Barra al Movimiento. The discontinuous passing of the cachapera-tortillera from the barrio to the bar to the Movement." Unpublished ms.

———. 1987. "Playfulness, 'World'-Traveling, and Loving Perception." *Hypatia* 2, no. 2: 3–19.

———. 1990. "Structure/Antistructure and Agency Under Oppression." *Journal of Philosophy* 87 (October): 500–507.

Lugones, María, and Joshua Price, N.d. "Dominant Culture: ed deseo por un alma pobre (the desire for an impoverished soul)." Unpublished ms.

McPherson, James Alan. 1974. "Indivisible Man." In Hershey 1974.

Murphy, Julien. 1995. "Beauvoir and the Algerian War: Toward a Postcolonial Ethics." In Simons 1995.

———. 1989. "The Look in Sartre and Rich." In Allen and Young 1989.

Neal, Larry. 1974. "Ellison's Zoot Suit." In Hershey 1974.

Osfosky, Gilbert, ed. (1969) *Puttin' On Ole Massa*. New York: Harper and Row.

Pateman. Carole. 1988. *The Sexual Contact*. Stanford: Stanford University Press.

Rodriquez, Luis. 1993. *Always Running: La Vida Loca: Gang Days in L.A.* New York: Simon and Schuster.

Roediger, David R. 1991. *The Wages of Whiteness*. New York: Verso.

Sartre, Jean-Paul. 1978. *Anti-Semite and Jew*. Trans. George J. Becker. New York: Schocken Books.

———. 1956. *Being and Nothingness*. Trans. Hazel E. Barnes. New York: Philosophical Library.

———. 1957. *Existentialism and Human Emotions*. New York: Philosophical Library.

———. 1974. *The Writings of Jean-Paul Sartre*. Trans. Richard C. McLeary. Ed. Michel Conant and Michel Rybalka. Evanston: Northwestern University Press.

Silko, Leslie Marmon. 1977. *Ceremony*. New York: Penguin.

Simons, Margaret A., ed. 1995. *Feminist Interpretations of Simone de Beauvoir*. University Park: Penn State Press.

Walzer, Michael. 1995. Preface to Jean-Paul Sartre, *Anti-Semite and Jew*, trans. George J. Becker. New York: Schocken Books.

Warren, Robert Penn. 1974. *Who Speaks for the Negro?* New York: Vintage. 1965.

Williams, Sherley Ann. 1987. *Dessa Rose*. New York: Berkeley Books.

Wittig, Monique. 1992. *The Straight Mind*. Boston: Beacon.

Wright, Richard. 1940, 1966. *Native Son*. New York: Harper and Row.

Zinn, Howard. 1990. *People's History of the United States*. Harper.

8

Sartre and de Beauvoir on Freedom and Oppression

Karen Green

1. A Paradoxical Partnership: Radical Freedom and Social Constraint

Feminists have been highly critical of Sartre's existentialism; existentialism is taken to be a philosophy of radical freedom, feminism is centrally a critique of oppression, their marriage has therefore seemed incongruous.[1] Yet, de Beauvoir's *The Second Sex,* which provided late twentieth-century feminism with many key concepts for analyzing women's oppression, announced itself as a work written from the perspective of an existentialist ethics.[2] Sartre's ethic of responsibility and bad faith apparently ignores oppression, so it has seemed to feminists that it could only have been by making existentialism "work beyond its means," to use

Le Doeuff's phrase, that de Beauvoir produced feminism from a philoso-phy that was "definitely not a feminism."[3] At the same time, de Beauvoir always insisted that she did nothing original in philosophy.[4] She said that her writings were applications and developments of Sartre's thought. She acknowledged him as the philosophically creative member of their part-nership, while she played the role of an acolyte faithfully following his itinerary, from *Being and Nothingness* to *Critique of Dialectical Reason.* From a feminist perspective, this humility is humiliating. The evidence points to what Le Doeuff has called a "Heloise complex" and it raises a philosophical conundrum.[5] How could one of feminism's greatest tri-umphs be the fruit of such unpromising ground?

A number of solutions to this conundrum have been proposed. One is that de Beauvoir's self-assessment was either consciously or unconsciously distorted. Perhaps it was the result of the all too familiar oppression of women, which she herself outlined so well.[6] Perhaps even de Beauvoir could not entirely shake off "history's lesson," that it is men who are great leaders, women who inherit culture from men. Or possibly, as Kate and Edward Fullbrook suggest, she only played at following Sartre, and hid her originality, like her promiscuity and bisexuality, in order to pro-tect herself.[7] Recent feminist scholarship is reaching a consensus that de Beauvoir's humility was unwarranted. But I will argue that the pendulum may have swung too far. Sartre's early philosophy was not as uncongenial to an analysis of oppression as has been claimed, and many of the key concepts in *The Second Sex* are prefigured in Sartre's 1946 essay, *Portrait of the Anti-Semite.*[8] My focus will be on Sonia Kruks's reading of the Sartre/de Beauvoir relationship. She overturns de Beauvoir's self-assess-ment by arguing that de Beauvoir taught Sartre the limitations of his early account of freedom, and was responsible for the evolution of his philosophy from *Being and Nothingness* to *Critique of Dialectical Reason.*[9] The Fullbrooks offer a more radical hypothesis: de Beauvoir was also the originator of the account of relations with Others to be found in *Being and Nothingness*. If they are right, it may seem less surprising that Sartre's early philosophy already contains the seeds of an account of oppression, but in what follows, I will be conservative and assume that Sartre was responsible for the texts that were published under his name.

Following de Beauvoir's own report that she had, in 1940, maintained against Sartre that from the point of view of freedom not every situation is equal, Kruks argues that with regard to the connected concepts of freedom and oppression, de Beauvoir led where Sartre followed. De Beauvoir never accepted that "the slave in chains is as free as his master." In works such as *Pyrrhus and Cinéas* and *The Ethics of Ambiguity*, she emphasized that the freedom of the individual depends on the freedom of others, and, most important, she challenged Sartre's assumption that "relations of otherness are conflictual relations between two *equal* freedoms."[10] Through her analysis of women as "locked into immanence by the situation *man* inflicts upon her," de Beauvoir provides us with a description of the way in which the "for-itself" can be turned into its opposite, the "in-itself," and thus radically departs from Sartre's notion of freedom.[11] Kruks suggests that, from the point of view of Sartre's philosophy, to say that there is a degradation of the for-itself is equivalent to saying that women are no longer conscious human beings. Such a statement is incoherent from a strictly Sartrean point of view. So, Kruks argues that we should make sense of de Beauvoir by reading her through the framework of Merleau-Ponty's ontology.[12]

For Merleau-Ponty, freedom exists as an embodied consciousness, "engorged with the sensible," and, because of its insertion into the material world, freedom can come in degrees. From this point of view the fall into immanence that is a degradation of existence into the in-itself ceases to be a philosophical problem. So although de Beauvoir never explicitly offered a critique of Sartre's notion of freedom, her account of oppression is claimed to be more coherent if we understand it as leaving Sartre's ontology behind.[13] This is plausible as an interpretation because de Beauvoir was well aware of Merleau-Ponty's work, and Sartre acknowledges it as having shown him the limitations of his earlier views. Kruks tells us that like Merleau-Ponty, de Beauvoir recognizes, well before Sartre, "that there can be no effective *individual* freedom in the face of oppression." This is an insight that she claims Sartre did not achieve until the late 1950s, when he introduced the notion of destiny and showed how oppression constitutes the life of the oppressed "in its totality."[14] But already in 1949 de Beauvoir had used the notion of "destiny" to describe woman's situation and had characterized the situation of the oppressed as a fall into immanence, which Kruks equates with Merleau-Ponty's "freedom devoid of any project."[15]

Superficially, this account of de Beauvoir's philosophical relationship with Sartre may be more appealing than her own. I will argue, however, that more light is shed on de Beauvoir's concepts, and in particular on her idea of a fall into immanence, if we read her work in the traditional manner as an application of structures first mapped out in *Being and Noth-*

ingness. Kruks's reading obscures the extent to which the account of women's oppression in *The Second Sex* draws on Sartre's earlier sketch of the oppression of the Jews. It masks certain deep inadequacies in de Beauvoir's most influential work that are the result of the limitations of the models of freedom and oppression that she shared with Sartre, and it risks attributing to her so little insight that she failed to understand the development of her own beliefs. Because de Beauvoir's work of the late 1940s shares so many features with Sartre's writing of this period it cannot be claimed to clearly preempt Sartre's views of a decade later. Rather, a close reading of Sartre brings into relief the points at which *The Second Sex* breaks down, and the reasons why Sartre and de Beauvoir finally renounced the point of view of existentialist ethics in favour of a philosophy of *praxis*.

In urging the merits of the traditional account of the relationship between Sartre's and de Beauvoir's existentialism, I do not want to deny the more general claim that, despite her disclaimers, de Beauvoir did produce philosophy. Even if Sartre was the source of many of de Beauvoir's ideas, Heidegger, and later Marx, were the source of many of Sartre's ideas. If total originality were a prerequisite for being a philosopher, nobody would pass muster. De Beauvoir takes the philosophy that is given its fullest exposition in *Being and Nothingness* and develops it in her own way, and in new directions. So she is a philosopher.[16] Nor do I want to assert that de Beauvoir taught Sartre nothing. It is inconceivable that the long intellectual collaboration between Sartre and de Beauvoir was not a two-way street.[17] There are, however, two implication of Kruks's paper that cannot be sustained. One is that de Beauvoir's notion of a fall into immanence cannot be understood within the framework of Sartre's ontology. The other is that the difficulties inherent in combining a philosophy of freedom with an account of oppression are already resolved in de Beauvoir's work. Rather, *The Second Sex* is a transitional work in which the ontological categories of *Being and Nothingness* are uneasily combined elements taken from Hegel, Engels, and Lévi-Strauss.

How then are we to solve the conundrum of a feminism that grows out of a philosophy that is in no way feminist? My answer is two pronged. Partly it revises the negative assessment of Sartre's early philosophy, captured by Le Doeuff's remark. In the next section I will show that there is more scope for an account of oppression within the ontological categories of *Being and Nothingness* than has generally been recognized. This potential is developed in somewhat different ways by de Beauvoir in *The Ethics of Ambiguity* and by Sartre in *Portrait of the Anti-Semite*, but key features of the structure of *The Second Sex* are original to Sartre's essay. At the same time, I question the positive interpretation placed on the account of oppression that is found in *The Second Sex*. There are inadequacies in the early model of oppression that are common to Sartre and de Beauvoir. These continue to reverberate throughout feminist debates on freedom and liberation. It is important to recognize this in order to clear the way for more cogent accounts of freedom, oppression, and the path to liberation.

2. De Beauvoir's Assessment: Phenomenology Enriched by the Social

Kruks's characterization of de Beauvoir's early essays as precursors of Sartre's later emphasis on concrete need do not accord with de Beauvoir's own understanding of her development. In *Force of Circumstance*, she says of *The Ethics of Ambiguity*, as she views it from the perspective of the early 1960s, that it is the one of all her books that irritates her most.[18] In speaking of the immediate postwar period, de Beauvoir concurs with Sartre's own assessment that the war had "shown him his own historicity" and had led him to think what he only later expressed, that "the true perspective is that of the most disinherited."[19] Yet he had not at this time "understood the fecundity of the dialectical idea and of Marxist materialism." Her evaluation of *Portrait of the Anti-Semite* is that "it shows how the phenomenological method can be enriched and made flexible by constant recourse to the social; but the concrete factual basis necessary to a history of anti-Semitism is not there."[20] This book already attempts to come to terms with the social situation of the Jew. But from the perspective of the 1960s, introducing the social into Phenomenology is not sufficient to have escaped idealism. By implication, de Beauvoir sees her own work of this period as attempting to introduce the social situation of individuals into the framework of existentialism, but in an inadequate way.

   The Ethics of Ambiguity attempts to extract a morality from *Being and Nothingness*. So, like *Existentialism Is a Humanism* it must forge a path from the separation of free consciousnesses to universal ethical principles. Such an ethic, says de Beauvoir, will assume that it is possible for individuals who are free and separate to "forge laws valid for all."[21] Sartre's attempt during this period to bridge the separation between individual consciousnesses was his ethic of authenticity, which tied morality to the pursuit of freedom as an end within the framework of a recognition of the Kantian principle that in choosing for oneself one chooses for all humanity. In her work, de Beauvoir develops the same theme, although she takes as much from Hegel as from Kant. But this does not prevent her from assessing her book as one that showed her to be at that time, like Sartre, insufficiently liberated from the idealist ideology of her class. Her irritation arises from the fact that she

> went to a great deal of trouble to present inaccurately a problem to which I then offered a solution quite as hollow as the Kantian maxims. My descriptions of the nihilist, the adventurer, the aesthete, obviously influenced by those of Hegel, are even more arbitrary and abstract than his, since they are not even linked together by a historical development. . . . I was in error when I thought I could define a morality independent of a social context. I could write a historical novel without having a philosophy of history, but not construct a theory of action.[22]

It is true, as Kruks points out, that in this text she shows how the freedom of the individual depends on the freedom of others.[23] Yet de Beauvoir does not see it as a precursor of a later turn to materialism, for her way of depicting this interdependence still takes too much from the bourgeois liberal tradition. Rather, she sees it as the equivalent, in her development, of Sartre's *Existentialism Is a Humanism* in his. It is a text that, despite the author's good political intentions, remains abstract and idealist.

Still, one might respond, *The Second Sex* goes well beyond *The Ethics of Ambiguity* in giving us an account of the concrete details of women's situation. If it is only here that de Beauvoir makes her mark, that will be sufficient. De Beauvoir certainly does not dismiss this work as irritating, but even with regard to it she has the following to say: "As for the content, I should take a more materialist position today in the first volume. I should base the notion of woman as *other* and the Manichaean argument it entails not on an idealistic and *a priori* struggle of consciences [*sic*] but on facts of supply and demand."[24] So, from her point of view even *The Second Sex* has not gone far enough in the direction of materialism. As we will see, this brief comment implies de Beauvoir's recognition of a fundamental weakness that *The Second Sex* shares with *Portrait of the Anti-Semite*. In the remainder of this essay I will seek to demonstrate that the model of oppression in de Beauvoir's work shares a number of important features with Sartre's account of the oppression of the Jews. De Beauvoir's work differs from Sartre's partly by virtue of an overlaying of themes from Hegel, Engels, and Lévi-Strauss. But her use of this material does not in the end rescue her book from the inadequacies of Sartre's early attempt to characterize the situation of the oppressed. These features of de Beauvoir's text obscure its similarity to Sartre's, but in the end they merely complicate a shared underlying model and do not constitute a clear break.

3. Concrete Situation in the Early Sartre

Kruks mentions Sartre's text briefly, citing as proof of her claim that Sartre thinks of relations of otherness as "conflictual relations between two equal freedoms" that "the Jew remains free in the face of the anti-Semite because he can choose his own attitude toward his persecutor."[25] But this cannot be enough to drive a wedge between the views of Sartre and de Beauvoir at this period. De Beauvoir also says that woman is "a free and autonomous being like all human creatures."[26] Indeed, in the *Ethics of Ambiguity* she speaks of the Negro slave or the women enclosed in a harem as possibly realizing, within the limitations of their situation, a "perfect assertion of their freedom."[27] Her perspective is that of an existentialist ethic that makes the ultimate end of existence the free transcendence of the present toward an open future.[28] She sometimes accuses women of bad faith, saying that men find in women more complicity than the oppressor usually finds in the oppressed, because the lies that she is told invite her to follow "the easy slope" of fleeing the anxiety that is the result of freedom and responsibility. Even when she can choose independence, it is agonizing for a woman to do so, and so instead she seeks to abandon herself in love.[29] All of this is Sartrean. It is true that de Beauvoir also suggests that society encourages women to take a certain attitude to their situation, and so the "choice" between good and bad faith is constrained by that situation.[30] But Sartre too sets out to explore the way in which the concrete situation of the Jews constrains their possibilities for authentic choice.

The most significant and shared feature of these two works resides in the fact that in each case the origin of oppression rests in a fundamental ontological attitude of the oppressor. As we saw, Kruks says that according to de Beauvoir woman is "locked into immanence by the situation *man* inflicts upon her," and she associates this with de Beauvoir's originality in showing how freedom can be turned into its opposite. But de Beauvoir's claim that the origin of woman's oppression resides in the fact that men have set her up as Other exactly mirrors Sartre's assertion that it is the anti-Semite who creates the Jew.[31] Because the Jew is flung into a situation that is created by the anti-Semite, the choices that are open to him are constrained: "He can choose to be brave or cowardly, sad or gay. . . . But he cannot choose not to be a Jew."[32] Kruks seems to have underestimated the extent to which Sartre's account of man as "a freedom within a situation" already brings with it a robust acknowledgment of the fact that the concrete realities of our existence constrain what is possible, and in particular, constrain the avenues for authentic choice. Even at this stage, Sartre's position is not that of the liberal democrat. What it means for man to be within a situation is "that he forms a synthetic whole with his biological, economic, political, cultural situation, and so on. He is not to be distinguished from it, since it moulds and determines his potentialities, but, inversely, it is he who gives the situation its sense by choosing to be what he is in and through it."[33] This means that, since there is a concrete difference between the situation of the Jew and that of the non-Jew, the democrat who wants to disregard this difference is little better than the anti-Semite.

In his discussion of the democrat, Sartre captures quite starkly the dilemmas that any theory of liberation must face up to, and that have been frequently interpreted, as Sartre interprets them, as showing the bankruptcy of liberal democratic models of universal man. The democrat, says Sartre, "rescues the Jew as a man, but annihilates him as a Jew":[34]

> He has no eyes for the concrete syntheses with which history presents him. He does not recognize the Jew, the Arab or the Negro, the bourgeois or the worker, but man alone, at all times and in all places the same as himself. He breaks up each collectivity into its individual elements. For him a physical body is the sum of a number of molecules, and a social body the sum of a

number of individuals. And when he speaks of an individual, he means a particular incarnation of those universal traits which make up human nature.[35]

Thus the democrat proposes a politics of assimilation. But, as has been increasingly reiterated during the past two decades by blacks, indigenes, Arabs, Jews, and feminists, assimilation denies the concrete differences between groups. It upholds an ideal of humanity that is itself white, male, and Christian, and so, more subtly, but no less destructively, provides the oppressed with options little better than those available under a regime of overt oppression. It is perhaps ironic that among feminists de Beauvoir has been criticized for offering women the kind of pseudo-liberation that Sartre has accused the democrat of offering the Jew. The rise of feminisms of difference has lead to the claim that de Beauvoir's version of liberation amounts to the adoption by women of a masculine subjectivity.[36] Very similar criticisms to those that Sartre levels against the democrat have been leveled against de Beauvoir. These criticisms are, in a sense, unchar- itable. Her book was intended to describe the concrete situation of women, and the forces that lead to one half of the population becoming women. And yet, as we will see, the criticisms are at the same time not entirely unjustified. Although de Beauvoir sets out to write a book about the specific situation of women, although she insists that women exist, and although she herself recognizes that male and female are not sym- metrical, but *man* designates humanity in general whereas woman is de- fined by limiting criteria, there are aspects of the theory that she shares with Sartre that preclude an adequate solution to the problem of libera- tion in a concrete situation of historical difference. Or, so I shall argue. Both Sartre and de Beauvoir are at this stage of their development aware of the real constraints imposed on individuals by their concrete situation. Both share an inadequate theory of the origin of those constraints. Both therefore fail to offer a satisfactory account of the possibilities for libera- tion. But before demonstrating these structural similarities it is worth clarifying Sartre's account of the human condition.

According to Kruks, for Sartre "relations of otherness are conflictual relations between two *equal* freedoms."[37] But this is at least tendentious as an interpretation of Sartre. Leo Fretz, for instance, claims: "The theory of the look as a basis for Sartre's conception of human conduct leaves no room for social intercourse in which *equal* subjects respect the ambiguity of human existence (facticity *and* freedom), with regard to themselves as well as to one another."[38] The outright contradiction between these two readings of Sartre appears stark, but it can be overcome in the following way. For Sartre there are two possible attitudes to the Other that result from the fact that our knowledge of the Other resides in the experience of objectification through the look. On the one hand we can take the attitude that is claimed to be involved in love, language, and masochism, and incorporate the Other's transcendence without denying it; or we can take the attitude that is involved in indifference, desire, sadism, and hate and transcend the other's transcendence. Roughly characterized, these are the positions of being-looked-at and being-a-look.[39] Whichever attitude we take we will not be treating the Other as an equal, but rather as the complimentary opposite of the self. And Sartre describes the situation as one in which "we shall never place ourselves on a plane of equality; that is, on the plane where the recognition of the Other's freedom would involve the Other's recognition of our freedom."[40] The very nature of our knowledge of the Other apparently precludes the possibility of any optimistic Hegelian resolution to the conflict between consciousnesses. So relations between people are never relations between equals.[41] Yet on the same page, Sartre describes the two attitudes as collapsing into each other in a circular movement that is never arrested. In *Being and Nothingness*, individuals are implicitly assumed to be equals in terms of their capacity to adopt either of these two opposing attitudes. There is only a passing recognition that certain social positions might fix individuals in the position of being-looked-at or being-a-look. But the structure of relationships between individuals that is described leaves open the possibility that some concrete situations are more conducive to one attitude than the other. It is exactly the recognition of this possibility that provides the basic model of the nature of oppression that is introduced in *Portrait of the Anti-Semite* and fleshed out in *The Second Sex*.

In a vague way, this possibility is already recognized in *Being and Nothingness*. In his discussion of "being-with," Sartre introduces the possibility of experiencing oneself as a member of an "us-object." We who are together looked at by a third and are seen as part of a complex object are collectively objectified. We feel shame for what we are in the Other's eyes. This, says Sartre, is the origin of class consciousness.[42] In sofar as we are members of a group toward whom others take an objectifying attitude we will be forced to experience ourselves as looked-at, as objects, rather than as a look. It is noteworthy that Sartre argues here that we cannot develop a stable sense of being a we-subject. Class consciousness is possible, but there is no clear place for solidarity. According to the description in these pages, our being with Others provides no escape from the fact that relations with others are conflictual.[43]

4. Sartre's Ontology in *The Second Sex*

The introduction to *The Second Sex* shows de Beauvoir's immersion in this background:

> The category of the *Other* is as primordial as consciousness itself (1:16/1:16–17). . . . we find in consciousness itself a fundamental hostility towards every other consciousness; the subject can be posed only in being opposed (1:17/1:18) . . . woman . . . finds herself in a world where men compel her to assume the status of the Other. They propose to stabilize her as object and to doom her to immanence since her transcendence is to be overshadowed and forever transcended by another ego (*conscience*) which is essential and sovereign. (1:31, 29)

Kruks tells us that de Beauvoir's notion of woman's immanence is the same as Merleau-Ponty's freedom devoid of any project. But de Beauvoir's phrases are heavily reminiscent of Sartre's description of the second attitude toward Others, that found in indifference, desire, sadism, and hate. This is the attitude that turns its look directly against the Other who looks, and in asserting itself as a freedom confronting the Other, makes "the Other a transcendence transcended—that is, an object."[44] If this is correct, then woman's immanence is a consequence of her being constrained by her concrete situation to take up the position of the looked-at rather than that of the one who looks.

The four objectifying attitudes that Sartre lists—indifference, desire, sadism, and hate—could serve as a feminist catalog of male attitudes toward women. But here there is a difference between de Beauvoir's account of women's situation and Sartre's account of the situation of the Jews. The objectifying attitude that the anti-Semite adopts toward the Jew is that of sadism and hate. Men's objectifying attitudes toward women are more varied and subtle. Nevertheless, with this proviso, " 'the eternal feminine' corresponds to 'the Jewish character.' "[45] The Jewish character is a myth constructed by the anti-Semite in order to rationalize the passion of hatred that he freely adopts and that provides the Manichean organizing principle of his world.[46] The mythic world of good and evil that the anti-Semite constructs is just one version of that everyday morality with which "respectable citizens" surround themselves in order to flee the ethical anguish that results from human freedom.[47] The anti-Semite justifies his existence by being the personification of good in the face of objective evil. "Anti-Semitism, in a word, is fear when faced with the human situation."[48] The oppression of the Jews arises out of the struggle between consciousnesses and the fear of freedom.

The Second Sex is less explicit, but one can find there a parallel explanation of the origin of misogyny. In Sartre's account of relations with others there is, as we saw, an element of equality. Although I cannot recognize the other as a free consciousness on the same plane as myself, I can change from one fundamental attitude to the other. Within this framework, the problem of explaining women's oppression becomes the problem of explaining why "women do not dispute male sovereignty."[49] How is it that men can maintain the attitude of transcending women's transcendence rather than experience themselves as us-objects for women? At this point certain Hegelian themes enter into de Beauvoir's text and cohabit rather unhappily with Sartre's account of human relations. Sartre begins by describing the emotional attitude of hatred that is adopted by the anti-Semite as a free choice in the face of the anguish of freedom. In her account of the history of sexual relations, de Beauvoir does not immediately resort to the claim that bad faith encourages men to objectify women, but borrows from Hegel the idea that it is in risking life that consciousness first becomes aware of itself.[50] This explanation of woman's fixation in the position of transcendence transcended comes perilously close to accepting that because woman's biological function is to reproduce life, rather than to risk it, she is arrested in a state of consciousness that is not self-conscious. This really would be to reduce woman to an in-itself, the opposite of being-for-itself. De Beauvoir immediately withdraws the implication. Woman is of course a transcendence, she says, but she is forced to transcend mere species life vicariously, through the heroic exploits of men. Yet this proffered "key" to the mystery of woman's submission is quite inadequate. It is disturbingly sexist.[51] Moreover, as Kruks has observed, it is incompatible with Sartre's account of consciousness. There is no place in Sartre's philosophy for a consciousness that is not self-conscious.[52] It is the consciousness of the self as an object of the Other's look that, according to Sartre, forces us to recognize the existence of another consciousness, but there is no obvious place in his philosophy, as there is in Hegel's, for a development of self-conscious-ness, out of mere consciousness, through the mediation of the threat of death at the hands of the other.[53] One might take this, as Kruks does, as evidence that de Beauvoir has indeed left Sartre behind. But, I will argue, the two somewhat different accounts of relations with others that are offered by Hegel and Sartre coalesce in de Beauvoir's text. The confusion is exacerbated by the influence of Lévi-Strauss.

De Beauvoir accepts Lévi-Strauss's claim that there never was a histor-ical matriarchy. She also quotes approvingly his assertion that marriage is a bond set up between men. And she notes, in this context, an ambigu-ity in the concept of otherness. On the one hand there is absolute alter-ity; one might think of this, in Sartrean terms, as the otherness of the in-itself. "To the precise degree that woman is regarded as the absolute Other—that is to say, whatever her magical powers, as the inessential—it is to that degree impossible to consider her as another subject."[54] De Beauvoir contrasts this with the Other who is similar to me and with whom it is possible to maintain reciprocal relations. On the other hand there is the Sartrean Other who is a subject whose subjectivity threatens mine. Although the transcendence of such an Other can be transcended and made an object, this will be an object that retains within it the marks of subjectivity. De Beauvoir's text seems to vacillate between these conceptions. On the one hand the question she raises—why has man transcended woman's transcendence?—assumes that woman is a tran-scendence. On the other hand it looks as though the explanation she gives implies that woman is not transcendent. It is men who have achieved transcendence through risking life and working on a nature that they have identified with woman. If this is the explanation, then the patriarchs are right, woman never creates but only inherits culture from men. Women do not challenge men's sovereignty because women are not subjects.

But this is hardly a solution to the problem posed, since that problem assumed that women are subjects. One can, however, read de Beauvoir's existentialist key in a slightly different way that is more in harmony with Sartre's account of relations with Others. Sartre argues, in *Being and Nothingness*, that we become aware of the Other in becoming aware of the self as an object for the Other. De Beauvoir infers that in a life-and-death struggle the hunter or fighter will be acutely aware of himself as an object for the beast or man that threatens to kill him in its own defense. If he succeeds in his goal he will have transcended its transcendence, but success is by no means guaranteed. So he will experience himself as an object for the Other, but feel passive, dependent on a Nature that dispenses life and death by chance.[55] At this stage, de Beauvoir's description of man's relation to the Other is reminiscent of Sartre's account of the attitude of language and love. Nature and woman are set up by man as the Mother Goddess whom he adores. Nature contains an uncontrollable magic. Language is a sacred object that "points to a transcendence beyond the world."[56] In the primitive stage of society man sets up life, Nature, and Woman as the essential; he chooses his alienation as an object that is dependent for its meaning on the transcendent Other, but this is an alienation to which he consents.[57] Sartre describes part of the instability of love as arising from the fact that the lover cannot hide from the fact that love, which is an alienated freedom, nevertheless is a free project. Love does not release the subject from responsibility for the self.[58] Analogously de Beauvoir describes the development of men's attitude to women as one that begins, while he is powerless and afraid, with his setting up woman as an Other who is venerated; and ends, as his power and consciousness of freedom grow, with his adopting the attitude that woman and nature are mere objects to be transcended.[59] What some historians had seen as a transformation of matriarchy into patriarchy, de Beauvoir interprets as a change on men's behalf from the first to the second of Sartre's fundamental attitudes to the Other.

So whereas Sartre introduces the objectifying attitude of the anti-Semite as the free choice of an inauthentic subject, de Beauvoir "explains" the objectifying attitude of men as resulting from their privileged biological position. If this is right, woman's development is retarded not because she lacks self-consciousness, but because nothing occurs to wrench her consciousness away from its solipsism, except man, who has already set her up as Other. There is a significant exegetical advantage to this interpretation. It allows us to understand why de Beauvoir describes woman's position as one of being locked in "immanence." In Sartre's early vocabulary the immanent is the subjective, the transcendent that which is beyond subjective appearance. Insofar as Sartre rejects idealism, objects, that is to say things-in-themselves, are not purely immanent.[60] This makes de Beauvoir's claim that woman is both object and immanent puzzling. It becomes less puzzling when we think of this immanence as the subjectivity of the solipsist. "It is the existence of other men which tears each man out of his immanence," says de Beauvoir.[61] Woman remains locked in immanence insofar as she fails to distinguish herself from her own subjective experience of the world. She experiences herself not as a transcendent consciousness beyond appearance, but identifies with her subjective image of herself. At the same time this image comes from the outside, from man. Men invented her.[62] Although the objectifying look of man exists for woman, it exists as an invitation to remain bound up in existing as the object looked at. The look is not a threat that needs to be overcome. Thus it fails to wrench woman from her immanence. From this point of view we can explain de Beauvoir's puzzling claim that woman fails to achieve transcendence as arising out of an ambiguity in the Sartrean notion of self-consciousness. On the one hand, the prereflective cogito ensures that consciousness is consciousness through and through, so already self-conscious. On the other hand, since there is only being and nothingness, there is nothing to know in consciousness. Insofar as I can know myself, I know myself as an object. It is the Other who reveals to me my existence as an object in the world. I can accept this object status, or I can reject it. It is only through rejecting the attitude that accepts that I am this object (and nothing more) that I can come to see myself as an object that nevertheless is not simply identical with itself, but that is a self on which I can work as a free creative project. This is the transcendence that the woman who is locked in immanence lacks.[63]

De Beauvoir defines an authentically ethical attitude as one that renounces mere being and assumes existence. By contrast the inauthentic attitude of the serious man is described as an escape from existence that makes itself mere being.[64] This vocabulary, and the possibility of degradation into mere being, are explained in thoroughly Sartrean terms in *The Ethics of Ambiguity*. To assume existence is to affirm one's liberty and the ambiguous split between being and nonbeing that is its foundation. To assume existence is to make oneself a lack of being in order that there should be being. By contrast, to accept the illusion that one is identical with being is a form of bad faith.[65] The slide into immanence is then a slide into a kind of subjectivity that affirms itself as mere being-in-itself, an object of sensory experience, in a world of subjective experience, rather than one that affirms itself as a free agent and transcendent negativity.

However, even the forgoing explanation of men's and women's asymmetrical opportunities for transcendence is not totally satisfying. Summing up the situation of women at the moment of prehistory at which she was revered, de Beauvoir says: "Being venerated and feared because of her fecundity, being *other* than man and sharing the disturbing character of the *other*, woman in a way held man in dependence upon her, while at the same time being dependent on him; the reciprocity of the master-slave relation was what she *actually* enjoyed, and through that fact she escaped slavery."[66] But it is well known that out of this reciprocity of master and slave Hegel described the emergence of the reciprocal of self-consciousnesses. Why does this not happen in the case of men and women? Early in the section devoted to myths, de Beauvoir provides an explanation. It is only possible for men to rise above the conflict between consciousnesses when an authentically moral attitude is attained. This attitude will come about through a conversion in which an individual renounces "being" and assumes his existence.[67] This is the conversion at which Sartre hints in a footnote at the conclusion of his discussion of concrete relations with others, and that he discusses at greater length in the *Notebooks for an Ethics*.[68] The two attitudes toward others described in *Being and Nothingness* are those that man adopts while in bad faith. From the point of view of the ethic at which Sartre hinted at the end of *Being and Nothingness*, the circle that captured men in these two attitudes could only be overcome by those who had undergone a conversion from bad faith to authenticity. The theme of conversion is also to be found in de Beauvoir's *Ethics of Ambiguity*, where she notes that, according to the existentialist, the resolution of the Hegelian conflict requires a conversion.[69] Ultimately then, it is because man is in bad faith that he chooses to make woman an object. In the pages that follow, de Beauvoir describes man's attitude to woman in language heavily reminiscent of Sartre's description of the second objectifying attitude, that of desire. Man "hopes to fulfil himself by carnally possessing a being, but at the same time confirming his sense of freedom through the docility of a free person."[70] So, despite all the historical explanations, in the end, men choose to treat women as objects, because, being in bad faith, they are afraid of freedom.

All the complexity of de Beauvoir's account of the origin of women's oppression amounts to little. Like Sartre's account of the oppression of the Jews, the bad faith of the oppressor is ultimately to blame. Like the Jew, woman is the imaginary product of the transcendent one who flees the ambiguity of incarnate freedom. At the conclusion of her discussion of the history of the women's movement de Beauvoir asserts: "Just as in

America there is no Negro problem, but rather a white problem; just as 'anti-Semitism is not a Jewish problem; it is our problem'; so the woman problem has always been a man's problem. We have seen why men had moral prestige from the start; they created values, mores, religions; never have women disputed this empire with them."[71] Sartre says that the Jew is not historical and has no history, De Beauvoir echoes that women have "no past, no history, no religion of their own."[72] Since the Jew flees from his situation as a Jew he is constantly afraid that certain characteristics deemed Jewish will be found in him. This kind of inauthenticity is more tempting for the Jew than for other men, and leads to an inferiority complex.[73] The Jewish situation also tends towards masochism.[74] De Beauvoir finds similar consequences flowing from women's situation as the Other set up by man. Women are tempted by the inauthentic choice of denying that they are women.[75] The young girl is inclined towards masochism, and it is an attitude more tempting to women that to men. Moreover, narcissism, a peculiarly feminine failing, evinces the same structure. In both I become fascinated by myself as an object for the Other.[76] Women's "justifications"—narcissism, love, and mysticism—all turn out to be forms of experiencing the self through the other's transcendence. Inauthentic woman has projects, but only projects in which she freely alienates her liberty, and provides herself with a justification in some transcendence outside herself.

The structural similaries that I have outlined make it abundantly clear that the philosophy of The Second Sex is an application, in the case of women, of a model of oppression that had been extracted from the ontological categories of Being and Nothingness. There is no need to turn to Merleau-Ponty in order to understand de Beauvoir's text. Indeed, de Beauvoir's use of the term immanence is only comprehensible if we reject the interpretation that takes it to be a mere synonym for "being-in-itself" and read it, in the light of Being and Nothingness, as referring to a certain kind of solipsistic immersion in the world of sensory experience; a form of being rather than of existing. It is true that there is more Hegel, more Marx, and more history in The Second Sex than there is in Portrait of the Anti-Semite, but if we compare de Beauvoir's work to the Notebooks for an Ethics, even this difference fades away. In de Beauvoir's work, Marxism and the history of woman's situation are only partly integrated into the ontological categories of Being and Nothingness. It is a work that belongs to a period of transition. In it the dialectic of history cohabits unhappily with an ethic of conversion and free choice. Sartre and de Beauvoir ultimately saw the inadequacies of this early model of oppression. It remains to show their descendents in some recent feminist texts.

5. Sartre's Problematic Structures in Contemporary Feminist Thought

There are three connected problems with this model of oppression that can be briefly stated. First, oppression is ultimately grounded in a moral failing of the oppressor. Second, the oppressed are faced with an invidious choice; Sartre extols authenticity, but his theory makes it look like an impossible option. Third, there is no place for the solidarity of the oppressed. These failings are, once again, clearest in Sartre's text, but once recognized, can be clearly seen in *The Second Sex* and the feminist philosophy that derives from it.

It is when Sartre discusses the possibilities for combating anti-Semitism that his essay is at its weakest, and its moralism most evident. Since the Jew is created by the anti-Semite, it is by changing the anti-Semite that the oppression can be lifted. But if the attitude of the anti-Semite is a free choice, adopted in bad faith, what could induce him to change? Logically, one is left with nothing but idealistic, moral exhortation. Sartre, however, changes tack, and brings into play an idea that he had hinted at earlier: anti-Semitism is a mystification that results from class conflict.[77] But this brings in a different and incompatible explanation. Either the anti-Semite chooses freely, or his views are the result of class conflict mystified. Which, one wants to say to Sartre, is it to be? Moreover, it is almost as though Sartre agrees with the democrat that the Jew is a fiction. Whereas the democrat thinks that the Jew is a fiction in the mind of the Jew, and wishes that the Jew would give up this fiction and see himself as the universal "man," Sartre argues that the Jew is a fiction in the mind of the anti-Semite. He will cease to exist once anti-Semitism is dispelled.[78] It is hardly flattering to the Jew to learn that his identity is nothing but that which the anti-Semite has created for him.[79] This consequence connects with the second failing. Authenticity involves accepting that one is a Jew, but how can one be a Jew if being a Jew is being what the anti-Semite says the Jew is? Either the analysis is not correct, and the Jew does exist independently of the anti-Semite, or authenticity looks in danger of collapsing into the attitude in which one identifies the self with the object one is for the Other. The free choice of affirming one's Jewishness will be tainted by a situation in which everything one does can count against one.[80] It is only on condition that members of the oppressed group can create for themselves a we-subject with which they can identify that they can establish a sense of solidarity. Yet there is little room in Sartre's early analysis for the development of such a we-subject.

These failings lead to some of the most outrageous and irritating claims in de Beauvoir's work. At the culmination of her discussion of the nineteenth-century feminist movement, which shared its origins with the French Revolution and culminated in the vote, de Beauvoir makes the claim, quoted earlier that "the woman problem has always been a man's problem." Some isolated individuals—she mentions Sappho, Christine de Pisan, Mary Wollstonecraft, and Olympe de Gouges—have protested "the harshness of their destiny" but not one of their successes could have been won "unless men had been quite disposed to submit to it. . . . Feminism itself was never an autonomous movement: it was in part an instrument in the hands of politicians, in part an epiphenomenon reflecting a deeper social drama."[81] This dismissive attitude toward, and lack of solidarity with, past women, flows logically from the Sartrean analysis. If woman is merely a transcendence transcended, an object created by the transcendence of men, then evidence of her transcendent activity must be an illusion. De Beauvoir's prescription for liberation is, it is true, not quite as idealistic as Sartre's. She sees that the oppressors cannot be expected to give up their privileges in an act of gratuitous generosity. Change will come about either through the revolt of the oppressed or through "the evolution of the privileged caste."[82] But like Sartre, she vacillates between incompatible alternatives. Either the oppressor makes a gratuitous gesture, or there is an unexplained revolt or an equally unexplained "evolution." Free choice and Marxist determinism are both appealed to, without any resolution offered of their incompatibility. De Beauvoir does see that for women to authentically assume their liberty requires revolt and a collective liberation.[83] And Sartre too alludes to the need for a Jewish revolt.[84] But the theory according to which oppression is maintained through myths created by the free choice of the oppressor makes it mysterious how the oppressed could achieve the sense of solidarity necessary for a collective revolt.[85] Of course, one might question whether Sartre's mature attempt to bridge this gap succeeded, but one does not find in de Beauvoir's work anything like Sartre's later synthesis of freedom and Marxism according to which men (and women too) make history just to the extent that it makes them.[86]

The asymmetry, in *Portrait of the Anti-Semite*, between the free choice of the anti-Semite and the constraint placed on the liberty of the Jew by that freely chosen attitude, lives on implicitly in certain strands of feminism. In the writings of feminist antipornographers one finds the assumption that man is a subject with autonomous desires who creates woman as a sexual object who desires her own self-annihilation.[87] In MacKinnon's text the link with de Beauvoir is explicitly acknowledged. The campaign therefore becomes one of moral reformation of a certain group of men. Desire and sadism are attitudes that men adopt and promulgate through pornography, which is taken to be an instrument for creating the submissive creature known as woman. There is a clear asymmetry. Men are autonomous and free, women socially constructed. MacKinnon, it is true, says that the category *male* is not a biological category, but a social one. Moreover, the subject is by definition male. But this itself leads to an impasse. Should biological women aspire to this social status? Very little effort is put into explaining why biological males tend to be the individuals who are in this social situation. This gives the impression that the origin of this fact must, after all, reside in a free choice or essential moral defect. So, the Manichean conflict between good and evil remains, and, in some writers, most notably Mary Daly, it is explicitly essentialized.[88]

The invidious nature of the choices available to the oppressed, if this model is accepted, are evident in recent feminist conflicts. This is evocatively expressed by both Le Doeuff and Irigaray.[89] As a woman, one cannot choose to be a male subject. But if women are just what men have set them up to be, one cannot choose to be a woman either. The debate between feminists of equality and feminists of difference gets caught between these two unacceptable poles. In her discussion of Freud, de Beauvoir had already described these two choices as "two modes of alienation."[90] What she in fact wanted was for women to choose authenticity; the complex acceptance of one's existence as both identical with and different from that which one is for others (oneself as material thing in the world). But the effect of her description of man's objectifying attitudes is, like the effect of *Being and Nothingness*, to leave one with the impression that one can only be either looking subject or object of a look. If the subject is masculine, then for woman transcendence is self-annihilation. Despite the fact that on one level this dilemma misrepresents de Beauvoir's intention, it is still a consequence of her account. If woman is *just* a creation of men, she, like the Jew, will cease to exist once society has become a kingdom of ends.[92]

The greatest failing of these early works is that, from their perspective, it is impossible to see how authenticity is to be concretely achieved. "One cannot be converted alone," writes Sartre in his *Notebooks*.[92] He will come to recognize that what is needed is social change, *praxis* grounded in one's membership of a group.[93] In the case of women this will involve solidarity with the others who are women. But, I have argued, this is not coherently available from within the perspective of *The Second Sex*. Like Sartre's work of the same period, the account of oppression offered is unable to give a satisfactory account of the possibility of radical political action.

So, Sartre's influence on de Beauvoir's account of oppression should not be ignored. We will understand the strengths and weaknesses of *The Second Sex* much better if we read it alongside Sartre's philosophical works of this period. As feminists we should not let our desire to recognize de Beauvoir's greatness get in the way of giving Sartre credit where credit is due. By the late 1940s Sartre and de Beauvoir were both deeply influenced by Marxism, but neither had given up the existentialist categories of *Being and Nothingness*, and neither had forged a satisfactory reconciliation of these two conflicting tendencies in their thought. Perhaps de Beauvoir was originally responsible for the account of the structure of our relations with others that Sartre had laid down in *Being and Nothingness*. But even if she was not, and the weight of future scholarship comes to concur with her claim that she followed Sartre's philosophy and internalized his thought, it would still be the case that she reexternalised it in a book that was more than anything a totalization and a *praxis*. What de Beauvoir taught Sartre was, perhaps, not so much in what she said, but in what she did. She showed, concretely, how political change can come about through the historically located activity of an individual who thematizes the situation of her class. Within the master-slave dialectic there is a dialectical inversion. Even if de Beauvoir began as acolyte and lover, she worked on her material, seeking an answer to the question, How does woman come into being? But the answer was itself an act of coming into being; an act that took the "master's" thought for its object, and transformed it into a new transcendent activity. Without de Beauvoir, Sartre's thought would now be largely outdated abstract speculation. It lives on in a developing, if sometimes inadequate and fragmented, feminist *praxis*.

Thus, ironically, one might say that now it is largely through her that Sartre attains a "real hold upon the world."[94]

Notes

1. Michèle Le Doeuff, "Simone de Beauvoir and Existentialism," *Feminist Studies* 6 (1980): 277–89; *Hipparchia's Choice*, trans. Trista Selous (Oxford: Blackwell, 1990).

2. Simone de Beauvoir, *Le Deuxième Sexe* (Paris: Gallimard, 1949); *The Second Sex*, trans. H. M. Parshley (Harmondsworth: Penguin, 1972), 1:31, 28. Where a text and its translation are cited, all page numbers will be to the French original first, the English translation second.

3. Le Doeuff, "Simone de Beauvoir and Existentialism," 287; *Hipparchia's Choice*, 62.

4. Margaret Simons, "Two Interviews with Simone de Beauvoir," in *Revaluing French Feminism*, ed. Nancy Fraser and Sandra Lee Bartky (Bloomington: Indiana University Press, 1992), 27–28; Simone de Beauvoir, *La Force de l'age* (Paris: Gallimard, 1960); *The Prime of Life*, trans. Peter Green (Harmondsworth: Penguin, 1965), 228–29, 220–21.

5. Le Doeuff, *Hipparchia's Choice*, 162.

6. Simons, "Two Interviews with Simone de Beauvoir," 27.

7. Kate Fullbrook and Edward Fullbrook, *Simone de Beauvoir and Jean-Paul Sartre: The Remaking of a Twentieth-Century Legend* (New York: Harvester Wheatsheaf, 1993), 122–27. As the Fullbrooks acknowledge, Margaret Simons had previously argued that de Beauvoir concentrated on relationships with others earlier than did Sartre (Margaret Simons, "Beauvoir and Sartre: The Philosophical Relationship," *Yale French Studies* 72 [1986]: 165–79). Yet Simons underplays the influence that Sartre's analysis of anti-Semitism had on *The Second Sex*, saying that Sartre does not there use the concept of the Other. With this I disagree. Although Sartre does not explicitly speak of the Other when discussing anti-Semitism, his analysis clearly derives from the characterization of concrete relations with Others developed in *Being and Nothingness*.

8. Jean-Paul Sartre, *Réflexions sur la question juive* (Paris: Gallimard, 1954); *Portrait of the Anti-Semite*, trans. Eric Mauny (London: Secker and Warburg. Lindsay Drummond, 1948).

9. Sonia Kruks, *Situation and Human Existence: Freedom, Subjectivity, and Society* (London: Unwin Hyman, 1990), 83–112; and "Simone de Beauvoir: Teaching Sartre About Freedom," *Sartre Alive*, ed. R. Aronsen and A. van den Hoven (Detroit: Wayne State University Press, 1991), 285–300, reprinted in *Feminist Interpretations of Simone de Beauvoir*, ed. Margaret Simons (University Park: Penn State Press, 1995), 79–95. Page references are to the reprint.

10. Kruks, "Simone de Beauvoir: Teaching Sartre About Freedom," 82–84; Simone de Beauvoir, *Pyrrhus and Cinéas* (Paris: Gallimard, 1944); and *Pour une morale de l'ambiguité* (Paris: Gallimard, 1947); *The Ethics of Ambiguity*, trans. Bernard Frechtman (New York: Citadel Press, 1962).

11. Kruks, "Simone de Beauvoir: Teaching Sartre About Freedom," 87; *Situation and Human Existence*, 101–2.

12. Ibid., 87–88.

13. Ibid., 88–90.

14. Ibid., 92.

15. Ibid., 93.

16. Le Doeuff, *Hipparchia's Choice*, 164; Simons, "Two Interviews with Simone de Beauvoir," 43.

17. Simone de Beauvoir, *La Force des choses* (Paris: Gallimard, 1963); *Force of Circumstance*, trans. Richard Howard (Harmondsworth: Penguin, 1968), 15, 12.

18. De Beauvoir, *La Force des choses*, 79–80, 77.

19. Ibid., 15–18, 13–15.

20. Ibid., 56–57, 52.

21. De Beauvoir, *Pour une morale de l'ambiguité*, 26, 18.

22. De Beauvior, *La Force des choses*, 80, 76.

23. Kruks, "Simone de Beauvoir: Teaching Sartre About Freedom," 83.

24. De Beauvoir, *La Force des choses*, 210, 202.

25. Kruks, *Situation and Human Existence*, 103, "Simone de Beauvoir: Teaching Sartre About Freedom," 84.

26. De Beauvoir, *Le Deuxième Sexe*, 1:31, 29.

27. De Beauvoir, *Pour une morale de l'ambiguité*, 56, 38. A significant difference between Sartre and de Beauvoir is evident here. De Beauvoir suggests that those who are totally oppressed are like children, and not morally at fault for accepting the values imposed on them. But while this amounts to a rejection of Sartre's claim that freedom implies responsibility, it does not involve the assertion that freedom is lost altogether. In fact, de Beauvoir goes on to say that as soon as circumstances change so that liberation is a possibility, those who fail to exploit it are morally at fault.

28. De Beauvoir, *Le Deuxième Sexe*, 1:31, 28–29.

29. Ibid., 2:480–85 and 2:565, 655–60 and 730.

30. Ibid., 1:39, 27.

31. Sartre, *Réflexions sur la question juive*, 176, 120.

32. Ibid., 108–10, 74–75.

33. Ibid., 72, 49.

34. Ibid., 68, 46.

35. Ibid., 66–67, 45.

36. Charlene Haddock Seigfried, "Gender Specific Values," *Philosophical Forum* 15 (1984): 425–42; "*Second Sex*, Second Thoughts," *Women's Studies International Forum* 8 (1985): 219–29.

37. Kruks, "Simone de Beauvoir: Teaching Sartre About Freedom," 84.

38. Leo Fretz, "Individuality in Sartre's Philosophy," *The Cambridge Companion to Sartre*, ed. Christina Howells (Cambridge: Cambridge University Press, 1992), 88.

39. Jean-Paul Sartre, *L'Être et le néant* (Paris: Gallimard, 1943); *Being and Nothingness*, trans. Hazel Barnes (London: Routledge, 1989), 430–31, and 479, 363 and 408.

40. Ibid., 479, 408.

41. At least, this is the case while people remain in bad faith. As we will see below, Sartre raises the possibility of a radical conversion that can overcome this state of affairs.

42. Sartre, *L'Être et le néant*, 491–92, 420.

43. Ibid., 495–503, 423–30.

44. Ibid., 448 and 405, 379 and 339.

45. De Beauvoir, *Le Deuxième Sexe*, 1:24, 23.

46. Sartre, *Réflexions sur la question juive*, 10–11 and 19 and 46–61, 7 and 13 and 32–41.

47. Sartre, *L'Être et le néant*, 75–76, 38.

48. Sartre, *Réflexions sur la question juive*, 65, 44.

49. De Beauvoir, *Le Deuxième Sexe*, 1:17 and 1:105, 18 and 93.

50. Ibid., 1:112, 96.

51. I have discussed the implicit sexism of de Beauvoir's view of history elsewhere *The Woman of Reason* (Continuum Press, 1995), 133–36.

52. Sartre, *L'Être et le néant*, 18–22, xxviii–xxxi.

53. Ibid., 294–99, 238–43.

54. De Beauvoir, *Le Deuxième Sexe*, 1:120, 102.

55. Ibid., 1:116–67, 100.

56. Sartre, *L'Être et le néant*, 442, 374.

57. De Beauvoir, *Le Deuxième Sexe*, 1:122–23, 104–5.

58. Sartre, *L'Être et le néant*, 442–45, 374–76.

59. De Beauvoir, *Le Deuxième Sexe*, 1:126–28, 106–9.

60. Sartre, *L'Être et le néant*, 23–24, xxxiii. This is in accord with the standard Kantian use of these terms.

61. De Beavior, *Le Deuxième Sexe*, 1:231, 171.

62. Ibid., 1:295, 218.

63. There is a difference between Sartre's and de Beauvoir's accounts of the relationship betwen the two attitudes. Sartre clearly says that they are at the same level (*L'Être et le néant*, 430–31, 379). De Beauvoir implicitly interprets the relationship between Sartre's first and second attitude as one of progress. Even if the objectifying attitude of men is the result of bad faith, she implies, that it is closer to free authentic transcendence than is woman's alienation of her freedom. This is, I think, a defect in her account. More consistently with Sartre's description of the two attitudes one should argue that men will not achieve authentic transcendence until they recognize that they are as dependent for their being on women's look as subjects whose look creates women. This is where de Beauvoir ends up, but she muddies the waters through her positive assessment of men's historic achievement of transcendence in comparison with that of women.

64. De Beauvoir, *Le Deuxième Sexe*, 1:232, 172, *Pour une morale de l'ambiguité*, 66, 46.

65. De Beauvoir, *Pour une morale de l'ambiguité*, 48–49, 34.

66. De Beauvoir, *Le Deuxième Sexe*, 1:231–32, 110.

67. Ibid., 1:232, 172.

68. Sartre, *L'Être et le néant*, 484, 412. Jean-Paul Sartre, *Cahiers pour une morale* (Paris: Gallimard, 1983); *Notebooks for an Ethics*, trans. David Pellauer (Chicago: University of Chicago Press, 1992), 16, 9. The theme of conversion in Sartre is discussed by Thomas Anderson, *Sartre's Two Ethics* (Chicago: Open Court, 1993) 33–35.

69. De Beauvoir, *Pour une morale de l'ambiguité*, 19–20 and 93, 13 and 66.

70. De Beauvoir, *Le Deuxième Sexe*, 1:233–34, 172–73, Sartre, *L'Être et le néant*, 461–66, 392–96.

71. De Beauvoir, *Le Deuxième Sexe*, 1:216, 159. On the last page of *Réflexions sur la question juive*, Sartre quotes Richard Wright's comment that there is no Negro problem, but a white problem. This comment originally appeared in *Action* in October 1946 and is reprinted in *Conversations with Richard White*, ed. Keneth Kinnamon and Michel Fabre (Jackson: University of Mississippi Press, 1993), 99.

72. De Beauvoir, *Le Deuxième Sexe*, 1:19, 19, Sartre, *Réflexions sur la question juive*, 103 and 112, 71 and 77.

73. Sartre, *Réflexions sur la question juive*, 113–30, 77–90.

74. Ibid., 131–33, 90–91.

75. De Beauvoir, *Le Deuxième Sexe*, 1:13, 14.

76. Ibid., 2:165–66, 2:474–75 and 2:533–34, 420–21, 650–51 and 700.

77. Sartre, *Réflexions sur la question juive*, 53 and 182–86, 36 and 124–46.

78. Ibid., 185, 126.

79. Contemporary criticism of Sartre's essay focused on this point. See Michel Contat and Michel Rybalka, eds. *Les Écrits de Sartre: Cronologie, bibliographie commenté* (Paris: Gallimard, 1970), 140.

80. Sartre, *Réflexions sur la question juive*, 133 and 169–75, 91 and 115–19.

81. De Beauvoir, *Le Deuxième Sexe*, 1:217, 159–60.

82. Ibid., 2:573–74, 738.

83. Ibid., 2:455, 639.

84. Jean-Paul Sartre, "Une Lettre de Jean-Paul Sartre," reprinted in Contat and Rybalka, *Les Écrits de Sartre*, 141.

85. Perhaps, however, given the difficulty of enlisting the oppressed in collective liberation movements, one might take this as evidence for the descriptive adequacy of this early analysis of the situation of the oppressed.

86. Jean-Paul Sartre, *Critique de la raison dialectique*, vol. 1. (Paris: Gallimard, 1960); *Critique of Dialectical Reason*, trans. Alan Sheridan-Smith (London: NLB, 1976), 180, 97.

87. Andrea Dworkin, *Pornography: Men Possessing Women* (London: Woman's Press, 1981), 99; Catharine MacKinnon, *Feminism Unmodified* (Cambridge: Harvard University Press, 1987), 50–55.

88. Mary Daly, *Gyn/Ecology: The Metaethics of Radical Feminism* (Boston: Beacon Press, 1978).

89. Le Doeuff, *Hipparchia's Choice*, 165; Luce Irigaray, *Speculum of the Other Woman* (Ithaca: Cornell University Press, 1985), 133.

90. De Beauvoir, *Le Deuxième Sexe*, 1:92–93, 82–83.

91. Some feminists are quite prepared to accept this consequence of the theory that woman is only a myth in the mind of man. One is Monique Wittig, who argues that liberation is becoming a nonwoman without thereby becoming a man (Monique Wittig, "One Is Not Born a Woman," in *The Straight Mind* [Boston: Beacon Press, 1992], 9–20). Another is Judith Butler, who argues that liberation does not require a belief in the real existence of women (Judith Butler, *Gender Trouble* [New York: Routledge, 1990]).

92. Sartre, *Cahiers pour une morale*, 16, 9.

93. Sartre, *Critique de la raison dialectique*, 357–58, 316–17.

94. De Beauvoir, *La Force des choses*, 211, 203.

9

Gender as Seriality

Thinking About Women as a Social Collective

Iris Marion Young

In the Summer of 1989 I worked in Shirley Wright's campaign for a seat on the Worcester School Committee. Shirley is African American in a city where about 5–7 percent of the population are African American, and 7–10 percent are Hispanic. As in many other cities, however, more than 35 percent of the children in the public schools are black, Hispanic, or Asian, and the proportion of children of color is growing rapidly. For more than ten years all six of the school committee seats have been held by white people, and only one woman has served, for about two years. In

I am grateful to Linda Alcoff, David Alexander, Sandra Bartky, Sonia Kruks, Lynda Lange, Bill McBride, Uma Narayan, Linda Nicholson, Vicki Spelman, and anonymous reviewers for *Signs* for comments on earlier versions of this article.

her announcement speech Shirley Wright pledged to represent all the people of Worcester. But she noted the particular need to represent minorities, and she also emphasized the importance of having a woman's voice on the committee.

A few weeks later a friend and I distributed Shirley Wright flyers outside a grocery store. The flyers displayed a photo of Shirley and some basics about her qualifications and issues. In the course of the morning at least two women, both white, exclaimed to me, "I'm so glad to see a woman running for school committee!" This African American woman claimed to speak for women in Worcester, and some white women noticed and felt affinity with her as a woman.

This seemed to me at the time an unremarkable, easily understandable affinity. Recent discussions among feminists about the difficulties and dangers of talking about women as a single group, however, make such incidents appear at least puzzling. These discussions have cast doubt on the project of conceptualizing women as a group, arguing that the search for the common characteristics of women or of women's oppression leads to normalizations and exclusions. While I agree with such critiques, I also agree with those who argue that there are pragmatic political reasons for insisting on the possibility of thinking about women as some kind of group.

Clearly, these two positions pose a dilemma for feminist theory. On the one hand, without some sense in which "woman" is the name of a social collective, there is nothing specific to feminist politics. On the other hand, any effort to identify the attributes of that collective appears to undermine feminist politics by leaving out some women whom feminists ought to include. To solve this dilemma I argue for reconceptualizing social collectivity or the meaning of social groups as what Sartre describes as a phenomenon of serial collectivity in his *Critique of Dialectical Reason* (1976). Such a way of thinking about women, I will argue, allows us to see women as a collective without identifying common attributes that all women have or implying that all women have a common identity.

I

Doubts about the possibility of saying that women can be thought of as one social collective arose from challenges to a generalized conception of gender and women's oppression by women of color, in both the northern and southern hemispheres, and by lesbians. Black, Latina, Asian, and indigenous women demonstrated that white feminist theory and rhetoric tended to be ethnocentric in its analysis of gender experience and oppression. Lesbians, furthermore, persistently argued that much of this analysis relied on the experience of heterosexual women. The influence of philosophical deconstruction completed the suspension of the category of "women" begun by this process of political differentiation. Exciting theorizing has shown (not for the first time) the logical problems in efforts to define clear, essential categories of being. Let me review some of the most articulate recent statements of the claim that feminists should abandon or be very suspicious of a general category of woman or female gender.

Elizabeth Spelman (1988) shows definitively the mistake in any attempt to isolate gender from indentities such as race, class, age, sexuality, and ethnicity to uncover the attributes, experiences, or oppressions that women have in common. To be sure, we have no trouble identifying ourselves as women, white, middle class, Jewish, American, and so on. But knowing the "right" labels to call ourselves and others does not imply the existence of any checklist of attributes that all those with the same label have in common. The absurdity of trying to isolate gender identity from race or class identity becomes apparent if you ask of any individual woman whether she can distinguish the "woman part" of herself from the "white part" or the "Jewish part." Feminist theorists nevertheless have often assumed that the distinctive and specific attributes of gender can be identified by holding race and class constant or by examining the lives of women who suffer only sexist oppression and not also oppressions of race, class, age, or sexuality.

The categories according to which people are identified as the same or different, Spelman suggests, are social constructs that reflect no natures or essences. They carry and express relations of privilege and subordination, the power of some to determine for others how they will be named, what differences are important for what purposes. Because it has assumed that women form a single group with common experiences, attributes, or oppressions, much feminist theorizing has exhibited privileged points of view by unwittingly taking the experience of white middle-class heterosexual women as representative for all women. Even when feminists attempt to take account of differences among women, moreover, they often manifest such biases because they fail to notice the race or class specificity of white middle-class women and how these also modify our gender. Much feminist talk about paying attention to differences among women, Spelman points out, tends to label only women of color or old women or disabled women as "different."

Chandra Mohanty believes that the "assumption of women as an already constituted, coherent group with identical interests and desires, regardless of class, ethnic or racial location, or contradictions, implies a notion of gender or sexual difference or even patriarchy which can be applied universally or even cross-culturally" (1991, 55). She believes that this category of "woman" as designating a single, coherent, already constituted group influences feminists to regard all women as equally powerless and oppressed victims. Rather than developing questions about how and whether women in a particular time and place suffer discrimination and limitation on their action and desires, questions that can then be empirically investigated, the assumption of universal gender categories bypasses such empirical investigation by finding oppression a priori. This tendency is especially damaging in the way European and American feminists think and write about women in the southern and eastern hemispheres. Assumptions about a homogeneous category of women helps create a homogeneous category of Third World women who stand as the Other to western feminists, who define Third World women as powerless victims of patriarchy.

Judith Butler draws more explicitly on postmodern theories to argue against the viability of the category of "woman" and of gender (1990). In a Foucauldian mode, Butler argues that the idea of gender identity and the attempt to describe it has a normalizing power. The very act of defining a gender identity excludes or devalues some bodies, practices, and discourses at the same time that it obscures the constructed, and thus contestable, character of that gender identity.

Feminism has assumed that it can be neither theoretical nor political without a subject. Female gender identity and experience delineate that subject. Feminist politics, it is assumed, speaks for or in the name of someone, the group women, who are defined by this female gender identity.

The category of gender was promoted by feminism precisely to criticize and reject traditional efforts to define women's nature through "biological" sex. In its own way, however, according to Butler, gender discourse tends to reify the fluid and shifting social processes in which people relate, communicate, play, work, and struggle with one another over the means of production and interpretation. The insistence on a subject for feminism obscures the social and discursive production of identities.

In one of the most important arguments of her book, Butler shows that the feminist effort to distinguish sex and gender itself contributes to such obscuring by ignoring the centrality of enforced heterosexuality in the social construction of gender. However variable its content is understood to be, the form of gender differentiation is always a binary opposition between the masculine and the feminine. Inasmuch as sexual difference is classified only as man and woman, then, gender always mirrors sex. The binary complementarity of this sex/gender system is required and makes sense, however, only with the assumption of heterosexual complementarity. Gender identification thus turns out not to be a culturally variable overlay on a given biological sex; rather, the categories of gender construct sexual difference itself. "Gender can delineate a *unity* of experience, of sex, gender and desire, only when sex can be understood in some sense to necessitate gender. The internal coherence or unity of either gender, man or woman, thereby requires both a stable and oppositional heterosexuality. Thus we see the political reasons for substantializing gender" (Butler 1990, 23).

This mutual reinforcement of (hetero)sex and gender as fixed categories suppresses any ambiguities and incoherences among heterosexual, homosexual, and bisexual practices. This unity of sex and gender organizes the variability of desiring practices along a single scale of normal and deviant behavior. Butler concludes that feminism's attempt to construct or speak for a subject, to forge the unity of coalition from the diversities of history and practice, will always lead to such ossifications. The primary task for feminist theory and politics is critical: to formulate genealogies that show how a given category of practice is socially constructed. Feminist discourse and practice should become and remain open, its totality permanently deferred, accepting and affirming the flows and shifts in the contingent relations of social practices and institutions.

These analyses are powerful and accurate. They identify ways that essentializing assumptions and the point of view of privileged women dominate much feminist discourse, even when it tries to avoid such hegemonic moves. They draw important lessons for any future feminist theorizing that wishes to avoid excluding some women from its theories or freezing contingent social relations into a false necessity. But I find the exclusively critical orientation of such arguments rather paralyzing. Do these arguments imply that it makes no sense and is morally wrong ever to talk about women as a group or, in fact, to talk about social groups at all? It is not clear that these writers claim this. If not, then what can it mean to use the term *woman?* More important, in the light of these critiques, what sort of positive claims can feminists make about the way social life is and ought to be? I find questions like these unaddressed by these critiques of feminist essentialism.

II

What is the genealogy of the essentializing discourse that established a normative feminist subject, woman, that excluded, devalued, or found deviant the lives and practices of many women? Like most discursive constructs, this one is overdetermined. But I suggest that one important source of the oppressive and paradoxical consequences of conceptualizing women as a group is the adoption of a *theoretical* stance. In large part feminist discourse about gender was motivated by the desire to establish a countertheory to Marxism, to develop a feminist theory that would conceive sex or gender as a category with as much theoretical weight as class. This desire employs a totalizing impulse. What *is* a woman? What *is* woman's social position such that it is not reducible to class? Are all societies structured by male domination, and of the same form or of variable forms? What are the origins and causes of this male domination?

These are all general and rather abstract theoretical questions. By "theory" I mean a kind of discourse that aims to be comprehensive, to give a systematic account and explanation of social relations as a whole. A theory tries to tell the way things are in some universal sense. From it one can derive particular instances or at least one can apply the theoretical propositions to particular facts that the theory's generalities are supposed to cover. A social theory is self-enclosed, in the sense that it offers no particular purpose other than to understand, to reveal the way things are.

Despite much work in the last twenty years to make such theories, feminists do not need and should not want theory in this sense. Instead, we should take a more pragmatic orientation to our intellectual discourse. By being pragmatic I mean categorizing, explaining, developing accounts and arguments that are tied to specific practical and political problems, where the purpose of this theoretical activity is clearly related to those problems (see, e.g., Bordo 1989). Pragmatic theorizing in this sense is not necessarily any less complex or sophisticated than totalizing theory, but rather it is driven by some problem that has ultimate practical importance and is not concerned to give an account of a whole. In this article I take the pragmatic problem to be a political dilemma generated by feminist critiques of the concept of "woman," and I aim to solve it by articulating some concepts without claiming to provide an entire social theory.

From this pragmatic point of view, I wish to ask, why does it matter whether we even consider conceptualizing women as a group? One reason to conceptualize women as a collective, I think, is to maintain a point of view outside of liberal individualism. The discourse of liberal individualism denies the reality of groups. According to liberal individualism, categorizing people in groups by race, gender, religion, and sexuality and acting as though these ascriptions say something significant about the person, his or her experience, capacities and possibilities, is invidious and oppressive. The only liberatory approach is to think of and treat people as individuals, variable and unique. This individualist ideology, however, in fact obscures oppression. Without conceptualizing women as a group in some sense, it is not possible to conceptualize oppression as a systematic, structured, institutional process. If we obey the injunction to think of people only as individuals, then the disadvantages and exclusions we call oppressions reduce to individuals in one of two ways. Either we blame the victims and say that disadvantaged people's choices and capacities render them less competitive, or we attribute their disadvantage to the attitudes of other individuals, who for whatever reason don't "like" the disadvantaged ones. In either case structural and political ways to address and rectify the disadvantage are written out of the discourse, leaving individuals to wrestle with their bootstraps. The importance of being able to talk about disadvantage and oppression in terms of groups exists just as much for those oppressed through race, class, sexuality, ethnicity, and the like as through gender (cf. Young 1990, chap. 2).

The naming of women as a specific and distinct social collective, moreover, is a difficult achievement and one that gives feminism its specificity as a political movement. The possibility of conceptualizing ethnic, religious, cultural, or national groups, for example, rarely comes into question because their social existence itself usually involves some common traditions—language, or rituals, or songs and stories, or dwelling place. Women, however, are dispersed among all these groups. The operations of most marriage and kinship forms bring women under the identity of men in each and all of these groups, in the privacy of household and bed. The exclusions, oppressions, and disadvantages that women often suffer can hardly be thought of at all without a structural conception of women as a collective social position. The first step in feminist resistance to such oppressions is the affirmation of women as a group, so that women can cease to be divided and to believe that their sufferings are natural or merely personal. Denial of the reality of a social collective termed *women* reinforces the privilege of those who benefit from keeping women divided (Lange 1991).

Feminist politics evaporates, that is, without some conception of women as a social collective. Radical politics may remain as a commitment to social justice for all people, among them those called women. Yet the claim that feminism expresses a distinct politics allied with anti-imperialism, antiracism, and gay liberation but asking a unique set of enlightening questions about a distinct axis of social oppression cannot be sustained without some means of conceptualizing women and gender as social structures.

The logical and political difficulties inherent in the attempt to conceptualize women as a single group with a set of common attributes and shared identity appear to be insurmountable. Yet if we cannot conceptualize women as a group, feminist politics appears to lose any meaning. Is there a way out of this dilemma? Recent feminist discussions of this problem have presented two strategies for solving it: the attempt to theorize gender identity as multiple rather than binary and the argument that women constitute a group only in the politicized context of feminist struggle. I shall argue now that both of these strategies fail.

Spelman herself explores the strategy of multiple genders. She does not dispense with the category of gender but, instead, suggests that a women's gender identity and gender attributes are different according to what race, class, religion, and the like she belongs to. Gender, she argues, is a relational concept, not the naming of an essence. One finds the specific characteristics and attributes of the gender identity of women by comparing their situation with that of men. But if one wishes to locate the gender-based oppression of women, it is wrong to compare all women with all men. For some women are definitely privileged when compared to some men. To find the gender-specific attributes of a woman's experience, Spelman suggests, one must restrict the comparison to men and women of the same race or class or nationality. Women of different races or classes, moreover, often have opposing gender attributes. In this reasoning, women as such cannot be said to be a group. Properly designated groups are "white women," "black women," "Jewish women," "working-class women," "Brazilian women," each with specific gender characteristics (Spelman 1988, 170–78).

In a recent paper Ann Ferguson proposes a similar solution to the contradictions and quandaries that arise when feminists assume that all women share a common identity and set of gendered attributes. "Instead of a concept of sisterhood based on a shared gender identity," she suggests, "it may be more helpful to posit different racial gender positions, and possibly different class gender positions. Processes of racialization in U.S. history have created at least ten gender identities informed with racial difference if we consider the various subordinate races: black, Latino, Native American, and Asian, as well as the dominant white race" (1991, 114–15).

There is much to recommend this concept of multiple genders as a way of describing the differentiations and contradictions in the social experience of gender. The idea of multiple genders highlights the fact that not all men are equally privileged by gender. It also makes clear that some women are privileged in relation to some men, a privilege that derives partly from their gender. It allows the theorist to look for race or class in specific gender interactions and expectations without essentializing them. Multiple gender conceptualization may also address the problems of binarism and heterosexism that Butler finds in gender theory. According to a concept of multiple genders, the gender identity of lesbians, for example, can be conceptualized as different from that of straight women.

Despite its promising virtues, the strategy of multiplying gender also has some dangers. First, it is just not true, as Spelman suggests, that gender relations are structured primarily within a class, race, nationality, and so on. A working-class woman's gendered experience and oppression is not properly identified only by comparing her situation to working-class men. Much of her gendered experience is conditioned by her relation to middle-class or ruling-class men. If she experiences sexual harassment at work, for example, her harasser is at least as likely to be a middle-class professional man as a working-class assembler or delivery man. Examples of such cross-class or cross-race relations between men and women can be multiplied. In such relations it would be false to say that the class or race difference is not as important as the gender difference, but it would be equally false to say that the cross-class or cross-race relations between men and women are not gendered relations. But if we conceive of an African American feminine gender, for example, as having one set of attributes in relation to African American men and another in relation to white men, one of two things results: either we need to multiply genders further or we need to draw back and ask what makes both of these genders womanly.

Second, the idea of multiple genders presumes a stability and unity to the categories of race, class, religion, and ethnicity that divide women. To conceptualize "American Indian woman" as a single identity different from "white woman," we must implicitly assume "American Indian" or "white" as stable categories. As Susan Bordo points out, feminist arguments against conceptualizing women as a single group often privilege categories of race or class, failing to challenge the appropriateness of these group categories (Bordo 1989). But the same arguments against considering these categories as unities can be used as the arguments against thinking about women as a unity. American Indians are divided by class, region, religion, sexuality, and ethnicity as well as by gender. Working-class people are divided by race, ethnicity, region, religion, and sexuality as well as by gender. The idea of multiple genders can solve the problems and paradoxes involved in conceptualizing women as a group only by presuming categorical unities to class and race.

This last point leads to my final objection to the idea of multiple genders. This strategy can generate an infinite regress that dissolves groups into individuals. Any category can be considered an arbitrary unity. Why claim that Black women, for example, have a distinct and unified gender identity? Black women are American, Haitian, Jamaican, African, Northern, Southern, poor, working class, lesbian, or old. Each of these divisions may be important to a particular woman's gender identity. But then we are back to the question of what it means to call her a woman. The strategy of multiple genders, then, while useful in directing attention to the social specificities of gender differentiation and gender interaction, does not resolve the dilemma I have posed. Instead, it seems to swing back and forth between the two poles of that dilemma.

Some feminist theorists propose "identity politics" as a different answer to the criticism of essentializing gender while retaining a conception of women as a group. According to this view, an identity *woman* that unites subjects into a group is not a natural or social given but rather the fluid construct of a political movement, feminism. Thus Diana Fuss agrees that *woman* cannot name a set of attributes that a group of individuals has in common, that there is not a single female gender identity that defines the social experience of womanhood. Instead, she holds, feminist politics itself creates an identity *woman* out of a coalition of diverse female persons dispersed across the world. "Coalition politics precedes class and determines its limits and boundaries; we cannot identify a group of women until various social, historical, political conditions construct the conditions and possibilities for membership. Many anti-essentialists fear that positing a political coalition of *women* risks presuming that there must first be a natural class of women; but this belief only makes the fact that it is coalition politics which constructs the category of women (and men) in the first place" (Fuss 1989, 36).

Interpreting the theoretical writings of several Black feminist writers, Nancie Caraway proposes a similar understanding of women as a group. She argues that unity and solidarity among women is a product of political discussion and struggle among people of diverse backgrounds, experiences, and interests who are differently situated in matrices of power and privilege. The process of discussion and disagreement among feminists forges a common commitment to a politics against oppression that produces the identity "woman" as a coalition. Thus, says Caraway, "identity politics advances a space for political action, praxis, justified by the critical *positioning* of the marginalized subjects against hierarchies of power— the Enlightenment promise of transcendence. . . . These emerging theories are codes about the fluid construction of identity. They are not racially specific; they speak to both white and Black feminists about the shared and differentiated faces of female oppression" (1989, 9).

The identity politics position has some important virtues. It rightly recognizes that the perception of a common identity among persons must be the product of social or political process that brings them together around a purpose. It retains a conception of women as a group that it believes feminist politics needs, at the same time clearly rejecting an essentialist or substantive conception of gender identity. There are, however, at least two problems with identity politics as a way to get out of the dilemma I have articulated.

Judith Butler points out the first. Even though identity politics' coalition politics and deconstructive discourse avoids the substantialization of gender, the dangers of normalization are not thereby also avoided. The feminist politics that produces a coalition of mutually identifying women nevertheless privileges some norms or experiences over others. Thus Butler suggests that feminist politics should be suspicious of settling into a unified coalition. The question of solidarity should never be settled, and identities should shift and be deconstructed in a play of possibilities that exclude no one.

My second objection to the idea that women are a group only as the construction of feminist politics is that it seems to make feminist politics arbitrary. Some women choose to come together in a political movement, to form themselves as a group of mutually identifying agents. But on the basis of what do they come together? What are the social conditions that have motivated the politics? Perhaps even more important, do feminist politics leave out women who do not identify as feminists? These questions all point to the need for some conception of women as a group prior to the formation of self-conscious feminist politics, as designating a certain set of relations or positions that motivate the particular politics of feminism.

III

Stories like Shirley Wright's race for school committee remind us that everyday language seems to be able to talk about women as a collective in some sense, even though women's experiences vary considerably by class, race, sexuality, age, or society. But Spelman, Mohanty, Butler, and others are right to criticize the exclusionary and normalizing implications of most attempts to theorize this everyday experience. We want and need to describe women as a group, yet it appears that we cannot do so without being normalizing and essentialist.

I propose a way out of this dilemma through a use of the concept of seriality that Sartre develops in his *Critique of Dialectical Reason*. I propose that we understand gender as referring to a social series, a specific kind of social collectivity that Sartre distinguishes from groups. Understanding gender as seriality, I suggest, has several virtues. It provides a way of thinking about women as a social collective without requiring that all women have common attributes or a common situation. Gender as seriality, moreover, does not rely on identity or self-identity for understanding the social production and meaning of membership in collectives.

One might well question any project that appropriates Sartrian philosophy positively for feminist theory (see Murphy 1989). Much of Sartre's writing is hopelessly sexist and male biased. This is certainly manifest in his theorization and functionalization of heterosexual relations. Perhaps more fundamentally, Sartre's early existentialist ontology presumes human relations as oppositional, egoistical, and basically violent. While his later philosophy on which I will draw is less individualistic than his early philosophy, the later thinking retains the assumption of human relations as latently violent. In it, boxing is a paradigm of the relation of self and other as mediated by a third.

Although Sartre's writing is sexist and his ontological assumptions about human relations tend to derive from masculine experience, I nevertheless have found the idea of seriality in particular, and its distinction from other kinds of social collective, of use in thinking about women as a collective. Linda Singer has talked about the feminist philosopher as a "Bandita," an intellectual outlaw who raids the texts of male philosophers and steals from them what she finds pretty or useful, leaving the rest behind (1992). I aim to approach Sartre's texts with the spirit of this Bandita, taking and rearticulating for my purposes the concepts I think will help resolve the dilemma I have posed. In doing so I need not drag all of Sartre with me, and I may be "disloyal" to him.

In the *Critique of Dialectical Reason,* Sartre distinguishes several levels of social collectivity by their order of internal complexity and reflexivity. For the purposes of addressing the problem of thinking about women as a social collective, the important distinction is between a group and a series. A group is a collection of persons who recognize themselves and one another as in a unified relation with one another. Members of the group mutually acknowledge that together they undertake a common project. Members of the group, that is, are united by action that they undertake together. In acknowledging oneself as a member of the group, an individual acknowledges oneself as oriented toward the same goals as the others; each individual thereby assumes the common project as a project for his or her individual action. What makes the project shared, however, is the mutual acknowledgment among the members of the group that they are engaged in the project together; this acknowledgment usually becomes explicit at some point in a pledge, contract, constitution, set of by-laws, or statement of purpose. The project of the group is a collective project, moreover, insofar as the members of the group mutually acknowledge that it can only be or is best undertaken by a group—storming the Bastille, staging an international women's conference, achieving women's suffrage, building an amphitheater (Sartre 1976, bk. 2, secs. 1, 2, and 3).[1]

So far in this article I have used the term *group* loosely, as does ordinary language, to designate any collection of people. Since my theorizing about women depends on Sartre's distinction between group and series, however, from now on in this article I shall reserve the term *group* for the self-consciously, mutually acknowledging collective with a self-conscious purpose. Much of an individual's life and action takes place in and is structured by a multitude of groups in this sense. Not all structured social action occurs in groups, however. As Sartre explains it, groups arise from and often fall back into a less organized and unself-conscious collective unity, which he calls a series.

Within Sartre's conception of human freedom, all social relations must be understood as the product of action. Unlike a group, which forms around actively shared objectives, a series is a social collective whose members are unified passively by the objects around which their actions are oriented or by the objectified results of the material effects of the actions of the others. In everyday life we often experience ourselves and others impersonally, as participating an amorphous collectives defined by routine practices and habits. The unity of the series derives from the way that individuals pursue their own individual ends with respect to the same objects conditioned by a continuous material environment, in response to structures that have been created by the unintended collective result of past actions.

Sartre describes people waiting for a bus as such a series. They are a collective insofar as they minimally relate to one another and follow the rules of bus waiting. As a collective they are brought together by their relation to a material object, the bus, and the social practices of public transportation. Their actions and goals may be different, and they have nothing necessarily in common in their histories, experiences, or identity. They are united only by their desire to ride on that route. Though they are in this way a social collective, they do not identify with one another, do not affirm themselves as engaged in a shared enterprise, or identify themselves with common experiences. The latent potential of this series to organize itself as a group will become manifest, however, if the bus fails to come; they will complain to one another about the lousy bus service, share horror stories of lateness and breakdowns, perhaps assign one of their number to go call the company, or discuss sharing a taxi.

Such serial collectivity, according to Sartre, is precisely the obverse of the mutual identification typical of the group. Each goes about his or her own business. But each is also aware of the serialized context of that activity in a social collective whose structure constitutes them within certain limits and constraints. In seriality, a person not only experiences others but also himself or herself as an Other, that is, as an anonymous someone: "Everyone is the same as the other insofar as he is Other than himself" (260). Individuals in the series are interchangeable; while not identical, from the point of view of the social practices and objects that generate the series, the individuals could be in one another's place. It is contingent that I am third in line for the bus today. Thus in the series individuals are isolated but not alone. They understand themselves as constituted as a collective, as serialized, by the objects and practices through which they aim to accomplish their individual purposes. Often their actions take into account their expectations of the behavior of others in the series whom they nevertheless do not encounter. For example, I ask for a later schedule at work so that I will miss the crowd of bus riders at the rush hour.

Sartre uses the example of radio listening to illustrate some of the characteristics of seriality. The collective of radio listeners is constituted by their individual orientation toward objects, in this case radios and their material possibilities of sound transmission. As listeners they are isolated, but nevertheless they are aware of being part of a series of radio listeners, of others listening simultaneously linked to them indirectly through broadcasting. One's experience of radio listening is partly conditioned by the awareness of being linked to others from whom one is separated and of serving as Other for them. Frequently the radio announcer explicitly refers to the serialized being of the listeners.

Sartre calls the series a practico-inert reality. The series is structured by actions linked to practico-inert objects. Social objects and their effects are the results of human action; they are practical. But as material they also constitute constraints on and resistances to action that make them experienced as inert. The built environment is a practico-inert reality. The products of human decision and action daily used by and dwelt in by people, the streets and buildings, are inert. Their material qualities enable and constrain many aspects of action.

Sartre calls the system of practico-inert objects and the material results of actions in relation to them that generate and are reproduced by serial collectives the milieu of action. The milieu is the already-there set of material things and collectivized habits against the background of which any particular action occurs. Thus for the series, commuters, for example, the milieu is the totality of the structured relations of the physical space of streets and rail lines, together with the predictable traffic patterns that emerge from the confluence of individual actions, together with the rules, habits, and cultural idiosyncracies of driving, riding, and walking.

Serialized action within the milieu results in *counterfinalities:* the confluence of individual intentional actions to produce a result that is counter to some purposes and that no one intended. Within a certain kind of milieu the series commuters will produce a gridlock; each individual driver pursues his or her own individual ends under material conditions that eventually makes a large cluster of them unable to move.

The collective otherness of serialized existence is thus often experienced as constraint, as felt necessities that often are experienced as given or natural. Members of the series experience themselves as powerless to alter this material milieu, and they understand that the others in the series are equally constrained. "A series reveals itself to everyone when they perceive in themselves and Others their common inability to eliminate their material differences" (277). At the same time, the material milieu and objects are conditions of enablement for action. Objectives can be realized only through the mediation of already there things, practices, and structures. A market is paradigmatic of such structured relations of alienation and anonymity that are felt as constraints on everyone. I take my corn to market in hopes of getting a good price, knowing that some people are trading on its price in a futures market and that other farmers bring their corn as well. We know that by bringing our large quantity of corn that we contribute to a fall in its price, and we might each play the futures market ourselves. But we are all equally as individuals unable to alter the collective results of these individual choices, choices that themselves have been made partly because of our expectations of what is happening to market prices.

Membership in serial collectives define an individual's being, in a sense—one "is" a farmer, or a commuter, or a radio listener, and so on, together in series with others similarly positioned. But the definition is anonymous, and the unity of the series is amorphous, without determinate limits, attributes, or intentions. Sartre calls it a unity "in flight," a collective gathering that slips away at the edges, whose qualities and characteristics are impossible to pin down because they are an inert result of the confluence of actions. There is no concept of the series, no specific set of attributes that form the sufficient conditions for membership in it. Who belongs to the series of bus riders? Only those riding today? Those who regularly ride? Occasionally? Who may ride buses and know the social practices of bus riding? While serial membership delimits and constrains an individual's possible actions, it does not define the person's identity in the sense of forming his or her individual purposes, projects, and sense of self in relation to others.

Thus far the examples of seriality have been rather simple and one-dimensional. Sartre's theoretical purpose in developing the concept, however, is to describe the meaning of social class. Most of the time what it means to be a member of the working class or the capitalist class is to live in series with others in that class through a complex interlocking set of objects, structures, and practices in relation to work, exchange, and consumption.

Class being does not define a person's identity, however, because one is a class member in a mode of otherness, otherness to oneself in one's subjectivity. If one says, "I am a worker," in naming serialized class being, this does not designate for one a felt and internalized identity but a social facticity about the material conditions of one's life. (To be sure, one can and many do say, "I am a worker," as a badge of pride and identity. But when this happens the class being is not experienced in seriality; rather, one has formed a *group* with other workers with whom one has established self-conscious bonds of solidarity.) As serialized, class lies as a historical and materialized background to individual lives. A person is born into a class in the sense that a history of class relations precedes one, and the characteristics of the work that one will do or not do are already inscribed in machines, the physical structure of factories and offices, the geographic relations of city and suburb. An individual encounters other members of the class as alienated others, separated from one through the materiality of the things that define and delimit his or her class being—the factory with its machines, the physical movements and demands of the production process, the residential districts, buses, and highways that bring the workers into contact. As class members the individuals are relatively interchangeable, and nothing defines them as workers but the practico-inert constraints on their actions that they find themselves powerless to change. "If you want to eat, then you have to get a job," expresses the anonymous constraints on anyone who lacks independent means of support.

Let me now summarize the major elements in the concept of seriality. A series is a collective whose members are unified passively by the relation their actions have to material objects and practico-inert histories. The practico-inert milieu, within which and by means of whose structures individuals realize their aims, is experienced as constraints on the mode and limits of action. To be said to be part of the same series it is not necessary to identify a set of common attributes that every member has, because their membership is defined not by something they are but rather by the fact that in their diverse existences and actions they are oriented around the same objects or practico-inert structures. Membership in the series does not define one's identity. Each member of the series is isolated Other to the Others, and as a member of the series Other than themselves. Finally, there is no concept of the series within attributes that clearly demarcate what about individuals makes them belong. The series is a blurry, shifting, unity, an amorphous collective.

Seriality designates a level of social life and action, the level of habit and the unreflective reproduction of ongoing historical social structures. Self-conscious groups arise from and on the basis of serialized existence, as a reaction to it and an active reversal of its anonymous and isolating conditions. Next I shall examine how gender is seriality and then explain the relationship between groups of women and the series, women.

IV

Applying the concept of seriality to gender, I suggest, makes the theoretical sense out of saying that "women" is a reasonable social category expressing a certain kind of social unity. At the same time, conceptualizing gender as a serial collectivity avoids the problems that emerge from saying that women are a single group.

As I explained earlier, seriality designates a certain *level* of social existence and relations with others, the level of routine, habitual action, which is rule-bound and socially structured but serves as a prereflective background to action. Seriality is lived as medium or as milieu, where action is directed at particular ends that presuppose the series without taking them up self-consciously.

Thus, as a series *woman* is the name of a structural relation to material objects as they have been produced and organized by a prior history. But the series *women* is not as simple and one-dimensional as bus riders or radio listeners. Gender, like class, is a vast, multifaceted, layered, complex, and overlapping set of structures and objects. *Women* are the individuals who are positioned as feminine by the activities surrounding those structures and objects.

The loose unity of the series, I have said, derives from the fact that individuals' actions are oriented toward the same or similarly structured objects. What are the practico-inert realities that construct gender? Clearly female bodies have something to do with the constitution of the series *women*, but it is not merely the physical facts of these female bodies themselves—attributes of breasts, vaginas, clitoris, and so on—that constructs female gender. Social objects are not merely physical but also inscribed by and the products of past practices. The female body as a practico-inert object toward which action is oriented is a rule-bound body, a body with understood meanings and possibilities. Menstruation, for example, is a regular biological event occurring in most female bodies within a certain age range. It is not this biological process alone, however, that locates individuals in the series of women. Rather, the social rules of menstruation, along with the material objects associated with menstrual practices, constitute the activity within which the women live as serialized. One can say the same about biological events like pregnancy, childbirth, and lactation.

The structure of the social body defining these bodily practices, however, is enforced heterosexuality. The meanings, rules, practices, and assumptions of institutionalized heterosexuality constitute the series, women, as in a relation of potential appropriation by men. Likewise the series *men* appears in the structures of enforced heterosexuality. The assumptions and practices of heterosexuality define the meaning of bodies—vaginas, clitorises, penises—not as mere physical objects but as practico-inert.

Even one so anti-essentialist as Gayatri Spivak locates heterosexuality as a set of material-ideological facts that constitute women cross-culturally. The material practices of enforced heterosexuality serialize women as objects of exchange and appropriation by men, with a consequent repression of autonomous active female desire. In Spivak's terms, "In legally defining woman as object of exchange, passage, or possession in terms of reproduction, it is not only the womb that is literally 'appropriated'; it is the clitoris and signifier of the sexed object that is effaced. All historical theoretical investigation into the definition of women as legal object—in or out of marriage; or as politico-economic passageway for property and legitimacy would fall within the investigation of the varieties of the effacement of the clitoris" (1987, 151).

Bodies, however, are only one of the practico-inert objects that position individuals in the gender series. A vast complex of other objects and materialized historical products condition women's lives as gendered. Pronouns locate individual people, along with animals and other objects, in a gender system. Verbal and visual representations more generally create and reproduce gender meanings that condition a person's action and her interpretation of the actions of others. A multitude of artifacts and social spaces in which people act are flooded with gender codes. Clothes are the primary example, but there are also cosmetics, tools, even in some cases furniture and spaces that materially inscribe the norms of gender. I may discover myself "as a woman" by being on the "wrong" dorm floor.

What usually structures the gendered relation of these practico-inert objects is a sexual division of labor. Though their content varies with each social system, a division of at least some tasks and activities by sex appears as a felt necessity. The division between caring for babies and bodies, and not doing so, is the most common sexual division of labor, over which many other labor divisions are layered in social specific ways. Other sexual divisions of tasks and activities are more arbitrary but, in practice, also felt as natural. (Think, e.g., about the genderization of football and field hockey in most American colleges.) The context of the sexual division of labor varies enormously across history, culture, and institutions. Where the division appears, however, it usually produces a multitude of practico-inert objects that constitute the gendered series. The offices, workstations, locker rooms, uniforms, and instruments of a particular activity presuppose a certain sex. The language, gestures, and rituals of exclusion or inclusion of persons in activities reproduce the divisions by attracting people to or repelling people from those activities.

In short, then, bodies and objects constitute the gendered series women through structures like enforced heterosexuality and the sexual division of labor. As I have interpreted Sartre's concept, being positioned by these structures in the series women does not itself designate attributes that attach to the person in the series, nor does it define her identity. Individuals move and act in relation to practico-inert objects that position them as women. The practico-inert structures that generate the milieu of gendered serialized existence both enable and constrain action, but they do not determine or define it. The individuals pursue their own ends; they get a living for themselves in order to have some pleasures of eating and relaxation. The sexual division of labor both enables them to gain that living and constrains their manner of doing so by ruling out or making difficult some possibilities of action. The bathroom enables me to relieve myself, and its gender-marked door constrains the space in which I do it and next to whom.

The practico-inert structures of the gender series are abstract in relation to individuals and to groups of individuals. They are possibilities and orientations for concrete actions that give them content.[2] The gender structures are not defining attributes of individuals but are material social facts that each individual must relate to and deal with. The subjective experiential relation that each person has, and sometimes groups have, to the gender structure, are infinitely variable. In a heterosexist society, for example, everyone must deal with and act in relation to structures of enforced heterosexuality. But there are many attitudes a particular individual can take toward that necessity: she can internalize norms of feminine masochism, she can try to avoid sexual interaction, she can affirmatively take up her sexual role as a tool for her own ends, she can reject heterosexual requirements and love other women, to name just a few.

In seriality, I have said above, the individual experiences herself as anonymous, as Other to herself and Other to the others, contingently interchangeable with them. Sometimes when I become aware of myself "as a woman" I experience this serial anonymous facticity. The serialized experience of being gendered is precisely the obverse of mutual recognition and positive identification of oneself as in a group. "I am a woman" at this level is an anonymous fact that does not define me in my active individuality. It means that I check one box rather than another on my driver's license application, that I use maxipads, wear pumps, and sometimes find myself in situations in which I anticipate a deprecation or humiliation from a man. As I utter the phrase, I experience a serial interchangeability between myself and others. In the newspaper I read about a woman who was raped, and I empathize with her because I recognize that in my serialized existence I am rapeable, the potential object of male appropriation. But this awareness depersonalizes me, constructs me as Other to her and Other to myself in a serial interchangeability rather than defining my sense of identity. I do not here mean to deny that many women have a sense of identity as women, an issue I will discuss in the next section. Here I only claim that the level of gender as series in a background to rather than constitutive of personal or group identity.

Sartre's main purpose in developing the concept of seriality is to describe unorganized class existence, the positioning of individuals in relations of production and consumption. Race or nationality can also be fruitfully conceptualized as seriality.[3] At the level of seriality racial position is constructed by a relation of persons to a materialized racist history that has constructed racially separated spaces, a racial division of labor, racist language and discourse, and so on. A person can and often does construct a positive racial identity along with others from out of these serialized positionings. But such racial identification is an active taking up of a serialized situation. Which, if any, of a person's serial memberships become salient or meaningful at any time is a variable matter.

Like gender structures, class or race structures do not primarily name attributes of individuals or aspects of their identity but practico-inert necessities that condition their lives and with which they must deal. Individuals may take up varying attitudes toward these structures, including forming a sense of class or racial identity and forming groups with others they identify with.

Thus the concept of seriality provides a useful way of thinking about the relationship of race, class, gender, and other collective structures, to the individual person. If these are each forms of seriality, then they do not necessarily define the identity of individuals and do not necessarily name attributes they share with others. They are material structures arising from people's historically congealed institutionalized actions and expectations that position and limit individuals in determinate ways that they must deal with. An individual's position in each of the series means that they have differing experiences and perceptions from those differently situated. But individuals can relate to these social positionings in different ways; the same person may relate to them in different ways in different social contexts or at different times in their lives.

A person can choose to make none of her serial memberships important for her sense of identity. Or she can find that her family, neighborhood, and church network makes the serial facts of race, for example, important for her identity and development of a group solidarity. Or she can develop a sense of herself and membership in group affiliations that makes different serial structures important to her in different respects or salient in different kinds of circumstances.

V

The purpose of saying that *women* names a series thus resolves the dilemma that has developed in feminist theory: that we must be able to describe women as a social collective yet apparently cannot do so without falling into a false essentialism. An essentialist approach to conceiving women as a social collective treats women as a substance, as a kind of entity in which some specific attributes inhere. One classifies a person as a woman according to whether that person has the essential attributes of womanness, characteristics all women share: something about their bodies, their behavior or dispositions as persons, or their experience of oppression. The problem with this approach to conceptualizing women as a collective is that any effort to locate those essential attributes has one of two consequences. Either it empties the category *woman* of social meaning by reducing it to the attributes of biological female, or in the effort to locate essential social attributes it founders on the variability and diversity of women's actual lives. Thus, the effort to locate particular social attributes that all women share is likely to leave out some persons called women or to distort their lives to fit the categories.

Conceptualizing gender as seriality avoids this problem because it does not claim to identify specific attributes that all women have. There is a unity to the series of women, but it is a passive unity, one that does not arise from the individuals called women but rather positions them through the material organization of social relations as enabled and constrained by the structural relations of enforced heterosexuality and the sexual division of labor. The content of these structures varies enormously from one social context to the next. Saying that a person is a woman may predict something about the general constraints and expectations she must deal with. But it predicts nothing in particular about who she is, what she does, how she takes up her social positioning.

Thinking of gender as seriality also avoids the problem of identity. At least since Nancy Chodorow developed her theory of the psychodynamics of mother-infant relations, gender has been understood as a mode of personal identity (1978). By identity, I mean one of two conceptions, which sometimes appear together. First, identity designates something about who persons are in a deep psychological sense. This is the primary meaning of identity in Chodorow's theory of gender identity. She argues that feminine gender identity gives women more permeable ego boundaries than men, thus making relations with other persons important for their self-conception. Many recent moral and epistemological theories have been influenced by this notion of gender identity and suggest that theories, modes of reasoning, and ways of acting tend to be structured by those feminine and masculine identities.

Second, identity can mean self-ascription as belonging to a group with others who similarly identify themselves, who affirm or are committed together to a set of values, practices, and meanings. This is the sense of identity expressed by theorists of identity politics. Identity here means a self-consciously shared set of meanings interpreting conditions and commitments of being a woman.

Criticisms of gender as identity in either of these senses are similar to criticisms of gender essentialism. This approach either leaves out or distorts the experience of some individuals who call themselves or are called women. Many women regard their womanness as an accidental or contingent aspect of their lives and conceive other social group relations— ethnic or national relations, for example—as more important in defining their identity. Many women resist efforts to theorize shared values and experiences specific to a feminine gender identity—in a caring orientation to relationships, for example—claiming that such theories privilege the identities of particular classes of women in particular social contexts. Even among women who do take their womanhood as an important aspect of their identity, the meaning of that identity will vary a great deal (cf. Ferguson 1991).

Thinking about gender as seriality disconnects gender from identity. On the one hand, as Elizabeth Spelman argues, at the level of individual personal identity there is no way to distinguish the "gender part" of the person from her "race part" or "class part." It may be appropriate, as Butler argues, to think of subjects or personal identities as constituted rather than as some transcendental origin of consciousness or action. It nevertheless would be misleading to think of individual persons as mixtures of gender, race, class, and national attributes. Each person's identity is unique—the history and meaning she makes and develops from her dealings with other people, her communicative interactions through media, and her manner of taking up the particular serialized structures whose prior history position her. No individual woman's identity, then, will escape the markings of gender, but how gender marks her life is her own.

Conceptions of gender as an identity, however, more often seek to name women as a group—that is, a self-conscious social collective with common experiences, perspectives, or values—than to describe individual identity. Conceiving gender as seriality becomes especially important for addressing this mistake. In Sartre's conceptualization, a group is a collection of persons who do mutually identify, who recognize one another as belonging to the group with a common project that defines their collective action. A series, on the other hand, is not a mutually acknowledging identity with any common project or shared experience. Women need have nothing in common in their individual lives to be serialized as women.

A relationship between series and groups does exist, however. As self-conscious collectives of persons with a common objective that they pursue together, groups arise on the basis of and in response to a serialized condition. The group in fusion is a spontaneous group formation out of seriality. When those who have waited for the bus too long begin complaining to each other and discussing possible courses of action, they are a group in fusion. Once groups form and take action, they either institutionalize themselves by establishing meetings, leaders, decision-making structures, methods of acquiring and expending resources, and so on, or they disperse back into seriality. Social life consists of constant ebbs and flows of groupings out of series; some groups remain and grow into institutions that produce new serialities, others disperse soon after they are born.

At its most unreflective and universal level, being a woman is a serial fact. But women often do form groups, that is, self-conscious collectives that mutually acknowledge one another as having common purposes or shared experiences. Let me give an example of a movement from women as a serial collective to a group of women. In her novel, *Rivington Street*, Meredith Tax vividly portrays the lives of Russian Jewish immigrant women in the Lower East Side of Manhattan at the turn of the century (1982). In one episode of the novel, some women in the neighborhood discover that a local merchant has manipulated the chicken market in order to make more profits. They talk with one another with anger and then go about their business. One of them, however, thinks a bit more in her anger and decides to act. She calls her three or four women friends together and tells them that they should boycott the butcher. The women organize a boycott by going from apartment to apartment talking to women. Gradually these neighborhood women, formerly serialized only as shoppers, come to understand themselves as a group, with some shared experiences and the power of collective action. When the boycott succeeds, they hold a street celebration and honor their leader, but then they quickly disperse back into the passive unity of the series.

The gendered being of women's groups arises from the serial being of women, as taking up actively and reconstituting the gendered structures that have passively unified them. The chicken boycott arises from the serialized condition of these women defined by the sexual division of labor as purchasers and preparers of food. While the gendered series *women* refers to the structured social relations positioning all biologically sexed females, groups of women are always partial in relation to the series—they bring together only some women for some purposes involving their gender serialized experience. Groups of women are usually more socially, historically, and culturally specified than simply women—they are from the same neighborhood or university, they have the same religion or occupation. Groups of women, that is, will likely, though not necessarily, emerge from the serialities of race and class as well as gender. The chicken boycotters live in the same neighborhood, speak the same Russian-Yiddish, and are passively united in a marginal working-class series in the class structure of Manhattan. All of these serialized facts are relevant to their story and partially explain their grouping.

The chicken boycott example shows a case of women grouping self-consciously as women and on the basis of their gendered condition, but the boycott is not feminist. There can be many groupings of women as women that are not feminist, and indeed some are explicitly antifeminist. Feminism is a particularly reflexive impulse of women grouping, women grouping as women in order to change or eliminate the structures that serialize them as women.

In order to clarify and elaborate the relation of series and group in understanding women as a collective, let me return to my story of Shirley Wright. In her announcement of her candidacy for school committee, when Shirley Wright says that she intends to represent women, she is referring to a gender series defined primarily by the sexual division of labor. *Women* names a position in the division of labor that tends to be specifically related to schools, the primary parent to deal with schools, at the same time that it names a position outside authority structures. In that speech Wright is not claiming a group solidarity among the women of Worcester, either around her candidacy or in any other respect, but is referring to, gesturing toward, a serial structure that conditions her own position and that she aims to politicize. To the degree that Shirley Wright aims to politicize gender structures in her campaign and on the school committee, she invites or invokes the positive grouping of women out of the gender series, but her candidacy speech neither names a group nor generates it. Her claiming to represent "minorities" is also a reference to a serial structure of race and racism that she claims conditions her position and that she aims to politicize.

The women who responded to my handing them a flyer with satisfaction at seeing a woman running are also serialized, as women, as voters. Their identification with Shirley Wright as a woman, however, makes for a proto-group. If some women are motivated to come together to form a "Women for Shirley Wright" committee, they have constituted an active grouping. In relation to the series women, or even to the series "the women of Worcester," the group is necessarily partial—it will probably attract only certain kinds of women, with only some kinds of experiences, and it will focus only on some issues.

In summary, then, I propose that using the concept of seriality and its distinction from the concept of a group can help solve the conundrums about talking about women as a group in which feminist theory has recently found itself. *Woman* is a serial collective defined neither by any common identity nor by a common set of attributes that all the individuals in the series share, but, rather, it names a set of structural constraints and relations to practico-inert objects that condition action and its meaning. I am inclined to say that the series includes all female human beings in the world, and others of the past, but how and where we draw the historical lines is an open question. We can also claim that there are also social and historical subseries. Since the series is not a concept but a more practical-material mode of the social construction of individuals, one need not think of it in terms of genus and species, but as vectors of action and meaning.

Unlike most groups of women, feminist groups take something about women's condition as the explicit aim of their action, and thus feminist groups at least implicitly refer to the series of women that lies beyond the group. Feminist politics and theory refer to or gesture toward this serial reality. Feminist reflection and explicit theorizing draw on the experience of serialized gender, which has multiple layers and aspects. Feminism itself is not a grouping of women; rather, there are many feminisms, many groupings of women whose purpose is to politicize gender and change the power relations between women and men in some respect. When women group, their womanliness will not be the only thing that brings them together; there are other concrete details of their lives that give them affinity, such as their class or race position, their nationality, their neighborhood, their religious affiliation, or their role as teachers of philosophy.

For this reason groupings of women will always be partial in relation to the series. Women's groups will be partial in relation to the series also because a group will have particular objectives or purposes that cannot encompass or even refer to the totality of the condition of women as a series. This is why feminist politics must be coalition politics. Feminist organizing and theorizing always refers beyond itself to conditions and experiences that have not been reflected on, and to women whose lives are conditioned by enforced heterosexuality and a sexual division of labor who are not feminist and are not part of feminist groups. We should maintain our humility by recognizing that partiality and by remaining open to inquiring about the facts of the series beyond us.

Notes

1. Sartre in fact distinguishes several levels of group: the group in fusion, the statutory group, the organization, and the institution. Each is less spontaneous, more organized and rule bound, and more materialized than the last. All come under the more general definition I am offering here, which is all that is necessary to develop my argument. Although my summaries of Sartre throughout this article leave out a great deal of detail, I believe they are nevertheless adequate to the text and sufficient for developing my argument.

2. In terms of Sartre's early work, I am here interpreting seriality as a condition of facticity that helps constitute a situation but in no way determines action. Action, the having of projects and goals, the realizing of ends, I am saying here, is what constitutes the identities and experiences of persons. Action is situated against a background of serialized existence, which means that it is constrained but neither general nor determined.

3. While Sartre does not thematize race as such, I think he provides grounds for understanding race positioning as seriality. He describes being Jewish as initially belonging to a series. As a social fact or social label, being Jewish in a society that marks or devalues Jews does not name some concept, a set of specific attributes a person must be identified as having in order to be classed as Jewish. In the social relation of being Jewish, there is no separate substance that Jews have in common that makes them Jews. The group label is never real, specific limited, here; it always names an alien otherness coming from elsewhere, from the facticity of "them," the anonymous others who say things about the Jews, who "know" what the Jews are: "In fact, the being-Jewish of every Jew in a hostile society, which persecutes and insults them, and opens itself to them only to reject them again, cannot be the only relation between the individual Jew and the antisemitic, racist society which surrounds him; it is this relation insofar as it is lived by every Jew in his direct or indirect relations with all the other Jews, and in so far as it constitutes him, through them all, an Other and threatens him in and through the Others. To the extent that, for the conscious, lived Jews, being-Jewish (which is his status to *non-Jews*) is interiorized as his responsibility in relation to all other Jews and his being-in-danger, out there, owing to some possible carelessness caused by Others who mean nothing to him, over whom he has no power and every one of whom is himself like Others (in so far as he makes them exist as such in spite of himself,) the *Jew*, far from being *the type* common to each separate instance, represents *on the contrary*, the perpetual being *outside-themselves-in-the-other* of members of this practico-inert grouping" (268). Sartre also discusses colonialism as a serial

social relation, mediated by an anonymous public opinion that constitutes racist discourse. He says that the most important thing about racist ideas and utterances is that they are not *thoughts*. Racism as operative in everyday life and as a medium of works and beliefs for reproducing practically congealed social relations of oppression and privilege is not a *system* of beliefs, thought through and deliberated. On the contrary, the racist language is unconsidered, uttered as the obvious, and spoken and heard always as the words of an Other. Everyday repeated stereotypes such as that Blacks are lazy or more prone to be aggressive, or that they prefer to stay with their own kind, "have never been anything more than this system itself producing itself as a determination of the language of the colonists in the milieu of alterity. And, for this point of view, they must be seen as material exigencies of language (the *verbal milieu* of all practico-inert apparatuses) addressed to colonialists both in their eyes and in those of others, in the unity of a gathering. . . . The sentence which is uttered, as a reference to the common interest, is not presented as the determination of language by the individual himself, but as his *other* opinion, that is to say, the claims to get it from and give it to others, insofar as their unity is based purely on alternity"(301).

References

Allen, Jeffner, and Iris Marion Young, eds. 1989. *Thinking Muse: Feminism and Modern French Philosophy*. Bloomington: Indiana University Press.

Bordo, Susan. 1989. "Feminism, Postmodernism, and Gender-Scepticism." In *Feminism/ Postmodernism*, ed. Linda Nicholson. New York: Routledge.

Butler, Judith. 1990. *Gender Trouble*. New York: Routledge.

Caraway, Nancie. 1989. "Identity Politics and Shifting Selves: Black Feminist Coalition Theory." Paper presented at American Political Science Association.

Chodorow, Nancy. 1978. *Reproduction of Mothering: Psychoanalysis and the Sociology of Gender*. Berkeley and Los Angeles: University of California Press.

Ferguson, Ann. 1991. "Is There a Lesbian Culture?" In *Lesbian Philosophies and Cultures*, ed. Jeffner Allen, 63–88. Albany: State University of New York Press.

Fuss, Diana. 1989. *Essentially Speaking*. New York: Routledge.

Lange, Lynda. 1991. "Arguing for Democratic Feminism: Postmodern Doubts and Political Amnesia." Paper presented to the meeting of the American Philosophical Association, Midwest Division, Chicago.

Mohanty, Chandra Talpade. 1991. "Under Western Eyes: Feminist Scholarship and Colonial Discourses." In *Third World Women and the Politics of Feminism*, ed. Chandra Talpade Mohanty, Ann Russo, and Lourdes Torres, 51–80. Bloomington: Indiana University Press.

Murphy, Julien. 1989. "The Look in Sartre and Rich." In Allen and Young.

Sartre, Jean-Paul. 1976. *Critique of Dialectical Reason*, trans. Alan Sheridan Smith, ed. Jonathan Ree. London: New Left Books.

Singer, Linda. 1992. *Erotic Welfare*. New York: Routledge.

Spelman, Elizabeth. 1988. *Inessential Woman*. Boston: Beacon.

Spivak, Gayatri Chakravorty. 1987. "French Feminism in an International Frame." In *In Other Worlds: Essays in Cultural Politics*. New York: Methuen.

Tax, Meredith. 1982. *Rivington Street*. New York: Morrow.

Young, Iris Marion. 1990. *Justice and the Politics of Difference*. Princeton: Princeton University Press.

10

Identity Politics and Dialectical Reason

Beyond an Epistemology of Provenance

Sonia Kruks

Feminists have given Jean-Paul Sartre a hard time. Although second-wave feminism has deemed the works of male thinkers as diverse as Marx, Freud, and Foucault worthy of serious if critical engagement, Sartre has for the most part been vilified when he has not been ignored. In one way this is perhaps surprising, for Simone de Beauvoir, "mother of us all,"

Some of the work on this essay was undertaken while I was a research associate at the Five College Women's Studies Research Center at Mount Holyoke College. My thanks to all there for assistance and support. A much earlier version of the paper was given at a colloquium of the Simon Silverman Center of Duquesne University. I acknowledge the work of the organizers of the colloquium, and I thank Hazel Barnes, Michèle le Doeuff and Monika Langer for their thought-provoking commentaries at that event. Others who have provided valuable comments include Kirstie McClure, Phyllis Morris, Bob Stone, Harlan Wilson, Iris Young, Linda Zerilli, and anonymous reviewers for *Hypatia*.

certainly acknowledged a debt to him. The central claim of *The Second Sex*—"one is not born a woman but becomes one"—presupposes Sartre's argument that "existence precedes essence": that human beings become what they are on the basis of no pre-given necessity or "nature." As a radically anti-essentialist philosophy of freedom, it would seem that Sartre's work ought, prima facie, still to have some relevance for feminism.

But this potential notwithstanding, there are also reasonable grounds for the hostility Sartre's work has evoked on the part of feminists. In the phenomenological psychology developed in *Being and Nothingness* (1943), the feminine is frequently equated with a "nature" that is not only unfree, but that threatens treacherously to suck "man" into its viscous embrace and destroy "his" freedom.[1] Moreover, although Sartre is certainly no orthodox Cartesian, it can be argued that in *Being and Nothingness* he in large measure replicates the Cartesian conflation of consciousness with freedom and posits a fundamentally autonomous, self-constituting subject. Between men—the bearers of such subjectivity—conflict and aggression are seen as ubiquitous; and society, insofar as it appears at all in Sartre's account of human existence, is essentially Hobbesian. In short, what many feminists have described as a distinctly masculinist conception of the self and "his" relation to others can be said to permeate *Being and Nothingness*.[2]

However, although it remains Sartre's best-known book, *Being and Nothingness* was by no means his last. The oppressive experiences of World War II (including time spent in a German prisoner-of-war camp and life in German-occupied Paris) and his involvement in non-Communist Left politics in the decades thereafter, led to significant reformulations of Sartre's earlier ideas. Along with Beauvoir—and arguably in part from her—Sartre learned of *la force des choses*, of the weight of systems of oppression, and of the intrinsically interdependent quality of human freedoms.[3] I argue in this essay that his greater focus on such issues, particularly in the *Critique of Dialectical Reason* (1960), gives aspects of his later work an enduring relevance for feminism. In particular, we should still turn to the *Critique* for insights that will help us address certain epistemological problems that have become acute with the development of feminist (and other) identity politics.

Since the late 1970s, second-wave feminism has undergone a marked reorientation: a shift away from its earlier demands to minimize distinctions between the sexes and a move, instead, toward a celebratory emphasis on women's differences from men. In what I will call global-difference feminism, modern Western culture as a whole has been depicted as fundamentally male in its individualism, competitiveness, and desire to dominate nature; in its denigration of emotions and the body; and in its faith in abstract, disembodied reason. By contrast, women—all women—have been celebrated for their connectedness with nature and with others—particularly through their maternal capacities—for their acceptance of the body, their more concrete and embodied ways of knowing and judging.

More recently, however, the argument for celebrating women's difference has been turned back against global-difference feminism. For increasingly in the last decade, many have pointed out that the rather grandiose and universal claims made about women's differences from men have obscured profound and frequently oppressive differences between women. Just as "humanist" voices, calling since the seventeenth century for the liberation of humankind, have turned out frequently to be speaking uniquely for certain male parts of humankind, so feminist voices turn out to have been speaking for only certain parts of womankind—primarily for white, middle-class, and heterosexual women. They have thus masked power relations and helped perpetuate divergences of interest between different kinds of women. By the mid-1990s feminists have come to recognize that women have radically different experiences from each other and speak with many different voices. Furthermore, they may also have widely divergent, or even directly conflicting, interests. In short, there has been a shift toward what I will call multiple-difference feminism.[4]

The "double turn" toward difference—the recognition of difference as occurring both between men and women and between women themselves—has marked an important advance in feminism. Above all, the ideological nature of bold universalistic claims, be they about the nature of "the human self" or "woman's self," about freedom, justice, truth, or progress, have been demonstrated with a thoroughness never dreamed of by Marx. It is not only each ruling class, as Marx said, which has "to represent its interest as the common interest of all members of society" ([1846] 1978, 174). Similarly, those who come to dominate by virtue of sex, race, or other characteristics will tend to represent their own interests in universalistic forms, thus masking oppression and silencing those who are subordinate. The valid goals of much recent multiple-difference feminism, particularly feminist identity politics, have been to expose such ideological maskings within the women's movement itself and to begin to create spaces of various kinds in which the previously silenced can speak.

Identity politics is important within feminism. It functions effectively both as a critique of existing power relations and as a project of self-empowerment for marginalized categories of women. Against the hegemonic claims and norms of feminism as a predominantly white, middle-class, and heterosexual movement, identity politics seeks to affirm the validity, indeed even the superiority, of different ways of being and knowing. Within feminism, black identity politics, along with that of other women of color, has functioned as a particularly powerful attack on global-difference feminism. As Audre Lorde pithily responded to Mary Daly's account of the universality of women's oppression: "The oppression of women knows no ethnic nor racial boundaries, true, but that does not mean it is identical within those differences . . . beyond sisterhood is still racism" (1984, 70). Black feminist identity politics has asserted that what might appear as universal forms of women's experience, be they motherhood or subjection to sexual violence, are not "the same" for all women. It also points out that white women are frequently complicit in the particular forms of oppression still experienced by black women: feminism itself can function as ideology, as a masking of power and privilege, as a means of empowering some women at the expense of others.

As a political critique of global-difference feminism, identity politics is indubitably valid. Since women are never women *tout court*, but are always situated also as members of a class, a race, an ethnic grouping, a sexual orientation, an age grade, and so on, it is dangerous to assume that the inequities and power relations that pertain to those other dimensions of social situation will not play out also between women. However, in its attempts to refute falsely universalizing knowledge claims, identity politics sometimes tends to replicate those aspects of global-difference feminism which have stressed the radical incommunicability of women's experience to men. Identity politics tends toward an excessive particularization and partitioning of knowledge, but now along the lines of race or ethnicity, for example, as well as gender. For such experience-based accounts of knowledge imply an epistemology of provenance: that is, the claim that knowledge arises from an experiential basis that is fundamentally group-specific and that others, who are outside the group and who lack its immediate experiences, cannot share that knowledge. As a corollary it is generally claimed that outsiders have no basis from which they can legitimately evaluate the group's claims about its knowledge, or those political or moral positions that it takes on the basis of that knowledge. In short, only those who live a particular reality can know about it; and only they have the right to speak about it.

Many groups that practice identity politics also advocate a politics of alliance or coalition with other groups, invoking the ideal of "bridging" differences once they are recognized and respected.[5] Commitments to coalition-work, to alliance, to solidarity across groups are, I believe, vital for any effective progressive politics in this day and age. However, the implications of an epistemology of provenance, if consistently pursued, threaten to undercut coalition politics or other forms of solidarity among women. The unintended end-point of an epistemology of provenance can be an acute and politically debilitating subjectivism, which belies the possibility of communication and common action across differences. It is this apparent contradiction within identity politics (and other forms of multiple-difference feminism) that concerns me in this essay.

Some identity politics has tended to assert global identities for a particular kind of women, arguing for example that all black women share culture, experience, and ways of knowing (Collins 1990; Brown 1988). However, such assertions tend in turn to be challenged as falsely universalistic. There is thus a tendency for identities increasingly to subdivide. For example, many lesbian women of color have come to identify themselves as having an identity distinct from that of other women of color and of other lesbians. Or, within the lesbian community, those who accept sado-masochistic practices proclaim themselves to have a different identity from those who do not (Phelan 1989, esp. Chap. 6). Since no woman can avoid living a plurality of identities, a central dynamic of identity politics is to move toward ever-shrinking identity groups, for which the logical terminus would have to be not merely subjectivism but solipsism, since no one person's set of experiences is identical to another's.[6]

Identity politics, as an epistemological position, thus threatens to leave us without the possibility of having the kind of common knowledge, or forming the kind of collective judgments, necessary for the development of broadly organized, feminist coalition politics such as its adherents often advocate. To exemplify: some consistent end-points of an epistemology of provenance would be to say, among other things, that those who do not experience domestic violence, or incest, or rape, or unwanted pregnancy, or even unequal pay, have no experiential basis from which to evaluate and speak about such issues. Statements such as these, which

I think very few feminists would want to endorse, are not of a different propositional order than the statements, commonly heard today, to the effect that white women have no basis or right to discuss the issue of sexism in black heterosexual relationships, or that Western women should take no position on clitoridectomy in Africa or the Middle East. The challenge identity politics now presents us with is this: to find a way to recognize the power-laden dangers of global-difference feminism and to affirm the importance of the existence of radical experiential differences, but to do so without embracing an epistemology of provenance. The problem is to find a way of acknowledging the claims to knowledge of particular identity groups without thereby wholly evacuating claims for a more general basis for knowledge, or more general visions and projects of emancipation.

To suggest a way out of this impasse I think it might be helpful to build on some of the insights of feminist standpoint theory. In this section of my essay I discuss the work of two theorists, Nancy Hartsock and Donna Haraway. In the next section I will use the later work of Sartre as a resource for further developing some of their insights.

Like identity politics, standpoint theory, for which the work of Nancy Hartsock (1983) is paradigmatic, insists on the epistemological validity of the experience of a particular oppressed group: women. But it does so while also concerning itself with a *general* human emancipatory project and with the formulation of claims about the world that are accessible and potentially valid beyond the experience of that particular oppressed group.

Hartsock appropriates for feminism aspects of a humanistic reading of Marxist epistemology. Marx had argued that dominant bourgeois accounts of reality are, as Hartsock puts it, "partial and perverse" (1983, 232) and that the proletariat, through theoretical and political practice, may rid itself of these accounts and formulate an epistemological standpoint of its own, one that is not merely different from the dominant one but which has an emancipatory potential. In so doing, it may make itself a "universal class," the vehicle not only of its own emancipation but of human emancipation more generally. Similarly, Hartsock argues, women may achieve a feminist standpoint that not only functions as an alternative to, or a critique of, "abstract masculinity," but which would involve "generalizing the human possibilities present in the life activity of women to the social system as a whole," and which would "raise, for the first time in human history, the possibility of a fully human community, a community structured by a variety of connections rather than separation and opposition" (1983, 247).

Hartsock argues that the possibility for the development of such a feminist standpoint is given *not* in women's subjective experience per se, but in their specific forms of life activity, or practices, within the social division of labor. She is careful to distinguish a *feminist* standpoint from the experience of women in general, for the latter frequently tends to be shaped by dominant male views and values, whose hegemony can be exposed only through a critical and self-critical feminist project. Equally importantly, a feminist standpoint also involves more than recognizing and valorizing the experiences of oppression, otherness, marginalization, of which identity politics also speaks. It involves a work of critical reflection on that experience and on the *social practices* out of which it is born. It aims to develop a critique of dominant knowledge claims and an alternative account of social reality on which a project of *general* human emancipation might be based.

Hartsock's standpoint theory, then, attempts both to show how knowledge emerges from specific practice-based experiences and to connect it with a broader epistemological universe and political agenda. But there are also difficulties with her work. As critics from both postmodern and identity politics positions have pointed out, Hartsock still tends to operate with an overly global conception of women's practice and experience, and thus to obscure differences and power inequities between women. As Marlee Kline puts it,

> Hartsock opens herself to the same charge of false generalization that she has raised against Marx from the perspective of gender. A feminist standpoint, when viewed from perspectives attentive to considerations of race, class, ethnicity, religion, sexual identity, physical ability, etc., appears limited and essentialist in the same way the proletariat [*sic*] perspective appears limited from a perspective attentive to considerations of gender. (1989, 38)

However, contrary to such criticisms, I do not think that the importance of differences between women is *necessarily* excluded from the central concerns of standpoint theory.[7] Because it begins from the social division of labor and from accounts of social reality that emerge from different social practices, there is nothing intrinsic to the theory that would preclude developing an account of a multiplicity of women's standpoints, each of which would overlap in some aspects and diverge radically in others. Hartsock's work can be developed in ways she did not initially undertake herself, in order to elaborate an account of multiple feminist standpoints that are neither identical nor yet wholly distinct. As Donna Haraway writes in her article, "Situated Knowledges": "There is no single feminist standpoint. . . . But the feminist standpoint theorists' goal of an epistemology and politics of engaged, accountable positioning remains eminently potent. The goal is better accounts of the world, that is 'science' " (1991, 196).

In this significant article, to which I now turn, Haraway recasts standpoint theory through postmodern problematics to argue for the importance of a multiplicity of different epistemological locations for a nondominative feminism. She also recognizes, however, the need for objective knowledge—by which I take her to mean knowledge that is at least partially shareable, publicly communicable and transmissible, about a world that is in some sense "real." Her question, which is also mine, is whether both a respect for different and divergent knowledges *and* some kind of account of objective—thus shareable—knowledge can be sustained at the same time.

Haraway suggests that they can both be sustained if we reconceptualize our notions of objectivity to take account, as feminism (and I would also add existential phenomenology) has taught us we should, of the embodied and situated nature of all knowing subjects. Objectivity is not to be confused with the traditional "god-trick" of "promising vision from everywhere and nowhere equally and fully" (191). Rather, she insists, objectivity is not about detachment but must emerge through the recognition of "particular and specific embodiment" and is "definitely not about the false vision promising transcendence of all limits and responsibility" (190). Thus to privilege embodied standpoints is not to embrace relativism or subjectivism. On the contrary, Haraway suggests, "The alternative to relativism is partial, locatable critical knowledges sustaining the possibility of webs of connections called solidarity in politics and shared conversations in epistemology" (191).

Haraway takes vision as a general metaphor for knowing. She argues that we do not need to conceive of vision as the disembodied and objectifying male gaze, but can instead use it to remind ourselves that knowing selves are always embodied and that our seeing/knowing is thus always located, partial, and perspectival. But Haraway, not unlike Hartsock, is at pains to stress that not all perspectives are equally valid in the struggle against domination: simply "being" of an oppressed or marginalized group does not automatically give one a privilege in formulating truth. Rather, she argues: "Not just any partial perspective will do. . . . We are also bound to seek perspective from those points of view, which can never be known in advance, which promise something quite extraordinary, that is, knowledge potent for worlds less organized by axes of domination" (192). However, such liberatory (my word) "partial perspectives" are not those of a simple identity politics, in which unproblematized, or self-identical, selves claim to present their own direct experience as reality: "Identity, including self-identity, does not produce science; critical positioning does, that is objectivity" (193).

For Haraway, the distinction between asserting an identity and assuming a *critical* positioning involves an awareness of the *mediated* nature of all experience and of the ways that power differentials permeate those mediations. "Vision is *always* a question of the power to see" (192). This power is not equitably distributed across humanity, but depends on our differential access to various prostheses, or optical technologies: "Vision requires instruments of vision; an optics is a politics of positioning. Instruments of vision mediate standpoints; there is no immediate vision from the standpoints of the subjugated" (193). Thus, she suggests, there is no such thing as "innocent 'identity' politics"—identity politics too is always implicated in power.

This far, I find Haraway's argument helpful. But important questions remain, concerning the mediated nature of knowing, to which her answers are less than adequate. Using vision as the metaphor for knowing has the advantage of emphasizing the embodied and situated nature of knowledge; and stressing that vision is never direct, but always mediated by "instruments of vision," has the virtue of pointing out that knowledge is never a simple "given" but is structured—and power-differentiated—by human artifice. But vision per se is also a limited metaphor for knowing, implying that knowledge is rather passively received through the senses and simply varies according to where we happen to be situated. Thus Haraway has additionally to introduce the notion of optics, of the politics of the production and differential distribution of instruments of vision, to make her metaphor work. But in doing so she actually intimates that we need another account of knowing: one based on human praxis. For the questions we have to ask about situated knowledges, in order to understand how they differ and yet might still give rise to forms of objectivity, must surely concern the following: How do people come to be situated such that they have different "partial perspectives"? Who makes the instruments of "vision" that enable them differentially to see/know the world? Who has which instruments and who controls access to their use? We need, in short, a fuller account of the *politics* of the production and distribution of seeing/knowing technologies that can be derived from vision as the primary metaphor for knowing. A theory that links the emergence of knowledges more directly to action is called for.

Another difficulty concerns the way Haraway characterizes the power-saturated technologies upon which situated knowledges depend. Mixing her metaphors with blithe abandon, Haraway suggests that the instruments, or technologies, of vision are above all semiotic: it is what she calls "a semiotic-material technology" that links "meanings and bodies" (192). But it is never clear in her account what justifies the hyphen here. Semiosis, could be described as a technology and as involving a "skilled practice" (194). But in what sense is this technology, or practice, "material"? Because it emerges from and affects bodies? Because it uses material analogues of such manufactured objects as the eye-glasses, microscopes, telescopes, or cameras of optics? We are not told. Haraway's insistence on the materially mediated nature of all knowledge, including knowledge of the located self, is of prime importance. But her conceptions of the material and of human-material interactions remain far too sketchy. I will turn shortly to Sartre's description of the emergence of the human world as a multiplicity of "practico-inert" totalizations of practices for a way of clarifying and developing her insights.

Although Haraway claims that from "partial perspectives" and "partial connections" there can emerge "webs of connection" and "shared conversations"—that is, forms of objective or partially shareable knowledge—her account never makes clear *how* it is that such connections and communications across difference are possible. What is it that is shared between the occupants of different "partial perspectives"? If we are able to make partial connections, what precisely are the connecting "parts," and why and how do they do the connecting? What needs to be explained is what is taken for granted here: "We do need an earth-wide network of connections, including the ability partially to translate knowledges among very different—and power-differentiated—communities," Haraway writes (187). I agree. But what is it that makes knowledges even "partially" translatable across radical differences? What enables escape from an epistemology of provenance? Haraway hints at a couple of answers, but develops neither very far. One is to do with the nature of selves; the other with the kinds of shared, or overlapping, milieux in which selves exist.

The first answer is that if we cease to view the self as unitary and stable, realizing that it is instead "split and contradictory" we will see that such a split self can join easily with other such selves: "The knowing self is partial in all its guises, never finished, whole, simply there and original; it is always constructed and stitched together imperfectly, and *therefore* able to join with another, to see together without claiming to be another. Here is the promise of objectivity" (193). It is an attractive metaphor: our rough edges, our seams, our openings perhaps, are the places where we can join with other and different selves. But, we must surely ask, *who* does the stitching together of this self? Is the self a kind of transcendental seamstress who sews her own parts together? If so, this self is perhaps more originary and cohesive than Haraway wants to admit; perhaps the self can even be conceived as a "project," as Sartre would put it.

Alternatively, with a certain further mixing of metaphors, the stitching together might be construed as an operation taking place on the self from without: automated sewing machines, which stitch us together, are parts of the "semiotic-material technology." Put less metaphorically, Haraway's second suggestion seems to be that what connects diverse knowing selves is, indeed, the existence of some common dimensions to their otherwise disparate lives. Experiences are never as radically distinct as either identity politics or postmodern notions of fracturing would imply because there are, after all, some elements common to all human lives—elements that make the communicability of experience across difference possible. Semiosis is one of these elements, but Haraway also points to others. She suggests at one point that gender is "a field of structured and structuring difference" (195). Feminism, she also tells us, must critically position itself in "inhomogeneous gendered social space" (195). But to talk of "a field" (even one of difference) and of "social space" (even if it is "inhomogeneous") is to posit an at least partially continuous social world that mediates between differently located selves and, as it were, underwrites their ability to communicate through the presence of common externalities.

In order for our partial perspectives to ground a situated objectivity they must be formulated from our different locations within something continuous, something in which all of us are embedded—be it field, social space, discourse, or some other medium. "Webs of connections" can arise across our diverse standpoints and identities *only* if the world mediates between them in some very general ways. Haraway implies as much, but her discomfort with anything that might be seen as universalizing discourse seems to leave her reluctant to explore explicitly how such general mediations might be constituted. Her project thus remains suspended in mid-air.

Haraway points us in the right direction by insisting that we need to seek ways of formulating objective knowledges that originate from, rather than obscure, differences and multiple standpoints and which acknowledge embodiment and location. But she offers us neither a sufficient account of selves, nor a sufficient account of how it is that the world mediates between them.

Re-enter the later Jean-Paul Sartre. In the *Critique of Dialectical Reason* ([1960] 1976), Sartre develops a theory of situated, practical subjectivity that can be of help in addressing the difficulties raised by an epistemology of provenance. What makes this theory of particular interest to feminism is Sartre's concern to defend particularity and difference while still exploring, at least as a heuristic device, the universalistic emancipatory vision of Marx. One of Sartre's main protagonists in the *Critique* is the "orthodox" Soviet-style Marxism that the French Communist Party still espoused in the late 1950s. Such a Marxism, Sartre charged, "is identical with Terror in its inflexible refusal to *differentiate;* its goal is total assimilation at the least possible effort. The aim is not to integrate what is different as such, while preserving for it a relative autonomy, but rather to suppress it" ([1960] 1968, 48).[8] Against such a totalitarian Marxism, Sartre seeks to elaborate a Marxist theory that would privilege differences while still exploring the possibility of a project of worldwide human emancipation.

To emphasize Sartre's sensitivity to difference is not, however, to deny that the *Critique* is still deeply flawed by sexism—it is! For example, Sartre's account of how social relations come to be constituted out of praxis simply ignores the whole area of reproduction, from pregnancy to childcare. In *Search for a Method*, Sartre criticizes orthodox Marxism for failing to recognize the importance of childhood: "Today's Marxists are concerned only with adults. Reading them, one would believe that we are born at the age when we earn our first wages," he writes ([1960] 1968, 62). Alas, the very same criticism can be leveled against the *Critique,* where both childhood and the various kinds of parxis involved in giving birth to and bringing up children are ignored. Moreover, those rare mentions of sexuality in the many hundreds of pages of the *Critique* treat it above all from a masculine point of view.[9] Even so, a selective appropriation of the *Critique* is worthwhile. For my purposes, Sartre's criticism of what he calls "analytic reason" and his development of an account of what he calls "dialectical reason"—that is, a reason which recognizes itself to be situated and to be able to grasp reality only from its own location—are of particular significance.

Analytic reason (or "positivist reason" as Sartre sometimes calls it), is the kind of reason that has also been subject more recently to postmodern critique as "Enlightenment" thought.[10] It lays the world out before itself as a set of objects for contemplation and dispassionate investigation. Analytic reason thus presupposes a knowing subject who stands, transcendent, outside the domain he or she investigates. It engages, in short, in Haraway's "god-trick," positing the theorist as the all-seeing spectator, the great panorama of history laid out at his or her feet. Against such a conception Sartre had written to Camus some years earlier that, "we are up to our eyebrows" in history ([1952] 1965, 77). In short, our vision is always from within or under, never from without or above. When analytic reason purports to study the world as if the theorist were not immersed in it, it functions ideologically: it serves to mask forms of oppression and exploitation by making the present human condition appear "natural" and thus not amenable to alternation ([1960] 1976, 820).

Against analytical reason, particularly as it has been used in Marxism to give a "scientific" account of the "laws of motion" of society, Sartre sets out to develop his account of "dialectical reason." Dialectical reason begins from the situation of an embodied and practically engaged self. It involves an investigation of the human world for which an individual situation is the point of departure but which, Sartre argues, can proceed far beyond our direct experience. It must begin from "the *life*, the objective being, of the investigator, in the world of Others" ([1960] 1976, 51).

But what then, we must ask, prevents Sartre also from slipping into relativism and an account of fragmented and incommunicable knowledges? If each of us comes to know the world and to theorize about it from our own particular historical and social location, do we not risk embarking, as with identity politics, on an epistemology of provenance which has solipsism at its worst-case terminus? For Sartre, the answer to such a question is, after much consideration, "no." Such particular, situated knowledges are, in principle, communicable and intelligible to others. But this possibility has to be systematically demonstrated, rather than, as in Haraway's work, rhetorically asserted.

The demonstration begins for Sartre from the examination of the purposive and transformative human activity that he calls *praxis*. Sartre defines praxis as "an organising project which transcends material conditions towards an end" ([1960] 1976, 734). In its most abstract form, praxis arises from our existence as organic entities: we need to engage in praxis in order to transform nature into means of survival that will ward off death. But in its more concrete manifestations, this kind of action generates not only the world of products (of use-values in Marxian terminology) but also less tangible phenomena, such as aspects of culture, forms of social organization, even language. In choosing praxis as his starting point Sartre differs significantly from many postmodern thinkers, who tend to grant constituting primacy to discourse. He differs also from advocates of identity politics, who generally begin not from action but from subjective experiences of shared oppression in order to construct an affirmative identity.

Like Hartsock, Sartre argues that an adequate social theory must start from what it is that human beings *do* in the world. He also argues that the specific characteristics of human practical activity must be the point of departure for accounting for the possibility of knowledge and reason. An adequate theory of situated knowledges, Sartre teaches us, cannot be developed primarily from Haraway's metaphor of vision. Although Sartre's exemplifications of praxis tend to involve primarily masculine activity, I think that the structure of praxis as he describes it applies also to uniquely female forms of activity. Insofar as becoming pregnant, giving birth and nursing are human actions, rather than natural functions, these too are not fundamentally different in structure from what Sartre calls praxis.[11]

Sartre begins his account of dialectical reason at the most abstract point possible, with praxis as a purely individual undertaking. However, this individualistic starting point is heuristically chosen, in order to be able to demonstrate that human action is in fact social through and through. "Critical investigation," as Sartre also calls dialectical reason, "will set out from . . . the individual fulfilling himself in his abstract *praxis*, so as to rediscover, through deeper and deeper conditionings, the totality of his practical bonds with others and, thereby, the structures of the various practical multiplicities" ([1960] 1976, 52).[12] Through what might initially appear a thoroughly subjectivist project, the study of one's own situated praxis, ever wider sets of social and historical processes may be made intelligible. It can be demonstrated that "there is no such thing as an isolated individual" ([1960] 1976, 677) and that it is possible for us (whoever "we" may be) to understand and communicate about kinds of human praxis radically different from our own. The relevance of such an undertaking to the issue of connections across differences between women is, I think, obvious.

Examining such abstract, individual praxis, Sartre identifies two sets of analytically distinct but always mutually implicated, indeed dialectical, properties that together account for the fact that praxis is always social. These sets of properties also justify the claim that situated knowledges can encompass realities far wider than the scope of our own direct experience. First, individual abstract praxis comes to discover that it is connected to that of others "in exteriority," through the mediations of what Sartre calls "the practical material field." Second, individual praxis involves "interior" qualities. It possesses a fundamental intelligibility because it is intentional: it requires a purpose, a project to transform something existing into a future possibility. As such *any* praxis has certain qualities that enable us, *reciprocally*, to recognize it *as* human praxis.

Connections in Exteriority

Any praxis, Sartre argues, has to involve a transformation of that segment of the world on which it acts, of its "practical material field." When it acts on the world, however, praxis also produces the "practico-inert": forms of worked matter, or externalized embodiments of praxis, which in turn will both mediate and constrain future praxis. These may then be encountered as forms of "exigency," which in part dictate the necessary forms of future praxis. Simply because it cannot take place without the mediation of the material world, praxis always produces something more and other than is intended, be it simple waste matter or changed social relationships. This process is compounded by the fact that even what might initially appear to be isolated and individual parxis never is.

As Sartre painstakingly demonstrates, praxis always takes place situated in a practical material field that brings it into mediation with other individual praxis. In the process, it brings social entities of various kinds into being, whether or not the individual actors are aware of it at the time. Moreover, this field is generally shaped by scarcities which compound the exigencies of praxis. Scarcity here does not mean merely an objective insufficiency of material goods. It encompasses also the threat or fear thereof (as in the dynamic that can create hoarding) or less-tangible lacks—of time, status, affection, or social recognition, for example. Thus a praxis such as child-care, or other forms of noncommodified "sex-affective production,"[13] also takes place in a field of scarcity.

Sartre gives the history of deforestation in China as a simple paradigmatic example of the material mediation of individual praxis conditioned by scarcity: individual peasants, seeking to increase their arable land, cut down trees. But in the process they *collectively* denuded the land, inducing massive flooding of the Yangtze river and ending up by reducing the total amount of arable land available. There was, says Sartre, "no joint undertaking." However, the transformation of each individual undertaking through its unanticipated mediation with other identical undertakings issued finally in a "joint result," which each encountered as the alienation (that is, the making other) of his or her own praxis ([1960] 1976, 163–64).[14] An analogue to Sartre's example would be the way that decisions by individual women in the United States to enter forms of traditionally female employment, such as the "caring" occupations, result in the consolidation of a segmented labor market, in which women tend increasingly to be locked into low status and poorly paid employment. Another example would be the outcomes of decisions made by many poor women in "third world" societies to give birth to a large number of children as a strategy for ensuring support in old age. Given existing economic inequities, such individual strategies may give rise to the "joint result," intended by none, of increasing pressure on resources and may, paradoxically, result in greater destitution in old age.

What is important in Sartre's example is that a simple social identity has come into being on the basis of apparently individual parxis: the Chinese peasants who produced deforestation constitute a "practical ensemble," Sartre's most general term for a set of human beings whose praxis connects them together through the mediation of the material world, whether or not they are aware of it. As the book proceeds, Sartre's examples deal with ensembles that are unified by an increasingly complex and socially constituted practical material field, be they a number of people waiting at a bus stop for a bus that might not have seats for all of them, a collection of people listening to a propaganda broadcast, consumers linked by the market, or workers competing for jobs.

Insofar as such ensembles are constituted through the mediations of the external field, whose practico-inert exigencies react back upon the further praxis of each of its individual members, Sartre describes the relationship of the members of such ensembles to each other as one of "seriality." That is, they are passively and unintentionally connected, each a victim of the unchosen links that alter the outcome of the praxis of each. Sartre uses the term "collective" to describe such an ensemble. By contrast, he uses the term "group" to describe individuals who come together in a more purposive and direct manner. Thus, in his analysis of the history of the French working classes, he depicts a complex set of dynamics between workers as collectives—individuals who are serialized, atomized, isolated and placed in competition with each other by the labor market—and workers as groups. Only the latter form organized and conscious nodes of resistance of various kinds (ranging from union activity to spontaneous participation in brief acts of sabotage to attempted revolution).

Sartre's account of collectives and of the serial relations of their members can help us to resolve issues about the identity of "women."[15] The identities of individual women, I suggest, are constituted in large measure "in exteriority," as members of multiple collectives (for example, as objects of male sexual desire, as consumers of particular kinds of products, as members of ethnic collectives, as pregnant females, as workers in a segmented labor market). Moreover, the relationship between women and feminism (Hartsock's *feminist* standpoint; Haraway's *critical* positioning) can be clarified by using Sartre's distinction between collectives and groups, that is, between passively mediated ensembles and intentionally created ones. Indeed, one could write a fascinating history of the feminist movement in the United States and its relationship to diverse ensembles of women by adapting Sartre's methods of analyzing class as collectives and as groups. However, my main point here is epistemological: the fact that individual praxes are materially and serially connected is a necessary pre-condition for the possibility that critical reflection about one's own praxis can extend into a wider investigation of society. It is not, however, in itself a sufficient condition.

Interiority and Reciprocity

Co-given with its exterior conditionings and mediations, praxis must also have what Sartre calls an "interior" dimension. If it had none, it would be some kind of blind force that we simply would not recognize as human action. However, this is not to say that praxis must be guided by a Cartesian consciousness, existing independently of the world it contemplates—or indeed by any kind of constituting consciousness. Far from it. As we have seen, Sartre anticipates feminist critiques of Western rationalism by rejecting the possibility of a de-situated and detached subject surveying the world as its object. Sartre's practical subject is not the disembodied propagator of the god-trick.

However, although consciousness is not autonomous, Sartre argues that any praxis, as a transformative engagement with the world, must necessarily involve intentional consciousness, even if it is often at a prereflective level. There is an embodied intentionality to human existence that is prior to both conscious knowledge and to discourse.[16] This also implies that perhaps the practical subject is not as "split" as Haraway's account of the subject suggests: there is a basic bodily intentionality that knits an existence together, integrating its multiple and apparently fragmentary collective identities, each of which is itself the outcome of a multiplicity of prior and present praxes.

In *Being and Nothingness* Sartre had argued (with a certain debt to Husserl) that consciousness is consciousness *of* something, that it cannot but intend an object. But now, in the *Critique*, where Sartre's concern is no longer consciousness per se but consciousness as the interior dimension of praxis, intentionality has additionally to do with the purposive quality of our apprehension of the world in which we are actively engaged. To talk of intentionality as purposive is not to say that our ends have always to be fully articulated prior to action. But it is to say that intentionality is what ensures that action is amenable to at least a degree of post hoc comprehension. Most important, since intentionality is a general structure of human action, this is also what enables the intelligibility of a particular practical action to be grasped, at least to some degree, by any other practical subject.[17] Even if we cannot grasp the full import of the praxis of another (or indeed of our own praxis), we can generally recognize that an intentional human project is taking place.

Sartre uses the term "reciprocity" to describe this mutual comprehension of each other's projects. It is important to point out that reciprocity need in no way denote empathy, such as subjective feelings of care or connection between human beings. "It cannot," says Sartre, "be based on a universal abstract bond, like Christian 'charity'; nor on an *a priori* willingness to treat the human person . . . as an absolute end; nor on a purely contemplative intuition revealing 'Humanity' to everyone as the essence of his fellows" ([1960] 1976, 109–10). Nor, one might add, can it be based on a mystical or emotional bond of "womanhood," such as one finds in some ecofeminist and other variants of global-difference feminism.

Reciprocity lies in no generic essence, feminine or otherwise. It emerges and endures only in the mutual encounter of specific praxes, where the recognition that others are engaged, like myself, in intentional projects of transformation of the practical material field may result in either reciprocal antagonism or in reciprocal solidarity, depending on whether our projects threaten each other or are complementary ([1960] 1976, 112–13).

Moreover, in relations of reciprocity each of us comes to recognize that the praxis of others actually *alters* our own praxis, through the mediations of the practico-inert. For example, the significance of what I have written in this essay will depend not only on what I believe to be its import but also on my situation within the collective of feminist theorists. Through future scholarship others may well return my thoughts to me profoundly altered—for either better or worse—even though this essay will remain "my" product. This process of alteration depends in turn on such practico-inert structurings of the field of academic production as the marketing and distribution of journals, the positioning of feminist scholarship within the institutions of American academia, and the hierarchies within feminist scholarship. Thus, as Haraway also insists, my relationship to you, the reader, is never one of directly communicating consciousnesses but rather of *materially mediated* selves.[18] Moreover, the material mediations are what enable the relationship to take place at all.

To make this point Sartre now criticizes Hegel's "master-slave dialectic"—which had been central to his own account of human relations in *Being and Nothingness*—as idealist: "Hegel . . . ignored matter as a mediation between individuals. Even if one uses his terminology, one has to say that while each consciousness is the counter-part of the Other, this reciprocity can take an infinity of different forms, positive or negative, and that it is the mediation of matter which determines these forms in every concrete case" ([1960] 1976, 113).

Such a reciprocal relationship may in some instances involve overcoming seriality to form groups engaged in a common praxis, including forms of common resistance to domination. Indeed, this has frequently been the case in the women's movement, when what are experienced by isolated women as private problems, such as the fear of rape or unwanted pregnancy, become the basis for group action. But an even more important point here, bearing on the issue of whether partial perspectives can give us "shared conversations" and objective knowledges, is that in those very different instances where relations of the most profound conflict of interests exist there must also be reciprocity. As Sartre points out, while denying the humanity of his slaves, a U.S. slave owner still had to recognize that they were, like him, practical subjects, who could choose either to put their labor and skills at his disposal or else to plot revolt or escape. "This is the contradiction of racism, colonialism and all forms of tyranny: in order to *treat a man like a dog*, one must first recognise him as a man" ([1960] 1976, 111).

The sexism of Sartre's statement notwithstanding, his point is vital: even in relations of profound antagonism, such as may of course exist not only between men and women but also between women of different races, ethnicities, social classes, sexual orientations, religions, and so on, a reciprocal comprehension of praxis exists. Indeed, if it did not exist, conflict or struggle would not be possible. Whether it be conflict between classes, as in Sartre's examples,[19] or strife between diverse collectives of women whose unequal power or contradictory interests pit them against each other in relationships of antagonism, struggle is possible *only* because we can reciprocally comprehend praxis as intentional action. Thus the claim to an exclusive domain of knowledge—the very core of an epistemology of provenance—is put into question through the very act of asserting that it exists.

Reciprocity, even when it is antagonistic, thus limits the tendency toward extreme subjectivism which I have argued is implicit in identity politics. An epistemology of provenance is shown to undermine itself. The investigation of one's own praxis, that is, one's own situated knowledge, may develop into wider knowledge of the praxis of others beyond the collectives or groups through which one directly acts.

Thus, to conclude by returning to Haraway's work, we can now see more clearly why it is indeed possible for the "webs of connections" that Haraway calls both "shared conversations" in epistemology and "solidarity" in politics to be created. If we conceive of the self not only as one of situated vision but also as a practical situated subject, one whose knowledge and whose reciprocal relations with others (be they antagonistic or solidaristic) come into being through praxis and its practico-inert mediations, we avoid the problems of global-difference feminism, which posits a pre-given and universal female essence. We also avoid the fragmenting tendencies implicit in identity politics, as well as other forms of multiple-difference feminism. It might be the case that it is impossible—as identity politics suggests—for others to know the subjective experiences, that is the "inner" emotions and feelings, of a particular woman or even an ensemble of women.[20] However, the fact that all of us engage in a diversity of praxes, mediated through the same or overlapping practical material fields, means that however different our worlds appear, and however antagonistic our interests really may be, reciprocity and the possibility of a mutual comprehension of each other's actions always remain possible.

And what of Haraway's call for standpoint theories and situated knowledges that are "potent for worlds less dominated by axes of domination"? Can we both value differences and pursue broader political agendas for human emancipation that transcend differences? Epistemology is political, since claims about knowledge involve the exercise of power; but politics functions along many other axes than that of knowledge claims and is not co-extensive with epistemology. Thus, to establish, as I have set out to do here, that knowledge must be both practical and situated—and that these are the very conditions for the possibility of a knowledge that is both particular and general—does not in itself give us a difference-sensitive yet general emancipatory politics. It is, however, a necessary element of such a politics.

Notes

1. For the first—and much cited—feminist critique of this, see Collins and Pierce (1973).

2. I have offered such a reading of Sartre's early work in Kruks (1990). For similar readings, see Nancy Hartsock's critique of the Sartrean elements in the thought of Beauvoir (Hartsock 1983, app. 2) and Lorraine (1990, chap. 4). A related critique is developed in Le Doeuff ([1989] 1991). However, for a defense of *Being and Nothingness* against such charges of masculinism see Barnes (1990). Barnes argues that although one can find plenty of sexist statements in *Being and Nothingness* they are merely contingent and not integral to Sartre's philosophy.

3. On Beauvoir's influence on Sartre, see Simons (1986) and Kruks (1991). For the argument that Sartre actually stole most of his ideas from Beauvoir, see Fullbrook and Fullbrook (1994).

4. Many advocates of this kind of feminism have rightly urged that differences between women should be conceived not as discrete and additive, but as multiplicative in their effects: "The modifier 'multiple' refers not only to several, simultaneous oppressions but to the multiplicative relationships among them as well" (King 1988, 270).

5. For early statements linking identity politics and coalition building, see Johnson (1983) and

Combahee Collective (1983). See also many of the writings in Moraga and Anzaldúa (1983). For more recent statements see essays in Anzaldúa (1990a) and Albrecht and Brewer (1990). Some advocates of identity politics have, of course, taken more separatist positions, but these are not my concern here.

6. An alternative tendency is to shift toward a postmodern emphasis on the fragmentary and unstable nature of the self. Although the postmodern notion of the self as fragmented and shifting well captures some of the complexities of identity today, it frequently tends to beg the question of how to characterize the "self" that experiences itself as multiple and unstable. Often a transcendental "self" is tacitly assumed, one that is capable of the meta-experience of itself as living its multiple identities. For example, Gloria Anzaldúa's statement, "This morning when I got up I looked in the mirror to see who I was (my identity keeps changing)" (Anzaldúa 1990b, 216), tacitly posits some kind of a core "I," or "self," which can observe (in the mirror) how its identities come and go. I address the difficulties of the conception of the fragmented or split self more fully in my discussion of Haraway below.

7. I thus disagree also with Sandra Harding's claim that "the importance of differences in women's politics . . . appears to be excluded from the central concerns of standpoint theories" (1986, 164). See also on this issue Alarcón (1990).

8. Sartre's *Search for a Method* ([1960] 1968) forms the prefatory essay to the original French version of the *Critique*, but it is published as a separate essay in English.

9. The most extended discussion of sexuality is to be found in the second volume of the *Critique* (Sartre [1985] 1991, 255ff.), published only posthumously.

10. Sartre himself has of course also been subjected to the charge of "Enlightenment" thinking, for example by Foucault and Derrida. For a review of Sartre's treatment at the hands of postmodern thinkers and a persuasive argument that Sartre's ideas have far more in common with many of them than they care to admit, see Howells (1992).

11. Sara Ruddick (1989) has creatively explored mothering as a practical activity which gives rise to its own specific knowledges and ways of thinking. See Emily Martin (1987) and the essays of Iris M. Young (1990), "Pregnant Embodiment" and "Breasted Experience," for materials from which to construct an argument that pregnancy, childbirth, and nursing are forms of praxis.

12. Sartre's style is consistently masculinist. The English translation of the book, which I use here and in subsequent quotations, has not attempted to render it more gender neutral and neither have I.

13. This useful concept is developed in Ferguson (1989).

14. One can also think of many environmental examples closer to home that fit Sartre's model, from the dustbowl to the destruction of forests through acid rain.

15. See Young (Chapter 9) for a fuller treatment of these issues. Young suggests that Sartre's account of serial collectives offers a way of talking about the category of "woman" without essentializing or reifying it.

16. Indeed, for Sartre discourse—like any other human artifact—is practically produced. It thus cannot have the constitutive primacy that is accorded to it in most postmodern theory. Although over all Sartre pays insufficient attention to the question of discourse in the *Critique*, I find the notion of discourse as praxis to be helpful: it places us in a less passive position in relation to discourses and enables us to raise questions about their origins.

17. When we cannot comprehend in any degree we tend to say that the other person is "mad," connoting that their behavior is not recognizably human to us. The project of some alternative psychiatry—notably that of R. D. Laing (1969)—is to reveal that there still is coherence and intentionality to what might appear to be non-intentional and unintelligible behavior on the part of psychotics.

18. This would also be the case if you were part of the audience at a conference where I was presenting this paper orally, or even if I were telling you my ideas in a one-on-one conversation, although the practico-inert mediations would be somewhat different in each case.

19. For the most part members of classes are, alas, male in Sartre's account. Where he does use an example concerning women workers, it is to exemplify a situation where alienation is so extreme that no effective choice is left to an impoverished woman worker who "chooses" an abortion over an impossible motherhood ([1960] 1976, 232–35).

20. But it might also be possible to comprehend purely subjective experiences in alternative ways, for example through poetry, dance, or music. Sartre's theory does not preclude other such forms of knowledge: he simply does not establish their formal possibility.

References

Alarcón, Norma. 1990. "The Theoretical Subject(s) of *This Bridge Called my Back* and Anglo-American Feminism." In *Making Face, Making Soul.* See Anzaldúa 1990a.

Albrecht, Lisa, and Rose M. Brewer, eds. 1990. *Bridges of Power: Women's Multicultural Alliances.* Philadelphia: New Society Publishers.

Anzaldúa, Gloria, ed. 1990a. *Making Face, Making Soul.* San Francisco: Aunt Lute Books.

Anzaldúa, Gloria. 1990b. "Bridge, Drawbridge, Sandbar or Island, Lesbians-of-Color Hacienda Alianzas." In *Bridges of Power: Women's Multicultural Alliances.* See Albrecht and Brewer 1990.

Barnes, Hazel E. 1990. "Sartre and Sexism." *Philosophy and Literature* 14:340–47.

Beauvoir, Simone de. [1949] 1989. *The Second Sex.* Trans. H. M. Parshley. New York: Vintage Books.

Brown, Elsa Barkley. 1988. "African-American Women's Quilting." In *Black Women in America.* See Malson et al. 1988.

Collins, Margery, and Christine Pierce. 1973. "Holes and Slime: Sexism in Sartre's Psychoanalysis." *Philosophical Forum* 5:112–27.

Collins, Patricia Hill. 1990. *Black Feminist Thought: Knowledge, Consciousness, and the Politics of Empowerment.* Boston: Unwin Hyman.

Combahee Collective. 1983. "The Combahee River Collective Statement." In *Home Girls: A Black Feminist Anthology.* See Smith 1983.

Ferguson, Ann. 1989. *Blood at the Root: Motherhood, Sexuality and Male Dominance.* London: Pandora Press.

Fullbrook, Kate, and Edward Fullbrook. 1994. *Simone de Beauvoir and Jean-Paul Sartre: The Remaking of a Twentieth Century Legend.* New York: Basic Books.

Haraway, Donna. 1991. "Situated Knowledges: The Science Question in Feminism and the Privilege of Partial Perspective." In *Simians, Cyborgs, and Women.* New York: Routledge.

Harding, Sandra. 1986. *The Science Question in Feminism.* Ithaca: Cornell University Press.

Hartsock, Nancy. 1983. *Money, Sex, and Power: Toward a Feminist Historical Materialism.* Boston: Northeastern University Press.

Howells, Christina. 1992. "Conclusion: Sartre and the Deconstruction of the Subject." In *The Cambridge Companion to Sartre,* ed. Christina Howells. Cambridge: Cambridge University Press.

Johnson, Bernice Reagon. 1983. "Coalition Politics: Turning the Century." In *Home Girls: A Black Feminist Anthology.* See Smith 1983.

King, Deborah K. 1988. "Multiple Jeopardy, Multiple Consciousness: The Context of a

Black Feminist Ideology." In *Black Women in America: Social Science Perspectives*. See Malson et al., 1988.

Kline, Marlee. 1989. "Women's Oppression and Racism: A Critique of the 'Feminist Standpoint.'" *Socialist Studies/Etudes Socialistes: A Canadian Annual* 5:37–64.

Kruks, Sonia. 1990. *Situation and Human Existence: Freedom, Subjectivity, and Society*. New York: Routledge.

———. 1991. "Simone de Beauvoir: Teaching Sartre About Freedom." In *Sartre Alive*, ed. Ronald Aronson and Adrian van den Hoven. Detroit: Wayne State University Press.

Laing, R. D. 1969. *The Divided Self*. New York: Pantheon Books.

Le Doeuff, Michèle. [1989] 1991. *Hipparchia's Choice*. Trans. Trista Selous. Cambridge, Mass.: Blackwell.

Lorde, Audre. 1984. *Sister/Outsider*. Freedom, Calif.: Crossing Press.

Lorraine, Tamsin. 1990. *Gender, Identity, and the Production of Meaning*. Boulder: Westview Press.

Malson, Micheline R. et al., eds. 1988. *Black Women in America: Social Science Perspectives*. Chicago: University of Chicago Press.

Moraga, Cherríe, and Gloria Anzaldúa, eds. 1983. *This Bridge Called My Back: Writings by Radical Women of Color*. New York: Kitchen Table, Women of Color Press.

Martin, Emily. 1987. *The Woman in the Body: A Cultural Analysis of Reproduction*. Boston: Beacon Press.

Marx, Karl. [1846] 1978. "The German Ideology." In *The Marx-Engels Reader*, ed. Robert Tucker. New York: Norton.

Phelan, Shane. 1989. *Identity Politics: Lesbian Feminism and the Limits of Community*. Philadelphia: Temple University Press.

Ruddick, Sara. 1989. *Maternal Thinking*. Boston: Beacon Press.

Sartre, Jean-Paul. [1943] 1966. *Being and Nothingness*. Trans. Hazel E. Barnes. New York: Washington Square Press.

———. [1952] 1965. "Reply to Albert Camus." In *Situations*. Trans. Benita Eisler. Greenwich, Conn.: Fawcett.

———. [1960] 1968. *Search for a Method*. Trans. Hazel E. Barnes. New York: Vintage Books.

———. [1960] 1976. *Critique of Dialectical Reason*. Vol. 1. Trans. Alan Sheridan-Smith. London: New Left Books.

———. [1985] 1991. *Critique of Dialectical Reason*. Vol. 2 (unfinished). Ed. Arlette Elkaïm-Sartre, Trans. Quintin Hoare. London: Verso.

Simons, Margaret. 1986. "Beauvoir and Sartre: The Philosophical Relationship." *Yale French Studies* 72:165–79.

Smith, Barbara, ed. 1983. *Home Girls: A Black Feminist Anthology*. New York: Kitchen Table, Women of Color Press.

Young, Iris M. 1990. *Throwing Like a Girl and Other Essays in Feminist Philosophy and Social Theory*. Bloomington: Indiana University Press.

———. 1994. "Gender as Seriality: Thinking About Women as a Social Collective." *Signs: Journal of Women in Culture and Society* 19(3): 713–38. See also Chapter 9.

11

Friendship and Feminist Praxis

Insights from Sartre's *Critique of Dialectical Reason*

Peter Diers

Why should an existentialist "critique of dialectical reason" interest us? On the surface, there does not seem to be anything peculiarly redeeming about dialectical reasoning that would specifically endear it to a feminist approach to philosophy. In fact, the dialectic might lend itself rather well to postmodern feminist criticisms of metanarratives, psychoanalytic feminist analyses of male-centered theorizing about alienation, general feminist concerns regarding the tendency to try to appropriate otherness not letting the other speak for herself, and so forth. Indeed a survey of Jean-Paul Sartre's works would contain no shortage of misogynist anecdotes that might make a feminist philosopher suspicious of theorizing on the basis of his reflections. However, one of the most redeeming features of Sartre's overall philosophy is that when played against itself, it reveals a position in which his own theories condemn his actual misogynist practices and often describe a corrective. But the question remains: what has Sartre's Marxist existentialism to do with feminist theory and practice? Why focus on the *Critique of Dialectical Reason?*

Sartre's most explicit goal in the introduction to the *Critique* is to justify the use of dialectical reason. That is, Sartre argues that the only way to make history intelligible is through the lens of historical materialism. But even more important for our concern is that the *Critique* is arguably the culmination of Sartre's lifelong project of advocating "freedom and socialism." Throughout his career, Sartre was concerned with the possibilities for and the nature of freedom within the context of larger social collectives.[1] Thus a major focus of the *Critique* is an analysis of the processes of social and political transformation that are required to create a situation of socialism and freedom.

The focus of the *Critique* may thus be seen as compatible with the goals of many feminist philosophers. We must of course note that not all feminists seek a classless society, but all agree upon the need to transform our existing culture into one in which women no longer wield a disproportionately low share of the economic, political, and social power. Precisely because of this focus on revolutionary praxis in feminist philosophy, Sartre's analyses of social and political transformation can be insightful for evaluating and improving feminist theory and practice. We will begin our study with a brief sketch of the various social entities that Sartre discusses in the *Critique*. Following this presentation, we will use his theoretical tools and insights to evaluate the relationship between friendship and feminist praxis in Marilyn Friedman's and Janice Raymond's works.

Friendship is one of the most significant social bonds that we form and participate in on a daily basis. The friendships we form often dominate the kind of lives we lead, the activities in which we engage, and even our methods of thought and speech. But friendship is a topic to which Sartre has devoted little attention in his writings, especially in the *Critique*. This deficiency is itself a weakness of the social theory that Sartre develops in the *Critique*. Thus an analysis of friendship, its place in our social existence, and its impact on history and political transformation would be a valuable addition to the study of Sartre's social philosophy.

Joseph Catalano has divided Sartre's social philosophy into three levels of explanation: the historical, local, and psychoanalytic. All three levels are operative at all times in our existence, but they may vary in importance and explanatory power depending upon the particular situation. The level of theorizing that dominates the *Critique* is the historical (though this is to be expected, especially if we consider the subtitle of the second volume, *The Intelligibility of History*). I assert that, contrary to Sartre, this focus on the historical level is a detriment to his overall project. Without an adequate study of the local level (especially friendships), our understanding of the historical level will be inadequate. In addition, such overemphasis will skew our perceptions of the local level. Therefore, friendship is an important element to consider in analyzing our social being and in developing a theoretical grasp of history and the social and political transformations which occur in history.

But why these particular feminist philosophers? They are neither existentialists, nor Marxists, nor dialecticians. I have chosen to study Friedman and Raymond because of the skill with which they link friendship and social and political transformation. Their work can be seen as building a bridge between the local and historical levels—a bridge that Sartre did not explicitly provide. It is precisely at this point that I offer Friedman's and Raymond's works as correctives and scaffolding for Sartre's mature social theory.

I. From the Individual to History: A Summary of the *Critique of Dialectical Reason*

The *Critique of Dialectical Reason* is presented in two volumes (the second posthumously published) roughly following the progressive-regressive method that Sartre put forth in *Search for a Method*. The first volume, subtitled *A Theory of Practical Ensembles*, develops a regressive approach to history. That is, Sartre sets out to dissect society into its various abstract components so that a set of theoretical tools can be developed for understanding the complexities of history in motion. The second volume, *The Intelligibility of History*, was intended to employ these tools in a progressive study of the workings of historical events. In other words, volume 1 takes a synchronic look at the various practical groupings that form society in general, and volume 2 suggests, through application, that dialectical intelligibility emerges diachronically as the result of the mediations between these general social entities.

After presenting a sketch of some of the theoretical motivations that will be used in the *Critique*, Sartre begins his synchronic analysis with the praxis of the lone individual.[2] This individual is primarily defined as a being of need. The human being is a lack that must be filled if it is to survive. We engage in praxis upon the practico-inert (the material world) in order to totalize (organize) it in such a way that it is more conducive to satisfying our needs. Thus Sartre may be seen as enriching his earlier account of human reality. In *Being and Nothingness*, human reality is described as a negation, a being-for-itself, that creates itself and organizes the world, being-in-itself, into meaningful configurations in a never ending attempt to be the foundation of its own being. In the *Critique*, human reality is a being of need that engages in praxis in order to totalize the practico-inert into systems that make the satisfaction of its needs easier.[3]

But the individual engaged in praxis soon learns that the world is not conducive to his or her praxis. Praxis is absorbed by the practico-inert and transformed into counterfinalities. That is, the materiality and inertia of the inorganic world deviate the individual's praxis in such a way that the result of his or her activity is never exactly the result that was intended. In fact, Sartre's conclusion is even more radical, namely, that the individual is ultimately ineffective and impotent in his or her own praxis. "Rugged Individualism" is at best a deceptive myth once the exigencies of the material world are clearly stipulated. Our individual praxis cannot succeed on its own. Sartre's most profound examples of counterfinalities include the periodic and devastating floods created by the deforestation of China by its peasant farmers and the impoverishment of Spain through the overabundance of new-world gold. Neither of these results was the intended purpose of the praxes, but nonetheless, because of the structures embedded in the practico-inert, praxis was turned against itself. All praxis, because it confronts the practico-inert, results in deviated praxis.

Sartre continues his synchronic analysis of history by looking to the level of social collectives. The first and most prevalent social unit that he discovers is the series.[4] The series is a passive gathering of individuals who all happen to be organized around a common object. They do not organize themselves around this object, but are content to allow the object to act upon them. Sartre uses the example of a bus stop. The people are in line waiting for the same object, the bus. They possess a "serial unity" because they are brought together by the demands of this bus (being at a specific place at a specific time, being a certain number in line, etc.). Their unity as a social collective is not derived by any interior (self-chosen) reason, but rather they are a passive unity where each person lives his or her place in the collective as a separate individual. I could be first in line; I could be last in line. The other and I are purely interchangeable. Thus, not only is the other experienced as an alterity in the series, my own being is an alterity because I am merely a passive activity. Sartre calls this pattern of action other-direction. The other, whether it be a material object, my membership in a series, another person, controls and directs my actions. I do not find the reason for acting within my own freedom.

But suppose the bus is late, and, in fact, becomes chronically late. Then it is possible that these isolated individuals would form a group in order to demand that their need for reliable and efficient bus service be met. The group enters the historical stage and humanity is born.[5] That is, the group provides the necessary power for freedom to overcome its domination by practico-inert structures so that it can change them. Practically speaking, the lone individual is powerless to oppose the dominance of the inhuman forces of the practico-inert. The series is the domination of the human by inhuman counterfinalities. But the "group-in-fusion" is a spontaneous gathering of formerly separated praxes that constitute themselves as the same in order to satisfy a perceived common need or defend themselves against a common threat.

Sartre's favorite example of the group-in-fusion is the storming of the Bastille that began what we call the French Revolution. The citizens of the Quartier Saint-Antione perceived that they were the potential targets of a massacre by the troops of Louis XVI. In the face of such a threat that constituted these citizens as a serial unity, an "apocalypse" occurred in which they became aware that the other could become the same. That is, they realized that the other possessed the same status of fear in relation to this perceived threat. In a spontaneous and unorganized movement, these citizens created their own internal unity to form a group whose practical goal was liberation from an oppressive power. The Bastille stood for them as the symbol of that power, which had to be defeated. And so, without hierarchical structures, each citizen became the same as the others by internalizing a common praxis—storm the Bastille. The group-in-fusion is the moment when freedom enters the historical scene in order to create for itself a successful satisfaction of its needs.

However, all does not go well for this group-in-fusion. Sartre notes that from its inception it is plagued by its very freedom. Because each citizen is free to join with others to form a group, he or she becomes aware that everyone, including him- or herself, is free to leave the group. Hence the significance of the term "group-*in-fusion*." Sartre adamantly maintains that there will always be an infinitesimal gap between the individuals who constitute a group. That gap is precisely the freedom embodied in each person's individual praxis. There are, for Sartre, no hyperorganisms; no social entities that transcend the individuals who compose them. At best, the members of a group are constantly trying to pull together their infusible freedoms. So as soon as the immediate need or threat that created the apocalyptic moment of the group-in-fusion disappears, fear of fragmentation and dissolution grips the members of the group. The possibility that the group will be reclaimed by the practico-inert is ever present. If too many members choose to leave, the group will collapse into a series once again.

In an attempt to circumvent this disaster, the members of the group seek a new structure that will ensure their continued status as a group praxis. This new structure is initiated by the pledge. Sartre says that the members take an oath to remain within the group in order to assure its permanence. They agree to continue the project that the group has begun, but, to enforce this promise, each member pledges to kill anyone who defects. The pledged group is created in an effort to provide a semblance of stability to a social unit that is grounded on each individual's spontaneous freedom. Ultimately, the pledge unfolds as the almost inevitable decay and degradation of the group back into the practico-inert, back into a series.

The reason that the pledge initiates the downfall of the group is that it creates what Sartre terms "fraternity-terror." Fraternity is the camaraderie that the members of the group create by virtue of their shared goals and praxis. Since the pledge, however, is based upon a fundamental promise of violence, the group members live their membership as terror. They fear their own fracturing from the group because of the death sentence that separation implies. Sartre argues that it is because of the equality with which the members of the group live the pledge and its terror that they can develop "friendship, love, and comradeship."[6] Sartre does not address any other modes in which friendship may arise within human society. Friendship is only analyzed within the context of fraternity-terror and the pledged group. It is here that the limitations of Sartre's analysis of friendship and the local level crystallize. There are no truly positive noncoercive sites within which friendships can develop and grow. This friendship via terror thus creates a tenuous situation that will generate the counterfinalities that will almost inevitably lead to further degeneration of the group and its praxis.

The further fracturing and dissolution of the group leads to an attempt to create an even more permanent structure, the institution. In order to produce a more effective and organized common praxis from the multiplicity of individual praxes composing the group, the institution is created to assign tasks and duties to each individual based on her qualifications. In addition, a hierarchy of authority establishes itself as the director of the common praxis of the group. This authority is maintained by the constant praxis of all of the group members. Sartre says that each individual "incarnates" the praxis of the sovereign authority. That is, in all of their separate and specially designated tasks, each group members is ultimately engaging in the praxis that the sovereign institution authorizes and organizes through its own "sovereign praxis." The intention is that the group become more unified by virtue of the fact that those controlling its praxis are unified. This drive toward a unification of the sovereign praxis often results in sovereignty being placed in the hands of a single individual. By the fundamental unity of his or her individual praxis, the sovereign unites the group because each group member incarnates the sovereign praxis by retotalizing the sovereign's directives. In other words, the institution becomes the highly complex manifestation of the sovereign's own individual praxis.

The problem that arises as a result of this consolidation of power is that a massive bureaucracy is created for the purpose of maintaining order within the institutionalized group. But here, Sartre says, alterity has reentered the group praxis. Each group member no longer directs his or her praxis but is instead directed by the praxis of the sovereign—each person is directed by the other. Other-direction, however, is one of the primary structures that we identified in the series—the reason for one's actions is no longer found within oneself. In the institution, other-direction manifests itself as an active passivity: the group members are still engaged in praxis (unlike in the series), but this praxis is almost wholly inward. Maintenance of the bureaucracy becomes the goal of the revolutionaries instead of the aim being transformation of the existing systems of oppression into a common freedom. Ultimately, the weight of the bureaucracy or the praxis of a counterrevolutionary group will result in a complete lapse into a new form of seriality. The group has, at best, merely succeeded in replacing one form of oppression for another.

This quite pessimistic attitude toward revolutionary praxis continues into volume 2 of the *Critique*. The second volume is intended to put together these social units that have just been dissected from living history back into a diachronic historical movement that makes the conflict of these social collectives intelligible. To that effect, Sartre must show that the competing praxes of two different groups results in a coherent and meaningful whole. That is, class struggle must be intelligible. The manuscript leaves off, however, without ever coming to an answer to that question, but before that point Sartre provides us with several interesting analyses.

He begins the work through an application of the concept of incarnation. He argues that the praxes of two boxers are intelligible to the extent that they incarnate the violence of the larger social collective of which they are a part. The movements of each boxer can only be comprehended when seen in relation to the other boxer within the larger situation of violence. Thus we can say that there is an intelligibility to these individuals' praxes precisely because they incarnate a larger social milieu. But this finding is itself not enough. To fully answer our initial question, we must show that the struggle between groups, series, institutions, and ultimately classes is intelligible, and that there will be no larger praxis to which we can appeal to account for this intelligibility. Thus, for *historical* intelligibility, we need to have "totalization without a totalizer."

Sartre continues the work with an analysis of the intelligibility of competing subgroups within a pledged group. He uses the example of the Bolshevik Revolution to illustrate his point, taking that revolution as a whole to be a form of pledged praxis that developed two conflicting subpraxes during its history. These subgroups became headed by Trotsky and Stalin. Sartre reveals with great clarity how the plan of "socialism in one country" was the result of these competing praxes. He pursues the history of the revolution, revealing how it followed the various stages of degeneration that he uncovered in the synchronic study. That is, as the revolution progressed, the members of the group came to realize that further fracturing would destroy the revolutionary praxis. In response to this threat, power became more and more concentrated in a hierarchical institution. Ultimately, when it became necessary, sovereignty was consolidated in one person—Stalin. The revolution needed the unity of a single sovereign praxis in order to maintain the unity of the various individual praxes within the group. But, as Sartre very clearly points out, the results were almost inevitably imperfect. *Stalinism* became the *deviation* of the revolutionary praxis. That is, even though Stalin was in some sense necessary for the revolution, Stalinism became a group praxis turned in upon itself until its very inertia created new forms of serial oppression.

After this analysis of the history of the Soviet Union under Stalin, the remainder of the second volume wanders its way through a series of scattered topics such as ontology and progress, and offers an outline for a study of the intelligibility of struggle in a country with a diffuse sovereignty (a capitalist democracy). The result is that the work never reaches an answer to the question with which it began: can history be made intelligible without a single totalizer? One may wonder why it was never completed, but suffice it to say that the results would have been quite interesting.

II. The *Critique of Dialectical Reason* Applied to Feminist Theory and Practice

Now that we have a sketch of Sartre's theory of social and political transformation, we can apply his analyses to feminist literature on revolutionary praxis. One obvious factor that Sartre immediately brings to our attention is that it must be a group (not an individual) that confronts an oppressive institution. An individual or a relatively few individuals is no match for the inertia contained in an institution. Institutions are the products of hundreds or thousands of individual praxes that have been solidified into structures that are taken for granted and not usually questioned by those who participate in them. Thus Sartre's thinking offers a corrective to narrowly conceived revolutionary praxis. Because we cannot deal with the entirety of feminist literature on revolutionary praxis, I have chosen to focus on the connection between feminist understandings of friendship and feminist praxis, especially since we can use these insights to see the weaknesses in Sartre's approach.

We will begin with an examination of Marilyn Friedman's work, *What Are Friends For?* In this text, Friedman develops an account of friendship that ultimately generates revolutionary praxis. She argues that interaction with friends can lead to social criticism that in turn can lead one to political activism. These friendships, based on an empathetic understanding of the other's point of view, encourage moral growth. This moral growth can provide the friends with the experience, knowledge, and strength necessary to work toward transforming oppressive structures and institutions in society.

Genuine friendship is a commitment to a particular person, and so one of the benefits is the intimate contact with that person's experience and his or her interpretation of it. Friendship allows us to expand the horizons of our own experience by sharing in the experiences of others. This expansion promotes a more sophisticated evaluation of our moral positions. Friedman argues that the moral growth in such friendships "is the profound sort that occurs when we learn to grasp our experiences in a new light or in radically different terms. It is the kind that involves a shift in moral paradigms, in the basic values, rules, or principles which shape moral thought and behavior."[7] Through this paradigm shift, genuine friendship can lead us toward social criticism and political action. When confronted with the particularity of a friend's experiences as well as with this friend's evaluation of his or her experiences, events that seemed unproblematic might be seen to be quite oppressive and solutions to problems that we thought to be adequate can be seriously called into question. The disruption in our moral thought can be a catalyst for finding new solutions to old problems and effective answers for new dilemmas.

In Friedman's analysis, "friendship is precisely a relationship that provides for the morally unimpaired expression of personal commitment. This is far less true of personal relationships that lack equality and mutuality."[8] In other words, Friedman is arguing that friendship is such a unique and important relationship in people's lives that it allows for the possibility of the kind of moral growth that can lead to a commitment to political praxis aiming to end certain forms of oppression. Many other types of relationships that we form are disrupted by unequal power dynamics, contractual expectations, or other disparities. Friedman concludes that "voluntary friendship has the potential to support unconventional values and deviant lifestyles, themselves a source of needed change in our imperfect social practices."[9] It is the empathy and personal commitment to another that is the foundation for friendship, according to Friedman. In Sartre's view, friendship is just a potential by-product of a political alliance. Friedman shows us that friendship can be a source of political transformation, opposed to Sartre's view of friendship as a secondary phenomenon. For Sartre, friends are those who help us in revolution, but for Friedman, friends form the basis of our affective lives and that foundation can then be built upon in the work for change in our larger social institutions. Friedman's analysis avoids much of the coercion and violence that Sartre packs into his analysis of that relationship.

But Sartre's analysis does demand that we provide an account of how these friends will experience their encounter with oppressive institutions and bureaucracies. On this score, Friedman's suggestions seem to lack sufficient depth to counter the problem of such entrenched hierarchies. To begin with, people who are willing to engage in genuine friendships are quite rare, and it takes considerable effort to start, develop, and maintain the kind of fruitful friendship that Friedman has in mind. But even after surmounting these initial difficulties, there is still no guarantee that revolutionary praxis will emerge. For example, one might find agreement on the problems but not on the solutions, and so the praxis that comes out of the relationship could be quite minimal. Even if there is an agreement about what is to be done, friends sometimes lull themselves into inactivity by theorizing too much. Friends may be all "talk" and no "action."

Another factor affecting the success of friendship as a source of revolutionary praxis is that the genuine friendships that Friedman describes are often efforts at an alternative to the traditional institutions rather than attempts to transform them from the inside. In other words, friendship might be seen as an isolationist move that discredits one's ability to criticize social institutions in the eyes of those who are participating in them. Those who preach "family values," for example, tend not to take seriously the "deviants" who, offering criticism of the marriage institution, refuse to get married. They say that those who criticize marriage do so because they do not know what it is really like or that their criticism proves that they are indeed deviants who should not be regarded as morally trustworthy individuals. In the end, the praxis of friends may fail to actually engage the oppressive institution itself.

On the other hand, if friends do participate in the various social institutions that they seek to critique, they can find the inertia of the institution daunting. Participating in an institution brings numerous traditional expectations and obligations into play. These expectations will be placed equally on all members of the institution including those who attempt to transform it. If the majority of individuals in a society place on friends strong expectations to follow traditional roles, norms, and values of the institutions they enter, the friends may not be able to carry out their intended praxis. Institutions demand that individuals incarnate the accepted praxis and not deviate from it. For example, even if a particular couple married with the expectations of living a balanced/egalitarian relationship, there will often be strong pressures on them to conform to the existing social norms for that institution. And, if they still persist in trying to make changes, they might still be labeled "agitators" by those seeking to uphold the traditional structure of the institution. Thus once engaged in revolutionary praxis on the institution, the friends are presented with social expectations that run counter to their intended praxis. Given such pressures, they may fall into those traditional roles or they may give up their quest to transform the institution.

Hence friends who desire to engage in revolutionary praxis often seem to be in a "catch-22" situation. If they do not participate in the institutions, their criticisms may be ignored because it is coming from "ignorant isolationists," but if they do participate in the institutions that they seek to critique, they may not be able to overcome the inertia of the social expectations that come with that participation. Thus, if we are to salvage the political activism that stems from Friedman's account of friendship, we must find a way to circumnavigate this dilemma.

The key to an escape lies in recognizing the difficulties of fighting against an institution. First, the institution is a form of pledged praxis that sees itself as self-justifying—"we have always done it this way." Second, the institution demands that individuals within its scope incarnate its praxis—it presents them with specific roles to fulfill. Third, these factors plus the inertia of the bureaucracy itself require that we take up praxis against it in the form of a group. A few scattered clusters of individuals cannot make the difference. What is needed is a concerted effort on the part of the oppressed to invent new ways of living in society.

Such a focus on group praxis that yet retains an emphasis on friendship appears in Janice Raymond's work A Passion for Friends. Raymond agrees with Friedman that friendships can bring about beneficial social and political change, but she goes further and asserts that without female friendships, feminism will not succeed. Raymond suggests that "the first goal of feminism is not to bring women and men together but to bring women together."[10] She argues that the primary aim of as well as means for feminist revolution will be "Gyn/affection."

Raymond states that "Gyn/affection connotes the passion that women feel for women, that is, the experience of profound attraction for the original vital Self and the movement toward other vital women."[11] Female friendship is more or less synonymous with Gyn/affection, but Raymond's emphasis is on the active and dynamic dimensions that such friendships can take. She claims that truly Gyn/affective relationships are both personal and political. When women gather together with other women there is not only the potential for personal strength through friendship, but because these friendships occur in heteroreality they ultimately have a political dimension as well. In other words, reality is currently constructed by men to serve their needs and desires (heteroreality), and one aspect of this construction is the notion that women together are women alone. Men have used women as scaffolding for their own political and social aims, and thus they do not see women together as a totality. In heteroreality, women are defined by and given a place only in relation to men. Thus Gyn/affection disrupts the traditional categories of heteroreality by revealing the power of women together. Women can form (and have formed) meaningful, satisfying, and happy relations with one another. These friendships can change (and have changed) the quality of life for the friends as well as beneficially impact the lives of those outside the friendship.

Raymond goes beyond Friedman's account of friendship by noting that the historical context of female friendship requires that it be political and not just personal. The power of these relationships can then effect change on the institutions that oppress women. Again, we see an analysis of friendship that offers us greater insight into its affective and local dimensions than that provided by Sartre. But what about our Sartrean concerns regarding the inertia of oppressive institutions? Raymond notes that it is not enough for feminists to form only friendships. Gyn/affection between scattered individuals will not transform society, but when many women bond together out of Gyn/affection, then positive change can result. Raymond argues that it is often necessary, especially within heteroreality, for women to create their own institutions that provide a woman-identified and woman-centered space. Her primary examples of such spaces are the convents of Western Christendom and the marriage resisters of China. Both groups established institutions that allowed for the flourishing of Gyn/affection, and because of the large numbers of women that these institutions supported, they were able to impact the surrounding culture, creating beneficial change.

The nuns and marriage resisters give positive content to the idea that "sisterhood is powerful." The convent allowed women not only to develop friendships, but also to receive an education, exercise their leadership abilities, avoid the stigma of the "loose woman" in heteroreality, as well as bring about social and political transformation. The marriage resisters in China created a space in which it was acceptable to avoid the traditional roles of wife and mother, which offered little or no freedom for women. These women established households of unmarried women for the purposes of supporting one another, and they generally worked in the silk industry. Through their collective power they were able to live independent of the traditional marriage institution. Hence, both the nuns and the marriage resisters created institutions that were conducive to the development of Gyn/affection.

By our Sartrean critical standards, Raymond has given us a more likely candidate for feminist praxis than has Friedman. Whereas Friedman's account seems to avoid institutional affiliations, Raymond notes that such affiliations are necessary given the state of heteroreality. On Raymond's view, when the friends confront the oppressive structures of patriarchy, they do so not in small scattered clusters, but as members of a group pledged to one another and to working toward a better world for one another. Because heteroreality is composed of oppressive institutions and bureaucracies, it cannot be battled alone. Only a group praxis can have the potential for revolutionary praxis.

But have we really found a solution to our dilemma? Can Gyn/affection, as Raymond has described it, provide an effective praxis against oppressive patriarchal institutions? The first thing that our Sartrean critique should note, and which Raymond does mention herself, is that the institutions that support Gyn/affection may themselves be hindrances to such friendships. That is, the phenomenon of other-direction that Sartre described as a part of institutions could lead to divisions between people rather than fostering connections. Raymond notes that agreed-upon rules established a certain degree of order that fostered convent community for the nuns, but when the rules became too restrictive and dogmatic they broke down that community.[12] But, if Sartre's evaluation of the progression of institutions is correct, such restriction and dogmatism may be almost inevitable. That is, as the leadership tries to maintain cohesion among the group members, they tighten the boundaries of acceptable individual deviations from the common praxis. If so, then virtually all institutions designed to provide a space for Gyn/affection will become unable to accomplish their initial goals.

In addition to this concern, Sartre's concept of "incarnation" can provide some insight into the decline of convents. Sartre argues that in a hierarchically structured institution, group members carry out the group praxis by incarnating the sovereign praxis into their own actions. This top-down control is aimed at keeping the group together, but it also makes the deviation of the group praxis more likely. In addition, it makes it easier for oppressive institutions within the culture to manipulate the group's praxis. The hierarchy of the convent made an easy target for those who wished to suppress its power. By decreeing that men could be leaders of women's religious orders but women could not lead men's religious orders, the male religious leaders were able to manipulate the actions of women within the convents. Because the group members incarnated the praxis of the sovereign and men became the sovereigns governing the women's religious orders, enforcing the rules of cloister and enclose became easier. Male religious authorities were able to deviate the praxis of the convents by manipulating that praxis from the top down. This is one of the primary dangers that Sartre's analysis of revolutionary praxis brings to light. Hierarchies concentrate power, but then that power can be more easily swayed toward ends that were not originally intended.

But perhaps Raymond's account of the marriage resisters can provide an antidote for avoiding an institution that is too hierarchically oriented. There was a mentoring system among the marriage resisters in which the older women assisted the younger in education, work, and community life. Seniority conferred leadership upon one of the women, but, as Raymond notes, there were no bureaucracies that held such structures in place. The organization of the group remained somewhat flexible depending upon the particular needs of those within the group. The marriage-resistance movement lasted for about one hundred years, but, as Raymond notes, the "collapse of the silk industry in the late 1930s paved the way for the communist extinction of the resistance movement."[13] Because these women required jobs outside the community to sustain their Gyn/affective relationships, when those jobs ceased to exist, the community could not survive.

By heterorelational standards, Raymond argues, these women's efforts would be seen as amounting to little or nothing. They were seen merely as deviants and agitators. Because they did not make any significant impact on the surrounding institutions, they have been viewed as ineffective in most scholarly research. But Raymond states that to treat the marriage resisters in this way is to deny the significance of the community that they fashioned for themselves. She argues that we need new Gyn/affective political standards for evaluating the success of such movements. In those standards, we would include a recognition of the quality of life that the women created for themselves and not merely focus on whether or not they effected great changes to the external institutions of the time.[14] If their practices led to a flourishing of Gyn/affective relationships that were noticed and perhaps had some impact on the surrounding culture, then they should be judged as important contributions to a history of women successfully working and living together.

But again, our Sartrean questions resurface: is this enough? Is it sufficient to examine the internal successes of a political movement without focusing primarily on its external success? It would seem that the very downfall of the marriage-resistance movement points toward an answer to our question. These women did not effect fundamental change in the surrounding institutions, particularly in regard to women's lack of participation in political power. As a result, once the economy on which their community was dependent collapsed so did the community itself. The women were mostly forced back into the traditional roles of wife and mother, although some did emigrate to other countries to maintain their lifestyle. Under Sartrean terminology, if the group does not succeed in transforming the existing institutions of oppression, its almost inevitable decay into seriality will leave the group members in the same state of oppression as before their efforts. They might enjoy a certain temporary peace from such oppression, but if the group is not externally focused, then it will eventually be eroded by the inertia of the existing bureaucracies. Thus, if we are looking to build a feminist future, we must work against the current patriarchal structures and not be content to form communities that merely run parallel to those structures. Eventually the larger, oppressive institutions of patriarchy will dissolve the conditions for the possibility of such Gyn/affective relations. There must be a direct engagement with existing oppression if it is to be overcome. Patriarchy demands that everyone incarnate its sovereign praxis, and if its demand is left virtually unchallenged, it will overpower revolutionary praxis. Ultimately, these institutions will so deviate feminist praxis within Gyn/affective communities that they will no longer support the types of relationships that they were intended to support.

It is at this point that we can suggest a space for men in the feminist movement. Historically speaking, male friendship has all too often been formed in an antiwoman context. Such male bonding against women has occurred in, among other places, military service, sports, the local bar, and political organizations. Men concerned with bringing about justice should critique and avoid any friendship that finds its source in male domination. By contrast, men can play a revolutionary role in assisting women in their quest to create new spaces for the equal exercise of social, political, and economic power. Women forming revolutionary friendships with men could be the catalyst that moves Gyn/affective institutions beyond merely providing temporary havens from patriarchy to a direct engagement with oppressive institutions. This is not to say that men are being placed in the role of savior or defender, a role that has historically been connected with that of master and abuser. Genuine friendships with male feminists may be an important step on the road to a truly feminist future.

III. Concluding Remarks

We have seen that Sartre's analysis of the processes of social and political transformation has interesting insights to offer to feminist praxis. Sartre's conceptions condemn to defeat any revolutionary praxis that is narrowly conceived. People must work in groups to overcome the inertia of currently existing institutions of oppression. But we have also seen that those groups themselves can become new forms of oppression or that their praxis can be deviated by demands on group members to incarnate the sovereign praxis of the dominant institutions. So what do we have left? Is there still hope for a feminist future?

We must note, in searching for answers to these questions, that we have only hinted at a feminist criticism of these Sartrean insights. That is, it seems likely that a feminist criticism of Sartre will reveal aspects of his account of revolutionary praxis that cannot accommodate certain feminist insights. Our clearest insight has been to point out the limitations of Sartre's view of friendship within the pledged group. The limited focus reveals a friendship that is based on political affiliation and not a deep personal commitment to another individual on an emotional and intellectual as well as a practical basis. Perhaps Sartre's starting points of ratiocinative intelligibility, need, fraternity-terror, and conflict between groups and individuals leads him to misconstrue the possible ways that individuals within a group can relate to one another and the manner in which groups can interact with the existing institutions. Nonetheless, Sartre does present us with a challenging reading of the forms that feminist revolution can take if it is to have a chance of succeeding.

Our Sartrean criticism requires a form of revolutionary praxis that avoids rigid hierarchicalization but still retains a vital connection with the institutions that it is trying to transform. An overly bureaucratic feminist praxis will either collapse under its own inertia or be more easily manipulatable by patriarchal practices. A nonhierarchical approach that does not directly confront the existing institutions is doomed to be reappropriated by them. Thus, if Sartre is correct, we need to articulate a theory of revolutionary praxis that remains flexible and yet is able to focus its energies outward toward transforming the current instruments of oppression.

Notes

1. One might wonder at this claim—that it was a career-long concern of Sartre's. Admittedly, *Being and Nothingness* suffers from an individualistic focus. Sartre's theory of the look with its combative consciousnesses looking at each other has trouble dealing with more complex social phenomena. But, at times, Sartre does deal well with the ways in which we play out our freedom in social contexts. The waiter in the café is an excellent example of how one might use one's freedom to play an expected social role at the expense of one's own creativity and spontaneity. Sartre develops these insights as he moves beyond *Being and Nothingness* to the *Notebooks for an Ethics*, *Saint Genet*, his 1950s political essays, *Search for a Method*, and finally the *Critique*.

2. Praxis, for Sartre, is the purposive action of the human agent in order to organize the material environment in which he or she is situated so as to satisfy his or her needs. The process of grasping and organizing the environment, the primary function of praxis, Sartre terms "totalization." The practical environment that is being organized by praxis is called the practico-inert. Thus, through praxis individuals (and groups) totalize the practico-inert in order to sustain themselves in being (existence).

3. Sartre himself makes such a link in the *Critique* (Jean-Paul Sartre, *Critique of Dialectical Reason*, vol. 1, trans. Alan Sheridan-Smith [London: Verso, 1976], 227n). In addition, he returns to this comparison in a more in-depth manner near the end of the unfinished manuscript for volume 2.

4. For an enlightening use of this concept of seriality in relation to feminist concerns see Iris Marion Young's "Gender as Seriality: Thinking About Women as a Social Collective," Chapter 9, this volume. She uses the idea of series to articulate a conception of "woman" that avoids essentialism and a substantial subject and yet retains the ability to capture the history of women's oppression as well as the possibilities for collective action against such oppression.

5. Sartre, *Critique*, 436.

6. Ibid., 438.

7. Marilyn Friedman. *What Are Friends For?* (Ithaca: Cornell University Press, 1993), 196.

8. Ibid., 214.

9. Ibid., 217.

10. Janice G. Raymond. *A Passion for Friends: Toward a Philosophy of Female Affection* (Boston: Beacon Press, 1986), 39.

11. Ibid., 7–8.

12. Ibid., 108.

13. Ibid., 136.

14. Raymond (141–45) notes five different questions that need to be asked in order for us to truly appreciate the accomplishments of Gyn/affective praxis. We need to evaluate the success of the marriage resisters in living in nonheterorelational ways, changes in the concept and reality of power that they created, their own new quality of life, their visibility to outsiders of the time, and the means by which they effected their distance from contemporary society.

12

The Beauvoir and Lévy Interviews

Toward a Feminine Economy

Guillermine de Lacoste

In the eyes of Sartre's colleagues at *Les Temps Modernes*, the stroke that left him bereft of his eyesight in March 1973 marked the termination of his forty years of creative, incisive philosophizing. I shall assert in this essay that during the last seven years of his life, Sartre found the dialogical format of the interview, which now became his sole means of expression, extremely well suited to the final formulation of his philosophy, which he had long ago converted from its original basic antagonism between persons, and which had been evolving toward openness to and dialogue with the other and toward a search for social solidarity. Two of the interview series of that period, those with Simone de Beauvoir and those with Benny Lévy, are especially important, not only because they shed much light on this particular phase of Sartre's thought, but because they help to put his entire philosophical trajectory in perspective.

The Beauvoir interviews took place over the summer of 1974, first in Paris then in Rome. Sartre had originally viewed them as the basis of a book that would be the continuation of *Les Mots*.[1] But he soon became totally involved in the Benny Lévy interviews, and seems to have forgotten about the publication of the Beauvoir interviews. She eventually published them in 1981, posthumously, as an appendix to *La Cérémonie des adieux*, her account of his last ten years.[2] The Lévy interviews were far more stimulating to Sartre, both because Lévy was a gadfly, continually challenging him, and because they were not about his past life and thought (as the Beauvoir interviews had been), but about the articulation of a social philosophy that he had been attempting to formulate for a number of years, with a number of ups and downs—due to its situatedness. The interviews took place on an ongoing basis from 1975 to 1980. They were originally to have been part of a book, *Pouvoir et liberté* totaling some eight hundred pages, which was scheduled to be published in 1980.[3] Sartre and Lévy opted to prepublish them in *Le Nouvel Observateur*, a leftist newspaper, under the title *Hope Now*, during three consecutive weeks in March 1980.[4] However, Sartre died a few weeks later.

Annie Cohen-Solal points out that everyone at *Les Temps Modernes* (with the exception of Gérard Horst), was thoroughly scandalized by the *Hope Now* text, for it did not conform to what they considered to be the real Sartre—and they tried to stop its publication.[5] Later, using the terminology of Olivier Todd in *Un Fils rebelle*,[6] Beauvoir accused Benny Lévy of forcibly leading astray an "old man" (*un détournement de vieillard*). She asserted that, in fact, since Sartre could not read what Lévy had written, he had been forced to reject himself (CA 150). The testimony of Jean Daniel, the editor of *Le Nouvel Observateur*, belies this assertion. Daniel relates that, prior to his publication of the interviews, Sartre himself had called him:

> His voice was loud and clear, and he spoke with extreme authority: "I believe you are quite troubled," he said, "My friends must have besieged you. Never mind them. I, Sartre, ask you to publish [the *Hope Now* text] in its entirety. If, however, you'd rather not do it, I'll publish it elsewhere; but I would be very grateful to you if you did it. I know my friends have gotten in touch with you, but their reasons for doing so are totally wrong. The itinerary of my thought eludes them all, including Simone de Beauvoir." Seldom had Sartre been as clear, as precise, as much in control of both his thought and his language. Besides when I called him

back to tell him about a minor mistake, and asked him if he had the text handy, he answered: "I have it right here in my head." And indeed, he knew it by heart." (S:L 514)

The Beauvoir interviews were also controversial, but for a reason opposite to that concerning the Lévy interviews. Geneviève Idt, for example, accuses Beauvoir of appending them to *La Cérémonie des adieux*, her almost clinical account of Sartre's last years, to show that in fact nothing had changed during those years in the topography of Sartre's relationships and of his ideas.[7] And Aronson suggests that Beauvoir "constructed" the traditional Sartre she wanted to show the world, as opposed to the outlandish, schismatic one of the Lévy interviews that she wanted to banish.[8]

Beauvoir herself asserts, in the brief introduction to the interviews, that they yielded no "unexpected revelations" (CA 163). Yet, in a certain section of the interviews, Sartre candidly discusses with her his fear of "abandon" to his body and to women throughout his life.[9] He states that this fear impeded him from reaching what he now sees as the ideal of reciprocity in love—the complete abandon/gifting of each lover to the other. As Beauvoir tries to help him to pinpoint the origin of this fear, he agrees that it was his fear of abandon to/by his mother. Then he goes on to explain that he tried to exorcize this subjective fear through aggressive war games that made him symbolic master of the objective world.

This whole section of the interviews, in which Sartre acknowledges for the first time that he had a deep neurosis and Beauvoir helps him to find the key to it, is critical to a fuller understanding of Sartre's total philosophical venture. If in this essay I ignore Descartes's, Husserl's, Heidegger's, Merleau-Ponty's, and Beauvoir's crucial influences on his thought,[10] and I concentrate instead on the extent to which his neurosis affected him personally and deeply influenced his entire thought, I am only following his own lead. For did he not devote hundreds of pages of *Saint Genet*, and thousands of pages of *The Family Idiot*, to a study of the effect of Genet's and Flaubert's "childhood socialization" on their thought"—and no one has done this for him.

Moreover, Sartre is here articulating what has been called by Hélène Cixous "a feminine economy" of reciprocal abandon in personal and eventually in social relationships. He links his failure to reach this ideal during most of his life to his neurosis, his fear of abandon. He also gives indications that the roots of his masculine economy of appropriation/

mastery of the world are that neurosis. Last, he intimates that he has now effected a complete reversal of his *Being and Nothingness* theories, according to which any attempt at a love relationship can only end in sadism or masochism. I shall give a full exposition of this reversal in the last section of this essay.

This reversal of Sartre's thinking about personal relationships corresponds closely to the changes in his sociopolitical thinking, which he had been trying to formulate for decades, and a sketch for which we now find in *Hope Now*, as well as in other interviews of this period, especially "Self-Portrait at Seventy." Now the desire for society, for sociality and solidarity, on the part of a consciousness that is interdependent with other consciousnesses, has replaced the desire to be and to appropriate the world, on the part of a monolithic independent consciousness (the for itself in *Being and Nothingness*). And the "fraternity" of "people bound to each other in feeling and action" (HN 91), has replaced the original conflict rooted in the objectifying propensity of the look. Moreover, Sartre insists on linking the new ideal of "fraternity" to what the French call the *matriciel*, the fact that we are all children of one mother, thus openly, if metaphorically, acknowledging that he has now completely overcome his neurosis—that is his fear of his mother's body and of his link to it.[12] The social and political are intimately linked to the personal here.

Both interviews indicate a full evolution in Sartre's thought from what is expressly—to use Cixous's terminology (which applies splendidly here)—a masculine economy, toward the articulation of an economy that is undeniably feminine in nature. It is on this evolution that I shall focus in this essay. Before I do so, I must explain why this categorization of Sartre's philosophy, first as masculine, then as feminine, does not lead to essentialism, and point out the characteristics that Cixous gives to these two economies.

I. Cixous's Distinction Between Feminine and Masculine Economies

Cixous herself tells us that far from placing woman and man in pigeonholes leading to essentialism, the distinction between the two economies opens up everyone's horizons—for her ideal is one of bisexuality or "the presence of both sexes" within each of us. She explains that "one can find these two economies in no matter which individual,"[13] in different proportions. She uses two different criteria for her distinction between the two economies. First, she sees one's relationship to pleasure as either masculine or feminine. In order to explicate the difference between the two relationships, she refers us to two stories that help define "the zones of libidinal emotional behavior" in which these relationships are determined—the story of the apple, and that of the quest for the Holy Grail.

For her, the story of "Eve and the Apple" is fundamental because it symbolizes each individual's relationship to the world, with its joys and its prohibitions/laws (EF 133). "The stakes are extremely simple," she writes. "It is a question of the apple: does one eat it or not? Will one enter into contact with the intimate inside of the fruit or not?" (EF 133). For Cixous, the story is simple also: on one side there is the law "which is absolute, verbal, invisible," and which is not, and facing it there is "the apple which is, is, is" (EF 133). It is a struggle between absence and presence, between negation and affirmation, between the abstract and the concrete. Eve is on the side of presence, of affirmation, of the concrete, of happiness. She symbolizes the feminine economy. In the quest for the Holy Grail, Perceval, a woman's son, with no father, is also on the side of innocence, of pleasure, of happiness. But after he is educated and "phallicized," he falls prey to the law, which is "anti-pleasure" (EF 135).

According to Cixous, one's path through life in one economy or the other, or partly in both, "depends on one's relationship to pleasure and the law," and on the way in which one responds to "this strange antagonistic relationship" (EF 135). This is not determined by anatomical sex. Rather, Cixous writes, it is established by history (both collective and individual), by "the cultural schema and the way the individual negotiates with these schema . . . adapts to them and reproduces them, or else . . . goes beyond them . . . and joins up or never joins up with the universe which I would call 'without fear or reproach' " (EF 135). In great part this depends on the possibility of one's "experience of the inside," on one's experience of capacity for other, on one's capacity for "positive receptivity" (EF 135).

The second criterion that Cixous uses to distinguish between feminine and masculine economies is that of attitudes toward giving. Within a masculine economy, the gift must bring a return on one's investment. This proprietary attitude is rooted in "man's desire to be (at) the origin."[14] It turns gifting to the other into an appropriation of the other. Its logic depends, as Susan Sellers explains, on "a differential process that entails opposition to and appropriation of whatever is thereby designated as other" (NBW 37). The creation of the opposition between "activity" and "passivity" to distinguish its most desirable activity from a feminine "passivity" or abandon of self, which is not desirable within a masculine economy, is the fruit of this differential process. It is because of this opposition that someone within a masculine economy feels the danger of being obligated by someone else's generosity. For "the moment you receive something," Cixous explains, "you are effectively open to the other, and, if you are a man, you have only one wish": to close off that openness by giving a gift in return.[15]

A feminine economy, on the other hand, "encourages giving as an affirmation of generosity."[16] For it, there is no calculation in gifting, which is for the pleasure of the other with no attempt "to recover one's expenses" (Cixous 1981, 44). What matters is what Susan Sellers calls in her introduction to a passage from *The Newly Born Woman* "the closer relationship to the m/other, the body and hence to love."[17] Within the framework of this economy, the inner face of giving is receiving, that is, opening up to the other in a positive receptivity. By opening up, one is, however, "open to being possessed . . . which is to say dispossessed of (oneself)" (NBW 42). This is what Cixous terms "the capacity to depropriate (oneself) without self-interest" NBW 44), and to be well on one's way in the process of de-selfing, or de-egoization, which she looks upon as a most positive, empowering process—yet as enabling greater reciprocity with the other.

II. The Roots of Sartre's Masculine Economy

In this section I shall show how these roots are in Sartre's neurosis, or in his fear of abandon to/by his mother. Contat and Rybalka were well aware of that neurosis. In a 1971 interview on *The Family Idiot*, they asked him whether his "discovery of Flaubert's neurosis" corresponded somewhat to the discovery of his own neurosis. Sartre's answer was evasive.[18] But by 1975 he had changed his attitude. He told Contat that he wanted to "yield [his] subjectivity" to him. However, he immediately backed out, for, as he said, "there are still things in me which refuse to be said" (SPS 13), such as "the sexual and erotic relations in my life" (SPS 31). We are therefore fortunate that in the Beauvoir interviews he was quite candid about his fear of abandon to his body, to women, and to his mother.

The importance of this fear first surfaces when Beauvoir is interrogating him about his subjective relation to his body ("la saisie subjective du corps") (CA 396). He explains to her that whereas many of his friends spoke about the joy of skiing or of swimming, he experienced only fear, of falling when skiing and of getting tired when swimming. For he never felt good in his body, never enjoyed it. She then reminds him that he always hated what he termed "abandon," relaxing on the grass or on the beach, much preferring to sit on a hard, sharp block of stone in a rather painful manner. "You seem to have had a moral refusal to abandon yourself to your body, and to have reacted to any possibility of it by a certain crispation," she tells him. And he agrees that indeed, abandon did not at all use to fit into his ideal of "what one should be," which greatly favored action dealing with the objective world (CA 397).

When Beauvoir tries to pinpoint the reason for the refusal of "all passivity," of all abandon, of all jouissance on Sartre's part, he concedes that as a child he had a horror of his mother's abandon. He does not specify in what this abandon consisted—only that it was a very rare occurrence, "poor woman!" he sighs. Beauvoir suggests, and Sartre acquiesces, that it may have been indulgence in food, as in the case of Madame Darbida in his short story "The Room."[19] It certainly seems, however, that Sartre's great fear of abandon all his life must have had deeper roots than his mother's fondness for sweets! We must therefore take seriously his mention in Les Mots of his desire as a child to have incest with a sister, most obviously his sister/mother. Were not he and his mother treated as children by her parents, and did they not sleep in twin beds in the same room for ten years? And Sartre writes that the years of World War I (during which he was a preadolescent) were heavenly for him: "My mother and I were the same age . . . and we were always together. She called me her knight attendant, her little man. I told her everything."[20] He also writes of their intimacies, their linguistic rituals, and their adolescent complicities. Fifty years later, he comments that "incest is the only family relationship which still moves me" (M 54). And Sartre's biographer, Cohen-Solal, is quite clear about Sartre's incestuous tendencies (S:L 29, 34, 38).[21]

The confrontation between the "law and the apple," described by Cixous, can help us better understand these tendencies. On one side, there is the "law," the incest taboo, which is invisible and negative, and which absolutely forbids sexual feelings between a son and his mother. Facing it, there is the "apple": an alluring, charming, nurturing, warm, playful woman, who has been Poulou's (young Sartre's) roommate since his infancy, and his daytime companion as well (until his tenth birthday), and who is infinitely desirable for him. She is sheer presence. And since Poulou, like Perceval, "is a mother's son, with no father" (EF 135), she holds for him the promise of eternal innocence, jouissance, happiness. However, society educates and phallicizes Poulou, as it had Perceval, and he likewise falls prey to the law, and to the masculine economy, which is anti-jouissance/happiness. Within that economy, receptivity, openness, and abandon to the other are reprehensible. And activity that separates one from the (m)other, thus creating an insular/autonomous self, is most attractive, along with the resulting violent connotations/confrontations. Poulou must try to repress the first and to develop the second.

From both the Beauvoir interviews and *Les Mots*, we learn that the young Poulou reacted to his fear of his mother's abandon, to what he saw as his vulnerability through physical/emotional abandon by symbolically exorcising it from his life. He made a ritual of playing at Pardaillon, the sword-wielding hero of Michel Zevaco's adventure series, who killed the hundreds of enemies who attacked him. Thus his body, which he stiffened in mock battle, became for him "a center of action, of mastery, dealing with the objective world." For whereas the relaxing of his body in abandon/enjoyment would have made Poulou vulnerable to incest, its stiffening protected him from this vulnerability. In the course of time this became a habit. He surmised that he had left behind the "subjectivity and passivity of his body," with its scary sensations and feelings, as well as any enjoyment of it (CA 400).

At first glance, Poulou's predicament may not appear very different from that of other boys in a patriarchal society when they discover that they are ambivalently, irresistibly attracted by their mother and repelled by her bodily functions. They develop a fear of embodiment and run away from this fear in a threefold movement: (1) by turning to their father's clean and neutral physicality; (2) by joining other boys in aggressive games of action and adventure; and (3) by looking for symbolic freedom in the social world outside the home.[22] For Poulou, however, the first two ways of escape were barred. He never knew his father, who had died when Sartre was an infant. The fact that, as he writes, his mother "was all mine" (M 24), and that conversely her acceptance of him was total, only complicated further his effort to run away from his fear of abandon to/by her.

And he was completely excluded by his peers, never accepted by a single group of boys playing Pardaillon in the Luxembourg gardens where his mother took him to play: "always imploring, always excluded," Sartre observes laconically fifty years later (M 111). He was therefore forced to play Pardaillon alone in his grandfather's study while his mother played the piano in the next room. This means that although he managed to repress the natural feelings of his body, the "soft" desire for abandon, by means of tough masculine action, he never experienced the social bonding, the fraternity that boys feel while fighting together against a fictitious enemy. This would have been the positive, salvific aspect of the Pardaillon games.

Later, however, during his adolescence in La Rochelle, young Sartre experienced much real violence.[23] This was a most difficult period for him. His mother had just remarried a certain Joseph Mancy, and for the first time in his life his possession of her was contested by another man. His desire for/fear of abandon to her, must certainly have been exacerbated. In the Beauvoir interviews, Sartre tells Beauvoir how sexually attracted he was to his mother when, at thirteen, he spent three weeks in the hospital, and she slept in the cot next to him. He made believe he was asleep, in order to watch her undress and see her naked (CA 373).

This time, young Sartre could try to escape from his desire/fear of abandon by real fighting. For the students at the La Rochelle lycée had two sets of enemies—the Catholic-school boys and the hoodlums who attended no school at all. Young Sartre was able to join the lycée students in fighting the hoodlums violently a number of times, and thus experience fraternity to a certain extent. But this fraternity was probably completely canceled out by the fact that he himself was the constant object of violence among his peers in the lycée, because he was a new boy from Paris, because of his small size, and probably also because of his ugliness. He was very often punched—much more than a fist in the nose, which was standard fare, he tells Beauvoir (CA 191). All in all, Sartre's experience of violence in La Rochelle led him to believe that "there had to be violence between men in their relationships," and made him dream at the École Normale a few years later of "a simple and violent philosophy" (CA 194).

We have seen that the first two routes of escape that boys usually take to distance themselves from their mother had been barred for Poulou. But a third route, the search for symbolic freedom in the social world, was open to him. Sartre lucidly explains in *Les Mots* how he was saved through writing, which his grandfather helped him discover when he was around eight. This became his route (long and arduous) of escape—then of recovery, first through the continuation of his repression of his desire for incestuous pleasures, associated with his mother, in *Nausea* and *Being and Nothingness*, the works of his masculine economy; then through his search for the comprehension of what he understood to be his deep neurosis, throughout the late 1940s and the 1950s and 1960s; and finally through the formulation of a thought akin to a feminine economy of reciprocity, rooted in the *matriciel*.

Sartre did all he could to hide his repression of incestuous pleasures, repression on which his would-be freedom and autonomy were founded—as Lacan suggests is the case with masculine subjects who are creating symbolic texts structured according to "the paternal law."[24] But eventually, having reached in the seventies what Cixous terms a "universe free of fear and guilt," he was ready for self-revelation (SPS 13, 14). In the meantime he left us a number of clues and it is these that I have used in my "sleuthing."

III. Sartre's Masculine Economy

Nausea can be read as the allegory of Poulou and young Sartre's own struggle against his desire for abandon to his mother and his repression of it. For Roquentin, the sudden uncontrollable giving in of his body to passivity/abandon is a completely negative experience, accompanied by strong nausea. The abandon of "all things" that "gently, tenderly, were letting themselves drift into existence like those relaxed women who burst out laughing and say 'It is good to laugh' in a wet voice,"[25] is a lure and a veneer, Roquentin thinks. When this veneer melts, what remains are "soft, monstrous masses, all in disorder—naked in a frightful, obscene nakedness" (N 172). Abandon is here definitely a *laisser-aller*, a letting-go in its negative connotation. Roquentin has lost the customary control/mastery that his rationality gave him—and existence has therefore "lost the harmless look of an abstract category" (N 172). It invades him, masters him, weighing on him like a great motionless beat (N 177). Only the stiffening of his body, as for activity (like Poulou/Pardaillon stiffening against his enemies), makes nausea temporarily vanish for a short while (N 38).

In *Being and Nothingness*, Sartre's struggle against his fear of incest, and his attempt to be in control of himself and of reality, is more metaphysically couched than in *Nausea*, and closer to Cixous's basic metaphorical opposition between the apple and the law. Here Sartre expresses and represses his fear of self-abandon to the presence of the apple—his fear of receptivity, of jouissance, of openness to the other—by the creation of two antagonistic categories, the in-itself, which like Cixous's apple *is, is, is,*[26] and the for-itself, which like Cixous's law is abstract and is not.

But since he wants to exorcise it from his system (his own body, not his philosophy!), Sartre makes the in-itself as unappealing and undesirable as possible. To begin with, he assures us that it has no place in his (masculine) economy, for it is simply *de trop* for all eternity. He also depicts it as exasperatingly inept, since it does not have the slightest trace of consciousness. And, although he speaks of its plenitude, it seems rather inoffensive, since it lets itself be appropriated and absorbed by the for-itself—most of the time.

Yet, almost at the end of *Being and Nothingness*, under the guise of the slimy, "which is softness pushed to its ultimate limit" (BN 608), the in-itself takes on a menacing and terribly frightening allure. For, although the slimy is soft and seemingly docile and manipulable, because it yields itself (abandons itself), the moment I think I possess it, "it possesses me" (BN 608) with a leechlike hold and a "moist feminine sucking." It attempts to trap the for-itself in a "poisonous possession," which harbors a horrible fear that the in-itself will absorb it in a "sickly-sweet feminine revenge" (BN 609), for being appropriated by it in knowledge as rape. And lest we question the probability that this text on the slimy is a metaphorical reference to Sartre's own fear of being seduced by his mother, and his mother abandoning herself to him and possessing him, he shortly refers to sexuality itself and to woman's obscenity because she is "in the form of a hole," appealing to be plugged or penetrated, in order to castrate man in the "amorous act" (BN 614).

It is therefore essential that the for-itself free itself from the in-itself through a clean rational activity. It thus takes on the abstract character and the negativity of the Cixousian masculine law, and is very clean: its goal is to withdraw from, disengage itself from, and transcend every situation, so that it will be beyond the control of the in-itself, or ever be

tempted to abandon itself to it. Its rationality complies with that direc-
tive. Since it creates itself through its nihilation of the is, it is not. There
is nothing in it. "It is as clean as a great wind."[27] Because of this, it is
totally free to choose its identity. Yet, it can never choose to be itself—for
it would annihilate itself in the process. The deep cleavage between itself
and itself, the absence that ironically Sartre calls "self-presence," is necessary to its existence.

There are two other aspects of the for-itself that situate it in the realm
of Cixousian masculine economy: first, the sheer activity through which
it creates its "original project" in its attempt to give meaning and value
to what it considers to be the passive impersonal world of the in-itself.
Second, there is its prehensive attitude to the world, its desire to be, as it
appropriates, controls, and tries to master the world through its project.

And of course, the for-itself's imperialistic stance continues as it relates to others, both on the personal and on the social level. It attempts
to appropriate their freedom and their world through the look. Since the
other necessarily retaliates, the result can only be conflict. The look is the
sword through which the adult Poulou-as-Pardaillon fights his enemies in
an eye-to-eye skirmish.

Under these conditions, the reciprocal gifting of love in a feminine
economy is an impossibility. For either the for-itself objectifies the other
and forces them to submit—in sadism, or the other objectify themselves
and submit to the for-itself—in masochism. A communal "we" is likewise
an impossible ideal, for which many hope in vain: social experiences in
which we are in community with the other as a "we" (subject) or as
an "us" (object), correspond to the two forms of objectification by the
look—being in the act of looking, or being looked at. "An intersubjective
totality [that] would obtain consciousness of itself as a unified subjectivity" (BN 428), is only a dream.

IV. The Beginnings of a Feminine
Economy—Personal Level

When it was published in 1980, *Hope Now* shocked the Sartrians, who
had chosen to ignore the indications that Sartre had long ago begun to
change his original positions. *Notebooks for an Ethics*, published posthumously in 1983 in France, and in 1992 in the United States, certainly

well indicates that Sartre had started to demolish much of the structure of *Being and Nothingness*, the core of his masculine economy of appropriation through the desire to be, and of conflict through the look, as early as 1947 or 1948 when he wrote the *Notebooks*. For we find here, with his studies of gifting, of the loss of ego, of the appeal, of generosity and authentic love almost instant immersion into a Cixousian feminine economy—although there are certainly a good many of the building blocks of a masculine economy still standing there, as we shall see shortly.

The twelve-page commentary on Marcel Mauss's *potlach* ceremony in his *Essai sur le don*, is extremely interesting, for here, twenty-seven years before Cixous's *Newly Born Woman* (1975) and forty-four years before Derrida's "Given Time: The Time of the King" (1992),[28] Sartre uses Mauss's *Essai* as a point of departure for a distinction between the spirit of a feminine and that of a masculine economy. Authentic gifting, he explains, is disinterested, gratuitous, with no motivation in the giving.[29] It "presupposes a reciprocity of recognition" (NE 369), that is, a recognition of the other's freedom. In its refusal of being caught up in proprietorship or mastery, it is an interhuman relation, which is freeing and liberating. And "its acceptance is as free as disinterested and unmotivated as the gift itself. Like the gift, it is freeing" (NE 370).

On the other hand, the *potlach* ceremony is the perfect example of a subjugating gift, within the masculine economy, since the ones receiving are "not free not to accept it" (NE 370). They are in fact under the obligation to receive it. It thus consists of a generosity whose aim is to alienate the donee. Through it, the one who gives the gift affirms his or her freedom against that of the donee. As Sartre comments, freedom functions here like the look, objectifying the donees and "mortgaging" them to themselves. "The act of gift-giving installs my freedom in the other as a subjective limit to the other's freedom" (NE 376).

Sartre's distinction between the two types of gifting is certainly very close to Cixous's distinction between feminine and masculine economies. His interpretation of the *potlach*'s alienating gifting gives us a deeper insight into the possibly subjugating aspect of gift giving, between a "superior" (husband, father, mother, colonialist) and an "inferior" (wife, child, or native).

But in a number of sections of the *Notebooks*, he further develops an ontology based on the feminine economy of gifting. Early on he writes that the structure of the gift implies "the recognition of the other's freedom" (NE 169), and later, that the reverse is also true, that "freedom exists only in giving, it devotes itself to giving itself" and to recognizing the other's freedom (NE 282). And Sartre recognizes, already at this early date in his evolution, that this recognition must be concrete, that it must deal with the other in their situation, and thus be "a comprehension."

Later in the *Notebooks*, he extends the recognition and the comprehension of freedoms to the love relationship, only adding the word "deeper" to recognition, and "reciprocal" to "comprehension" (NE 414). But he explains that this comprehension can only happen when one manages to get rid of one's ego, which separates one from oneself and consequently from the other. And Sartre surprises us by writing in a tone at once Zen and Derridian, "The ego exists to lose itself. It is the gift" (NE 418). He is here deconstructing himself, three decades before Jacques Derrida would begin his own deconstruction.

It is in this vein that Sartre insists that love is not an appropriation—but rather an unveiling/creating. "In pure generosity, I assume myself as losing myself, so that the fragility and finitude of the other exists absolutely as revealed within the world" (NE 507). I actually make myself the one through whom the loved one's finitude finds safety. And Sartre enumerates the different roles I as lover take to ensure this: that of guarding the loved one's finitude, that of protecting him from danger, that of savior, secretly acquiescing his fragility and secret weakness (NE 508).

But there are problems here in terms of Sartre's evolving feminine economy. First his statement that there is no love "without reciprocal comprehension of freedoms" (NE 414) is juxtaposed between two other statements stressing that "to bring about a love which would surpass the sadisdic/masochistic . . . dialectic subjugation of freedom . . . would be to make love disappear" (NE 414). This is a return to the masculine economy of *Being and Nothingness*. We all know too well that love often does revert to the subjugation of freedoms—but we certainly must hope that this is not an absolute necessity. Also, Sartre's depiction of the lover as "creator" of the extremely fragile, vulnerable "finitude/object" of the loved one, who depends on the lover almost for his very being, makes the lover into a Pygmalion.[30] Although Sartre means to show here the receptivity of the lover to the loved one, the overly active, overprotective attitude of the lover certainly replicates Sartre's own difficulties in his relationships with women.

Sartre did not continue his discussion of gifting and authentic love and would not return to it until the 1970s interviews with Beauvoir, Lévy, and others. In *Saint Genet*, however, we find carefully hidden in this lengthy book a very strong Cixousian statement on love. Here Sartre insists that love is a total acceptance of the loved one, including the most contingent dimensions of that person's body. Genet loves Decarnin totally—even in the body lice he receives from him—for "one loves nothing, if one does not love everything."[31] And Sartre reiterated his position in an interview with Francis Jeanson in 1965. He tells Jeanson that in *Saint Genet*, love "is not a fact of death (as in *Being and Nothingness*) but a fact of life." It is "the acceptance of the total person including his viscera."[32] But when Jeanson asks Sartre why he had not dealt with that positive force of love at length in any of his later works, Sartre replied that he had not had the occasion to do so!

Yet Sartre had spent the seventeen years since *Notebooks* feverishly writing about the attempt of several individuals (including himself) at comprehending their own conditioning—in *Saint Genet, The Freud Scenario*, and *Les Mots*. And he would spend the next seven years dealing with Flaubert's conditioning in an even more extensive way. Obviously, after *Notebooks* (aside from his separate evolution on the sociopolitical level, which I shall examine shortly), Sartre still needed to work on the personal problems that he had not fully resolved through the writing of *Nausea* and *Being and Nothingness*. There, as we saw, he had repressed his fear of abandon by calling it an undesirable "passivity," and foisting it onto nature and to the in-itself—and simultaneously creating an absolutely free, lucid, active, unsituated consciousness to control it. Now, having come to the realization that consciousness is thoroughly entangled with what he calls *le vécu* (lived experience), he gives a very different meaning to the term "passivity," which becomes a person's lack of response to the conditioning of her consciousness by various circumstances. And, especially important, he adopts the notion of "neurosis" as a most significant factor affecting consciousness in such a willy-nilly fashion that we can never "know" their influence on us, we can only attempt to "comprehend" them. Sartre defines "lived experience" as "the terrain in which the individual is perpetually overflowed by himself and his riches, and consciousness plays the trick of determining itself by forgetfulness."[33] A little later, he explains that this terrain is "precisely the ensemble of the dialectic process of psychic life, in so far as this process is obscure to itself, because it is a constant totalization, thus necessarily a totalization which cannot be conscious of what it is" (IT 41). If I am not conscious of the totalization, I cannot know it, I can only try to comprehend it.

The distinction that Sartre makes here between "knowledge" and "comprehension" helps us better understand what he means by "lived experience." He explains that we can know an idea, or a practical conduct, but we can only comprehend a passion, or "lived experience." Flaubert spoke of the *indisable* (the unsayable), by which he meant "precisely the kind of comprehension of oneself which cannot be named and which perpetually escapes one" (IT 41). Neuroses are among the psychic fact that are "neither named nor known." They are the result of wounds suffered in the process of living one's childhood, and although they are bandaged again and again by society, they go on bleeding until they are comprehended (IT 42).

According to Sartre, we can begin to comprehend this *indisable*, these neuroses, in an individual through an assessment of the total way in which that individual has been conditioned historically, socially, psychologically, biologically and linguistically. Sartre's basic stance is that one must continually react to the passivity implied by one's conditioning. Thus, for example, although passivity was always "a deep hidden wound" in Flaubert, he had to try incessantly to heal it, that is, to assume it:[34] "We are lost during childhood, methods of education, the parent-child relationship and so on, are what create the self. But, it's a lost self," Sartre said about Flaubert (IFI 116). But it is certain that he was also thinking about his own conditioning and neurosis. For, as Rudolph Allers well saw, Sartre's inability to abandon himself was a deep neurosis. In fact, he greatly resembled the neurotic described by Adler who is "unable to abandon himself even for a minute."[35]

My conjecture is that Sartre was able to come to a comprehension of his own conditioning, of his own neurosis, by writing extensively about other neurotic persons who had been conditioned by their circumstances: Genet, Freud, Flaubert. In the process, he certainly learned that neuroses are shaped by each individual's experience, that, for example, whereas Flaubert's neurosis compelled him to give in to passivity and to forego activity, his own (Sartre's) neurosis compelled him, on the contrary, to fear abandon and to turn to frantic intellectual activity. Having comprehended all this, he would finally, in 1974, be able to candidly discuss with Beauvoir his ideal of self-abandon in love.

V. Difficult Exit from a Masculine Economy—Social Level

For Sartre, the development of the social sphere toward a feminine economy did not correspond to that of the personal sphere, which was a sudden and rather substantial conversion from one economy to the other, in the *Notebooks*. The sociopolitical notions discussed there: society, oppression/alienation, and violence, are still thoroughly ensconced in the masculine economy of the look, with the exception of the notion of the authentic appeal.

In a fairly long passage of the *Notebooks*, Sartre views society as existing only when "I become conscious of it" through the look (NE 111). For I become a mail clerk at the post office only through the look of those waiting in line for my services. And since I cannot possibly coincide with the meanings of these looks, I am just as oppressed by society as I was by the look of one individual. And in turn, I oppress other individuals functioning in society.

Sartre also views cases of deeper oppression, that of the native by the colonialists, of the black man by the white or of the child by the parent in the same manner—as a result of the look that is of being "seen" as other. And again the oppression is reversible: the other in turn looks at me as other. Those I alienate also alienate me. Likewise, when he discusses violence, Sartre finds that the slave's alienation is due to the look of the master—who through it wants to suppress the slave's consciousness. And terrorist violence arises because, in turn, the slave wants to suppress the power of alienation of the master. He tries to escape the master's look by destroying any future and by living in the present. Interestingly, at this point, in 1948, Sartre does not legitimize the violence of the slave and views it as a dead end (NE 399–404).

In between these discussions on society, oppression, and violence that are based on the look, Sartre has sandwiched a discussion of the "authentic appeal," probably because it relates as much to the notions of gifting and love he has examined as it does to the social. The notion of the authentic appeal, which consciously reaches beyond all inequalities "toward a human world where any appeal of anyone to anyone will always be possible" (NE 285), is stunning in its idealistic yearning for solidarity close to the Cixousian philosophy. Here, Sartre is still in the crystal-clear waters of his newly discovered ideal, in which the personal and the social blend completely, but which has not yet been made concrete, has not dealt with the other in his or her situation, has not yet become a "comprehension." This ideal is certainly very close to the notion of "fraternity" that Sartre will discuss with Lévy in *Hope Now*. Moreover, it does not have any of the sexist connotations that critics find in the notion of "fraternity." But more than thirty years will flow between it and *Hope*

Now, and Sartre will have to wade through much murky water (of con-
cretization, of involvement in situations—his involvement with commu-
nism and especially with the Algerian war), before being able to return
to this ideal in a new form.

In the next twelve years, Sartre keeps searching for the solidarity implied in the appeal—in spite of the rampant alienation he finds everywhere—through a socialized comprehension of the way in which
individuals in various milieus are able to react more or less well to the
passivity implied in the shaping of their personalities and their lives by
all kinds of circumstances. In *Saint Genet*, he explores the passivity, that
is, the social circumstances, that have alienated Genet. And he infers
that real reciprocity is "concealed by the historical conditions of class
and race, by nationalities, by the social hierarchy" (SG 635). In *Communists and Peace*, Sartre sees the alienation of the working class as the result
of their passivity within social and economic structures. And he urges
"community of action" as a means of reaching solidarity—for it is "not
in isolation that each [will] become a person."[36]

In *Search for a Method*, Sartre's further development of the notion of a
"socialized comprehension" moves in the direction of a feminine economy. "To grasp the meaning of any human conduct, it is necessary to
have at our disposal what German psychiatrists and historians have called
'comprehension.' But what is involved here is neither a particular talent,
nor a special faculty of intuition,"[37] Sartre writes in that essay. It is rather
the capacity for participating in another's feelings, ideas or situations. As
Sartre explains it in an interview on *The Family Idiot*, comprehension
requires empathy and therefore suspension of moral judgments. It deals
with notions that define things from the inside (subjectivity), not with
concepts in knowledge, which does so from the outside (objectivity).
Thus comprehension is both noncognitive and nonobjective (IFI 113).

Due to the essential role that Sartre suddenly gives to violence, the
Critique of Dialectical Reason takes a complete turn away from a feminine
economy. He is still looking for solidarity and would like to find it in the
notion of fraternity: ("He and I are brothers"),[38] to which he gives a
central importance in this work. But he himself recognizes that the "links
of reciprocity" in the "fraternity" of the fused group are ambivalent, as
well as the fact that there is in it only a "resemblant solidarity" (CDR
437). This ambivalence has usually been explained as a result of the oath
of fidelity that each member of the group takes, and that actually implies
violence, since this fidelity connotes the promise to kill any brother sus-

pected of breaching the oath, (thus the term of *fraternité-terreur* that Sartre uses).

In fact, the notion of "fraternity" in the *Critique* is violent through and through. For the formation of the fused group always takes place through a violent activity, such as the storming of the Bastille (which Sartre discusses in detail). The solidarity of the group, its "fraternity," is really a union in violence based on the initial violence against those perceived as the oppressors.[39] Sartre is returning here to the master/slave masculine economy of violence of the *Notebooks* (except that here he sees it as the only viable solution). He has left behind the (feminine economy) notion of comprehension he has been developing for years. Discussing the Algerian war of independence in the *Critique*, he writes that "the only possible way out was to confront total negation with total negation, violence with equal violence" (CRD 733). The natives simply adopted the despair in which they had been maintained by the colonialists. "The violence of the rebel was the violence of the colonialist" (CRD 433).

And in his preface to Frantz Fanon's *The Wretched of the Earth*, his language is even more radical. He asserts that the violence of the male colonialists consisted in the dehumanization of the natives, and in the buying of their own manhood at the natives' expense.[40] And in turn, the natives could rediscover their "lost innocence" only through violence— through the killing of the colonialists. "They are brothers inasmuch as they have killed," Sartre asserts there.[41]

Sartre had been radicalized through his immersion in the violent atmosphere in which France found itself at the time of the decolonialization of Algeria. The people who thought their lives depended on keeping Algeria as a colony were pitted against those who envisioned an Algeria free of imperialism. Sartre, who sided, of course, with the second, smaller group, became intellectually involved in defending it. But the little solidarity he thus shared with the Algerian rebels was dearly bought at the cost of being the "most hated man in France." He suffered in fact a number of assassination attempts from extremists, who called him a traitor to France.

It was not until he joined the Maoists, or *la gauche prolétarienne*, after May 1968, that he had the chance to finally experience the "fraternity" or concrete solidarity he had been longing for, ever since he had been rejected by the children playing at Pardaillon in the Luxembourg gardens, but that he had experienced neither with the communists in the early

1950s nor with the Algerian rebels. The Maoists had been inspired by his noncommunist Marxism. He now gave them his time and his money and they accepted him as one of them. When their leader, Pierre Victor (as Benny Lévy was then known), asked Sartre to edit his newspaper—*La Cause du Peuple*—the two soon became intimate. And when Sartre hired Victor/Lévy as a reader after the onset of his blindness, they began an exchange of ideas that was most vitalizing for Sartre and that became the (unpublished) controversial text of *Pouvoir et liberté* and its published fragment *Hope Now*.

VI. Sartre's Feminine Economy—Personal Level

The ideal of abandon in love that Sartre discusses with Beauvoir in the 1974 interviews is the culmination of his own personal trajectory, and it is certainly very close to the Cixousian feminine economy. There, Sartre tells Beauvoir that due to his fear of abandon, he never abandoned himself to any of the women with whom he had relationships. And he says explicitly that whereas in a good sexual relationship, each one takes and is taken, he took but did not allow himself to be taken, he did not give himself to the other. He performed the active, objective part of the act, but left out the passive, subjective aspect that would have involved self-abandon and jouissance on his part. The reason for this, he explains to Beauvoir, is that there existed within him a cleavage (*une coupure*), which made him resist abandon. This also led to "a cleavage between what the other could receive and give" in relation to him, and therefore to the impossibility of reciprocity between both of them (CA 400).

At one point in the interviews, Beauvoir suggests to Sartre that the overdevelopment of his active side, the fact that he was "pure activity" and that the other was "pure passivity," led to self-control and coldness on his part. He agrees and adds "almost to a slight taste of sadism, since in the end the other was yielded and I was not." "I was not!" he ponders, but goes on, "I was, but what was yielded was nothing to me, since at that very moment I was the active principle" (CA 415). Beauvoir comments that the other was thus "reduced to the state of object, whereas the norm would be reciprocity," and he fully agrees (CA 415).

It could be said that these ideas cannot be those of the Sartre we know, that Beauvoir must be manipulating him in order to get him to say what she wants, and that Sartre's words here have therefore no validity. Sartre's stance is strongly corroborated, however, by what he told a number of other interviewers during those years. In an interview with the feminist Catherine Chaine, for example, Sartre reaffirms and reinforces the notion of reciprocal giving and receiving that he discussed with Beauvoir. "Tenderness one receives, tenderness one gives, the two are linked and there only exists a general tenderness, both given and received," he told her.[42]

Likewise, in his interview with Michel Contat, "Self Portrait at Seventy," Sartre says that in relationships with women, which involve sexuality, "the subjective and the objective can be given together," and "the whole of what one is can be present" (SPS 65). Each of us must work toward the eventual complete "uncovery of the subjective" (SPS 63).

In another interview with Catherine Clément (the feminist who is co-author with Hélène Cixoux of The Newly Born Woman), Sartre attributes sensibility and the subjective to woman and rationality and the objective to man. But he says that there are "men-women" who have "more subjectivity." This makes for androgyny, and Sartre does not hesitate to tell Clément: "I am certainly androgynous myself,"[43] thus reaffirming for himself Cixous's and Clément's ideal of bisexuality. He also asserts his growing "femininity" to Jean Le Bitoux and Gilles Barbedette of Le Gai Pied; when they question him about Mathieu's and Roquentin's lack of virility, he comments: "Those correspond more or less to what I ask about myself."[44]

Sartre's last "personal" philosophy definitely belongs to a Cixousian feminine economy[45] according to which (1) there exists the possibility of mutual self-giving in love; (2) the lived body is gender-free (being both active and passive, and masculine and feminine); and (3) abandon is being deconstructed so that Dallery's words about Beauvoir's notion of abandon apply well to Sartre's: it is "not negative, not mindless, not even passive."[46] In fact, like Cixous's "de-selfing," it is most positive and empowering.

VII. Sartre's Feminine Economy—Social Level

"I am writing a work which will completely transform what I have thought in philosophy," Sartre told Michel Sicard barely a year before his death.[47] He is speaking of course about the final transformation of his thought from what I have called his masculine economy of *Being and Nothingness* and *Critique of Dialectical Reason* to the feminine economy he had initiated as early as the *Notebooks*. As we have seen, however, he had great difficulty formulating the latter, especially in the social realm, to "make good" his 1947 notion of the appeal—until the last five years of his life.

But in *Hope Now*, he is finally able to replace the monolithic, independent, isolated for-itself "which had no reciprocal, no other" with a consciousness that is "necessarily linked to and often is even engendered by the presence of another—or even momentarily by the absence of that other—but in all events by the existence of another" (HN 71). Each individual thus depends on all other individuals—and we are ethically conscious only if we recognize our relationship with the other, if we consider ourselves as "self for the other" (HN 71).

Sartre repeats this new vision again and again in various interviews of that period: (1) to Sicard—that ontologically, consciousnesses are not isolated, they interpenetrate each other;[48] (2) to *Libération*: "persons are linked to each other, to act and to think together";[49] and (3) to Leo Fretz: a society without power is ethical because "a new form of freedom is established, which is the freedom of reciprocal relations of persons in the form of a 'we.' "[50]

In other interviews of that period, Sartre also attributes transparency to the new intersubjective ethical consciousness. He tells Michel Contat about the importance of transparency—of speaking about our innermost being—and of offering up our subjectivity to the other. And he imagines a time in the future when a new form of sociality will allow each person to abandon him- or herself completely to someone else, who will reciprocate (SPS 11, 13). In an interview with Catherine Clément, he says that there are signs that can allow us to hope that one day humans shall be transparent to one another. This transparency would/will depend of course on a "mutual waiving of inhibitions, of repression, and of the need of secrecy,"[51] and on great openness to the other, implying mutual recognition of freedoms. Buisine looks at this stance as an attempt on Sartre's part to recover the "transparent innocence of childhood."[52] But Eléonor Kuykendall points out that it is in sharp contrast to the appropriate stance of consciousness of *Being and Nothingness*. For in transparency there is no control whatsoever of one's apprehension of the other.

Rather, there is an "abandonment of reflective control," which is the new basis of moral action. The ground for morality is other than rational.[53]

And effectively, in *Hope Now*, Sartre keeps pointing to a bond among people, which is more basic than sociality (or, for that matter, than rationality). It is a primary relationship, a "gift" or a feeling that we must rediscover (for originally everyone shared in it) (HN 90). That gift, that feeling, is that of fraternity, which must be allied with action and extended to include all of humanity (HN 93). Sartre explains to Lévy that when "fraternity" happens within a closed group, however, violence arises if/when other groups breach that group, or it breaches them. Violence is thus "the very opposite of fraternity" (HN 93). It is interesting to note in passing the great similarity between Sartre's distinction between the "fraternity" of closed groups prone to violence and the open "fraternity" that extends to all humanity, and Henri Bergson's distinction between a closed society "whose members hold together, caring nothing about the rest of humanity," and the open society that embraces in principle all humanity.[54]

Lévy responds to Sartre's articulation of his new ideal of nonviolence by harrassing him about his proviolence stance in Algeria, telling him that after he wrote his preface to Fanon's *Wretched of the Earth*, exhorting the Algerians to violence, "you went back to Poulou playing war games, sword in hand, in the living room while his mother played the piano." And Sartre replies (most meaningfully, as we shall see shortly), "Don't forget, Poulou was fighting for himself and against the bad guys" (HN 94).

Before I discuss how I think Sartre reached his nonviolence stance, I must discuss a most controversial but extremely relevant point that Sartre has made earlier: that "fraternity" is a primary relationship because birth is the same phenomenon for all people—we are all born of the same mother (*HN* 87). As Aronson notes, Lévy tries eight different times to get Sartre to say that he is speaking about a myth, but Sartre refuses to admit this. As I mentioned earlier, the French call this section *le matriciel*, or "the mother as matrix." It is a subject that Sartre discussed at length for a number of years with Jeannette Colombel. He was particularly interested in the birth process and in the relationship of the infant, and the young child, to his or her mother.[55] Now Sartre tells Lévy that woman has the womb that gives life, the breasts that nourish and the back that carries. The father, on the other hand, has a very small role. He merely gives his seed, like Sartre's father—no doubt as far as Sartre is concerned! (HN 90).

For Sartre's critics, *le matriciel* has proved to be the most baffling section of *Hope Now*. But I have shown throughout this essay that there is an
intimate link between Sartre's philosophical trajectory and his evolving
attitude toward his neurosis (which was the result of his original relationship with his mother). From that perspective, his final emphasis on *le
matriciel* is the final synthesis of his personal evolution and his philosophical trajectory. For it represents Sartre's final coming to terms with young
Poulou's fear of abandon to/by his mother, and his fear of the body, especially the female body.

Now Sartre has been able to overcome his fears and to "comprehend"
his neurosis. Instead of running away from his fear of abandon to his
mother, he acknowledges it. There is no more need of Pardaillon games
for Poulou/Sartre because there are no more "bad guys" (fear of feelings,
fear of the body, and fear of abandon to these). There is therefore no
need of violence to fight the "bad guys." Now "men" are "brothers" in
action because of their relationship to a(n) (m)other. This enables Sartre
to move away from the closed society of the patriarchy with its primarily
rational order or patriarchal law, and go back to "the original primary
relationship" with its emphasis on feeling; away from what Spinoza calls
natura naturata (traditional societies), back to *natura naturans* (nature
itself) or should we not say *natura nurturans*?[56]

Sartre is completely at peace with himself and exudes this peace. After
his death, Le Bitoux and Barbedette of *Le Gai Pied* wrote in a eulogy of
his "stupefying freshness" and "extraordinary kindness."[57] He has almost
fulfilled his 1947 *Notebooks* ideal of "getting rid of one's ego," and that of
the appeal, which coincides so well with Cixous's vision of the de-selfing
or de-egoization. He has joined up with what Cixous termed "a universe
without fear or remorse" (EF 135). And he wants to extend this feeling
to all of "mankind." He is at this point in his life close to those whom
Bergson calls the "exceptional men" (or women) who have incarnated
an open or complete morality, and now appeal to others to try to fulfill
it—the "sages," the "prophets," the "arahants," and "others beside."[58]

Thus he finds great similarities between Lévy's messianism, which is
about "the beginning of the existence of men who live for each other"
(HN 110) and his own vision, in which human beings will live more
humanely in relation to one another. But the great difference, he tells
Lévy, is that whereas Lévy believes that his messianism will be instituted
from above, by God, his own vision will be carried out from below, by a
revolution.

In *Hope Now*, as well as in other interviews of the 1970s, it seems obvious that Sartre cannot have in mind a violent revolution, for this would contradict his new ideal of "fraternity," which is against violence. He is speaking therefore about a peaceful revolution that will entail not only a change in economic conditions from scarcity to abundance, but the transformation/conversion of human behavior, in the direction of greater altruism, the beginning of transparency between persons, and the hope (and therefore the commitment to try to bring this about) that this ideal will be realizable at some point in the future.[59]

Reactions to the possibility of such a revolution were negative in the past and are still just as negative today. In 1932, Bergson wrote that one "cannot prevail over egoism by recommending altruism," and that "a mystic society embracing all of humanity" is not realizable in the future.[60] In 1983, Di Capra called Sartre's notion of transparence an ill-conceived "visionary utopia";[61] and recently, in 1996, McBride wrote that in today's "quasi-hopeless mess," Sartre's view that we must have "hope now" is naive indeed![62]

As we can observe in the last *Hope Now* interview, however, Sartre is most sensitive to the fact that today the world seems "ugly, evil, and hopeless," and he tells Lévy that because of it he is undergoing "the calm despair of an old man who will die in that despair" (HN 110). Yet, he continues—he knows that he will "die in hope"—in a hope that is grounded. I see that grounding as his experience of the possibility of genuine solidarity with the other and his perception and conviction of the value of this experience in his search for a more complete humanity. It is this hope and this grounding, with all that we have seen it entails, that places Sartre's final thought within the perspective of a feminine economy.[63] And his vision is not as unrealizable, as utopian, or as naive as it appears from within the frame of mind of a masculine economy.

Notes

1. Jean-Paul Sartre, "Self-Portrait at Seventy," interview with Michel Contat, in *Life/Situations: Essays Written or Spoken* (New York: Pantheon Books, 1976), trans. Paul Aster and Lydia Davis from the French "Autoportrait à soixante-dix ans," in *Situations 10* (Paris: Gallimard, 1974), 21. Hereafter as SPS.

2. Simone de Beauvoir, *La Cérémonie des adieux, suivi de Entretiens avec Jean-Paul Sartre* (Paris: Gallimard, 1981), trans. Patrick O'Brian, *Adieux: A Farewell to Sartre* (New York: Pantheon Books, 1984). Hereafter as CA.

3. Thomas W. Busch, *The Power of Consciousness and the Force of Circumstances in Sartre's Philosophy* (Bloomington: Indiana University Press, 1990), 98.

4. Jean-Paul Sartre and Benny Lévy, *Hope Now: The 1980 Interviews*, with an introduction by Ronald Aronson (Chicago: University of Chicago Press, 1996), trans. Adrien van den Hoven from *J. P. Sartre: Entretiens avec Benny Lévy, L'Espoir Maintenant, Le Nouvel Observateur* (10, 17, and 24 March 1980). Hereafter as HN.

William McBride has pointed out that it was with the publication of *Hope Now* that Benny Lévy abandoned the pseudonym of "Pierre Victor," which he had been using until that time for political purposes (William McBride, *Sartre's Political Theory* [Bloomington: Indiana University Press, 1991] 202).

5. Annie Cohen-Solal, *Sartre: A Life* (New York: Pantheon Books, 1987), trans. Anne Cancogni from *Sartre 1905–1980* (Paris: Gallimard, 1983), 652. Hereafter as S:L.

6. Olivier Todd, *Un Fils rebelle* (Paris: Grasset, 1981), 15.

7. Geneviève Idt, "Simone de Beauvoir's Adieux: A Funeral Rite and a Literary Challenge," in *Sartre Alive*, Ronald Aronson and Adrian van den Hoven, eds. (Chicago: Chicago University Press, 1991).

8. Ronald Aronson, introduction to Sartre and Lévy, *Hope Now*, 9.

9. The translator of *La Cérémonie des adieux*, Patrick O'Brian, has chosen to translate the French *abandon* as "letting go," except in one instance when he translates "l'abandon est présent" (Beauvoir, *La Cérémonie*, 402) as "surrender, abandon, letting go, is present" (Beauvoir *Adieux*, 316), using two other synonyms together with *abandon* to lessen its impact. It is true that in the past, androcentrism gave the word *abandon* pejorative implications. It was seen as a weakness in women and taboo in men. But because, in the above text, Sartre has rehabilitated the term, its use in this paper is imperative.

Philippe Lejeune, in his *Moi Aussi*, considers as by far the most interesting this section of the Beauvoir interviews in which Sartre discusses his neurotic relationship to his body and to women (Paris: Seuil 1986, 161ff).

10. All of which have been discussed at length by a large number of critics.

11. Of course, as Margaret Simons has well shown, it was Beauvoir who introduced Sartre to the importance of the great influence of childhood socialization on a person's life and thought. Beauvoir's role here in getting Sartre to understand the same thing in regard to himself is vital. Cf. Margaret Simons, "Beauvoir and Sartre: The Philosophical Relationship," *Simone de Beauvoir: Witness to a Century. Yale University French Studies* 72 (1986): 173–78.

12. Both William McBride and Eléonor Kuykendall have objected to Sartre's use of the term "fraternity" because of its limiting and sexist connotation. According to McBride, it limits Sartre in his search for "the community of free human beings, freely entered into and maintained" (of Abandonment and Hope in Light of Sartre's Last Words," 333). And according to Kuykendall, Sartre's link of "fraternity" to the *matriciel* implies "the brothers' non-reciprocal dependence upon the mother's nurturance" ("Sartre on Violence and Fraternity," 293). Both articles in *Sartre's Life, Times, and Visions du Monde*, ed. William McBride (New York: Garland, 1997).

In order to include these objections—with which I agree—in my text, I shall always put "fraternity" in quotations marks, unless it is within a direct quote from Sartre.

13. Hélène Cixous, "Extreme Fidelity," in *Hélène Cixous Reader*, ed. Susan Sellers (New York: Routledge, 1994), 197–205. Hereafter as EF.

14. Hélène Cixous, *The Newly Born Woman*, co-authored with Catherine Clément, trans. from *La Jeune Née*, 1975, in Cixous, *Hélène Cixous Reader*, 39. Hereafter as NBW.

15. Hélène Cixous, "Castration or Decapitation," *Signs: Journal of Women in Culture and Society* (1981): 50.

16. Alan D. Schrift, "Rethinking Exchange: Logics of the Gift in Cixous and Nietzsche," *Philosophy Today* 40 (Spring 1996): 201.

17. Susan Sellers, introduction to Cixous, *Newly Born Woman*, 40.

18. Jean-Paul Sartre, "Interview à propos de l'Idiot de la Famille, avec Michel Contat et Michel Rybalka," *Le Monde* (14 May 1971). Hereafter as IFI.

19. Jean-Paul Sartre, *Intimacy and Other Stories* (New York: New Directions, 1948), trans. Lloyd Alexander from the French *Le Mur* (Paris: Gallimard, 1939).

20. Jean-Paul Sartre, *Les Mots* (Paris: Gallimard, 1964), 177. Hereafter as M.

21. Cf. also Josette Pacaly's *Sartre au miroir: Une lecture psychanalytique de ses récits biographiques* (Pairs: Klincksik, 1980, currently out of print); and Jean-François Louette's "Ecrire l'universel singulier" in *Pourquoi et comment Sartre a écrit les mots*, under the direction of Michel Contat (Paris: Presses Universitaires de France, 1977).

22. Ernest Becker, *The Denial of Death* (New York: Free Press, 1973), 39–40; Demaris Wehr, *Jung and Feminism Liberating Archetypes* (Boston: Beacon Press, 1989), 111.

23. It is William McBride who alerted me to the importance of young Sartre's experience of violence during his years at La Rochelle. Cf. William McBride, *Sartre's Political Philosophy*, 19.

24. Judith Butler, *Gender Trouble Feminism and the Subversion of Identity*. New York: Routledge, 1990), 43–50.

25. Jean-Paul Sartre, *Nausea* (New York: New Directions, 1964), trans. Lloyd Alexander from *La Nausée* (Paris: Gallimard, 1938). Hereafter as N.

26. Cf. "the in-itself is what it is," in Jean-Paul Sartre, *Being and Nothingness* (New York: New York Philosophical Library, 1956), trans. Hazel Barnes from *L'Etre et le néant* (Paris: Gallimard, 1953), LXV. Hereafter as BN.

27. Jean-Paul Sartre, "Intentionality: A Fundamental Idea of Husserl's Phenomenology," trans. Joseph Fell, *Journal of the British Society for Phenomenology* (May 1970): 4–5.

28. Jacques Derrida, 1992. "Given Time, the Time of the King," *Critical Enquiry* (Winter 1992): 161–87.

29. Jean-Paul Sartre, *Notebooks for an Ethics* (Chicago: University of Chicago Press, 1992), trans. David Pellauer from *Cahiers pour une morale* (Paris: Gallimard, 1983), 368. Hereafter as NE.

30. It is interesting to note that Beauvoir actually accused Sartre of being a Pygmalion with the women he loved (CA 90). Hazel Barnes, in "Sartre's War Diaries: Prelude and Postscript," says that Sartre himself recognized that fact. "He regarded each woman as raw material to be molded into a form in which he as creator might find his image in the work he had created" (In McBride, *Sartre's Life, Times, and Visions du Monde*, 106).

31. Jean-Paul Sartre, *Saint Genet: Comédien et martyr* (Paris: Gallimard, 1952), 532. Hereafter as SG.

32. Francis Jeanson, *Sartre dans sa vie* (Paris: Seuil, 1974), 232.

33. Jean-Paul Sartre, "The Itinerary of a Thought," in *Between Existentialism and Marxism* (New York: Pantheon Books, 1974), trans. John Mathews from *Situation 8 et Situation 9* (Paris: Gallimard, 1972), 39. Hereafter as IT.

34. Jean-Paul Sartre, *The Family Idiot* (Chicago: University of Chicago Press, 1981), trans. Carol Cosman from *L'Idiot de la famille* (Paris: Gallimard, 1971).

35. Rudolph Allers, *Existentialism and Psychiatry* (Springfield: Charles Thomas, 1961), 117.

36. Jean-Paul Sartre, *Communists and Peace* (New York: Braziller, 1969), trans. Mark Fletcher and John Kleinschmidt from *Les Communistes et la paix, Situation 2* (Paris: Gallimard, 1964), 94.

37. Jean-Paul Sartre, *Search for a Method* (New York: Random House, 1958), trans. Hazel Barnes from *Questions de méthode* (Paris: Gallimard, 1964).

38. Jean-Paul Sartre, *Critique of Dialectical Reason* (London: Humanities Press, 1976), 437. Hereafter as CDR. Trans. Alan Sheridan-Smith from *Critique de la raison dialectique* (Paris: Gallimard, 1960). Hereafter CRD.

39. Kuykendall, "Sartre on Violence and Fraternity," 290.

40. Frantz Fanon, *The Wretched of the Earth*, preface by Jean-Paul Sartre, trans. Constance Farrington (New York: Grove Press, 1968).

41. Ibid., 19.

42. Jean-Paul Sartre, interview with Catherine Chaine: "Sartre et les femmes," *Le Nouvel Observateur* (31 January 1977), 74–76, 81.

43. Jean-Paul Sartre, "La Gauche, le désespoir, et l'espoir," interview with Catherine Clément, *Le Matin*, 10 November 1979.

44. Jean-Paul Sartre, interview with Jean Le Bitoux and Gilles Barbedette, *Le Gai Pied* 13 (April 1980), 1, 11–14.

45. I am speaking here about the deep core of Sartre's final thought—not his language, which is still often sexist because he has not learned the correct feminist terminology. He thus uses such words as "man," "mankind," "fraternity," although he is actually speaking about a postpatriarchal society. He also speaks about "rationality" as belonging to man, although he means the masculine side of all of us.

46. Arleen Dallery, 1985. "Sexual Embodiment: Beauvoir and French Feminism," *Women's Studies International Forum* 8(3):199.

47. Jean-Paul Sartre and M. Sicard, "L'Ecriture et la publication" (interview) *Obliques* 18–19 (1979): 15.

48. Sartre and Sicard, "L'Ecriture et la publication."

49. *Libération* (6 January 1979).

50. Leo Fretz, "An Interview with Jean-Paul Sartre," in *Jean-Paul Sartre: Contemporary Approaches to His Philosophy*, ed. Hugh J. Silverman and Frederick A. Elliston (Pittsburgh: Duquesne University Press, 1980), 236.

51. Jean-Paul Sartre, "Entretien avec Jean-Paul Sartre: Propos recueillis par Catherine Clément," *L'Arc*, November 1979, 34.

52. Alain Buisine, *Laideurs de Sartre* (Lille: PUF, 1986), 48.

53. Kuykendall, "Sartre on Violence and Fraternity," 292.

54. Henri Bergson, *The Two Sources of Morality and Religion* (New York: Doubleday, 1935), 266, 26.

55. Jeannette Colombel, *Sartre ou le parti de vivre* (Paris: Grasset, 1981), 16.

56. Bergson makes this interesting reference to Spinoza in his discussion of the closed and open societies (*Two Sources*, 58).

57. Jean Le Bitoux, and Gilles Barbedette, *Libération* (Spring 1980), special issue on Sartre.

58. Bergson, *Two Sources*, 34.

59. In "Self-Portrait at Seventy" (13), he tells Contat that the "real revolution" will entail "change in the economic, cultural and affective relations among men."

60. Bergson, *Two Sources*, 361, 84.

61. For transparence would necessarily lead, according to Di Capra, to "a society as unlivably hellish as an opaquely closed society" (Dominick Di Capra, "Sartre and the Question of Biography," in McBride, *Sartre's Life, Times and Visions du Monde*, 178.

62. William L. McBride, 1996. review of "Jean-Paul Sartre and Benny Lévy, Hope Now," *Radical Philosophy Review of Books* 14:19 McBride, who read the present essay before its publication, qualified my statement in the following way: "What I said was naive, if you look closely at my review, was the belief in historical progress" (Letter to the author, 10 July 1997).

63. Bergoffen says something quite similar about Beauvoir's vision, which she (Bergoffen) calls "feminist because it attends to the value that (according to Beauvoir) women have recognized and protected throughout the history of the patriarchy—the value of the bond." And Bergoffen sees the possibility of a nonpatriarchal society as residing "in the hope that the value of the bond will be recognized by both men and women and will become for both sexes the source of a new vision of reciprocity, sexuality, love and the couple" (Debra Bergoffen, *The Philosophy of Simone de Beauvoir: Gendered Phenomenologies, Erotic Generosities* [Albany: SUNY Press, 1997], 7.

13

Sartre and the Links Between Patriarchal Atheism and Feminist Theology

Stuart Z. Charmé

To discuss a possible link between the thought of Jean-Paul Sartre and some of the central figures of feminist theology in one breath is to immediately be confronted by two serious obstacles. The first relates to the word "feminist" and the second to the word "theology." Many aspects of Sartre's early existentialist philosophy have been criticized for their implicit and sometimes explicit sexist assumptions. Feminist philosophers were quick to note the problems with a theory where the transcendent, creative, liberating power of consciousness was characterized as masculine—in contrast to the inert, passive quality of nature and the body, which Sartre often depicted as distinctly feminine. His association with Simone de Beauvoir notwithstanding, Sartre's early writings showed signs of horror and disgust in the face of the female body. It is not hard to find elements in his work of the hierarchical ordering of culture over nature, and mind over body, that have been used to justify the patriarchal subordination of women in the development of most civilizations. Although some Sartre scholars have argued that the thrust of Sartre's positions is feminist despite various unfortunate and embarrassing sexist lapses, first impressions are often hard to change.[1]

Hazel Barnes offers a sympathetic reading that considers the sexist images in *Being and Nothingness* and elsewhere in his work to be incidental to a philosophy that otherwise "demands feminism as one of its natural consequences."[2] Michèle Le Doeuff, however, finds fault not only with Sartre's philosophical categories per se, but also with how they are put to use. She notes that Sartre used these categories to create a picture of human relations based on domination and submission, in contrast to Simone de Beauvoir, who put them in the service of feminist analysis.[3] Le Doeuff identifies the futile "desire to be God" that Sartre described as the underlying desire of human reality as nothing more than the white male desire to dominate and be a god to others. In this reading, the ghost of the transcendent male God whose death Sartre announced still haunts his view of humanity. There is some truth in both these positions. Surely, the overall thrust of Sartre's philosophy implies a feminist agenda of women's empowerment and a critique of sexist forms of bad faith. At the same time, too much of Sartre's images, metaphors, and discourse is tainted by sexist assumptions to allow it to be dismissed as incidental or trivial. Nonetheless, it is intriguing to consider that in the area of religion, Sartre's work contains ingredients necessary to feminist theology that are largely lacking in the thought of Simone de Beauvoir.

To use the word "theology" in relation to Sartre may initially evoke even more surprise than the word "feminist," for Sartre never wavered during his life from a complete rejection of God as both philosophically problematic and existentially irrelevant to human life. For the most part, Sartre stood shoulder to shoulder with both Freud and Marx on the issue of religion, which he presented as an avenue of escape for those too weak or too frightened to confront human life honestly and directly.

How then can this patriarchal atheist have anything in common with feminist theology? The answer to this question requires correcting a number of prevailing misunderstandings about Sartre. First, his thought changed considerably during the course of his life. The dualistic model of *Being and Nothingness* was eventually abandoned.[4] Second, and most important for my argument, Sartre's attitude toward religion was far more complex than is usually recognized. Unlike Simone de Beauvoir, whose hostility to her Catholic upbringing became a generalized rejection of all religion, Sartre took a position that was far more nuanced. His atheism was directed at a particular model of the Christian deity and should not be construed as an automatic rejection of alternative models of the divine or religions symbolism in general.[5] Indeed, as I have demonstrated elsewhere, Sartre's work is permeated by a wide variety of religious themes and metaphors.[6] Ironically, while Simone de Beauvoir and her use of Sartrean ideas in *The Second Sex* had a direct, profound influence on the first wave of analyses of women's place in religion, it was Sartre—and definitely not Beauvoir—who may have been more sympathetic to various developments in feminist theology, had he been aware of them during his life.

Feminists have to a great extent agreed that Western religious tradition is sexist and oppressive to women. For antireligious feminists, such as Simone de Beauvoir, religion is obsolete, a stage on the path of humanity's evolution that must be surpassed. From this point of view, the notion of "feminist religion" or "feminist theology" is an oxymoron. Other feminists, however, reject the sexism of Western religion without rejecting religion *tout court*. Despite this sexism in traditional religion, these religious feminists maintain the value of ritual, symbol, and myth for all human beings.[7]

Sartre's autobiography made clear (to anyone who had not already noticed) the profound affinities he felt between his own thought and religion, despite his youthful rejection of the possibility of God. He described himself there as a "weed on the compost of Catholicity; my roots sucked up its juices and I changed them into sap."[8] In religious matters as elsewhere, it is often the case that out of the refuse of discarded symbols and ideas, new forms begin to grow. So it would not be inappropriate to call Sartre a "religious weed," knowing full well that what constitutes a weed and what constitutes a flower is a matter of choice, taste, cultural convention. There is a big difference between being "religious" in the sense of having faith commitments to a particular religious tradition and seeing religious issues, images, and metaphors as an area of interest, fascination, and intellectual struggle. Surely, neither Sartre nor Beauvoir was religious in the former sense. In the latter sense, however, Sartre was compelled by religion in a way that Beauvoir never was. Where Beauvoir only saw stinking garbage in the "compost of religion," Sartre found nourishment for his own budding vision of reality.

The Antireligious Feminism of Beauvoir

It was Beauvoir's hostility to religion that contributed to her violent reaction to the now infamous interviews with Sartre by Benny Lévy that
occurred in the final months of Sartre's life. She reports that she was
"horrified by the nature of the statements extorted from Sartre."[9] What
seemed to shock Beauvoir most was the thought that Sartre could possibly have found anything in common with someone like Lévy, whose
worldview, Beauvoir described with palpable disgust, "had become spiri-
tualistic and even religious."[10] Indeed, in the series of interviews that
Beauvoir appended to her reflections on Sartre's final years and death,
she insisted that Sartre put his atheism on the record once more. Sartre
complied, though it is clear that his atheism was directed toward a very
specific view of God as a transcendent being who contemplates the world,
causes it to exist, and is the foundation of all moral values. Near the end
of her interview, Beauvoir summarized her take on Sartre's ideas, and
certainly her own. She told Sartre: "You think that the way for man to
cure himself—to do away with his alienation—is first of all not to believe
in God."[11] To a great extent, Sartre agreed with Beauvoir. The road to
freedom and authenticity, he claimed, "leads from belief in God to atheism, from an abstract morality divorced from space and time to concrete
commitment."[12] At the same time, however, it a simplistic error to equate
religion with belief in the traditional view of God, for Sartre himself
recognized that during certain historical periods, religion has offered the
only available expression to oppressed groups.[13]

The most obvious impact of Sartre on the feminist study of religion is
mediated through Simone de Beauvoir's classic work *The Second Sex*.[14]
Beauvoir's analysis of the cultural and historical status of women took
Sartre's existentialist model of human reality as its starting point. She
exhaustively demonstrated how the transcendent quality of what Sartre
called *being-for-itself* and the immanent quality of *being-in-itself* have been
ascribed to people along gender lines. She devoted particular attention
to the ways in which religion has assigned women a negative role associated with the immanent, uncontrolled power of nature, whereas men
(like God) have seen themselves as transcendent and dominant over nature. Applying these two principal Sartrean themes—the dualisms of
transcendence/immanence and self/other—to the analysis of religion,
Beauvoir documented how man has historically identified with the first

element in each of these dualisms, whereas woman has been relegated to the second element of each pair. Man's transcendent consciousness is thus defined as the norm for the self, whereas woman's immanent bodily nature is defined as relative and incidental to him, in other words, his Other.[15]

Sartre rejected the idea of God because he felt that a Creator who determined human nature according to this Creator's own will made genuine human freedom impossible. Simone de Beauvoir analogously agreed that if it is man who assumes a godlike position of defining the nature of woman, then she, too, is denied freedom and an autonomous sense of self. As Rosemary Ruether has observed, if God is male, then male is God.

In the late 1940s, as Beauvoir was preparing *The Second Sex*, Sartre was also examining how the concept of the Other was used to oppress racial and ethnic groups as well as women. Beauvoir's book was published in 1949, three years after Sartre's *Anti-Semite and Jew* and one year after his essay "Black Orpheus," on black poets and the concept of negritude. It is obvious that Sartre and Beauvoir discussed their developing analysis of the Other with each other during this same period. Beauvoir applied this idea in some detail to the interpretation of women's place in religion, and even Sartre himself referred to this subject in his notebooks from 1947–48.[16]

In *The Second Sex*, Beauvoir's attitude toward religion is uniformly negative and critical. Religion emerges as one of the prime societal instruments of women's alienation and oppression. It legitimizes male privilege and essentializes women in positions of inferiority. Beauvoir began with Sartre's notion of human freedom as the means by which human beings create projects that enable them to transcend their given situations. In *The Second Sex*, she argued that women's power of transcendence has been crushed by men and their cultural creations, such as religion; as a result, women are "doomed to immanence."[17] Beauvoir was doubly critical of religion, since in addition to the philosophical objection to the idea of God that she shared with Sartre, she saw religion solely as a male phenomenon, albeit one that affects women in a profoundly negative way. Beauvoir claimed that women, *qua* women, "have no past, no history, no religion of their own."[18] They are marginalized observers of a drama in which men are the prime actors. According to Beauvoir, women lack myths or symbols of their own that could give expression to their own projects; "they still dream through the dreams of men. Gods made by males are the gods they worship."[19] Of course, many feminists would take issue with this point, and much feminist work of the past twenty years has been dedicated to reconstructing women's past, women's history, and aspects of women's religious life that are not determined by men.

Beauvoir painted a relentlessly bleak picture of the destructive impact of religion on the lives of women, beginning with the tribal prehistory of human civilization. Even in these earliest social units, women were reduced to natural, biological functions, in other words, to repetitious, cyclical immanence, while men alone claimed true existential subjectivity. Men set goals for themselves that allowed them to transcend both their "animal nature"[20] and the present moment of time. The beginnings of religion celebrate and sacralize male accomplishment in all manner of ritual and festival. In addition, man's mastery and transcendence of nature is reflected in his mastery and transcendence of women. Even if religion was officially "neuter" at first, focused on "some asexual totem,"[21] it still was a product of men.

When maternity became sacralized in agricultural societies, women appeared to achieve a new level of prestige. According to Beauvoir, the mother's role as the one who nourishes and brings new life into being was of paramount importance. Women were assimilated to the earth; all nature is like a mother. "We may suppose then that in a mystical sense the earth belonged to the women; they had a hold, at once religious and legal, upon the land and its fruits."[22] But Beauvoir insisted that even during this stage of civilization, women's role was never seen as intrinsically creative; rather it was something involving magical, mysterious powers that men both respected, feared, and surrounded with taboos. "In woman was to be summed up the whole of alien Nature," she wrote.[23] Sartre himself made the same point about this stage of civilization in his notebooks around this time: "Woman is the pure Other. . . . Her body is mysterious and horrifying at the same time that it is attractive."[24]

Beauvoir could find little of positive worth for women in the appearance of female fertility goddesses in certain early periods, because the Goddess or Earth Mother remained a male-defined embodiment of the otherness of nature. "It was *beyond* the human realm that her power was affirmed, and she was therefore *outside* of that realm."[25] She acknowledged that the Goddess embodied certain nourishing and powerful qualities associated with women. However, the Goddess does not offer a model of genuine creativity for women because She is the apotheosis of Being, the immanence that man seeks to lose himself in. These female images of nature are all manifestations of bad faith to Beauvoir, for they deny the nothingness at the core of human beings. In time, moreover, all the goddesses of antiquity were dethroned by men, who needed to transcend their fear and powerlessness in the face of nature, and "it was to be the male principle of creative force, of light, of intelligence, of order, that he would recognize as sovereign."[26]

Images of the divine thus changed from an ambivalent representation of the Other, to a projection of male ideals of power, mastery, and intelligence. Sartre seems to have absorbed some of Beauvoir's conclusions about the emergence of goddesses in early agricultural societies. When he briefly discussed goddesses, he shared Beauvoir's appraisal that they meant little for women, whose status might sometimes have been better in such societies than in more "civilized" societies, but often was much worse. Woman is possessed by men, alienated as other, and then oppressing and alienating to men in return. "This other causes fear, is magic, is the same sex as the mother goddesses whom one fears. Possessed, this Other possesses. She is possessed because she is Other, this is one way of reacting against Otherness. But because she is a possessed Other, she possesses in her turn."[27] In short, primitive agricultural society, far from being a matriarchal utopia, is reciprocally alienated, though the alienation originally derives from men, who have decided that they are alienated from woman. In typically exaggerated fashion, Sartre summarizes the situation in primitive societies as "completely alienated" and every person is "totally an oppressor and totally oppressed."[28]

As the *Second Sex* unfolded, it was not hard for Beauvoir to catalog the numerous ways in which religions with male gods, such as Judaism and Christianity, continued, expanded, and deepened the oppression of women. Because the history of religion is the history of male subjugation of the women as Other, it is no wonder that Beauvoir offered no possibility of a religious life that might support human authenticity. Indeed, the ultimate expression of existential transcendence, authentic creativity, and assuming full responsibility for one's life required liberating oneself from the gods and the need for religion. Far from religion ever expressing women's freedom and aspirations, it represents a double alienation for women, first as females whose subordination has been religiously reified and sacralized, and second, as human beings, who remain infantilized by religion. Beauvoir could not envision any alternative forms of religion that were tolerable. After she said good-bye to religion in her adolescence, Beauvoir did not look back. Religion is crippling and oppressive for women, who learn to embrace it only out of masochism.[29] To be a religious woman is simultaneously to be alienated, oppressed, and in bad faith. Women who participate in religion merely internalize the otherness that has been projected onto them by men, thereby making it impossible to claim their own subjectivity. They become the objects that men have made them into. This is an inauthentic attitude toward religion, in which, as Ruether once put it, a woman hugs the chains that enslave her.

Deirdre Bair notes that Beauvoir associated religion with her mother, who was a devout Catholic, and atheism and skepticism with her father. "The young Simone who thought 'like a man' had no trouble rejecting her mother's 'womanly' attitude."[30] Though inspired to a great extent by Beauvoir's work, Mary Daly ultimately parted company because of a "psychological detachment from religious belief" in Beauvoir that contributed to the acuity of her critique of religion but also was responsible for the limitations of her attitudes toward it.[31] Sartre was well aware that even a rejected religion is part of one's historical situation that colors one's view of things. Despite her rejection of the church, Beauvoir's understanding of religion remained fairly Catholic throughout her life. Much more than Beauvoir, Sartre acknowledged the continuing influence religious ideas had on how he viewed the world.[32]

Interpretations of Simone de Beauvoir have undergone considerable changes in the past decade, particularly regarding her intellectual and philosophical debt to Sartre. During the same period that Sartre's reputation has plummeted in many intellectual circles, a number of Beauvoir interpreters have tried to distance her from Sartre and insist on her distinct philosophical perspectives.[33] Others have engaged in a wholesale rejection of Beauvoir in what some commentators have seen as a parallel oedipal revolt against the powerful parent figure, much as a new generation of French philosophers did to Sartre.[34] I do not wish to get involved in that debate except to point out the differences in their attitudes toward religion beneath the level of their shared atheism.

The Existentialist Roots of Feminist Theology

Certainly, most religious feminists accept Beauvoir's analysis of the corruption of Western patriarchal religion. Unlike Beauvoir, however, they do not consider this critique tantamount to rejecting the power of religious symbols and myths in general. Indeed, the aim of feminist theologians is to provide models for alternative forms of feminist religion in a way that retains some degree of authenticity for women. In *Womanspirit Rising*, Carol Christ and Judith Plaskow's influential reader on feminist approaches to religion, authentic religion moves beyond sexist tradition and begins with the validation of female experience.

I suggest that Sartre, given the opportunity, would have appreciated this path. Sartre's critique of the patriarchal God whose transcendent gaze objectifies all human efforts cleared the way for alternative religious symbols. Although Sartre never wavered in his atheism, neither did his fascination with religious symbolism and imagery, particularly when it was rooted in the concrete experience of those who had also been victimized by religion.

Despite Beauvoir's impatience with religion, the Sartrean critique laid out in *The Second Sex* provided the background for some of the original work by the two central figures in feminist theology in the United States, Mary Daly and Rosemary Ruether. Feminist theologians to some extent have been partners with those, like Sartre, who proclaim the death of the abstract, male, creator God. Their work has been characterized as providing new "discourses of resistance" to the dominant discourse of the Western theological tradition.[35] Mary Daly's first two books, *The Church and the Second Sex* (1975) (an obvious homage to *The Second Sex*) and *Beyond God the Father* (1973) dismiss God as an "hypostatized transcendence" or fixed image of Supreme Male Being. In a move inspired by Paul Tillich, Daly suggested a fundamental change in the thinking about God by calling God by a dynamic verb implying "becoming," rather than by a static noun. For Daly, "the women's revolution . . . is an ontological, spiritual revolution, pointing beyond the idolatries of sexist society and sparking creative action in and toward transcendence. It has everything to do with the search for ultimate meaning and reality, which some would call God."[36] For Daly, this ultimate meaning requires questioning all religious symbols and institutions and not accepting prefabricated morals and ideas. She agreed with Sartre's rejection of the traditional image of God as Creator and Judge as well as of the ethical system based on this idea.[37]

The first moment in feminist theological work is usually a negative, iconoclastic breaking of idols, the images of God that are merely reified forms to legitimate the oppressive status quo.[38] Daly, like Beauvoir and Sartre, recognized the temptation to live in bad faith, to refuse authenticity, and "to avoid the experience of nothingness."[39] She refused to take refuge in either submission to a paternalistic deity or the comfort of belief in an afterlife.[40] The result is redemptive iconoclasm, an antinomian rejection of existing images and ideologies. Daly is no less an atheist than Sartre when it comes to any God that is a projection used to justify exploitation and oppression. If God language is to be used, it must refer to a totally different model of God that affirms identity for women rather than erases it. Any faith in traditional patriarchal religion would only constitute bad faith.

Daly and others have argued that because Western theology reflects the experience of men rather than women, women now need to develop their own symbols and expressions in the realm of religion, as elsewhere. Surely, Sartre would have been just as sympathetic to this problem for women as he was with other groups who found themselves forced to speak through the linguistic and cultural lenses of other dominant groups. This was the iconoclastic power he found in the writing of Jean Genet, the black poets of negritude, and other would-be revolutionaries. They, like Daly, understood the need, in Daly's words, to "castrate' the language of patriarchy.[41] Sartre similarly described both how Genet used language to subvert the sexuality of respectable society, as well as how the black poets stripped whites of their illusions of civilization and forced them to see their own nakedness.[42]

If Mary Daly, rather than Benny Lévy, had interviewed Sartre at the end of his life or if Simone de Beauvoir had been able to envision a postpatriarchal feminist religious ideology when she and Sartre summed up their lives in the interviews gathered in *Adieux: A Farewell to Sartre,* one could imagine very different outcomes for these conversations. As a product of the overall feminist critique of cultural and institutional sexism, feminist theology is grounded in a political commitment to women's empowerment. This committed or "engaged" (*engagé*) stance is likely one that Sartre would have supported. Just as Sartre believed that political engagement set apart authentic literature from that which merely reflected back the social status quo, surely it would be possible for a politically engaged religious position to escape the weaknesses and bad faith of traditional religion. If Sartre could have imagined a form of "committed religion" (*réligion engagé*), it would have to include the same kind of liberatory perspective that he found appealing in the messianic theme in Judaism, which envisions a new social order to replace the present flawed and oppressive system.[43]

Religion, Feminism, and Authenticity

The possibility of authentic feminist religion, something for which Beauvoir left little opening, can be constructed on the basis of a number of clues that Sartre gives through his career. In his autobiography, *The Words*, he explained the displacement of his religious feelings into literature. This admission was mostly intended to unmask the bad faith behind Sartre's sense of literary mission. However, his description of the ideal of "engaged" literature, an idea he never renounced, offers a hint of the possibility of "engaged" religion. In *What is Literature?*, Sartre maintained that literature will no longer be alienated when it recognizes its concrete situatedness and ceases to be concerned with abstract humanity or a timeless reader.[44] It will describe a society free of oppressions where "the separation of the temporal and the spiritual" has been healed.[45] Sartre claimed that the temporal (the concrete lives of people) and the spiritual (the values and goals being defended by writers) have been alienated in societies throughout history, and that writers have usually been on the side of the oppressors.

It would be easy to substitute the word "religion" for "literature" in Sartre's discussion, not only on the grounds that religion has contributed to alienation and oppression throughout history, but also because an engaged religion, like engaged literature, can be an analogical, metaphorical form of discourse that aims at revealing new aspects of the world to its participants. Literature (and religion, we might add) is authentic and legitimate when it challenges received ideas and hierarchies. Committed literature, like authentic religion, is based on what Sartre called "spiritualization," by which he meant an experience of "renewal" that enables people who read a book "to get their bearings, to see themselves and see their situation"[46] in all its concrete complexity, yet challenged and questioned. He contrasted this open-ended, dynamic process with traditional religion's static contemplation of "the heaven of established values" and "adoration of the spiritual."[47] Authentic religion, like authentic literature, must deal with spiritualization, not with the spiritual.

Feminist theology is in the tradition of the liberation theology that developed among black theologians and Latin American theologians who found inspiration in the biblical condemnation of the sins of injustice and oppression and who speak of salvation in terms of social and political liberation, and earthly justice. Among Latin American theologians this tradition was heavily influenced by a Marxist critique of economic and political inequities. This type of religious perspective actively rejects the racism, classism, and sexism that identify and oppress certain groups as Other. This is the bad faith of traditional religion. Liberation demands that marginalized groups reclaim their voices, refuse to be Other for those holding traditional oppressive ideologies, and address the concrete experience of oppressed groups, in order to develop an authentic sense of self in relation to others.[48]

Sartre's argument at the end of *Anti-Semite and Jew* took a similar position. What he called "concrete humanism" meant that Jews, blacks, Arabs, women and all other people must participate and be recognized by society as "concrete persons."[49] Noting the case of women in particular, Sartre demanded that woman be granted her rights in society "as a woman . . . , with her womanly intuitions and concerns, in her full character of a woman."[50] It follows that a Jewish woman or a Muslim woman or an African woman will need to assume and reconcile her full concrete cultural, religious, and gender identities. Feminist theology shares Sartre's challenging of the universalism of liberalism, and demands that the diversity and difference in humanity be recognized. It follows the Sartrean imperative of becoming conscious of the situation of being a woman and determining what kind of meaning to give to it. It unveils the ways in which women have been oppressed by religion and identifies "salvation" with the transformation of the world through the overcoming of oppression and dehumanization. In this existentialist vein, Mary Daly writes that liberation or authenticity requires that woman "first become conscious of her situation. . . . Once conscious of her real situation, she can be free to become whatever she makes of herself."[51]

Raising the possibility of engaged, feminist religion that preserves and supports existential authenticity rests on the notion that it is sexist, patriarchal religion that is an alienating obstacle to authenticity, not religion *per se*. Many feminist women have struggled to find a way to assume both their identities as women and as members of religious/cultural communities. Judith Plaskow, for example, sees feminist Judaism as something that can emerge at the boundaries of mainstream sexist Judaism after claiming its own voice and challenging the authority of tradition.[52]

Expressing oneself authentically, concretely, and with awareness of one's situation requires developing new forms to embody the meaning of one's self. Carol Christ notes that much of the new feminist spirituality has involved producing new stories to help women understand themselves. Christ writes: "Without stories a woman is lost when she comes to make the important decision of her life. She does not learn to value her struggles, to celebrate her strengths, to comprehend her pain. Without stories she cannot understand herself. Without stories she is alienated from those deeper experiences of self and world that have been called spiritual or religious. She is closed in silence. The expression of women's spiritual quest is integrally related to the telling of women's stories. . . . Women often live out inauthentic stories provided by a culture they did not create."[53] Stories become sacred not because they deal with deities, but because they provide orientation in relation to "the boundaries against which life is played out, the forces against which a person must contend, or the currents in whose rhythms she must learn to swim. . . . They may ground a person in powers of being that enable her to challenge conventional values or expected roles."[54] Christ's notion of a woman's "spiritual quest" resembles what Sartre called a person's fundamental project. Both processes include experiences of nothingness, insights, stories that structure and name the meaning of life in "a spiral of ever-deepening but never final understanding."[55] From this point of view, women's spirituality is the unfolding of authenticity, not an alienating obstacle to it as Beauvoir and Sartre feared religion could be.

For Carol Christ, feminist theology is about creating an alternative symbol system to that of God the Father, which has only legitimated male authority and kept women in a state of dependence. She describes the importance of the symbol of the Goddess without implying any ontological or metaphysical claims. The symbol of the Goddess represents an affirmation of female power. Christ cautions about raising question of whether the Goddess is really out there or not, noting a variety of positions among women. For some, she says, "the Goddess is definitely not 'out there,' . . . the symbol of a divinity 'out there' is part of the legacy of patriarchal oppression, which brings with it the authoritarianism, hierarchalism, and dogmatic rigidity associated with biblical monotheistic religions."[56] The symbol of the Goddess also aids the affirmation of the female body, and its connection to the processes of life and death. It represents a positive model of relationship for women. Stories of the "Goddess" are crucial symbols of female authenticity, reclaiming not only the female voice and body, but also women's connections with each other and with nature. "To speak the word 'Goddess' after many centuries of silence is to reverse age-old patterns of thinking in which male power and female subordination are viewed as the norm."[57] It is as much a political statement as a theological one.

African Spirituality and Feminist Religion

Although Sartre did not directly address the issue of women's spirituality in a positive sense, his writings about African spirituality and the reclamation of "negritude" provide an interesting analogy. "Black Orpheus," an essay written around the time that Beauvoir was writing *The Second Sex*, analyzes the concept of negritude that was popular among certain black writers at that time. The essay is not without its difficulties, and has been criticized for falling into a romanticized and essentialized image of the African. Nonetheless, Sartre's approach to the religious elements in this material provides a valuable contrast to his more well-known atheism, and a parallel to issues in more recent feminist theology.

The alienation from the world of nature and the body has been a frequently criticized element of Western religion. Because of the universal association of women with nature, alienation from nature has most often been expressed in terms of the devaluation of all that is female, and devaluation of women reinforces alienation from nature. In some respects, Sartre's portrayal of the worldview of negritude and the black poets is virtually the same as Beauvoir's description of the agricultural stage of religion that focused on women. However, Beauvoir has no nostalgia for tribal harmony with nature or for a religious view that celebrates it, since that worldview represents being "arrested at a primitive state of civilization." It is the progress of civilization that moves from woman and religion to man and action. Beauvoir writes, "The religion of woman was bound to the reign of agriculture, the reign of irreducible duration, of contingency, of chance, of waiting, of mystery; the reign of *homo faber* is the reign of time manageable as space, of necessary consequences, of the project, of action, of reason."[58]

Although mastering a world of nature that has been demystified by human desire and will sounds existentially preferable to this prior "religion of woman," Sartre did not view the transition as unproblematically as Beauvoir did. Writing at approximately the same time as Beauvoir, Sartre warned that white European culture had developed a purely technological, mechanical relation toward nature in which nature, treated purely in an external way, had become lifeless. The white man is merely an engineer, like the Christian God who creates merely by intellectual conception and act of will. The result is that the white man has become alienated; he remains only on the surface of things, "unaware of life."[59] The black man, in contrast, refused to be *homo faber*; he trusts in life and waits. He understands nature to be more like the body of a mother Goddess whose creative power is "an enormous perpetual birth; the world is flesh and the son of flesh; on the sea and in the sky, on the dunes, on the rocks in the wind, the Negro finds the softness of human skin, he rubs himself against the sand's belly, against the sky's loins."[60]

Unlike Beauvoir, who associated waiting with passivity, Sartre associated it with a healthy harmony with nature, and with androgynous images that combine "the dynamic feeling of being an erect phallus, and the more deaf, more patient, more feminine one of being a growing plant."[61] African religion, Sartre observed, preserves a "carnal" connection between man and nature. The black sees himself as a child of nature and flesh of her flesh, yet he also understands nature as a sexual partner to be penetrated and impregnated.[62]

Are these images of nature just hopelessly simple-minded ways of thinking by those people whose civilization is not as advanced as Europe's? Beauvoir seemed to think so, and even Sartre was usually critical of the magical thinking of tribal religion.[63] In this case, however, Sartre uncharacteristically admired the black poets' primitive identification with the sacred time of their ancestors. These poets were not simply indulging in inauthentic magical thinking. What is striking about the black poets, in contrast perhaps to primitive societies, is that they embrace *both* a spiritual relation to nature *and* a revolutionary political stance. It was from the standpoint of their own cultural images and myths that they protested European cultural imperialism and highlighted the weaknesses of the supposedly more advanced civilization. It was this political dimension that made these images of nature far from innocent. The black poets rejected the white man's religion that was used as an excuse for the suffering that colonialism brought.[64]

There is a dramatic difference in Sartre's attitude toward Greco-Roman religion and gods, as depicted in plays such as *The Flies* and *The Trojan Woman*, and the religion of third-world colonized and decolonized peoples today. Sartre recognized that religious ideas and images arise out of a particular historical situation. Greco-Roman religion is clearly that of the conqueror, violently imposed on peaceful people. In the name of Greek culture and enlightenment, peoples' cities were burned, their young men sacrificed, and their pastoral existence destroyed. In *The Flies*, Jupiter/Zeus is a cruel and vengeful god who terrorizes humanity to keep them ignorant of their freedom. Such gods are symbolic of oppression. Submission to them and the religion that surrounds them can only be maintained in bad faith. Orestes' heroism stems from his rejection of the gods, their values, and the guilt they demand.

On the other hand, Sartre especially appreciated the deconstructive, transgressive qualities of black poetry that challenged the dualistic, hierarchical thinking of white Christian civilization. By privileging day over night, and white over black, Christianity has invoked the structure of the universe to legitimate racial inferiority for the black, just as the dualism and spirit and nature had legitimized the inferiority of women. But negritude uses blackness to challenge hierarchies by positing "a secret blackness in white, a secret whiteness in black."[65] Ultimately, Sartre wanted to recognize the possibility of an entirely different cosmology and ontology, as well as "a certain affective attitude toward the world,"[66] all of which relativized Sartre's own European culture and the image of nature most common in his own work. As Enzo Neppi observes, for Sartre, "man and nature are not opposed in an irreducible manner. Their separation is not an original ontological structure, but only a moment in the process of being. While the black is the Other of Nature [the phallus], he remains the Same [a fragment of her maternal flesh]."[67]

It is true that Sartre's analysis of negritude combines attitudes toward nature attributed to women in agricultural societies with a revolutionary attitude toward white Christian culture that parallels the perspective of some feminist theologians, but there are also some important differences. Sartre clearly found the black's closeness to nature and instinct both attractive and authentic, whereas he was far more negative about women as symbols of nature and fertility. His portrait of the African is certainly guilty of some uncritical exoticizing that has been common among many European thinkers. Sartre's imagery about Africans is also strongly masculine, despite its appeals to androgyny.

Whatever the limitations of "Black Orpheus," however, it does demonstrate Sartre's willingness to consider religious symbols as part of a critique of other religious ideologies. In saying this, it is important to note that Sartre was hardly expressing a desire to embrace a Mother Goddess as an object of religious belief. But such religious symbols are useful poetic expressions of underlying ideologies.

The feminist theology of Rosemary Ruether shares Sartre's and Beauvoir's critique of Western religion's dualistic hierarchy of religious themes associated with the ideas of transcendence and immanence. Unlike Beauvoir, who saw little of value in the agricultural societies' worship of Mother Goddesses, but closer to Sartre in his treatment of African religion in contrast to Christian theology, Ruether accused the rise of patriarchal religions of heightening the polarization of self/other, male/female, and self/nature. Patriarchal religion symbolically represents the struggle of the male ego to rise above its bondage to nature, a process that is symbolically expressed in the conquest of the mother figure.[68] The result is the rise of a transcendent male deity who stands in contrast to the feminine world of nature, leading inevitably to widespread alienation between man and woman, between humanity and nature, and between God and the world. The problem is not merely the legitimization of sexism by religion, but its legitimization of all hierarchical relations within society—"aristocracy over serfs, masters over slaves, king over subjects, racial overlords over colonized people."[69] At the same time, however, Ruether wished to acknowledge from the same tradition, the evolving prophetic consciousness that challenges hierarchy.

The Symbol of the Goddess and the Evolution of Sartre's Thought

To a certain extent, the "desire to be God" that was the focus of Sartre's early analysis expressed a futile desire to heal the gulf between the in-itself and for-itself, between transcendence and immanence, a gulf that Sartre deemed unbridgeable. Whereas Daly avoided all personal God language, Ruether, like many other feminist theologians, has turned to the symbol of the Goddess as an expression of this reintegration. Although Ruether is impressed with the symbol of the Goddess as an expression of the divine that women can relate to, "she has no interest in engaging in new mythologizations or reified hypostatizations of female 'essence.'"[70]

Ruether offers a feminist concept of God/ess that is more symbolic and analogical than literal. Like the symbol of Africa for the black poets of negritude in their quest for selfhood, the Goddess symbolizes rediscovered selfhood and the human impulse toward liberation and freedom for women. She writes, "God/ess is not the creator and validator of the existing hierarchical social order, but rather the one who liberates us from it, who opens a new community of equals."[71] This symbol of God/ess must draw from the experiences of women, working people, and marginalized groups, she continues. The goal is not to posit a loving mother figure to complement a powerful sovereign father figure. "Most of all, images of God/ess must be transformative, pointing us back to our authentic potential and forward to new redeemed possibilities."[72] Ultimately, the symbol of God/ess must be a symbol of "the harmonization of self and body, self and other, self and world. It is the *Shalom* of our being."[73] In short, this religious symbol functions equivalently to the negritude Sartre analyzed in the black poets, as a concrete expression of the rejection of alienation and oppression and the movement to liberation and authenticity. Ruether explains, "The liberating encounter with God/ess is always an encounter with our authentic selves resurrected from underneath the alienated self. It is not experienced against, but in and through relationships, healing our broken relations with our bodies, with other people, with nature. We have no adequate name for the true God/ess, the 'I am who I shall become.' "[74] This new model of resurrected humanity closely resembles a direction that Sartre also was pursuing in his final years. The "I am who I shall become" is a perfect image for Sartre's model of authentic human existence.

It is true that Ruether is less theological than other feminist religious thinkers. Marsha Hewitt has argued that Ruether's work is more of a "feminist *critical theory of religion*" than a "feminist *theology*."[75] Her goal is to deconstruct the patriarchal elements of Western religion, but then to reconstruct images and symbols with emancipatory potential that will "resonate with nonreligious theories of human liberation."[76] As Hewitt notes,

> Although Ruether uses explicit theological language, she does so more as a vehicle that expresses her utopian vision of an alternative, socialist, humanist, and feminist society than as a direct attempt to reformulate substantive theological claims. . . . Ruether's analysis of specific forms of oppression and injustice takes place within a utopian vision of transformed humanity in right relation with itself and with nature. This vision is articulated in

> symbolical theological language that is at the same time dis-
> tinctly nontheological. . . . The negation of theology is the shat-
> tering of the illusions that sustain and legitimate suffering;
> through the negation of theology, the liberating power of religion
> has a chance of being released, not directly as religion, perhaps,
> replete with doctrine and ritual, but as utopia realized in concrete
> history.[77]

This use of religious language and symbols for nontheological purposes is
precisely the type of approach that Sartre engaged in throughout his life.
Ruether's feminist conclusions are likewise suggestive of the kind of position Sartre was grasping for in the last stage of his life.

By the end of his life, Sartre had suggested that the desire to be God,
to be *causa sui* (which he saw as rooted in Christian tradition), should
not be seen as the sole goal of human life.[78] He referred to another fundamental desire connected to transformed relations between people according to a new ethical standard. "And the ethical modality implies that we
stop wanting to have being as a goal, we no longer want to be God, we
no longer want to be *ens causa sui*. We are looking for something else."[79]

Much of the ferment and creativity in recent feminist theology involving the image of the Goddess has not been about metaphysical claims or
beliefs about a female transcendent deity. Rather it is about "looking for
something else," finding resonant symbols that can embody an affirmation of the legitimacy of female power and a model for nonoppressive,
nonheirarchical human relations. I think Sartre's reevaluation of the
mother-child relation in his work on Flaubert and his own restless search
for new perspectives leaves open the possibility that the sort of imagery
some feminist theologians have experimented with would have been quite
attractive to him.

Feminist theologians have been sensitive to the interconnection between theological concepts and primordial family relationships. The patriarchal family and patriarchal religion mutually support each other.
Feminist theology has posed a challenge at both levels. In his work on
Flaubert, Sartre provided his own challenge to the psychological roots of
traditional religion. Sartre's emphasis on the importance of the preoedi-
pal relation with the mother provides a different model for spirituality
than the male paternal lawgiver. What turns out to be psychologically
pivotal to the development of one's religious worldview is not merely the
projection of the father and his authority, as Freud would have it. Rather,

claimed Sartre, it is the "valorization" of a child by his (her)[80] parents' love, especially his (her) mother, that is crucial for a healthy attitude toward the world later. If a child feels purpose and direction to his (her) life, "it is because the parents' love, their creation and expectation, creation for future delight, has revealed his existence to him as a movement toward an end."[81] For Jean Genet, argued Sartre, the absence of "the indissoluble intimacy of mother and nursling"[82] transformed his existential relation to the world and poisoned his relations with others. Although Sartre insisted that life's meaning is not predetermined in any sense by a transcendent deity, he noted that the *experience* of life as meaningful depends upon family and societal factors that predate the dawn of self-consciousness about life. Sartre wrote,

> Thus we must repeat these absurd formulas back to back: "life has a meaning," "it hasn't any," "it has what we give it," and understand that we will discover our ends, the non-sense or sense of our lives, as realities anterior to that awakening of consciousness, anterior perhaps to our birth and prefabricated in the human universe. The meaning of life comes to the living person through the human society that sustains him and through the parents who engender him, and it is for this reason that he always remains a non-sense as well. . . . When the valorization of the infant through life is accomplished badly or too late or not at all, maternal inadequacy defines experience as non-sense. . . . Briefly, the love of the Other is the foundation and guarantee of the objectivity of the individual's value and his mission; this mission becomes a sovereign choice, permitted and evoked in the subjective person by the presence of self-worth. If this is lacking, life presents itself as pure contingency.[83]

Not only is this a considerable retreat from the early existentialist view that life is totally absurd and that the individual ego alone acts unilaterally to give it whatever meaning it may have. It also suggests that theological formulations reflect and contribute to the valorization of the self. Just as Sartre saw the idea of negritude, including its theological components, as an attempt to support positive valorization of the black self, he would have understood feminist theology as an analogous effort to support the valorization of women's sense of self.

By the end of his life, Sartre's quest for a model of authentic brotherhood or communion among people had moved away from the fraternity of brothers who unite in violence against oppression, which he had described in the *Critique of Dialectical Reason*.[84] Although he continued to look forward into the future for the realization of a new society based on a new form of morality, much as the biblical prophets did, he turned back to a prebiblical period, to a tribal view of totemism for a model of human interconnection. Sartre saw hope for real human community by recapturing the sense of the Mother Goddess as totem. In one of the most suggestive passages from the Lévy interviews, Sartre said, "When I see man, I think: he has the same origin as myself, like me he comes from Mother Humanity, let's say, Mother Earth as Socrates says, or Mother."[85] In the interview, Benny Lévy objected to this mythological turn in Sartre's thinking and continued to heckle him. But Sartre persisted.

> For every person, birth is the same phenomenon as it is for his neighbor to such a degree that, in a certain way, two men talking to each other have the same mother. Not the same mother empirically, of course, but a mother without eyes, without a face. . . . To belong to the same species is, in a way, to have the same parents. In that sense we are brothers.
>
> . . . the great concept of the clan, its womb-like unity— starting with an animal, for example, that is supposed to have engendered them all—is what we must rediscover today, for that was true fraternity. In a sense it was a myth, no doubt about it, but it was also a truth. . . .
>
> . . . all men are brothers in the clan inasmuch as they are born of the same woman, who is represented by the totem. They are all brothers in the sense that they came from one woman's womb, and ultimately, at that moment, the individuality of the woman is not at issue. It's a woman who simply has the womb that will give life, the breasts that will nourish, perhaps the back that will carry.[86]

It is safe to say that this perspective in Sartre's thought is neither the result of interviewer influence nor senility, for it is consistent with a variety of other thoughts from earlier stages in his work. At the same time, the long-searched-for Sartrean ethics may have more in common with feminist ethics than has been previously appreciated.[87]

Erich Fromm's distinction between oppressive forms of "authoritarian religion" and more humanly authentic "humanistic religion" resembles the nuance in Sartre's views on religion that I have been trying to un-cover.[88] In his *Art of Loving*, Fromm associates the idea of unconditional, all-enveloping mother love with a religious system very different from patriarchal religion, which makes love dependent on obedience to laws. This model of love is neither controlled nor acquired. It is based on equality and family. One is loved just for being a child of the mother. "All men are equal, because they all are the children of a mother, because they all are children of Mother Earth."[89] For feminist theology as well, the symbol of the mother represents a different quality of relation to the Other. Nelle Morton writes of the symbolic meaning of the Mother: "Or-igin from a common womb was regarded the closest possible bond and originally the only true form of kinship. When the womb came to mean the Great Womb of the Creator, the term *stranger* was not known. To injure any human being or animal was a special crime."[90]

It is perhaps ironic that Sartre's own intellectual itinerary brought him to a place where feminist reconsiderations of the image and ethical implications of the Mother Goddess intersected with his own budding ethical vision of what might lie beyond the critique of patriarchal reli-gion. It is unfortunate that neither Benny Lévy, who was in the process of discovering the power of his own Jewish religious and ethical tradition, nor Simone de Beauvoir was able to appreciate Sartre's ongoing struggle to find an authentic way to respond to the potentially liberating power of religious images and ideas. As a result, both of them tended to misunder-stand, in different ways, the meaning of this seemingly aberrant direction in Sartre's thought. Sartre's final thoughts may have reflected a new turn in his thinking, but it was one that was thoroughly Sartrean nonetheless and consistent with many earlier threads in his work.

Notes

1. See Linda Bell's *Rethinking Ethics in the Midst of Violence: A Feminist Approach to Freedom* (Lanham, Md.: Rowman and Littlefield, 1993).

2. Hazel Barnes, "Sartre and Sexism," *Philosophy and Literature* 14, no. 2 (October 1990), 346.

3. Michèle Le Doeuff, *Hipparchia's Choice* (Oxford: Blackwell, 1991), 48.

4. Cf. Jean-Paul Sartre, "The Itinerary of a Thought," in his *Between Marxism and Existentialism* (New York: Pantheon Books, 1974), 33–64.

5. A number of commentators have noted parallels between Sartre's ideas and those of Bud-dhism, for example.

6. Cf. my *Meaning and Myth in the Study of Lives: A Sartrean Approach* (Philadelphia: University of Pennsylvania Press, 1983), and *Vulgarity and Authenticity: Dimensions of Otherness in the World of Jean-Paul Sartre* (Amherst: University of Massachusetts Press, 1991).

7. Carol Christ and Judith Plaskow, eds., *Womanspirit Rising* (New York: Harper Books, 1979), 1.

8. Jean-Paul Sartre, *The Words* (New York: Fawcett, 1969), 157.

9. Simone de Beauvoir, *Adieux: A Farewell to Sartre* (New York: Pantheon Books, 1984), 119.

10. Beauvoir, *Adieux*, 119.

11. Beauvoir, *Adieux*, 445.

12. Jean-Paul Sartre, *Sartre on Theater* (New York: Pantheon Books, 1976), 228.

13. Sartre wrote: "What struck me when I was studying the Reformation was that there is no heresy to which some form of social unrest is not, basically, the key, but it is expressed in an ideology appropriate to the times. The Cathars, the Anabaptists, the Lutherans, and the rest are invariably some oppressed group seeking to express itself, but doing do in a religious form, because the age would have it so" (*Sartre on Theater*, 228).

14. Recently, there have been those interpreters of Beauvoir who seek to distance her work from that of Sartre, emphasize her independence, or even suggest that it was she who was the creative inspiration behind Sartre's thought. I am not convinced by much of this revisionist interpretation, particularly the recent biography by Kate and Edward Fullbrook, *Simone de Beauvoir and Jean-Paul Sartre: The Remaking of a Twentieth-Century Legend* (New York: Basic Books, 1994), chapter 5.

15. Simone de Beauvoir, *The Second Sex* (New York: Bantam Books, 1961), xvi.

16. Jean-Paul Sartre, *Notebooks for an Ethics* (Chicago: University of Chicago Press, 1992), 379.

17. Beauvoir, *The Second Sex*, xxvi. Some interpreters have suggested that Beauvoir's distaste for immanence and cyclicality is one-sided and Eurocentric, for such ideas are quite consistent with the orientation of various Eastern religions. Her ideal of transcendence, moreover, is based on a linear sense of time and becoming that may be more typically male than female. Cf. Josephine Donovan, *Feminist Theory* (New York: Continuum, 1994), 126.

18. Beauvoir, *The Second Sex*, xix. Beauvoir's position sounds very similar to Sartre's in his description of Jews, which was written during the same period. Jews, he claimed, lacked any common history, language, or culture of their own (*Anti-Semite and Jew* [New York: Schocken Books, 1965], 66–67). The weakness of this position in regard to Jews, or Beauvoir's on women, is evident and has been the target of much criticism.

19. Beauvoir, *The Second Sex*, 132.

20. Beauvoir, *The Second Sex*, 58.

21. Beauvoir, *The Second Sex*, 60.

22. Beauvoir, *The Second Sex*, 62.

23. Beauvoir, *The Second Sex*, 63.

24. Sartre, *Notebooks for an Ethics*, 379.

25. Beauvoir, *The Second Sex*, 65.

26. Beauvoir, *The Second Sex*, 70.

27. Sartre, *Notebooks for an Ethics*, 379.

28. Sartre, *Notebooks for an Ethics*, 379–90. Although there is considerable controversy among feminist theologians about the meaning of ancient Goddess worship, some see Beauvoir's positions as unnecessarily critical. Feminist theologians have been attracted to the symbol of the Goddess as an expression of an integrated relation to nature in contrast to the ideal of transcendence of nature proposed by Sartre and Beauvoir as the central characteristic of human reality. Cf. Andrea Nye's *Feminist Theory and the Philosophies of Man* (New York: Routledge, 1988), 111.

29. Beauvoir, *The Second Sex*, 134–40.

30. Deirdre Bair, *Simone de Beauvoir: A Biography* (New York: Summit Books, 1990), 62.

31. Mary Daly, *The Church and the Second Sex* (New York: Harper and Row, 1975), 73.

32. Cf. Sartre, *Between Existentialism and Marxism* (New York: Pantheon Books, 1975), 155–60.

33. Cf. *Feminist Approaches to Simone de Beauvoir*, ed. Margaret A. Simons (Penn State Press, 1995).

34. Dorothy Kaufman McCall, "Simone de Beauvoir: Questions of Difference and Generation," *Yale French Studies* 72 (1986): 131.

35. Mary McClintock Fulkerson, *Changing the Subject: Women's Discourses and Feminist Theology* (Minneapolis: Fortress Press, 1994), 323.

36. Mary Daly, *Beyond God the Father* (Boston: Beacon Press, 1973), 6.

37. Christ and Plaskow, *Womanspirit Rising*, 213.

38. "Theologies that hypostatize transcendence, that is, that objectify God as a *being*, legitimate the existing status quo" (Daly, *Beyond God the Father*, 9).

39. Daly, *Beyond God the Father*, 23.

40. Carol Christ also speaks of the experience of nothingness as a indispensable questioning of conventional ideas (*Diving Deep and Surfacing: Women Writers in Spiritual Quest* [Boston: Beacon Press, 1980], 14).

41. Daly, *Beyond God the Father*, 9.

42. See my discussion in Charmé, *Vulgarity and Authenticity*, chapters 6–7.

43. See my discussion in Charmé, *Vulgarity and Authenticity*, chapter 8.

44. Jean-Paul Sartre, *What is Literature?* (New York: Philosophical Library, 1949), 157.

45. Sartre, *What is Literature?* 157.

46. Sartre, *What is Literature?* 158.

47. Sartre, *What is Literature?* 158.

48. Donovan, *Feminist Theory*, 129.

49. Sartre, *Anti-Semite and Jew*, 146.

50. Sartre, *Anti-Semite and Jew*, 146.

51. Daly, *The Church and the Second Sex*, 73.

52. Judith Plaskow, *Standing Again at Sinai* (San Francisco: Harper and Row, 1990).

53. Christ, *Diving Deep and Surfacing*, 1; on a Sartrean view of the role of narrative in the construction of the authentic self, see my *Meaning and Myth*.

54. Christ, *Diving Deep and Surfacing*, 3.

55. Christ, *Diving Deep and Surfacing*, 14. Cf. my *Meaning and Myth* on the image of the spiral, 65–66.

56. Carol Christ, "Why Women Need the Goddess: Phenomenological, Psychological, and Political Reflections," in Christ and Plaskow, *Womanspirit Rising*, 278.

57. Christ, *Diving Deep and Surfacing*, 129–30.

58. Beauvoir, *The Second Sex*, 70.

59. Jean-Paul Sartre, "Black Orpheus," *Massachusetts Review* 6 (1964–65): 38.

60. Sartre, "Black Orpheus," 40.

61. Sartre, "Black Orpheus," 40.

62. Sartre, "Black Orpheus," 40–42.

63. Sartre had studied the work of Levy-Bruhl on primitive mentality, of which he found evidence in modern society in emotional consciousness, anti-Semitism, and other forms of bad faith.

64. When Sartre visited Cuba, he was very impressed with the African religion that had been preserved underground, despite persecution by the church. Eventually poor whites became attracted to some of these religious rites. This sort of religious ritual and dance, which Sartre saw staged in a Havana theater, was a religious act that flowed from the situation of these blacks (Jean-Paul Sartre, "Epic Theater and Dramatic Theater," in *Sartre on Theater*, 79–83). For the duration of the performance, Sartre was swept up in the experience of something alien to him but that momentarily represented all religions. "It in fact contested every particular form of religion, because it was all religions" (84).

65. Sartre, "Black Orpheus," 28.

66. Sartre, "Black Orpheus," 36.

67. Enzo Neppi, Le Babil et la caresse: Pensée du maternel chez Sartre (New York: Peter Lang, 1995), 16.

68. Rosemary Ruether, New Woman, New Earth: Sexist Ideologies and Human Liberation (New York: Seabury Press, 1975), 25.

69. Rosemary Ruether, Sexism and God-Talk (Boston: Beacon Press, 1983), 61.

70. Marsha H. Hewitt, Critical Theory of Religion: A Feminist Analysis (Minneapolis: Fortress Press, 1995), 177.

71. Ruether, Sexism and God-Talk, 69.

72. Ruether, Sexism and God-Talk, 69.

73. Ruether, Sexism and God-Talk, 71.

74. Ruether, Sexism and God-Talk, 71.

75. Hewitt, Critical Theory of Religion, 175.

76. Hewitt, Critical Theory of Religion, 176.

77. Hewitt, Critical Theory of Religion, 205–6.

78. Jean-Paul Sartre, Hope Now (Chicago: University of Chicago Press, 1995), 59.

79. Sartre, Hope Now, 157.

80. Sartre's examples of disturbances in this process of valorization are all males, and he does not account for the likelihood of gender differences in how the process unfolds in boys versus girls. However, I think Sartre's underlying point about the centrality of valorization, whatever form it takes, transcends gender difference.

81. Jean-Paul Sartre, The Family Idiot (Chicago: University of Chicago Press, 1973), 1: 133.

82. Jean-Paul Sartre, Saint Genet (New York: Pantheon Books, 1963), 7.

83. Sartre, The Family Idiot, 1: 134–35.

84. Jean-Paul Sartre, Critique of Dialectical Reason (London: Verso, 1991), 437.

85. Sartre, Hope Now, 90.

86. Sartre, Hope Now, 87–89.

87. See my "Different Voices in Sartre's Ethics," Bulletin de l'Association Américaine de Philosophie de Langue Française 5 (Summer–Fall 1992): 264–80.

88. Cf. Erich Fromm, Psychoanalysis and Religion (New Haven: Yale University Press, 1950), 34–64.

89. Erich Fromm, The Art of Loving (New York: Harper, 1956), 65.

90. Nelle Morton, "The Dilemma of Celebration," in Christ and Plaskow, Womanspirit Rising, 161.

Selected Bibliography

Al-Hibri, Azizah, and Margaret A. Simons, eds. *Hypatia Reborn: Essays in Feminist Philosophy*. Bloomington: Indiana University Press, 1990.

Allen, Jeffner, "An Introduction to Patriarchal Existentialism, A Proposal for a Way out of Existential Patriarchy." First published in *Philosophy and Social Criticism* 9 (1982). Also in Allen and Young, *The Thinking Muse: Feminism and Modern French Philosophy*, and in Allen, *Sinuosities: Lesbian Poetic Politics*.

———. *Sinuosities: Lesbian Poetic Politics*. Bloomington: Indiana University Press, 1996.

Allen, Jeffner, and Iris Marion Young, eds. *The Thinking Muse: Feminism and Modern French Philosophy*. Bloomington: Indiana University Press, 1989.

Anderson, Thomas C. *The Foundation and Structure of Sartrean Ethics*. Lawrence, Kans.: Regents Press of Kansas, 1979.

———. *Sartre's Two Ethics: From Authenticity to Integral Humanity*. Chicago: Open Court, 1993.

Aronson, Ronald. *Jean-Paul Sartre: Philosophy in the World*. New York: Schocken Books, 1980.

Aronson, Ronald, and Adrian van den Hoven, eds. *Sartre Alive*. Detroit: Wayne State University Press, 1991.

———. *Sartre's Second Critique*. Chicago: University of Chicago Press, 1987.

Barnes, Hazel, E. "Beauvoir and Sartre: The Forms of a Farewell." *Philosophy and Literature* 9, no. 1 (1985): 21–40.

———. *An Existentialist Ethics*. New York: Knopf, 1967.

———. "Personal Recollections." *Sartre Studies International* 1, no. 1/2 (1995): 45–56.

———. *Sartre*. New York: Lippincott Press, 1973.

———. *Sartre and Flaubert*. Chicago: University of Chicago Press, 1981.

———. "Sartre and Sexism." *Philosophy and Literature* 14 (1990): 340–47.

———. *The Story I Tell Myself: A Venture in Existential Autobiography*. Chicago: University of Chicago Press, 1997.

Bartky, Sandra Lee. *Femininity and Domination: Studies in the Phenomenology of Oppression*. New York: Routledge, 1990.

Beauvoir, Simone de. *L'Amérique au jour le jour*. Paris: Mohrien, 1948. Translated as *America Day by Day*, by P. Dudley. New York: Grove, 1953.

———. *La Cérémonie des adieux suivi de Entretiens avec Jean-Paul Sartre, Août–Septembre*

1974. Paris: Gallimard, 1981. Translated as *Adieux: A Farewell to Sartre*, by P. O'Brian. New York: Pantheon, 1984.

———. *Le Dieuxième Sexe*. Vols. 1 and 2. Paris: Gallimard, 1949. Translated as *The Second Sex*, by H. M. Parshley. New York: Knopf, 1952; Vintage, 1989.

———. *Les Écrits de Simone de Beauvoir*. Ed. Claude Francis and Fernande Gontier. Paris: Gallimard, 1979.

———. *La Force de l'âge*. Paris: Gallimard, 1960. Translated as *The Prime of Life*, by P. Green. Cleveland: World Publishing, 1962.

———. *La Force des choses*. Paris: Gallimard, 1963. Translated as *Force of Circumstance*, by R. Howard. New York: Putnam, 1965.

———. *Journal de guerre: Septembre 1939–Janvier 1941*. Edited by Sylvie Le Bon de Beauvoir. Paris: Gallimard, 1990.

———. *Lettres à Sartre*. Vols. 1 and 2. Edited by Sylvie Le Bon de Beauvoir. Paris: Gallimard, 1990. Edited and translated as *Letters to Sartre*, by Q. Hoare. New York: Little, Brown, 1992.

———. "Littérature et métaphysique." *Les Temps Modernes* 7:1153–63, 1946. Reprinted in Simone de Beauvoir, *L'Existentialisme et la sagesse des nations*, 89–107. Paris: Nagel, 1948.

———. *Mémoires d'une jeune fille rangée*. Paris: Gallimard, 1958. Translated as *Memoirs of a Dutiful Daughter*, by J. Kirkup. Cleveland: World Publishing, 1959.

———. *Pour une morale de l'ambiguïté*. Paris: Gallimard, 1947. Translated as *The Ethics of Ambiguity*, by B. Frechtman. New York: Philosophical Library, 1948.

———. *Tout compte fait*. Paris: Gallimard, 1972. Translated as *All Said and Done*, by P. O'Brian. New York: Putnam, 1974.

Bell, Linda A. "Boredom and the Yawn." *Review of Existential Psychology and Psychiatry* 17, no. 1 (1980–81): 91–100.

———. "Loser Wins: The Importance of Play in a Sartrean Ethics of Authenticity." In *Phenomenology in a Pluralistic Context*, ed. William L. McBride and Calvin O. Schrag, 5–13. Albany: State University of New York Press, 1983.

———. *Rethinking Ethics in the Midst of Violence: A Feminist Approach to Freedom*. Totowa, N.J.: Rowman and Littlefield, 1993.

———. "Sartre: Alienation and Society." *Philosophy and Social Criticism* 6 (Winter 1979): 409–22.

———. *Sartre's Ethics of Authenticity*. Tuscaloosa: University of Alabama Press, 1989.

Bergoffen, Debra. *The Philosophy of Simone de Beauvoir: Gendered Phenomenologies, Erotic Generosities*. Albany: State University Press of New York, 1997.

Boschetti, Anna. *Sartre e "Les Temps Modernes": L'Impresa intellectuale*. Baci: Edizioni Dedalo, 1985. Translated into French as *Sartre et "Les Temps Modernes": Une entreprise intellectuelle*. Paris: Les Éditions de Minuit, 1985. Translated into English as *The Intellectual Enterprise: Sartre and "Les Temps Modernes,"* by Richard C. McCleary. Evanston: Northwestern University Press, 1988.

Braidotti, Rosi. *Patterns of Dissonance: A Study of Women in Contemporary Philosophy*. New York: Routledge, 1991.

Busch, Thomas W. *The Power of Consciousness and the Force of Circumstances in Sartre's Philosophy*. Bloomington: Indiana University Press, 1990.

Butler, Judith. *Gender Trouble: Feminism and the Subversion of Identity*. New York: Routledge, 1990.

———. *Subjects of Desire: Hegelian Reflections in Twentieth-Century France*. New York: Columbia University Press, 1987.

Cannon, Betty. *Sartre and Psychoanalysis: An Existentialist Challenge to Clinical Metatheory*. Lawrence: University Press of Kansas, 1991.

———. "Sartre, Transcendence and Education for Equality." In *Women's and Men's Liberation: Testimonies of Spirit*, ed. Leonard Grob, Riffat Hassan, and Haim Gordon, 181–200. Westport, Conn.: Greenwood Press, 1991.

Catalano, Joseph S. *A Commentary on Sartre's "Critique of Dialectical Reason."* Vol. 1. Chicago: University of Chicago Press, 1986.

———. *Good Faith and Other Essays: Perspectives on a Sartrean Ethics*. Lanham, Md.: Rowman and Littlefield, 1996.

Celeux, Anne-Marie. *Jean-Paul Sartre, Simone de Beauvoir: Une expérience commune, deux écritures*. Paris: Librairie Nizet, 1986.

Chanter, Tina. *Ethics of Eros: Irigaray's Rewriting of the Philosophers*. New York: Routledge, 1995.

Charmé, Stuart. "Authenticity, Multiculturalism, and the Jewish Question." *Journal of the British Society for Phenomenology* 25, no 2 (1994): 183–94.

———. *Meaning and Myth in the Study of Lives: A Sartrean Perspective*. University of Pennsylvania Press, 1984.

———. *Vulgarity and Authenticity: Dimensions of Otherness in the World of Jean-Paul Sartre*. Amherst: University of Massachusetts Press, 1991.

Christophe, Marc A. "Sex, Racism, and Philosophy in Jean-Paul Sartre's *The Respectful Prostitute*." *College Language Association Journal* 24, no. 1 (1980): 76–86.

Cohen-Solal, Annie. *Sartre: A Life*. Translated by Anna Cancogni, edited by Norman MaCafee. New York: Pantheon Books, 1987.

Collins, Margery L., and Christine Pierce. "Holes and Slime: Sexism in Sartre's Psychoanalysis." *Philosophical Forum* 5 (1973): 112–27. Also in *Women and Philosophy: Toward a Theory of Liberation*, ed. Carol C. Gould. and Marx W. Wartofsky, 112–27. New York: G. P. Putnam's Sons, 1976; and in *Women in Western Thought*, ed. Martha Lee Osborne, 319–22. New York: Random House, 1979.

Comesaña, Gloria. "Analisis de las figuras femeninas en el treatro de Sartre." *Rev Filosof* (Venezuela) 9 (1980): 103–33.

Connell, R. W. "Class, Patriarchy, and Sartre's Theory of Practice." *Theory and Society* 11, no. 3 (1982): 305–20.

Contat, Michel, and Michel Rybalka. *Sartre: Bibliography 1980–1992*. Bowling Green, Ohio: Bowling Green State University, Philosophy Documentation Center, 1993.

———. *The Writings of Jean-Paul Sartre*. 2 vols. Trans. R. McCleary. Evanston: Northwestern University Press, 1974.

Davis, Howard. *Sartre and "Les Temps Modernes."* Cambridge: Cambridge University Press, 1987.

Dobson, Andrew. *Jean-Paul Sartre and the Politics of Reason: A Theory of History*. Cambridge: Cambridge University Press, 1993.

Doubrovsky, Serge. "Phallotexte et gynotexte dans *La Nausée*: Feuillet sans date." In *Sartre et la mise en signe*, ed. Michael Issacharof and Jean-Claude Vilquin, 31–55. Paris: Klincksieck; Lexington, Ky.: French Forum, 1982.

Farr, Anthony. *Sartre's Radicalism and Oakeshott's Conservatism: The Duplicity of Freedom*. New York: Macmillan, 1998.

Flynn, Thomas R. *Sartre, Foucault, and Reason in History: Toward an Existentialist Theory.* Chicago: University of Chicago Press, 1997.

———. *Sartre and Marxist Existentialism.* Chicago: University of Chicago Press, 1984.

Fourny, Jean-Francois, and Charles Minahen, eds. *Situating Sartre in Twentieth-Century Thought and Culture.* New York: St. Martins Press, 1997.

Frie, Roger. *Subjectivity and Intersubjectivity in Modern Philosophy and Psychoanalysis: A Study of Sartre, Binswanger, Lacan, and Habermas.* Lanham, Md.: Rowman and Littlefield, 1997.

Friedlander, Judith. "The Anti-Semite and *The Second Sex*: A Cultural Reading of Sartre and Beauvoir." In *Women in Culture and Politics,* ed. Judith Friedlander et al., 811–96. Bloomington: Indiana University Press, 1986.

Fullbrook, Kate, and Edward Fullbrook. *Simone de Beauvoir and Jean-Paul Sartre: The Remaking of a Twentieth-Century Legend.* New York: Harvester Wheatsheaf, 1993.

Gordon, Hayim, and Rivca Gordon. *Sartre and Evil: Guidelines for a Struggle.* Westport, Conn.: Greenwood Press, 1995.

Gordon, Lewis Ricardo. *Bad Faith and Antiblack Racism.* Atlantic Highlands. N.J.: Humanities Press, 1995.

Guerlac, Suzanne. *Literary Polemics: Bataille, Sartre, Valéry, Breton.* Stanford: Stanford University Press, 1997.

Harvey, Robert. *Search for a Father: Sartre, Paternity, and the Question of Ethics.* Ann Arbor: University of Michigan Press, 1991.

Hayim, Gila J. *The Existential Sociology of Jean-Paul Sartre.* Amherst: University of Massachusetts Press, 1980.

Hoagland, Sarah Lucia. *Lesbian Ethics: Toward New Value.* Palo Alto, Calif.: Institute of Lesbian Studies, 1988.

———. "Some Thoughts About Heterosexualism." *Journal of Social Philosophy* 21, no. 2/3 (1990): 98–107.

Howells, Christina, ed. *The Cambridge Companion to Sartre.* New York: Cambridge University Press, 1992.

———. *Sartre: The Necessity of Freedom.* New York: Cambridge University Press, 1988.

Idt, Geneviève, ed. *Études Sartriennes.* Paris: Université de Paris X, 1990.

Jaggar, Alison. *Feminist Politics and Human Nature.* Totowa, N.J.: Rowman and Allanheld, 1983.

Jameson, Fredric, ed. *Sartre After Sartre.* Yale French Studies, no. 68, 1985.

Jardine, Alice. "Death Sentences: Writing Couples and Ideology." In *The Female Body in Western Culture,* ed. Susan R. Suleiman, 84–96. Cambridge: Harvard University Press, 1987.

Jeanson, Francis. *Sartre and the Problem of Morality.* Trans. R. Stone. Bloomington: Indiana University Press, 1981.

Joseph, Gilbert. *Une si douce occupation: Simone de Beauvoir et Jean-Paul Sartre 1940–1944.* Paris: Albin Michel, 1991.

Keefe, Terry. "Simone de Beauvoir and Sartre on 'mauvaise foi.' " *French Studies* 34, no. 3 (1980): 300–314.

König, Traugott, ed. *Sartres Flaubert Iesen: Essays zu "Der Idiot der Familie."* Reinbek bei Hamburg: Rowohlt, 1980.

Kristeva, Julia. *Sens et non-sens de la revolte.* Paris: Fayard, 1996.

Kruks, Sonia. "Simone de Beauvoir: Teaching Sartre About Freedom." In *Feminist Interpre-*

tations of Simone de Beauvoir, ed. Margaret Simons, 79–96. University Park: Penn State Press, 1995.

———. *Situation and Human Existence: Freedom, Subjectivity, and Society*. London: Unwin Hyman, 1990.

Kuykendall, Eleanor H. "Sartre on Violence and Fraternity." In *Sartre: An Investigation of Some Major Themes*, ed. Glynn Simon, 22–36. Aldershot, Brookfield USA: Avebury Gower, 1987.

Lamouchi, Nourredine. *Sartre et le Tiers-Monde: Rhétorique d'un discours anticolonialiste*. Paris: L'Harmattan, 1996.

Lilar, Suzanne. *A propos de Sartre et de l'amour*. Paris: Éditions Bernard Grasset, 1967.

Le Doeuff, Michèle. *L'Étude et le rouet*. Paris: Seuil, 1989.

———. *Hipparchia's Choice: An Essay Concerning Women, Philosophy, etc.* Trans. Trista Selous. Oxford: Blackwell, 1991.

———. *L'Imaginaire philosophique*. Paris: Payot, 1980. Trans. as *Philosophical Imaginary*, by Colin Gordon. Stanford: Stanford University Press, 1990.

McBride, William L. *Sartre's Political Theory*. Bloomington: Indiana University Press, 1991.

———, ed. *The Development and Meaning of Twentieth-Century Existentialism*. Vol. 1 of *Sartre and Existentialism: Philosophy, Politics, Ethics, the Psyche, Literature, and Aesthetics*. New York: Garland, 1997.

———, ed. *Existentialist Background: Kierkegaard, Dostoevsky, Nietzsche, Jaspers, Heidegger*. Vol. 2 of *Sartre and Existentialism: Philosophy, Politics, Ethics, the Psyche, Literature, and Aesthetics*. New York: Garland, 1997.

———, ed. *Existentialist Ethics*. Vol. 5 of *Sartre and Existentialism: Philosophy, Politics, Ethics, the Psyche, Literature, and Aesthetics*. New York: Garland, 1997.

———, ed. *Existentialist Literature and Aesthetics*. Vol. 7 of *Sartre and Existentialism: Philosophy, Politics, Ethics, the Psyche, Literature, and Aesthetics*. New York: Garland, 1997.

———, ed. *Existentialist Ontology and Human Consciousness*. Vol. 4 of *Sartre and Existentialism: Philosophy, Politics, Ethics, the Psyche, Literature, and Aesthetics*. New York: Garland, 1997.

———, ed. *Existentialist Politics and Political Theory*. Vol. 6 of *Sartre and Existentialism: Philosophy, Politics, Ethics, the Psyche, Literature, and Aesthetics*. New York: Garland, 1997.

———, ed. *Sartre's French Contemporaries and Enduring Influences*. Vol. 8 of *Sartre and Existentialism: Philosophy, Politics, Ethics, the Psyche, Literature, and Aesthetics*. New York: Garland, 1997.

———, ed. *Sartre's Life, Times, and Vision du Monde*. Vol. 3 of *Sartre and Existentialism: Philosophy, Politics, Ethics, the Psyche, Literature, and Aesthetics*. New York: Garland, 1997.

McCall, Dorothy Kaufmann. "Simone de Beauvoir, *The Second Sex*, and Jean-Paul Sartre," *Signs* 5 (1979): 209–23.

McCulloch, Gregory. *Using Sartre: An Analytical Introduction to Early Sartrean Themes*. New York: Routledge, 1994.

Monteil, Claudine. *Simone de Beauvoir: Le mouvement des femmes*. Montréal, Québec: Stanké, 1995.

Morris, Phyllis Sutton. "Sartre on the Self-Deceiver's Translucent Consciousness." *Journal of the British Society for Phenomenology* 23, no. 2 (1992): 103–19.

———. *Sartre's Concept of a Person: An Analytic Approach*. Amherst: University of Massachusetts Press, 1976.

————. "Self-Creating Selves: Sartre and Foucault," *American Catholic Philosophical Quarterly* 70, no. 4 (1996): 537–50.

Mui, Constance. "Sartre's Sexism Reconsidered." *Auslegung* 16, no. 1, (1990): 31–41.

Murphy, Julien S. "The Look in Sartre and Adrienne Rich." *Hypatia* 2, no. 2 (1987): 113–24; reprinted in Allen and Young, *The Thinking Muse: Feminism and Modern French Philosophy*, 101–12.

Nahas, Hélène. *La Femme dans la littérature existentialiste*. Paris: Presses Universitaires de France, 1957.

Nye, Andrea. *Feminist Theory and the Philosophies of Man*. New York: Routledge Press, 1988.

————. *Philosophy and Feminism: At the Border*. New York: Simon and Schuster Macmillan, 1995.

Peters, Hélène. *The Existential Woman*. New York: Peter Lang, 1991.

Quinn, Bernard J. "The Authentic Woman in the Theater of Jean-Paul Sartre." *Language Quarterly* 10, no. 3–4 (1972): 39–44.

Rajan, Marie-France Juneau. "Transcultural Nursing: A Perspective Derived from Jean-Paul Sartre," *Journal of Advanced Nursing* 22: (1995) 450–55.

Ranwez, Alain D. *Jean-Paul Sartre's "Les Temps Modernes": A Literary History 1945–1952*. New York: Whitston, 1981.

Rybalka, Michel, Michel Contat, Yan Cloutier, and Laura Piccioni. *Sartre: A Bibliography 1980–1992*. Bowling Green: Bowling Green State University Press, 1997.

Santoni, Ronald E. *Bad Faith, Good Faith, and Authenticity in Sartre's Early Philosophy*. Philadelphia: Temple University Press, 1995.

Sartre, Jean-Paul. *L'Affaire Henri Martin*. Paris: Gallimard, 1953.

————. *L'Âge de raison*. Paris: Gallimard, 1945. Translated as *The Age of Reason*, by Eric Sutton. New York: Knopf; London: Hamish Hamilton, 1947.

————. *Baudelaire*. Paris: Gallimard, 1946. Translated as *Baudelaire*, by Martin Turnell. New York: W. W. Norton, 1972.

————. *Cahiers pour une morale*. Paris: Gallimard, 1983. Translated as *Notebooks for an Ethics*, by David Pellauer. Chicago: University of Chicago Press, 1992.

————. *Les Carnets de la drôle de guerre*. Paris: Gallimard, 1983, 1995. Translated as *The War Diaries*, by Quintin Hoare, New York: Pantheon Books, 1985.

————. *Les Chemins de le liberté*. Vol. 2, *Le Sursis*. Paris: Gallimard, 1945. Translated as *The Reprieve*, by Eric Sutton. New York: Knopf, 1947.

————. *Les Chemins de le liberté*. Vol. 3, *La Mort dans l'âme*. Paris: Gallimard, 1949. Translated as *Troubled Sleep*, by Gerald Hopkins. New York: Knopf, 1950.

————. *Critique de la raison dialectique*. Vol. 1, preceded by *Questions de méthode*. Paris: Gallimard, 1960. Translated as *The Critique of Dialectical Reason*, by Alan Sheridan-Smith, London: Verso, 1976. *Search for a Method*. New York: Knopf, 1963.

————. *Critique de la raison dialectique*. Vol. 2. Paris: Gallimard, 1985. Translated as *Critique of Dialectical Reason*, vol. 2, by Quintin Hoare. London: Verso, 1991.

————. *Le Diable et le bon Dieu*. Paris: Gallimard, 1951. Translated as *The Devil and the Good Lord and Two Other Plays*, by Kitty Black. New York: Knopf, 1960.

————. *Entretiens sur la politique*. In collaboration with Gérard Rosenthal and David Rousset. Paris: Gallimard, 1949.

————. *Esquisse d'une théorie des émotions*. Paris: Hermann, 1939. Translated as *The Emotions: Outline of a Theory*, by Bernard Frechtman. New York: Philosophical Library, 1948.

————. *L'Etre et le néant: Essai d'ontologie phénoménologique*. Paris: Gallimard, 1943. Translated as *Being and Nothingness: An Essay on Phenomenological Ontology*, by Hazel Barnes. New York: Philosophical Library, 1956.

―――. *L'Existentialisme est un humanisme*. Paris: Nagel, 1946. Translated as *Existentialism and Humanism*, by Philip Mairet. London: Methuen, 1973.

―――. *Huis clos*. Paris: Gallimard, 1944. Translated as *No Exit*, in *No Exit and The Flies*, by Stuart Gilbert. New York: Knopf, 1948.

―――. *L'Idiot de la famille: Gustave Flaubert de 1821 à 1857*. Vols. 1 and 2, Paris: Gallimard, 1971; Vol. 3, Paris: Gallimard, 1972. Translated as *The Family Idiot: Gustave Flaubert, 1821–1857*, vols. 1–5, by Carol Cosman. Chicago University of Chicago Press, 1981, 1987, 1989, 1991, 1993.

―――. *L'Imaginaire*. Paris: Gallimard, 1940. Translated as *The Psychology of the Imagination*, by Bernard Frechtman. New York: Washington Square Press, 1966.

―――. *L'Imagination*. Paris: Presses Universitaires Françaises, 1936. Translated as *Imagination: A Psychological Critique*, by Forrest Williams. Ann Arbor: University of Michigan Press, 1979.

―――. *Kean, ou désordre et génie*. Paris: Gallimard, 1954. Translated as *Kean, or Disorder and Genius in The Devil and the Good Lord and Two Other Plays*, by Kitty Black. New York: Knopf, 1960.

―――. *Lettres au Castor et à quelques autres*. Vol. 1. Edited by Simone de Beauvoir. Paris: Gallimard, 1983. Translated as *Witness to my Life: The Letters of Jean-Paul Sartre to Simone de Beauvoir, 1926–1939*, by Lee Fahnestock and Norman MacAfee. New York: Charles Scribner's, 1992.

―――. *Lettres au Castor et à quelques autres*. Vol. 2. Edited by Simone de Beauvoir. Paris: Gallimard, 1983. Translated as *Quiet Moments in a War: The Letters of Jean-Paul Sartre to Simone de Beauvoir, 1940–1963*, by Lee Fahnestock and Norman MacAfee. New York: Charles Scribner's Sons, 1993.

―――. *Les Mains sales*. Paris: Gallimard, 1948. Translated as *Dirty Hands*, by Lionel Abel. New York: Knopf, 1949.

―――. *Mallarmé: La lucidité et sa face d'ombre*. Paris: Gallimard, 1986. Translated as *Mallarmé, or the Poet of Nothingness*, by E. Sturm, University Park: Penn University Press, 1988.

―――. *Morts sans sépulture*. Paris: Gallimard, 1946. Translated as *Men Without Shadows*, by Kitty Black. London: Hamish Hamilton, 1949.

―――. *Les Mots*. Paris: Gallimard, 1963. Translated as *The Words*, by Bernard Frechtman, New York: Braziller, 1964. New York: Vintage Books, 1981.

―――. *Les Mouches*. Paris: Gallimard, 1943. Translated as *The Flies*, in *No Exist and The Flies*, by Stuart Gilbert. New York: Knopf, 1948. In *No Exit and Three Other Plays*, New York: Vintage Books, 1955.

―――. *La Nausée*. Paris: Gallimard, 1943. Translated as *Nausea*, by Lloyd Alexander. New York: New Directions, 1948.

―――. *Nékrassov*. Paris: Gallimard, 1955. Translated as *Nekrassov*, by Sylvia and George Leeson. New York: Knopf, 1960. Also in *The Devil and the Good Lord and Two Other Plays*, translated by Kitty Black. New York: Knopf, 1960.

―――. *Oeuvres romanesques*. Edited by Michel Contat and Michel Rybalka. Bibliothèque de la Pléiade, Paris: Gallimard, 1981.

―――. *On a raison de se révolter*. With Philippe Gavi and Pierre Victor. Paris: Gallimard, 1974.

―――. *La Putain respectuesuse*. Paris: Gallimard, 1946. Translated as *The Respectful Prosti-*

tute, in *Three Plays*, translated by Kitty Black. New York: Knopf, 1949. In *No Exit and Three Other Plays*, translated by Stuart Gilbert. New York: Vintage Books, 1955.

————. *Réflexions sur la question juive*. Paris: Gallimard, 1946. Translated as *Anti-Semite and Jew*, by George T. Becker. New York: Schocken Books, 1948.

————. *Saint Genet, comédien et martyr*. Paris: Gallimard, 1952. Translated as *Saint Genet, Actor and Martyr*, by Bernard Frechtman. New York: Braziller, 1963; New York: Pantheon Books, 1983.

————. "Sartre Talks of Beauvoir." Interview with Madeleine Gobeil. In *Critical Essays on Simone de Beauvoir*, ed. Elaine Marks, 15–18. Boston: G. K. Hall, 1987.

————. *Le Scénario Freud*. With a preface by J.-B. Pontalis. Paris: Gallimard, 1984. Translated as *The Freud Scenario*, by Quintin Hoare. Chicago: University of Chicago Press, 1986.

————. *Les Séquestrés d'Altona*. Paris: Gallimard, 1959. Translated as *The Condemned of Altona*, by Sylvia Leeson and George Leeson, New York: Knopf, 1961.

————. *Situations 1*. Paris: Gallimard, 1947.

————. *Situations 2*. Paris: Gallimard, 1948. "Qu' est-ce que la littérature?" translated as *What is Literature?* by Bernard Frechtman. New York: Harper and Row, 1965.

————. *Situations 3*. Paris: Gallimard, 1949.

————. *Situations 4*. Paris: Gallimard, 1964. Translated as *Situations*, by Benito Eisler, New York: Braziller, 1965.

————. *Situations 5*. Paris: Gallimard, 1964.

————. *Situations 6*. Paris: Gallimard, 1964.

————. *Situations 7*. Paris: Gallimard, 1965. "Le Fantôme de Staline" translated as *The Ghost of Stalin*, by Martha H. Fletcher. New York: George Braziller, 1968.

————. *Situations 8*. Paris: Gallimard, 1972. Translated as *Between Existentialism and Marxism*, by John Matthews. New York: Pantheon Books, 1974.

————. *Situations 9*. Paris: Gallimard, 1972. Translated as *Between Existentialism and Marxism*, by John Matthews. New York: Pantheon Books, 1974.

————. *Situations 10*. Paris: Gallimard, 1976. Translated as *Life/Situations*, by Paul Auster and Lydia Davis. New York: Pantheon Books, 1977.

————. *Un Théâtre de situations*, ed. Michel Contat and Michel Rybalka, Paris: Gallimard, 1972. Translated as *Sartre on Theater*, by Frank Jellinek, New York: Pantheon Books, 1976.

————. *La Transcendance de l'Ego*. Paris: Vrin, 1937. Translated as *The Transcendence of the Ego*, by Forrest Williams and Robert Kirkpatrick. New York: Noonday Press, 1957.

————. *Les Troyennes*. Paris: Gallimard, 1965. Translated as *Euripides' The Trojan Woman*, by Ronald Duncan. New York: Knopf, 1967.

————. *Verite et existence*. Paris: Gallimard, 1989. Translated as *Truth and Existence*, by Adrian van den Hoven and edited by Ronald Aronson. Chicago: University of Chicago Press, 1992.

Sartre, Jean-Paul, and Benny Lévy. *L'Espoir maintenant: les entretiens de 1980*. Lagrasse: Editions Verdier, 1991. Translated as *Hope Now: The 1980 Interviews*, by Adrian van den Hoven. Chicago: University of Chicago Press, 1996.

Schilpp, P. *The Philosophy of Jean-Paul Sartre*. La Salle, Ill.: Library of Living Philosophers, 1981.

Scriven, Michael. *Sartre and the Media*. New York: St. Martin's Press, 1993.

Sicard, M. "Interférences: Entretien avec Simone de Beauvoir et Jean-Paul Sartre." *Obliques* 18–19 (1979): 325–29.

Siegel, Liliane. *In the Shadow of Sartre*. Translated by Barbara Wright. London: Collins, 1990.

Silverman, Hugh, and Frederick Elliston, eds. *Jean-Paul Sartre: Contemporary Approaches to His Philosophy*. Pittsburgh: Duquesne University Press, 1980.

Simons, Margaret A. "Beauvoir and Sartre: The Philosophical Relationship." *Yale French Studies*, no. 72 (1986): 165–79.

———, ed. *Feminist Interpretations of Simone de Beauvoir*. University Park: Penn State Press, 1995.

Singer, Linda. *Erotic Welfare: Sexual Theory and Politics in the Age of Epidemic*. New York: Routledge, 1992.

Stewart, Jon. ed. *The Debate Between Sartre and Merleau-Ponty*. Evanston: Northwestern University Press, 1998.

Stone, Robert V., and Elizabeth A. Bowman. "Dialectical Ethics: A First Look at Sartre's Unpublished 1964 Rome Lecture Notes," *Social Text: Theory/Culture/Ideology* 15 (Winter/Spring 1986): 195–215.

———. "Sartre's Morality and History: A First Look at the Notes for the Unpublished 1965 Cornell Lectures," in *Sartre Alive*, Ronald Aronson and Adrian van den Hoven, eds. Detroit: Wayne State University Press, 1991.

Verstraeten, Pierre. ed. *Sur les écrits posthumes de Sartre*. Bruxelles: Université de Bruxelles, 1987.

Wider, Kathleen V. *The Bodily Nature of Consciousness: Sartre and Contemporary Philosophy of Mind*. Ithaca: Cornell University Press, 1977.

Winock, Michel. *Le Siècle des Intellectuels*. Paris: Seuil, 1997.

Wood, Philip R. *Understanding Jean-Paul Sartre*. Columbia: University of South Carolina Press, 1990.

Young, Iris Marion. *Dilemmas of Gender, Political Philosophy, and Policy*. Princeton: Princeton University Press, 1997.

———. *Justice and the Politics of Difference*. Princeton: Princeton University Press, 1990.

———. *Throwing Like a Girl and Other Essays in Feminist Philosophy and Social Theory*. Bloomington: Indiana University Press, 1990.

Contributors

HAZEL E. BARNES, emerita professor of philosophy at the University of Colorado, translated Sartre's *Being and Nothingness* (Pocket Books, 1983) and has written extensively on French existentialism. Her most recent book is *The Story I Tell Myself: A Venture in Existentialist Autobiography* (University of Chicago Press, 1997).

LINDA A. BELL is professor of philosophy and director of the Women's Studies Institute at Georgia State University in Atlanta, Georgia. In addition to her work in feminist theory, she studies, teaches, and publishes in the areas of existentialism, ethics, and continental philosophy. She has published numerous articles and three books: the first an anthology of philosophers' statements about women, *Visions of Women* (Humana Press: 1983), the second a development of an ethics from the writings of Jean-Paul Sartre, *Sartre's Ethics of Authenticity* (University of Alabama Press, 1989), and the third an existentialist feminist ethics, *Rethinking Ethics in the Midst of Violence: A Feminist Approach to Freedom* (Rowman & Littlefield, 1993). A fourth book was co-edited with David Blumenfield: *Overcoming Racism and Sexism* (Rowman & Littlefield, 1995). She is presently developing a number of essays into a collection dealing with experience and its role in philosophizing.

STUART Z. CHARMÉ is professor of religion at Rutgers University (Camden). He is the author of two books on Sartre, *Meaning and Myth in the Study of Lives: A Sartrean Perspective* (University of Pennsylvania Press, 1984) and *Vulgarity and Authenticity: Dimensions of Otherness in the World of Jean-Paul Sartre* (University of Massachusetts Press, 1991). His current research deals with the religious dimensions of Sartre's work as well as the evolution of Sartre's understanding of Jewish identity.

PETER DIERS is an ABD graduate student at Purdue University. The working title of his dissertation project is "The Limitations of Individualism in Social Explanation: The Case of Sartre and a Feminist Revision." His major philosophical interests are in the area of social and political philosophy.

KATE FULLBROOK is professor of literary studies at the University of the West of England, Bristol. EDWARD FULLBROOK is a freelance writer with interests in economics, philosophy, and fiction. They are the joint authors of *Simone de Beauvoir and Jean-Paul Sartre: The Remaking of a Twentieth-Century Legend* (Basic Books, 1994) and *Simone de Beauvoir: A Critical Introduction* (Blackwell, 1998) as well as many articles and reviews.

KAREN GREEN is a senior lecturer in philosophy at Monash University in Melbourne, Australia, where she teaches courses on feminism and Sartre. She recently published *The Woman of Reason: Feminism, Humanism, and Political Thought* (Continuum, 1995), a history and defense of feminist humanist thinking. She has contributed articles to *Hypatia's Daughters: Fifteen Hundred Years of Women Philosophers*, ed. Linda L. McAlister (Indiana University Press, 1996) and to numerous philosophy journals.

SARAH LUCIA HOAGLAND is the author of *Lesbian Ethics: Toward New Value* (Institute of Lesbian Studies, 1988) and co-editor of *For Lesbians Only: A Separatist Anthology* (Onlywomen, 1988). She is professor of philosophy and women's studies at Northeastern Illinois University in Chicago.

SONIA KRUKS is the Danforth Professor of Politics at Oberlin College, where she teaches political philosophy and feminist theory. She is the author of *The Political Philosophy of Merleau-Ponty* (Humanities Press, 1981) and *Situation and Human Existence: Freedom, Subjectivity and Society* (Routledge, 1990) as well as numerous articles on Sartre, Beauvoir, and other thinkers. She is currently completing a book manuscript on phenomenology and feminism.

GUILLERMINE DE LACOSTE is former professor of philosophy at Newton College of the Sacred Heart. She holds a doctorate from the Sorbonne. Her interest in Sartre dates back to her Fulbright student days in Paris, but her involvement in feminism began much later, at the time of Beauvoir's death. She has published numerous articles in *Philosophy Today*, *Simone de Beauvoir Studies*, *Claudel Studies*, and *Bulletin de Société Americaine de Philosophe de Langue Francaise*.

THOMAS MARTIN wrote his contribution for this collection while he was a Ph.D. student at the School of Philosophy, University of New South Wales, in Sydney, Australia. He now holds a Post-Doctoral Research Fellowship in the Department of Philosophy, Rhodes University, in Grahamstown, South Africa. His research interests include the usefulness of Sartrean philosophy to feminist theory, racism, multiculturalism and self-deception.

PHYLLIS SUTTON MORRIS received her Ph.D. in philosophy from the University of Michigan. She taught philosophy at Kirkland College in New York, Hamilton College, and LeMoyne College, and has been a visiting professor at the University of Michigan-Dearborn, University of Michigan-Flint, and most recently, Oberlin College. She co-founded with William McBride the Sartre Society of North America in 1985 and was the North American book review editor for the new journal *Sartre Studies International*. She is the author of *Sartre's Concept of a Person: An Analytic Approach* (University of Massachusetts Press, 1976) as well as numerous articles on Sartre, including "Self-Creating Selves: Sartre and Foucault," in *American Catholic Philosophical Quarterly* 4 (1996): 537–49.

CONSTANCE MUI is an associate professor of philosophy at Loyola University in New Orleans. She has published articles in phenomenology and ontology, Sartre, Strawson, and feminism. In addition to teaching philosophy, she teaches courses in women's studies and is one of three founders of the interdisciplinary women's studies program at Loyola University.

JULIEN S. MURPHY is professor of philosophy and associate dean of the College of Arts and Sciences at the University of Southern Maine-Portland, where she teaches courses in feminist theory, continental philosophy, and medical ethics. She is the author of *The Constructed Body: AIDS, Reproductive Technology, and Ethics* (SUNY Press, 1995) and numerous articles on feminist medical ethics as well as on continental philosophy, including recent pieces in *Feminist Interpretations of Simone de Beauvoir*, edited by Margaret Simons (Penn State Press, 1995), and *Em-*

body Ethics: Recent Feminist Advances, edited by Anne Donchin and Laura McPurdy (Rowman and Littlefield, 1999).

IRIS MARION YOUNG is professor of public and international affairs at the University of Pittsburgh, where she teaches ethics, political philosophy, and women's studies. Her most recent book is titled *Intersecting Voices: Dilemmas of Gender, Political Philosophy, and Policy* (Princeton University Press, 1997).

Index